10/11

G000074931

Constraints and Resources in
Natural Language Syntax and Semantics

Studies in Constraint-Based Lexicalism

A series edited by
Miriam Butt, *University of Konstanz*
Andreas Kathol, *University of California, Berkeley*
Tracy Holloway King, *Xerox Palo Alto Research Center*
Jean-Pierre Koenig, *State University of New York at Buffalo*
Sam Mchombo, *University of California, Berkeley*

The aim of this series is to make work in various nonderivational, lexicalist approaches to grammar available to a wide audience of linguists. In approaches of this kind, grammar is seen as the interaction of constraints from multiple dimensions of linguistic substance, including information about syntactic category, grammatical relations, and semantic and pragmatic interpretation.

Studies in
Constraint-Based Lexicalism

Constraints and Resources in Natural Language Syntax and Semantics

edited by
Gosse Bouma
Erhard Hinrichs
Geert-Jan M. Kruijff
Richard Oehrle

CSLI
PUBLICATIONS
Center for the Study of
Language and Information
Stanford, California

Copyright © 1999
CSLI Publications
Center for the Study of Language and Information
Leland Stanford Junior University
Printed in the United States
03 02 01 00 99   5 4 3 2 1

Library of Congress Cataloging-in-Publication Data

Constraints and resources in natural language syntax and semantics /
edited by Gosse Bouma ... [et al.].
p.   cm. — (Studies in constraint-based lexicalism)
Includes bibliographical references and index.

ISBN 1-57586-221-2 (cloth : alk. paper)
ISBN 1-57586-222-0 (pbk. : alk. paper).

1. Grammar, Comparative and general—Syntax.
2. Head-driven phrase structure grammar.
3. Semantics. I. Bouma, Gosse, 1961–   .
II. Series.
P291.C577   1999
415—dc21   99-34322
CIP

CSLI was founded early in 1983 by researchers from Stanford University, SRI International, and Xerox PARC to further research and development of integrated theories of language, information, and computation. CSLI headquarters and CSLI Publications are located on the campus of Stanford University.

CSLI Publications reports new developments in the study of language, information, and computation. In addition to lecture notes, our publications include monographs, working papers, revised dissertations, and conference proceedings. Our aim is to make new results, ideas, and approaches available as quickly as possible. Please visit our web site at
http://csli-www.stanford.edu/publications/
for comments on this and other titles, as well as for changes and corrections by the author and publisher.

Contents

Contributors

EMILY BENDER: Department of Linguistics, Stanford University, Stanford CA 94305-23150 USA, bender@csli.stanford.edu

OLIVIER BONAMI: URA 1028, UFRL, case 7003, Campus Jussieu, 75251 Paris Cedex 05, France, Olivier.Bonami@linguist.jussieu.fr

BERTHOLD CRYSMANN: Universität des Saarlandes, Computerlinguistik Geb. 17.2, Postfach 151150, D-66041 Saarbrücken, crysmann@coli.uni-sb.de

FRANK VAN EYNDE: Centre for Computational Linguistics, KU Leuven, Maria Theresiastraat 21, 3000 Leuven, Belgium, frank@ccl.kuleuven.ac.be

DAN FLICKINGER: Center for the Study of Language and Information, Stanford University, Stanford CA 94305, USA, danf@csli.stanford.edu

DANIELE GODARD: CNRS, Silex, Université Lille 3, BP149, 59653 Villeneuve d'Ascq, France, Godard@Univ-Lille3.fr

HERMAN HENDRIKS: Research Institute for Language and Speech OTS, Utrecht University, Trans 10, 3512 JK Utrecht, The Netherlands, Herman.Hendriks@let.uu.nl

ERHARD W. HINRICHS: Seminar für Sprachwissenschaft, Universität Tübingen, Wilhelmstr. 113, D-72074 Tübingen, Germany, eh@sfs.nphil.uni-tuebingen.de

ANDREAS KATHOL: Department of Linguistics, 1203 Dwinelle Hall, UC Berkeley, Berkeley, CA 94720, USA, kathol@socrates.berkeley.edu

LAURA KALLMEYER: Sonderforschungsbereich 441, *Linguistische Datenstrukturen: Theoretische und empirische Grundlagen der Grammatikforschung*, Universität Tübingen, Köstlinstr. 6, D-72074 Tübingen, Germany, lk@sfs.nphil.uni-tuebingen.de

RUTH KEMPSON: School of Oriental and African Studies of the University of London, Thornhaugh Street, Russell Square, London, WC1H 0XG, rk@soas.ac.uk

JEAN-MARIE MARANDIN: URA 1028, UFRL, case 7003, Campus Jussieu, 75251 Paris Cedex 05, France, Marandin@ccr.jussieu.fr

WILFRIED MEYER-VIOL: Department of Computer Science, King's College, Strand, London, WC2R 2LS, meyervio@dcs.kcl.ac.uk

JENS MICHAELIS: Institut für Linguistik, Universität Potsdam, Postfach 60 15 53, D-14415 Potsdam, Germany, michaelis@ling.uni-potsdam.de

PAOLA MONACHESI: Utrecht University, Research Institute for Language and Speech OTS, Trans 10, 3512 JK Utrecht, The Netherlands, Paola.Monachesi@let.uu.nl

MICHAEL MOORTGAT: Utrecht University, Research Institute for Language and Speech OTS, Trans 10, 3512 JK Utrecht, The Netherlands, Michael.Moortgat@let.uu.nl

TSUNEKO NAKAZAWA: Language and Information Sciences, University of Tokyo, 3-8-1 Komaba, Meguro-ku, Tokyo 153, Japan, tsuneko@boz.c.u-tokyo.ac.jp

RICHARD OEHRLE: 256 Mansfield Road, Ashford, CT 06278-1411 USA, oehrle@linc.cis.upenn.edu

GERALD PENN: Seminar für Sprachwissenschaft, Universität Tübingen, Wilhelmstr. 113, D-72074 Tübingen, Germany, gpenn@sfs.nphil.uni-tuebingen.de

FRANK RICHTER: Seminar für Sprachwissenschaft, Universität Tübingen, Wilhelmstr. 113, D-72074 Tübingen, Germany, `fr@sfs.nphil.uni-tuebingen.de`

MANFRED SAILER: Seminar für Sprachwissenschaft, Universität Tübingen, Wilhelmstr. 113, D-72074 Tübingen, Germany, `mf@sfs.nphil.uni-tuebingen.de`

ED STABLER: UCLA Linguistics Department, 3125 Campbell Hall, Los Angeles CA 90095-1543, USA, `stabler@ucla.edu`

CHRISTIAN WARTENA: Institut für Linguistik, Universität Potsdam, Postfach 60 15 53, D-14415 Potsdam, Germany, `wartena@ling.uni-potsdam.de`

Introduction

GOSSE BOUMA, ERHARD HINRICHS,
GEERT-JAN KRUIJFF, AND RICHARD OEHRLE

The papers in this volume represent a broad spectrum of contemporary theoretical and empirical linguistic concerns. Although they flow from somewhat different research paradigms and draw on a variety of different perspectives, they reflect the fact that the paradigms and perspectives represented share important common ground, especially with regard to the role of logical, mathematical, and computational concepts and techniques in linguistic analysis.

A touchstone of these views can be found in the famous passage from the preface of Chomsky (1957), which emphasizes the heuristic role of formalization in clarifying linguistic analyses, especially in a way that will support empirical testing and possible falsification.

> ... The search for rigorous formulation in linguistics has a much more serious motivation than mere concern for logical niceties or the desire to purify well-established methods of linguistic analysis. Precisely constructed models for linguistic structure can play an important role, both negative and positive, in the process of discovery itself. By pushing a precise but inadequate formulation to an unacceptable conclusion, we can often expose the exact source of this inadequacy and, consequently, gain a deeper understanding of the linguistic data. More positively, a formalized theory may automatically provide solutions for many problems other than those for which it was explicitly designed. Obscure and intuition-bound notions can neither lead to absurd conclusions nor provide new and correct ones, and hence they fail to be useful in two important respects.

The work reported here—across the various linguistic perspectives represented—still respects this view, which takes formalization as a useful accompaniment to linguistic theorizing. But in many respects, the place of logic, mathematics, and computation in this work goes deeper: subsequent developments have brought about a keener appreciation of how linguistic composition can be modeled as a form of grammatical deduction, how linguistic processing is essentially a form of computation, and how such ideas yield new and interesting connections between linguistic theory and practice, on the one hand, and results and theoretical developments in logic, in computation, and in the increasing connections between these two basic fields. Indeed, the trends in linguistic theory represented by the key words *constraints* and *resources* of our title correspond broadly to the most obvious duality in both logic and computation—namely, to the model-theoretic and the proof-theoretic perspectives, respectively, a distinction whose importance in the theory of computation has increased in time, as well. At the same time constraint-based and resource-sensitive theories of grammar share a lexicalist approach to linguistic theorizing. It is therefore fitting to include this volume in a book series that is intended to make available a broad range of linguistic, foundational and computational research in lexicalist linguistic frameworks.

Following the practice of G. J. Caesar and C. S. Peirce, we have divided the matter at hand into three parts. The first contains papers from the HPSG paradigm, papers whose formal focus falls on the formulation of linguistic constraints and the investigation of how suitably formulated constraints interact in the characterization of linguistic form and interpretation. The second part contains papers that draw on the proof-theoretical perspective in which the composition of linguistic structures is modeled as a form of resource-sensitive deduction in a grammatical logic. The third part contains formal investigations—investigations of grammatical structure and computation over grammatical structures. In the paragraphs that follow, we shall briefly describe the contents of each paper and situate it in the broader context of current linguistic theory.

Part I: HPSG

Bender and Flickinger's paper *Diachronic Evidence for Extended Argument Structure* presents a diachronic study of clauses in English that are headed by *as if*, *as though*, and *like*. They show that such clauses underwent a historical change from adjuncts to complements. This finding lends further support to recent proposals in HPSG to include certain adjuncts in the (extended) argument structure list of words. Bender and Flickinger argue that the inclusion of postverbal adjuncts in the argument structure of verbs provided the basis for the reanalysis of *as if*, *as though*, and *like* adjuncts as verbal complements. More generally, the paper exemplifies how the lexicalist perspective of HPSG, with highly-structured lexical representations motivated by synchronic considerations, can also provide an explanatory basis for certain types of syntactic change.

Bonami, Godard, and Marandin's contribution *Constituency and Word Order in French Subject Inversion* proposes an analysis in terms of *domain union* for French subject inversion in extraction contexts. In particular, they aim to provide an account for the fact that the subject may not only follow the VP, but also appear in between a verb and its complements. Their proposal steers a mid-course between a movement analysis based on extraposition of complements, and an analysis based on a flat sentential phrase structure in combination with *argument inheritance*. A domain-union analysis provides a phrase structure for subject-inverted sentences which is isomorphic to that of non-inverted sentences, thus avoiding a number of problems which arise in a flat phrase structure account. At the same time, domain union is more restricted than extraposition of complements, thus accounting for the bounded nature of inversion.

Crysmann's paper *Morphological Paradoxa in Fox* proposes a linearization-based HPSG account of complex verbs in Fox (Mesquakie), an Algonquian language spoken in Iowa. Complex verbs in Fox provide an interesting case study for the morphology-syntax interface. With respect to inflection and derivation they behave as single morphological units. At the same time, pre-verb and verb appear to be syntactically independent, since syntactically derived words can intervene between them. In order to account for their syntactic behavior Crysmann hypothesizes that complex verbs introduce more than one domain object (in the sense of Reape 1994 and Kathol 1995) into the syntax. Inflectional and derivational effects are then treated as morphological constraints on lists of domain objects.

Hinrichs and Nakazawa's contribution *VP Relatives in German* offers syntactic evidence in favor of a double-extraction analysis of German VP relatives: extraction of the entire relativized VP and extraction of the relative pronoun within the extracted VP. This double-extraction analysis is realized by two filler-head rules: the Filler-Head Relative Clause ID Rule, which licenses extraction of relativized VPs, and the Filler-Head Relative VP ID Rule, which is responsible for the internal extraction of relative pronouns within the VP. Following Sag's recent HPSG account of relative clauses in English (Sag, 1997), the authors treat the finite verb as the lexical head of the relative clause, thereby obviating the need for an empty relativizer (Pollard and Sag, 1994), which was mainly motivated as a placeholder for the semantic information contributed by the relative clause.

Kathol's paper *Restricted Modification and Polycategorial NPs in English* provides a critical evaluation of the conventional syntactic wisdom that restrictive nominal modifiers attach at the $\overline{\text{N}}$-level. The conclusion is that, at least within a theory such as HPSG, there is little evidence for assuming $\overline{\text{N}}$-attachment, and an analysis based on attachment at the NP-level is in fact to be preferred. He then turns to the broader issue of NP-internal structure in general, and develops a proposal in which both determiners and nouns are subtypes of *nominal*. This accounts for the fact that in some cases it seems most convenient to treat the noun as the head of NP, whereas in other cases the evidence points towards an analysis in which the determiner is the head.

Monachesi's contribution *The Syntactic Structure of Romanian Auxiliary (and Modal) Verbs* investigates the properties of Romanian auxiliaries. Auxiliaries in Romanian are always strictly adjacent to the main verb. In contrast to French or Italian, no adverb or subject can intervene between the two. This provides evidence for an analysis in which the auxiliary and main verb form a verbal complex. The distribution of pronominal clitics supports this analysis. Clitics which can be prefixed to their host, are always prefixed to the auxiliary—never to the main verb—a situation which can be accounted for by assuming that auxiliaries and verbs form a complex in which the auxiliary inherits the complements of the verb through *argument composition*. Modal verbs differ from auxiliaries in that adverbs may intervene between a modal and a subordinate verb. On the other hand, clitic climbing is possible. This suggests that modals do attract the arguments of their subordinate verbs through argument composition but that they do not head a verbal complex.

In Penn's paper *A Generalized-Domain-Based Approach to Serbo-Croatian Second Position Clitic Placement*, domain union plays a prominent role as well. Penn investigates second position clitics in Serbo-Croation, and argues that both prosodic and syntactic constituency constrain the possible placements of these clitics. He develops a theory of domain union which generalizes earlier work by Reape and Kathol. In particular, a notion of *compaction* of word order domains is proposed which is inspired by the theory of topological fields, and which can handle situations where prosodic and syntactic constituency are not isomorphic.

Van Eynde's paper *Major and Minor Pronouns in Dutch* proposes a distinction between major and minor categories. Major categories can act as the head of a non-vacuous phrasal projection, whereas minor categories cannot. In HPSG, the distinction can be implemented by assuming that the sort *cat* has *major* and *minor* as subsorts, and that only the former licences the valence features which are crucial for selecting syntactic dependents. Van Eynde applies his idea to Dutch full and reduced pronouns, and argues that the latter are minor categories. This accounts for the fact that reduced pronouns, in contrast to full pronouns, cannot be modified by adjectives, relatives, or appositions. Furthermore, a number of phenomena, such as the fact that reduced pronouns cannot be topicalized or conjoined may be accounted for in terms of this distinction. The paper concludes with the observation that the distinction also makes sense from a semantic point of view: only reduced pronouns in Dutch can act as expletives and can be interpreted generically.

Part II: Resource-sensitive approaches

Hendriks's paper *Contour and Structure: A Categorial Account of Alignment* achieves two notable goals. First, it integrates intonational aspects of topic and focus (in English) into a deductive approach to grammatical composition. Second, it shows how this perspective accommodates both lexical and phrasal constructions, thus resolving a theoretical conundrum of prosodic morphology. The focus of the paper is on two critical assumptions. The first is that both phonological words and syntactically composed phrases constitute *headed structures*, which can be modeled (following Moortgat and Morrill 1991) by a multi-modal system containing two independent versions of the non-associative Lambek calculus **NL**: one left-headed and one right-headed. The second is that intonational phenomena can be regarded as the consequence of a correspondence between proofs and phonological terms, exactly analogous to the familiar Curry-Howard correspondence between proofs and λ-terms. Hendriks concludes by showing how this basic system can be extended by modal operators and modally-sensitive type declarations to a system that accommodates a broader range of English intonational contours.

In *Topic and Focus Structures: The Dynamics of Tree Growth*, Kempson & Meyer-Viol advance a cross-linguistic typology of a variety of syntactic structures involving forms of topicalization or left-dislocation, based on simple and general assumptions about incremental processing and pronominal resolution. Incremental processing is modeled dynamically by the construction of tree-structures constrained by the order of lexical elements and the requirements on structure that they impose, as specified in a modal tree description language. Topic and focus structures have a natural characterization from this perspective, based on underspecified tree-descriptions. The different ways in which these underspecified representations can be updated in the course of incremental processing leads directly to the proposed typology of topic and focus structures, with additional consequences for the analysis of cross-over phenomena.

Moortgat's paper, *Constants of Grammatical Reasoning*, views grammatical composition from a deductive perspective and investigates the properties of an appropriate form of grammatical inference. Two basic questions that arises are: what are the constants, if any, of grammatical logic? and how are these constants compatible with the apparent structural variation that different natural languages display? To answer these questions, Moortgat draws on two converging logical traditions, Linear Logic and Lambek Calculus, which have focused attention on the impact of the 'structural rules' governing occurrences and multiplicities (Weakening and Contraction) and structural configurations (Permutation and Associativity), and shown how these operations can be locally controlled through modal operators. This leads Moortgat to a simple universal architecture for grammatical logic: the core is a family of unary and binary products; each product is associated with a corresponding family of implications, connected to the products by the residuation/adjointness laws which yield directly the familiar logical operations of *modus ponens*, the Deduction Theorem, and more. The lexicon of a grammar consists of a set of type declarations. Proofs can be interpreted according to the Curry-Howard correspondence, which associates each proof with a term of the typed λ-calculus in a way that has interesting consequences for the division of semantic labor between lexical specification and compositional syntactic structure. Finally, structural variation can be introduced by the addition of language-particular structural rules and interaction postulates (drawn from a universally available set). On this basis, Moortgat shows how the striking syntactic distinctions between Dutch and English extraction patterns can be elegantly characterized.

Oehrle's paper, *Binding as Term Rewriting*, investigates one way in which the general principles of dynamic semantics can be integrated with a multi-modal system of categorial grammar to provide an account of binding phenomena. Dynamic interpretation is based on two related properties: interpretation is context-dependent and context-affecting. Expressions can be characterized by their properties with respect to these two parameters; taking contexts to be structured objects makes this approach applicable to the variety of anaphoric expressions which have been the focus of binding theories in many different frameworks. Integration of this approach to binding with a system of grammatical inference requires that an account be given of how contexts are assembled and how communication between an expression and the context it depends upon and acts on is achieved. There are a number of ways to do this. The one developed in the paper uses a system of term rewriting, controlled via modal distinctions in the categorial system. The paper concludes with a discussion of how this approach extends to quantification, and an application of this extension to a puzzle involving quantification and cross-over.

Part III: Formal and Computational Issues

Kallmeyer's contribution *Synchronous Local TDGs and Scope Ambiguities* presents a formal account of the syntax-semantics interface for natural language grammars in the framework of *local Tree Description Grammars*, an extension of the Tree Adjoining Grammars. Syntactic and semantic representations are each formalized as underspecified tree descriptions in a local TDG. The two types of representations are linked by a synchronization relation between the two local TDGs. Tree descriptions in local TDGs allow an underspecification of the dominance relation between nodes in trees and thereby provide suitable underspecified representations for scope ambiguities. Since local TDGs are subject to a locality condition on derivations island constraints on quantifier scope follow naturally from the formalism and do not need to be stipulated. Kallmeyer illustrates the resulting treatment of scope ambiguities by a natural language fragment that includes quantifiers and relative clauses.

In *LIGs with Reduced Derivation Sets*, Michaelis and Wartena investigate a weakly context-free subclass of linear indexed grammar (LIG), called *unidirectional indexed grammar* (UIG), and its extended version. The linguistic interest in LIGs (and weaker forms thereof) is that they provide a simple model for investigating movement phenomena. The authors examplify this with WH-movement and Dutch cross-serial dependencies. More formally, in a LIG derivation each nonterminal has a stack of indices associated to it. This stack is passed on to exactly one daughter when the nonterminal gets rewritten. The authors investigate the consequences of restricting the set of possible candidates for inheritance of the index stack. For example, if the grammar only contains production rules that require the stack to be passed on following the rightmost branches only, then a right linear indexed grammar (RLIG) is obtained. RLIGs are weakly equivalent to context-free grammars, and provide an intuitively simple model for extraction in SVO-languages. Similarly, left linear indexed grammars (LLIGs) can be obtained. RLIG and LLIG can be combined into a UIG, in which the stack can be passed on either over the leftmost child or the rightmost child, with the restriction that direction can only be changed if the stack is empty. As a formal model, UIGs are closely related to the tree insertion grammars (TIGs) which are a kind of restricted tree adjoining grammars (TAGs). UIGs are still context-free, as the authors prove. The authors conclude the paper by constructing an extended version of UIGs, so-called EUIGs, which can be proven to have a weak generative capacity that is properly in-between CFLs and LILs. These grammars provide a formal model for SOV-languages. That way, the authors shed some light on the nature of non-local dependencies in natural languages.

Richter, Sailer, and Penn's paper *A Formal Interpretation of Relations and Quantification in HPSG* presents a formal language RSRL, a relational extension of the *Speciate Reentrant Logic* (SRL) introduced by King (1989). RSRL provides a formal semantics for the language introduced by Pollard and Sag to formalize HPSG grammars. The main innovations of RSRL, compared to SRL, is the treatment of relations and quantification that are used frequently in the statement of HPSG principles. Particularly noteworthy is the semantics of quantification that the authors develop. Quantification is restricted to components of a given linguistic object, rather than ranging over all or some objects in a given model.

Stabler's paper *Remnant Movement and Complexity* uses the phenomenon of 'remnant movement'—displacement of a constituent containing one or more traces of other displacements—to motivate a simple, spare formalism for grammars in the Minimalist framework. In this formalism, a grammar is just a pair $\langle Lex, \mathcal{F} \rangle$, with *Lex* a set of expressions and $\mathcal{F}$ a set of (partial) structure-building functions. In the grammars of interest here, lexical expressions consist of sequences of syntactic features associated with the phonological and semantic properties. And there are just two structure-building functions: *merge* and *move*, each with the interesting property that a pair of features of opposite polarity is canceled in each constructive step. Stabler shows how this formalism accommodates the seemingly complex Hungarian analyzed as an instance of remnant movement by Koopman and Szabolcsi (1998), and concludes with some observations involving the expressive power of the formalism, its affinities with other grammatical formalisms, and a revealing information-theoretic complexity measure that it supports.

Sources

The chapters of this book stem from papers originally presented at three recent and closely related conferences. In July 1997, the annual HPSG conference was held in Ithaca in conjunction with the LSA Summer Linguistics Institute at Cornell University. A month later, the third in a series of annual conferences on Formal Grammar took place in Aix-en-

Provence, during the weekend before the start of the ninth European Summer School in Logic, Language and Information (ESSLLI IX). When the organizers of these two conferences realized that they were planning to hold separate follow-up conferences in Saarbrücken in August 1998 in conjunction with ESSLLI X, they combined their plans and collaborated on the organization of the Joint Conference on Formal, Head-Driven, and Categorial Grammar (FHCG-98). Most of the papers included stem from the latter conference. The contributions by Hendriks, Kallmeyer, and Oehrle are based on presentations at the Formal Grammar conference, and the contributions by Hinrichs and Nakazawa and Penn are based on presentations at HPSG-97. A number of other papers derived from presentations at the latter conference are to be found in Volume 1 of the present series, *Lexical and Constructional Aspects of Linguistic Explanation* (Webelhuth et al., 1999).

Our goal in shaping this volume was to select high-quality papers whose content and exposition were such that they would be accessible to scholars both within and across the research traditions represented here and to a broader audience as well. The reviewing and editing process strongly favored papers that could be published without substantial revisions, thus allowing the publication of these papers relatively soon after the original conferences had taken place.

Acknowledgments

The editors would like to thank the authors for timely submission of their contributions, often on the basis of minimal instructions and LaTeX support from our side. We also thank the external reviewers for their cooperation and detailed comments on the submitted papers: their contribution to the result has been critical. Glyn Morrill has provided an essential impetus for the Formal Grammar meetings and we have benefited from his counsel in numerous ways. For assistance in proofreading the manuscript, we are grateful to Dr. Stephanie Schwarz.

Finally, we are indebted to the series editors, in particular Andreas Kathol, for assistance in the editing and reviewing process, and for arranging the publication of this volume within the *Studies in Constraint-Based Lexicalism* series. CSLI has provided us with LaTeX support in a variety of ways, and cooperated graciously and efficiently with our projected publication deadlines.

Gosse Bouma
Erhard Hinrichs
Geert-Jan Kruijff
Richard Oehrle

References

Chomsky, N. 1957. *Syntactic Structures*. The Hague: Mouton & Co.

Kathol, A. 1995. *Linearization-Based German Syntax*. Ph.D. thesis, Ohio State University.

King, P. 1989. *A Logical Formalism for Head-Driven Phrase Structure Grammar*. Ph.D. thesis, University of Manchester.

Koopman, H. and A. Szabolcsi. 1998. *Verbal Complexes*. UCLA. Forthcoming.

Moortgat, M. and G. Morrill. 1991. *Heads and Phrases: Type Calculus for Dependency and Constituent Structure*. OTS Research Paper. University of Utrecht: Research Institute for Language and Speech.

Pollard, C. J. and I. A. Sag. 1994. *Head-Driven Phrase Structure Grammar*. Chicago: University of Chicago Press.

Reape, M. 1994. Domain union and word order variation in German. In J. Nerbonne, K. Netter, and C. J. Pollard, eds., *German in Head-Driven Phrase Structure Grammar*, no. 46 in CSLI Lecture Notes, pages 151–197. Stanford University: CSLI Publications.

Sag, I. A. 1997. English relative clause constructions. *Journal of Linguistics* 33(2):431–483.

Webelhuth, G., J.-P. Koenig, and A. Kathol. 1999. *Lexical and Constructional Aspects of Linguistic Explanation*. Stanford: CSLI Publications. Distributed by Cambridge University Press.

Part I

HPSG

1

Diachronic Evidence for Extended Argument Structure

EMILY BENDER AND DAN FLICKINGER

1.1 Introduction

In this paper we examine the historical development of a certain class of clauses from adjuncts into complements and argue that the nature of this change lends support to recent proposals (by Miller (1992) and others) within the Head-driven Phrase Structure Grammar framework (Pollard and Sag, 1994) which place certain adjuncts on the argument structure lists of words. Our hypothesis is that these clauses started historically as adjuncts with meaning similar to that of a neighboring complement, and took advantage of their position on the argument structure list to supplant that complement.

The clauses in question are those headed by *as if, as though,* and *like,* as illustrated in the following examples.

(1)   a. It appears as if Kim will be late.
       b. It sounds as though Kim will be late.
       c. It looks like Kim will be late.

In section 1.2 we will present evidence that these clauses are, in fact, complements.[1] Section 1.3 outlines their historical development and shows how an analysis of adjuncts as extended arguments leads to a natural modeling of that development. Section 1.4 addresses some further interesting properties of these elements in the synchronic grammar.

---

[1] While other authors discuss *as if* phrases with the underlying assumption that they can be complements, to our knowledge no one has previously justified this position.

Constraints and Resources in Natural Language Syntax and Semantics.
Gosse Bouma, Erhard W. Hinrichs, Geert-Jan M. Kruijff, and Richard T. Oehrle.

1.2 Evidence of complementhood

In this section, we will first establish that phrases marked by *as if*, etc.[2] are selected complements of the verbs they follow. We then consider the possibility that *as if*, etc. have also undergone a change in categorial status to become complementizers. This would be further evidence for the complement status of *as if* phrases, as (given Sag's (1997) analysis of relative clauses) complementizers never head modifiers.

As discussed in Przepiórkowski (forthcoming), several criteria have been used to define the classes adjunct and complement and the different criteria do not pick out the same classes. Here, we assume a variant of Tesnière's (1959) functional criterion: Complements are those things that are selected by the verb in its 'off the shelf' lexical entry; all other dependents are adjuncts.[3]

There are several fundamental differences between complements and adjuncts relevant to this discussion. First, it follows from our statement of the functional criterion that complements can fill an argument role in the semantics of the selecting head, while adjuncts never do.[4] Next, there are the two standard tests of iterability, which is not useful here, and *do so* substitution. A third useful contrast is the direction of selection: heads select for their complements, while adjuncts select what they will modify. A fourth contrast is that extraction from complements is less constrained than extraction from adjuncts. The final difference we consider is a semantic one, which comes to light in how certain ambiguous sentences retain or lose readings in different syntactic, semantic, and pragmatic conditions. On all of these criteria, certain uses of *as if* phrases qualify as complements rather than adjuncts.

A corpus search of North American newspapers[5] and 18th to early 19th century English prose fiction[6] was undertaken to discover which verbs might be taking *as if* phrases as complements. The following list of verbs was compiled on the basis of frequency of co-occurrence with *as*

---

[2]Henceforth, the term '*as if* phrases' will be used to refer to phrases headed by *as if*, *as though* and *like*.

[3]Przepiórkowski forthcoming provides a formalization of this distinction in HPSG.

[4]This view is not completely uncontroversial. For example, Grimshaw 1990 presents an analysis of the passive *by* phrase as a special kind of adjunct which restricts the interpretation of the argument that it is associated with, but does not itself satisfy an argument structure position. Even on this analysis, Grimshaw shares our central assumption that only complements directly fill argument positions, so the distinction between complements and adjuncts is maintained, though the classification of passive *by* phrases is in dispute.

[5]From the North American News Text Corpus, available from the Linguistic Data Consortium at www.ldc.upenn.edu.

[6]In Stanford University's Academic Text Service's collection.

if phrases and of the apparent intended meanings of attested examples involving the verbs and *as if*.[7],[8]

(2)

Verb class	Members
Verbs of perception	look, seem, appear, sound, feel, strike
Verbs of deception	make, behave, act, go about, shew, feign, pass off, make believe
Verbs of insinuation	hint, intimate, insinuate
Verbs of construal	understand, consider, construe
Verbs of caring	think of, treat, love, feel for, bring up, look after
Verbs of expression	talk, write, speak

As the verbs of perception can appear with expletive subjects, they can be used to show that *as if* phrases are complements by the first test. In (1) and (3), the only phrase that could be filling an argument position of the verb is the *as if* phrase.

(3) Prince Henriquez fell ill of a malignant Distemper, Medicine was at a loss, **it seem'd as if Art were no more,** the Physicians could find no Drugs of sufficient Heat to throw out the Distemper; without which, inevitable Death was all that could be expected. (M. Manley, *The New Atalantis*, 1709)

Given that most semantic predicates introduced by verbs have at least one argument position, the *as if* phrases must fill that argument position. As indicated above, we take being a selected complement to be a necessary condition for filling a semantic argument position. It follows that these phrases must be complements and not adjuncts.[9]

Next we turn to the two standard tests. We know that *as if* phrases can be adjuncts and we want to establish that they can also be complements, so the fact that they can iterate is not informative. This leaves only *do so* substitution. *Do so* is said to be a pro-form that stands

---

[7]*As though* is somewhat less frequent than *as if* in the corpora, from the earliest uses of these constructions. It is attested for at least one verb in each class except for the verbs of insinuation and construal. Since *like* is both harder to search for and more recent, this list is based on *as if* and *as though*. The similar distribution of *like* may be established on the basis of native speaker intuitions.

[8]The verb *be* is also attested in such uses. We take this to be less interesting, however, as *be* takes as complements many kinds of phrases that most verbs do not.

[9]Note that filling an argument role is a sufficient but not necessary criterion for being a complement rather than an adjunct, since there are on the one hand semantically empty arguments like expletive *there*, and on the other hand complements like obligatory adverbials which might combine semantically as do ordinary modifiers. Examples are found in Levin's (1993) verb class 47.6 (p.255), showing the contrast *The book lay on the table* but **The book lay*.

for a verb, plus all of its arguments, plus possibly some adjuncts. This accounts for the contrast in (4).

(4) a. Kim ate an apple and Sandy did so (*a pear) too.
     b. Kim ate an apple quickly and Sandy did so slowly.

We find parallel examples with *as if* phrases, as in (5).[10]

(5) a.#Kim talked as if the Ice Age had ended in the tenth century, and Sandy did so as if it had ended in the sixth.
     b. Kim ran as if the street were on fire and Sandy did so as if it were made of molasses.

The third contrast employs selectional restrictions.[11] All through their history, these phrases have been able to function as modifiers. In their role as modifiers, they are relatively unselective, and appear with a wide variety of verbs, including all of the verbs listed in (2) above. This is illustrated in (6). Notice that in these sentences, the subcategorization requirements of the verbs are filled with other material:

(6) a. Kim seems sad, as if something bad has happened.
     b. Kim appears to be happy, as though today were a holiday.
     c. Kim sounds angry, like we did something bad.
     d. Kim hinted that there would be a test tomorrow, as if there could be a test on a holiday.
     e. Kim strikes me strongly as likely to win, as if I had some premonition.
     f. Kim treats Bob like a brother, like the world would end if anything happened to him.

On the other hand, it is only a small set of verbs that can take *as if* phrases as complements, and semantically similar verbs can show different behavior in this regard. Of the verbs listed in (2), the verbs of perception except for *strike*, the verbs of deception, and the verbs of expression can be shown by either the first test or the fourth (see below) to take *as if* phrases as complements. The verbs of insinuation and construal and the verb *strike (one)* are attested in 18th-19th century prose fiction in suggestive examples, but are no longer grammatical with

---

[10]We mark (5a) as # instead of * because it does have a highly implausible interpretation involving intransitive *talk*; cf. the discussion of our fifth contrast below, especially of examples (13–14).

[11]While selectional restrictions might often follow from the semantic selection of an argument by a head, this test is distinct from the first one because the correlation has idiosyncratic exceptions.

as if complements.[12,13] (7) gives examples of these verbs from the 18th-19th century corpus.

(7) a. You seem to hint, **as if** you were to be in Town soon. (M. Davys, *Familiar Letters betwixt a Gentleman and a Lady*, 1761)

  b. I must put in a Caution however, here, that you must not understand me **as if** I let my Friend the Quaker into any Part of the Secret History of my former Life; (D. Defoe, *Roxana*, 1724)

  c. It strikes me **as if** it would do exactly. (J. Austen, *Mansfield Park*, 1814)

As shown in (6), *as if* phrases are relatively unselective as adjuncts. That only a small class of verbs allows what, on the strength of other tests, we are calling the complement use shows that the direction of syntactic selection in those cases is from the verb to the *as if* phrase. Thus, the third contrast adds its weight to the conclusion that they are complements.

The fourth distinction between adjuncts and complements involves the possibility of extraction from the phrase in question; extraction from complements is quite generally possible, while extraction from certain adjuncts is highly restricted. So while locative and temporal adjuncts freely allow extraction, a wide range of adjuncts do not, unless they occur in parasitic gap constructions.[14] In general, modifier phrases with an internal clausal complement do not permit ordinary extraction; consider the contrast in grammaticality for the following two examples:

(8) a. The president that he looked as if he was imitating was Ford.
  b.*The president that he fell as if he was imitating was Ford.

In the second, ungrammatical example, the *as if* clause is clearly an adjunct modifying the intransitive *fell*, and here the extraction of the object of *imitating* is blocked. In the first example, the extraction of the object is fine, as predicted on our account where this *as if* phrase is a complement of the verb *looked*.

---

[12]The judgment of ungrammaticality is supported by the fact that the sentences now sound archaic, and by the fact that the collocations are not attested in the modern newspaper corpora studied.

[13]As for the other verbs in (2), it is difficult to determine whether *as if* phrases following them are adjuncts or complements.

[14]In the extensive literature on parasitic gaps, the borders of grammaticality for extraction from certain adjuncts remain in dispute, but it is enough for our purposes to note that the underlying assumption in that line of research is that some adjuncts do systematically prohibit extraction.

Our fifth argument is based on a class of ambiguous sentences involving *as if* phrases. In each case, one reading is licensed by a structure in which the *as if* phrase serves as a complement, and the other by a structure in which it serves as a modifier. The ambiguity of sentences such as (9a) alone is intriguing. More telling, however, is that these sentences retain or lose readings due to syntactic, semantic, and pragmatic effects in a way characteristic of the structures we have posited.

The syntactic effect is illustrated in (9) and (10).

(9) a. She behaved as though she expected to get a cookie.
     b. As though she expected to get a cookie, she behaved.

(10) a. He started to talk as if he already felt the drug's effects.
      b. As if he already felt the drug's effects, he started to talk.

The (a) examples have both the modifier reading and the complement reading. For instance, (9a) could mean either 'she behaved *well*, as she would if she thought she would get a cookie by doing so' (modifier reading) or 'her behavior was such that one observing her would think she expected to get a cookie' (complement reading). The (b) examples have only the modifier reading. This suggests that while modifier *as if* phrases can appear with the expected free distribution of adjuncts, the one route to sentence initial position open to complements—viz., extraction—is not available to *as if* phrases. Here the *as if* phrases pattern with complementizer phrases headed by *whether* and *for*, leaving only *that*-phrases eligible for fronting in topicalized constructions:

(11) a. Kim wondered whether Sandy would stay.
        *Whether Sandy would stay, Kim wondered.
      b. Kim wanted very much for Sandy to stay.
        *For Sandy to stay, Kim wanted very much.
      c. Kim already knew that Sandy would stay.
        That Sandy would stay, Kim already knew.

If both readings of (9a) and (10a) were based on structures with modifier *as if* phrases, this contrast based on position would be unexpected, since most post-VP modifiers can also appear sentence-initially.

The semantic effect involves negative polarity items, and is illustrated in the two examples in (12), which only have the modifier reading.[15]

(12) a. She behaved as if anyone would notice.
      b. He continues to talk as if anyone was listening.

While a thorough explanation of this interaction with polarity phenom-

---

[15]In these cases, the comma intonation following the verb is required, but in fact it is also strongly preferred for the modifier readings for (9a) and (10a).

ena is beyond the scope of this paper, these data do seem to support our hypothesis. If *as if*, etc. undergo a semantic change in becoming complementizers (as discussed below), then it is plausible that their NPI-licensing properties would also change. In that case, the complement structures are ruled out for these sentences on semantic grounds, and only the modifier structures remain.

Finally, we turn to a pragmatic effect, which plays on the fact that the different valences for *behave* and *talk* correspond to slightly different meanings. By making the *as if* phrases pragmatically incompatible with the semantics of the intransitive variants of these verbs, we can create sentences with only the complement readings. Further evidence that this test is distinguishing between adjunct and complement readings comes from combining it with the syntactic test discussed above. As expected, the topicalized examples are infelicitous.

(13) a. He behaved as if he'd never been taught any manners.
      b.#As if he'd never been taught any manners, he behaved.

(14) a. She talks as though the ice age ended in the 1700s.
      b.#As though the ice age ended in the 1700s, she talks.

The above evidence establishes that *as if* phrases can be complements selected by a verb. We turn now to the classification of the lexical heads of these phrases as complementizers. The other possible categories are clause-taking preposition (like *before* or *after*), or subordinating conjunction (like *since* or *because*).

Evidence for a classification as complementizers comes from the semantic contributions of the lexical items in question. Prepositions and subordinating conjunctions both introduce a two-place predicate into the semantics, as shown in (15).

(15) a. Kim left before Sandy arrived.
      b. Kim has been here since Sandy arrived.

In both sentences in (15) the complement clause *Sandy arrived* introduces an event variable which serves as one argument of the two-place relation. The event variable of the main clause serves as the other.

In contrast, there is no second argument for the complement *as if* phrases in (16).[16]

(16) It looks as if/as though/like Sandy will win.

---

[16]We assume, uncontroversially, that the subject *it* is expletive, a position reinforced by the ungrammaticality of examples like that in (i).

(i) *After three appearances on daytime talk shows, the Smiths persuaded it to look like they were still a couple.

We claim that at least in examples like (16) (for another kind, see the discussion near (30) below), *as if*, etc. bear only a one-place predicate. As such, they are similar to the complementizers *if* and *whether*, which introduce the one-place predicate of question semantics:[17]

(17) Kim wonders if/whether Sandy left.

By analogy with verbs like *rely* which take a PP complement but treat the preposition as semantically empty, one could argue that the *if* in (17) was still a subordinating conjunction (SC), whose semantics was similarly ignored by the selecting verb. However, this assumption would force the complication of the lexical entry for *wonder*, which would then have to select either for a CP or for an SC-headed phrase, and in the latter case take the subordinator's complement's semantics as its own semantic argument. While both approaches are consistent with the data, the simpler solution provides a lexical entry for *if* as a complementizer, avoiding an awkward disjunction in the entry for verbs like *wonder*. The same reasoning holds for the *as if* class, given the following alternations:

(18) a. It seems/appears that Sandy has left already.
      b. It seems/appears as if Sandy has left already.

Again, to avoid such a disjunction in the lexical entries for *seem* and *appear*, we maintain that *as if* has an entry as a complementizer, in addition to its adjunct-heading entry as a subordinator.[18] A further benefit of this classification is that we can maintain the generalization about clause-

---

[17]See Ginzburg and Sag 1998 for a semantic framework for these complementizers which employs the notion of a specific *message* introduced in each clause.

[18]Some interesting cross-linguistic data given below from the analogous Dutch construction (provided by an anonymous reviewer) supports classifying the equivalent lexical entries as prepositions rather than as complementizers. (i) gives examples of a Dutch *alsof* phrase as a complement and as an adjunct.

(i) a. Het leek   alsof het sneeuwde.
         It   seemed as-if it   snowed
         'It seemed as if it were snowing.'
     b. Het leek   gek,   alsof het sneeuwde.
         It   seemed weird, as-if it   snowed
         'It seemed weird, as if it were snowing'

The reviewer points out that while Dutch does not allow extraction out of PPs (whether argument or adjunct), it does have long-distance extraction from complement clauses. And, interestingly, there is no extraction from complement *alsof* phrases, providing strong evidence for their classification as PPs.

(ii) a. Wie denk je   dat ik zag?
          who think you that I saw?
          'Who do you think I saw?'
      b. *Wie leek   het alsof hij haatte?
          Who seemed it   as-if he hated?
          Intended: 'Who did it seem as if he hated?'

taking prepositions and subordinators that the phrases they project are not selected as complements of verbs (apart from the copula *be*). We should also underscore that this classification of *as if* as a complementizer rather than as a preposition is independent of our central argument regarding the historical change of these phrases from adjunct to complement.

1.3 Historical development

Having established that *as if, as though*, and *like* clauses can be complements, we come to the second point of the paper: The historical development of these lexical items lends support to recent proposals, including Miller (1992), Przepiórkowski (1999), Przepiórkowski (forthcoming), and Bouma et al. (1998), that put post-verbal adjuncts together with complements on a single list in the feature structures for signs. In this paper, we adopt the version of this proposal that allows lexemes with 'off the shelf' argument structures to license instances with those argument structures extended to include post-verbal adjuncts. We argue here that such a structure lends itself to an account of how certain clauses in English converted from adjuncts to complements.

1.3.1 Representations

We posit the following representations for verbs modified by *as if* phrases. (19) gives a partial description of the lexeme *look*. (20) gives a partial description of one possible instantiation of that lexeme.[19]

(19)
$$
\begin{bmatrix}
\text{PHON} & \langle \text{look} \rangle \\
\text{SYNSEM} \mid \text{LOC} \mid \text{CONT} &
\begin{bmatrix}
look\_rel \\
\text{DESCRIBED} & \boxed{1} \\
\text{DESCRIPTION} & \boxed{2}
\begin{bmatrix}
property \\
\text{INST} & \boxed{1}
\end{bmatrix}
\end{bmatrix} \\
\text{ARG-ST} & \langle \text{NP}_{\boxed{1}}, \text{AP}[\text{CONT } \boxed{2}] \rangle
\end{bmatrix}
$$

---

    c. *De zanger die hij klonk   alsof hij nadeed was Pavarotti.
          The singer that he sounded as-if he imitated was Pavarotti
          Intended: 'The singer that he sounded as if he was imitating
          was Pavarotti.'

However, the historical data discussed below show that the construction is a recent phenomenon in English. Therefore, as the construction developed independently in English and Dutch, it is not surprising that the relevant lexical entries acquired different properties in the two languages.

[19]More precisely, the description in (20) is a more specified description of one of the many models that satisfies the description in (19).

(20)
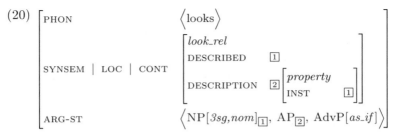

$$\begin{bmatrix} \text{PHON} & \langle \text{looks} \rangle \\ \\ \text{SYNSEM | LOC | CONT} & \begin{bmatrix} look\_rel \\ \text{DESCRIBED} & \boxed{1} \\ \text{DESCRIPTION} & \boxed{2}\begin{bmatrix} property \\ \text{INST} & \boxed{1} \end{bmatrix} \end{bmatrix} \\ \\ \text{ARG-ST} & \langle \text{NP}[\textit{3sg,nom}]_{\boxed{1}}, \text{AP}_{\boxed{2}}, \text{AdvP}[\textit{as\_if}] \rangle \end{bmatrix}$$

The specifics of the adjuncts of any given instantiation of (19) are 'unified in' when the word appears in a sentence, such as (21).[20]

(21) Kim looks sad, as if something bad has happened.

We propose that a historical change took place sometime in the 17th century, where adjuncts introduced by *as if* were reanalyzed as complements for certain classes of verbs. Summarizing the account that follows, this change took the form of speakers hearing one of these verbs in the right kind of context, and deducing from it a new lexeme, as in (22).

(22)
$$\begin{bmatrix} \text{PHON} & \langle \text{look} \rangle \\ \\ \text{SYNSEM | LOC | CONT} & \begin{bmatrix} look\_rel \\ \text{DESCRIBED} & \boxed{1} \\ \text{DESCRIPTION} & \boxed{2}\begin{bmatrix} property \\ \text{INST} & \boxed{1} \end{bmatrix} \end{bmatrix} \\ \\ \text{ARG-ST} & \langle \text{NP}_{\boxed{1}}, \text{AdvP}[\textit{as\_if}]_{\boxed{2}} \rangle \end{bmatrix}$$

1.3.2 Textual evidence

Because *as though* is rare throughout the historical corpora available, and *like* developed much later, we will concentrate in this section on the development of *as if*.

In the Helsinki Corpus,[21] the first apparent uses of *as if* as a complementizer do not appear until the late 1600s, although the phrase *as if* shows up in other uses much earlier. All of the examples in the Helsinki Corpus involve the verb *look*, and only one is a clear-cut case:

(23) I believe ye Parliament is like to sitt longer than was expected
    for ye differences between ye houses are so widened, and yett itt
    is so necessary they should come to some composure before they

---

[20] On this view of the relation between lexemes and instances, the ARG-ST attribute on the lexeme must either be by default a doubleton list, or must be underspecified for the length of the list. Either approach would be consistent with the assumptions we make here.

[21] Available from ICAME at www.hd.uib.no/corpora.html.

part that itt looks **as if** their sitting would yett bee of a month's continuance at least. (J. Sommers, letter to the Earl of Essex, June 1, 1675)

Example (23) is a clear-cut case because the subject of *look* is an expletive and there are no other candidates for the complement of the verb.

There are two other possible examples, given in (24).

(24)   a. I had forgot to tell you, that those who are nobly born of that country, are so delicately cut and raised all over the fore-part of the trunk of their bodies that it looks **as if** it were japan'd, the works being raised like high point around the edges of flowers. (A. Behn, *Oroonoko*, 1688)

   b. The Fellow looks **as if** he were broke out of Bedlam. (G. Farquhar, *The Beaux Stratagem*, 1707)

In both of these examples, but especially in (24a) it appears that the sense of *look* involved is the one synonymous with *appear* (as opposed to the one similar to *glance*), which, according to the *OED* (Simpson, 1992) is attested as early as 1400. Since *look* in that sense otherwise takes as complements phrases that usually function as modifiers, the innovation is the extension to clausal complements.

There are no examples of *seem* taking an *as if* clause as a complement in the Helsinki Corpus; the *OED* cites the following example from 1673.

(25) Stay, there's a Dance beginning, and she seems **as if** she wou'd make one. (Dryden, *Love in Nunnery*, iii. ii, 1673)

Taking this as evidence that *look* and *seem* were the first verbs to take *as if* clauses as complements, how might that innovation have occurred? A possible path is suggested by the examples in (26), both from the same period of the Helsinki Corpus as the above examples:

(26)   a. This seemed to be done in distrust of the privy council, **as if** they might stifle his evidence; which to prevent, he put in safe hands. (G. Burnet, *History of Charles II*, c.1700)

   b. But methinks, the Seat of our Family looks like Noah's Ark, **as if** the chief part on't were design'd for the Fowls of the Air, and the Beasts of the Field. (J. Vanbrugh, *The Relapse: Or Virtue in Danger*, c.1696)

In these examples, *seem* and *look* have their complement requirements saturated by other phrases; in each case the *as if* phrase is an adjunct. In (26b) the adjunct provides an elaboration of the semantic content supplied by the PP complement of *look*, where the PP and the adjunct phrase have a similar semantic type. Given the semantic compatibility, only the syntactic subcategorization constraints of *look* prevent the *as if* phrase from serving directly as a complement.

Now recent work (cited above) on the treatment of post-verbal adjuncts within the HPSG framework provides motivation from several languages for placing certain adjuncts on the argument structure lists of words. This provides the basis for improved accounts of phenomena including word order variation, scope, and distribution of clitics. On this account both complements and post-verbal modifiers are sisters of the verb under a single VP, subject to ordering constraints.

Following this approach, both *like Noah's Ark* and *as if the chief part ... Field* will be on the ARG-ST list of *looks* in the (26b) example, although only the former is semantically selected by *looks*. Further, as noted above, both express similar semantic information, and both have similar semantic types, namely two-place relations with both an internal and an external argument, where the external argument is filled by the subject in a predicative construction and otherwise by the modified phrase.[22] Given this structure for the ARG-ST attribute of the lexical entry *look*, it would be a simple step of lexical reanalysis for the *as if* phrase to usurp the position of the existing predicative complement, giving rise to a new lexical entry for *look* which omits the old complement and instead links the semantically equivalent *as if* phrase to the relevant position in the semantic structure.

In this newly added lexical entry, the syntactic dependency between the verb and the *as if* phrase has been reversed: the *as if* is now selected by the verb as its complement, opposite from the original structure in which the *as if* phrase selects for the verb phrase that it modifies. We assume that the semantic contribution of the *as if* phrase remained unchanged initially, since it was on the strength of its semantic similarity to the original predicative phrase that the *as if* phrase began its career as a complement.

The new complementizers could not, however, have remained unchanged as semantic two-place relations. As we have seen, in modern English, they also occur in sentences with expletive subjects, where there is no second argument to fill the relation.

---

[22]To illustrate with a simple case, the PP *on the table* can appear either as a modifier (ia) or as a predicative (ib):

(i)   a.   The book on the table is red.
        b.   The book is on the table.

In both cases, the external argument of *on* is the book.

(27) a. "It doesn't seem **like** anything could tarnish Chemical Waste's growth prospects," she says. (*Wall Street Journal*[23])

b. It was then that Northrop filed suit against the Koreans – in what the House investigators claim was an attempt to make it look **as if** Northrop had been swindled. (*Wall Street Journal*)

Hence at least in these entries for *seem* and *look* the *as if* phrase must be only a one-place relation semantically, and the simple additional change needed would be for *as if* to be reanalyzed as a complementizer like *that* and *whether*. Evidence consistent with this reanalysis can be found in the historical spread of expletive subjects through these constructions.

An example illustrating an intermediate step is given in (28).

(28) Does not all this look **as if** some unseen power, who guides our actions, had set a ... (F. C. Sheridan, *Memoirs of Miss Sidney Bidulph* 1761)

Here, the subject is not expletive but instead refers to the situation in general. That is, the subject is still referential, but not very informative. Such examples may have participated in the bleaching of the second argument from the relation introduced by *as if*.

1.3.3 Why it has to be extended argument structure

In this section, we have seen how the notion of extended argument structure leads to a plausible account of the historical change we are investigating. We now briefly consider an alternative account in order to establish that our diachronic investigation actually provides support within a general lexicalist framework for extended argument structure.

On our account, the reanalysis of *as if* phrases from adjuncts to complements is mediated by the mapping between lexeme and instance, where the lexeme specifies subcategorized-for complements, and where the associated instance(s) can extend the lexeme's argument structure to include VP adjuncts. In the reanalysis we propose, the learner hears a sentence like (26b) where the extended argument structure for the word *looks* has two elements (in addition to the subject), takes the PP *like Noah's Ark* to be an adjunct, and the *as if* phrase to be the complement. Both the old lexeme for *look* and the novel lexeme can employ the same binary semantic relation.

In contrast, if the representation of extended argument structure

---

[23]Excerpts from the *Wall Street Journal* are from 1989. The texts examined in this case were included in the raw text portion of the Penn Treebank II, available from the LDC at www.ldc.upenn.edu.

were not available in the grammar, then the change would require that the language learner again hypothesize an instance with two elements on the argument structure (in addition to the subject), but now the associated lexeme would also have to have both complements, which means that a novel three-place semantic predicate would have to be introduced. This innovation is unmotivated, since the old lexical entry was only two-place, and the new entry soon establishes its usage as only a two-place relation, meaning the three-place predicate would have had a very short life. What the notion of extended argument structure allows us to do is to provide a simpler account of the steps involved in the historical change of *as if* clauses from adjuncts to complements, without having to juggle the arity of the semantic predicates for the verbs which effect this change.

This kind of argumentation underlines how the precision of HPSG descriptions can contribute to historical linguistics. In other applications of formal grammar to historical issues (e.g., Lightfoot's (1991) application of the Principles and Parameters framework to historical change) the coarse granularity of the synchronic descriptions restricts the granularity of the possible diachronic explanations.

1.4 Future work

There are, as expected, numerous lexical idiosyncrasies in the distribution of *as if* complementizer phrases in modern English, with some verbs taking a wide range of CPs, and others being much more highly restrictive.

(29)   a. It seems as if Kim could win.
           It seems that Kim has won.
       b. It sounds as if Kim could win.
           *It sounds that Kim won.
       c.*It strikes me (as likely) as if Kim could win.
           It strikes me (as likely) that Kim could win.

Such idiosyncrasy is to be expected given our lexicalist treatment of these *as if* phrases as subcategorized-for complements, but the nature of the constraints on selection in (29b) and (29c) is not clear. In general the selection of CP complements appears to be semantic, which suggests that the *as if* CPs introduce a semantic type distinct from *that* CPs, yet with a common supertype distinct from, e.g., interrogative CPs. More work will be needed to fit this distinction into a framework like that of Ginzburg and Sag (1998).

These novel complementizers also appear in at least one construction unlike those involving the more familiar complementizers *that, whether,* and *for*. When there is a non-expletive subject of the higher verb, it tends to be coindexed with the subject of the CP. Examples like the following were analyzed in earlier transformational accounts by means of a transformation called "Richard" (introduced by Rogers 1971) which ensured the identity of the higher and lower subjects.

(30)   a. Sara seems as if she could win.
          *Sara seems as if I could win.
       b. Sara sounds like she's tired.
          *Sara sounds like I'm tired.

However, this coindexing with the subject is not obligatory, showing that there is not a simple control relation holding between the higher verb and the *as if* complement:

(31)   a. They look like someone just died.
       b. You sound as if I never mentioned this to you.
       c. He acts like the whole world is against him.

But these complementizers do appear in at least one construction which requires a raising analysis, with an expletive *there* subject in both the higher and lower clauses:

(32)   a. There sounds like there's going to be a riot.
       b.*There sounds like it's going to rain.
       c.*There sounds like we've lost.

We envision capturing the range of data by positing three separate valence patterns for each of these verbs. The first pattern, illustrated in (29), has expletive *it* as the subject and an *as if* clause complement, with no further constraints on the complement. The second pattern, illustrated in (30) and (31) has a non-expletive subject, and *as if* complement, and a constraint on the pragmatic relation between the subject and complement the details of which we leave to future research. The third pattern, illustrated in (32), has expletive *there* as the subject and requires that the *as if* clause also have expletive *there* as its subject. This matching of the subject can be carried out by means of the AGR feature. As such, the pattern in (32) provides additional evidence supporting the need for an AGR feature at the top phrasal node in a clause, carrying the agreement properties of the clause's subject, as argued in Bender and Flickinger (1999), since those agreement properties must be visible to the higher verb in (32).

1.5   Conclusion

In this paper, we have shown that the historical development of *as if* phrases from adjuncts into complements supports recent arguments for putting adjuncts with complements on the argument structure list of the selecting head. We provided a brief sketch of how the reanalysis of *as if* phrases from adjuncts to complements and then to CPs may have taken place given these assumptions, and supplied data from historical and contemporary corpora which support our analysis. Our larger goal has been the exploration of how the explanatory devices of a lexicalist framework like HPSG, developed for synchronic analysis, can be used in the arena of historical change.

Acknowledgments

Bender's contribution to this paper is based upon work supported under a National Science Foundation Graduate Research Fellowship. Any opinions, findings, conclusions, or recommendations expressed herein are those of the authors and do not necessarily reflect the views of the National Science Foundation. Flickinger's contribution was funded both by the German Federal Ministry of Education, Science, Research and Technology (BMBF) in the framework of the Verbmobil Project under Grant FKZ:01IV7024, and by the National Science Foundation under grant number IRI-9612682. This paper has benefited from discussions with Elizabeth Traugott and Ivan Sag, and from a careful reading by Adam Przepiórkowski. We are grateful for the counsel provided by an anonymous reviewer, who also provided us with the related data from Dutch. All errors remain our own.

References

Bender, E. and D. Flickinger. 1999. Peripheral constructions and core phenomena: Agreement in tag questions. In G. Webelhuth, J.-P. Koenig, and A. Kathol, eds., *Lexical and Constructional Aspects of Linguistic Explanation*, pages 199–214. Stanford: CSLI.

Bouma, G., R. Malouf, and I. A. Sag. 1998. Satisfying constraints on extraction and adjunction. Groningen University and Stanford University.

Ginzburg, J. and I. A. Sag. 1998. English interrogative constructions. Hebrew University of Jerusalem and Stanford University.

Grimshaw, J. 1990. *Argument Structure*. Cambridge, Mass: MIT Press.

Levin, B. 1993. *English Verb Classes and Alternations: A Preliminary Investigation*. Chicago: University of Chicago Press.

Lightfoot, D. 1991. *How to Set Parameters: Arguments from Language Change*. Cambridge, MA: The MIT Press.

Miller, P. 1992. *Clitics and Constituents in Phrase Structure Grammar*. New York: Garland.

Pollard, C. and I. A. Sag. 1994. *Head-driven phrase structure grammar*. Chicago: Chicago University Press.

Przepiórkowski, A. 1999. On case assignment and "adjuncts as complements". In G. Webelhuth, J.-P. Koenig, and A. Kathol, eds., *Lexical and Constructional Aspects of Linguistic Explanation*, pages 231–245. Stanford: CSLI.

Przepiórkowski, A. forthcoming. On complements and adjuncts in Polish. In R. D. Borsley and A. Przepiórkowski, eds., *Slavic in HPSG*. Stanford: CSLI.

Rogers, A. 1971. Three kinds of physical perception verbs. In *Proceedings of the Chicago Linguistics Society*, pages 206–222.

Sag, I. A. 1997. English relative clause constructions. *Journal of Linguistics* 33(2):431–483.

Simpson, J., ed. 1992. *Oxford English Dictionary Online*. Oxford: Oxford University Press.

Tesnière, L. 1959. *Éléments de syntaxe structurale*. Paris: Klincksieck.

2

Constituency and Word Order in French Subject Inversion

OLIVIER BONAMI, DANIÈLE GODARD AND JEAN-MARIE MARANDIN

2.1 Introduction

Subject NP inversion is a very common phenomenon in French.[1] It comes in three varieties, which are not clearly distinguished in the linguistic tradition although they have different properties: (i) inversion in extraction contexts (1); (ii) heavy subject NP inversion (2); (iii) inversion in spatio-temporally dependent clauses, instantiated in three contexts: time adverbials (3a), subjunctive complements (3b), and sentences with a thetic interpretation in a narrative (3c).

(1) Voici le texte qu'a écrit **Paul**.
    'Here is the text that Paul wrote.'

(2) Ont accepté notre proposition **les députés de la majorité ainsi que les non-inscrits**.
    'The MPs of the majority as well as the nonregistered ones have accepted our proposal.'

(3) a. Dès que se lève **le soleil**, le coq chante.
       'As soon as the sun rises, the rooster sings.'
    b. Je veux que soit invitée **Marie**.
       'I want that Marie be invited'
    c. (Alors) arriva **Marie**.
       '(Then,) Marie arrived.'

---

[1] We call 'subject NP inversion' what has been called 'stylistic inversion' since Kayne 1972. Note that it differs sharply from clitic subject inversion as shown there. Throughout this paper, inverted subjects are typeset in boldface.

Constraints and Resources in Natural Language Syntax and Semantics.
Gosse Bouma, Erhard W. Hinrichs, Geert-Jan M. Kruijff, and Richard T. Oehrle.

	inverted NP	subject	object
1. binding of *se*	yes	yes	no
2. quantitative *en* construction	no	no	yes
3. bare Qs *tous, beaucoup*	no	yes	no
4. floating *beaucoup (... de N)*	no	no	yes
5. *de N* in negative context	yes	no	yes
6. *combien* extraction	yes	no	yes
7. number agreement with finite V	yes	yes	no
8. person agreement with finite V	no	yes	no

FIGURE 1 Properties of subjects, objects and inverted NPs in ETI

In this paper, we restrict our attention to the first variety, extraction-triggered inversion (ETI). It has been known (since Kayne and Pollock 1978, Milner 1978, Zaenen 1983) that inversion is allowed along extraction pathways. We present a novel analysis of the phenomenon which is couched in a linearization-based HPSG framework and crucially relies on new data concerning inversion in embedded clauses.[2] Essentially, the analysis is as follows: the constituent structure of the inverted sentence is identical to that of the usual non inverted sentence (an NP VP construction) and the position of the subject NP is due to the union of the VP word order domain into that of the sentence. This analysis easily extends to another case, locative inversion, which has not been recognized as an instance of ETI in previous studies.

2.2   Properties of inverted subjects

Subject inversion is possible in all well-known extraction contexts in French: relatives, *wh-* interrogatives or exclamatives, clefts, PP topicalizations. In this section, we illustrate the general properties of ETI with relative clauses.

Preverbal subjects in French contrast with postverbal objects in a number of ways. Since the inverted NP in extraction contexts shares properties with both, the question of its grammatical function is not trivial. The relevant observations are summarized in Figure 1 (See Marandin 1997 and references therein).

Like noninverted subjects and unlike objects, the inverted NP can bind the anaphor *se* (4). Objects but not subjects allow the quantitative *en* construction; the inverted NP patterns with subjects (5). The same bare Qs that can be objects can be inverted subjects (6). The

---

[2]We leave aside the information structure and discourse properties which have been the main focus of the grammatical tradition (e.g., Le Bidois 1950). See Lambrecht and Polinsky 1997 for a crosslinguistic analysis and Bonami et al. 1998 which shows that subjects in extraction-context inversions cannot be topics in French.

floating $Q \ldots de\ N$ construction, which is available for objects but not for subjects, is impossible for the inverted NP (7). Like objects but unlike noninverted subjects, the inverted NP can take the form $de\ N$ in negative contexts (8). The interrogative determiner *combien*, which can be extracted out of an object but not out of a noninverted subject, can be extracted from the inverted NP (9). And finally, while objects never agree with the finite verb in French, and preverbal subjects agree both in number and person, the inverted NP only agrees in number with the verb (10).[3]

(4) le   miroir où   se$_i$ voit **Paul**$_i$
the mirror where SE sees Paul
'the mirror where Paul sees himself'

(5)*les livres qu' en ont lu   **trois**
the books that EN have read three
'the books which three of them read'

(6) a. Certains/quelques-uns viendront.
'Some (of them) will come.'

   b. Paul connait certains/*quelques-uns.
'Paul knows some (of them).'

   c. un problème que connaissent **certains /*quelques-uns**
a problem that know   some   some
'a problem that some (of them) know'

(7)*l' année où   sont beaucoup parus   **de best-sellers**
the year where are   many   published DE best-sellers
'the year during which many best sellers were published'

(8) une maison où   ne viennent plus   jamais **d' enfants**
a   house where NE come   no-more never DE children
'a house where kids do not come anymore'

(9) Combien   sont venus **de clients** aujourd'hui?
How-many are come DE clients today
'How many clients came today?'

(10) l' immeuble où   habitaient /*habitions **Marie et   moi**
the building where lived-3.PL   lived-1.PL Marie and I
'the building where Marie and I lived'

---

[3]This difference between number and person agreement is not specific to NP inversion. Similarly, the infinitival complement in causative constructions does not agree in person with a postverbal causee (*On a fait se/*nous lever tôt mon frère et moi* 'They made my brother and me wake up early').

In order to make sense of this complex pattern, we propose to rely on the case/function distinction: the inverted NP can be analyzed either as an accusative subject or as a nominative object. While most of the properties in Figure 1 are compatible with either analysis, the restriction on bare quantifiers unexpectedly favors an accusative subject analysis of the inverted NP. The behavior of bare Qs in general points to a constraint on case rather than on grammatical function.

The distribution of bare Qs is extremely intricate. They divide into two groups: (a) those which can be objects: *beaucoup* 'a lot' (in its non-human and non-anaphoric use: *Il apportera beaucoup en travaillant au projet* 'he will contribute a lot by working on the project'), *certains* 'some' and *chacun* 'each' (which is human or anaphoric: *Dieu examine chacun avec indulgence* 'God examines each person leniently'), *tout* 'everything' and *rien* 'nothing' (which are non-human and non-anaphoric); (b) those which cannot be objects: *beaucoup* 'many' (if anaphoric or with human reference), cardinals, *quelques-uns* 'a few', *tous* 'all'. Neither group forms a natural class with respect to quantification, anaphoric/non-anaphoric use or human/ non-human reference. The restrictions must be encoded on the lexical items themselves: some bare Qs simply fail to have an accusative form (Abeillé and Godard 1998).

Going back to ETI, the crucial observation is that those bare Qs that can be inverted NPs are precisely those which can be objects (6). This follows if inverted NPs are accusative, and is problematic if they are nominative. However, inverted NPs cannot be accusative complements, or they would not differ from objects. Thus, inverted NPs are accusative subjects (see also Abeillé 1997).

More precisely, if inverted NPs in ETI were accusative complements, they would only differ from objects in their position on ARG-ST. Such an analysis does not allow for a straightforward treatment of the constraints on quantitative *en*: on this approach, the ungrammaticality of (5) would result from a constraint stating that *en* cannot be linked to the first member of the ARG-ST. But this cannot be correct, since in other constructions, we do find *en* linked to the first member of the ARG-ST. This is the case in some instances of variety (iii) inversion (see section 2.1).

(11) a. Entrèrent trois hommes.
         'Three men came in.'

      b. En entrèrent trois.
         EN came-in   three
         'Three of them came in.'

Since the postverbal NP in (11a) has properties untypical of objects (e.g.

it agrees in number with the verb), we need a four way rather than a three way distinction: between noninverted subject NPs, inverted NPs in ETI, postverbal NPs in sentences such as (11), and objects. In our analysis, the first are nominative subjects (and the first member of the ARG-ST), the second accusative subjects (and the first member of the ARG-ST), the third accusative complements which are the first member of the ARG-ST[4] and the fourth accusative complements which are not the first member of the ARG-ST (that is, objects). The quantitative *en* construction is restricted to complement NPs.[5]

Given the analysis of the inverted NP in ETI as an accusative subject, we can account for the other properties of the inverted NP in the following way. (i) All and only subjects can bind the anaphor *se*. (ii) The form *de N* is always accusative, a constraint which accounts for observations 5 and 6 in Figure 1. (iii) Floating *beaucoup* can only be linked to an object. (iv) Finally, agreement data do not correlate with a subject/object contrast; rather they suggest that the verb always agrees in number with the first item on ARG-ST, but only agrees in person with a subject preceding it.

2.3 Inversion and phrase structure

2.3.1 A problem of word order

It has long been observed that the inverted subject in ETI can be linearized not only after the VP, but also between the verb and one of its complements:

(12) a. la lettre qu' enverra à la direction **le patron**
the letter that send-FUT to the management the boss
'the letter that the boss will send to the management'

b. la lettre qu'enverra **le patron** à la direction

This fact can be accounted for in two different ways. ETI sentences can be assumed to have a flat structure, the inverted subject being a sister of the lexical verb and of its complements.[6] Since the order between NP and PP is unconstrained in French (modulo discursive factors), the two orders in (12) would be accounted for directly. Alternatively, one may assume that either the NP or the PP is extraposed.[7]

---

[4]This is the analysis we adopt for what is essentially an unaccusative realization of verbs.

[5]This analysis correctly predicts that predicative NP complements allow the quantitative *en* construction (*Un chef, il ne veut pas en devenir un* 'He does not want to become a leader').

[6]Such an analysis requires positing a new phrase type *head-subject-complements*.

[7]This is the standard hypothesis in transformational analyses. Depending on the specific proposal, the subject NP is assumed to be either right adjoined to the VP,

However, none of these analyses can account for the word order illustrated in (13), a piece of data which has not been brought to light in previous studies. When the embedded V[*inf*] is slashed, the higher subject may occur between the embedded V and its complements. Note the potentially unbounded distance between the main verb and the VP among whose constituents the inverted subject is found.

(13) a. le   livre que pouvait recommander **le patron du**
          the book that could   recommend   the head   of-the
          labo à cet étudiant
          lab   to this student
          'the book that the head of the lab could recommend to this student'

      b. le   livre que croyait pouvoir recommander **le patron**
          the book that thought can   recommend   the head
          du   labo à cet étudiant
          of-the lab   to this student
          'the book that the head of the lab thought he could recommend to this student'

2.3.2 A problem for extraposition

An extraposition analysis for (13) would have to assume that extraposition is unbounded. Figure 2 illustrates this fact: the PP has to cross two VPs (or S) boundaries. The dashed lines indicate different conceivable attachments for the inverted subject. Note that generating the subject in a different 'base' position does not solve the problem since the PP has to be extraposed in any case to yield the right order.

But extraposition is clearly clause-bounded in French. Example (14) illustrates the well-known fact that extraposition of a relative clause out of an NP is clause-bounded.

(14) a. Je demanderai [à rencontrer [des lecteurs qui ont aimé
          I ask-FUT   À meet   DES readers who have liked
          mon livre]] à mon éditeur.
          my book to my   publisher
          'I will ask my publisher to meet readers who have liked my book.'

      b.*Je demanderai à rencontrer des lecteurs à mon éditeur qui ont aimé mon livre.

An extraposition analysis of (13) would involve a hypothetical PP extraposition. Example (15) shows that the purported PP extraposition

---

or in its base position, which is to the left or to the right of the VP (see de Wind 1995 and references therein for discussion).

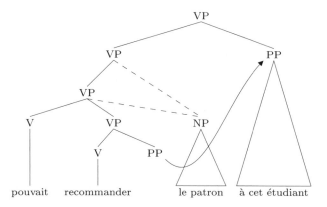

FIGURE 2 Extraposition analysis for (13a)

would similarly have to be clause-bounded. Accordingly, the extraposition analysis cannot account for the contrast between the acceptability of (13) and the unacceptability of (15b).

(15) a. Le patron du   labo [disait [travailler sur ce   sujet]
          the head of-the lab   said   work   on this subject
          [à   ses collaborateurs]].
          to his collaborators
          'The head of the lab said he worked on this subject to his collaborators.'
      b.*Le patron du labo disait travailler à ses collaborateurs sur ce sujet.

2.3.3   Problems for flat structures

Another possibility would be to assume a flattened structure for the main VP in (13), as in Figure 3:[8] in the spirit of e.g., Hinrichs and Nakazawa (1994), we could assume that the verb whose subject is inverted is a composition verb inheriting the arguments of its infinitival V complement. This would create a flat structure with the inverted subject at the same level as the V[*inf*], thus allowing the unusual position of the inverted subject. Such an analysis encounters three serious empirical problems.

Non-inherited arguments. First, it is not clear what type of arguments would be inherited by the verb whose subject is inverted. In

---

[8]The flat structure seems to be the only purely phrase-structural option: to account for the data in (13) with a hierarchical complementation, we would have to postulate a new type of 'upside down' unbounded dependency where the subject of the main verb would be at the same level as the complements of the V[*inf*].

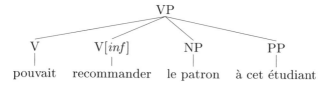

FIGURE 3 Flat structure analysis for (13a)

causative constructions, which have been argued to instantiate a flat complementation (e.g., Abeillé et al. 1998), pronominal clitics are inherited by the head verb which is their host (16). This is not the case in ETI (17), since the clitic argument only occurs on the downstairs verb.

(16) a. Paul le fera   lire aux   étudiants.
          Paul it make-FUT read to-the students
          'Paul will make the students read it.'

    b.*Paul fera le lire aux étudiants.

(17) a.*un message que   lui   veut envoyer **Paul**
          a message which to-him wants send   Paul
          'a message which Paul wants to send to him'

    b. un message que veut lui envoyer **Paul**

Hence, the purported composition verb in ETI would inherit only the canonical complements from its V[*inf*] complement. However, this turns out not to be the correct generalization.

The floating Q *beaucoup* is inherited by composition verbs (auxiliaries and causative verbs) as shown by its occurrence between the auxiliary and the past participle *fait* (18a). The inverted NP is perfectly compatible with such inheritance (18b).

(18) a. les étudiants auxquels le   prof   de math en a
          the students to-whom the teacher of math EN has
          beaucoup fait   faire
          many   made do
          'the students whom the math teacher made do many (exercises)'

    b. les étudiants auxquels en a beaucoup fait faire **le prof de math**

On the other hand, *beaucoup* cannot climb out of a VP whose head is not a composition verb. Subject inversion does not modify this behavior.

(19) a.*les étudiants auxquels le   prof   de math a   beaucoup
          the students to-whom the teacher of math has many

voulu   en donner
wanted EN give
'the students to whom the math teacher wanted to give many (exercises)'

b.*les étudiants auxquels a beaucoup voulu en donner **le prof de math**

Accordingly, the putative argument-composition *vouloir* in (19b) does not inherit *beaucoup*, although *beaucoup* is canonical. The flat structure analysis would have to prevent not only clitics but also canonical bare Qs from being inherited. Such a stipulation would be unfortunate, since clitics and bare Qs are precisely the items whose distribution gives a strong argument in favor of a flat structure for causatives and auxiliaries; thus the putative composition verbs in ETI would be unable to inherit any of the items for which there is independent evidence of inheritance.

Binding. The binding data present a second challenge for argument composition. The expression *l'un ... l'autre* is an anaphor which must be bound by an o-commanding argument in every ARG-ST list where it occurs, as shown by its behavior in causatives. In (20a), both arguments of the V[*inf*] (*des patients*, *l'un après l'autre*) are inherited by *faire*; the anaphor is bound on both the ARG-ST of *s'occuper* and *faire*. On the other hand, in (20b), the cliticized antecedent *en* is 'trapped' on the downstairs verb and fails to occur on the ARG-ST of *faire*.[9] Thus *l'un après l'autre* is not bound on the main verb's

(20) a. Sa rigueur   le   fera   s' occuper [des   patients]$_i$
        His orderliness him make-FUT SE take-care of-the patients
        [l' un après l'   autre]$_i$.
        the one after the other
        'His orderliness will make him take care of the patients one after the other.'

    b.*Sa rigueur   le   fera   s' en$_i$ occuper
        His orderliness him make-FUT SE EN take-care
        [l' un après l'   autre]$_i$.
        the one after the other
        'His orderliness will make him take care of them one after the other.'

If NP inversion were due to composition, we would expect (21b) to be similarly unacceptable: the cliticized antecedent (*les*) of the anaphor *l'un ... l'autre* only belongs to the ARG-ST of *mélanger*. If the anaphor

---

[9]We follow Abeillé *et al.*'s 1998 analysis where composition-*faire* can take a complement hosting clitics if one of them is an inherent clitic such as the reflexive in *s'occuper*.

were inherited by the higher verb, it would be unbound. But (21b) is grammatical; thus, *l'un ... l'autre* should not be inherited in ETI sentences.

(21) a. On a   perdu le   tube dans lequel notre préparateur
       We have lost   the tube in   which our   assistant
       avait pensé   les$_i$ mélanger [les unes avec les autres]$_i$.
       had   planned them mix   the ones with the others
       'We have lost the tube in which the assistant had planned to mix them together (the colors).'

   b. On a perdu le tube dans lequel avait pensé les$_i$ mélanger **notre préparateur** [les unes avec les autres]$_i$.

VP marking. The third problem for the composition analysis resides in the combined properties of adverbs and the marking system of infinitival VPs (Abeillé and Godard, 1997). The bare quantifier *tout* adjoins to the left of the V[*inf*] (Abeillé and Godard, 1998). On the other hand, an adverb such as *fréquemment* adjoins to the left of VP[*inf*] rather than V[*inf*]; this is shown by the fact that it cannot occur between *tout* and the verb (22).[10]

(22) a. Il   se résigne à fréquemment tout expliquer à   ses élèves.
       He SE accepts À frequently   all   explain   to his students
       'He accepts to explain frequently everything to his students.'

   b.*Il se résigne à tout fréquemment expliquer à ses élèves.

Certain verbs subcategorize for a VP 'marked' with *de* or *à*. That such elements combine with a VP is shown by their occurrence to the left of *fréquemment* (23a). We analyze them as phrasal affixes realized on the leftmost branch of the VP, in the spirit of Miller (1992). Crucially, subject inversion does not affect their position (23b).

(23) a. C' est un problème que notre médiéviste se résigne à
       It is a problem that our   medievalist SE accepts À
       fréquemment expliquer aux   étudiants de première année.
       frequently   explain   to-the students of first   year
       'It's a problem that our medievalist accepts to explain frequently to first year students.'

   b. C'est un problème que se résigne à fréquemment expliquer **notre médiéviste** aux étudiants de première année.

These data raise difficulty for a flat structure analysis because the notion of a VP leftmost branch disappears at the same time as the VP

---

[10]Note that this is not a scope problem: *Paul a tout expliqué à ses étudiants fréquemment* can mean that for each thing Paul explained to his students, he explained it frequently.

disappears. Without a VP constituent, it is impossible to account for the fact that the affix *à* occurs on the leftmost adjunct, if there is one, and on the V otherwise.[11] On the other hand, the data follow from the independently motivated analysis of *de* and *à* provided the main verb in ETI constructions takes a VP complement as it does in noninverted sentences.

We thus conclude that argument composition is an inadequate treatment for long-distance inversion.

2.4 A domain-union analysis

In our approach, the constituent structure of an ETI sentence is not different from that of a noninverted sentence. Subject inversion is the consequence of a different word order domain configuration. Specifically, we adopt Reape's (1994) domain union framework, and we assume that in inverted sentences, the slashed VP's word order domain gets unioned into the S domain. Having presented the data in more detail, we propose a treatment involving verb subtypes which we connect with domain union, and we give the major relevant linear precedence statements.

2.4.1 More data

Inversion is licensed by a gap in an NP.

(24) a. Combien   sont venus **de clients** ?
       How-many are   come DE clients
       'How many clients came?'

   b. une brosse à habits dont   se recourbait **la poignée**
      a   brush to clothes of-which SE bent   the handle
      'a clothes brush the handle of which bended'

It is never completely acceptable with verbs taking a complement sentence, whether the gap is local or inherited (*contra* Kayne and Pollock 1978); the complement sentence itself can of course be inverted (26).

(25) a.*l' étudiant à qui disait **Marie** qu' elle ne viendrait pas
       the student   to who said   Marie that she NE come   not
       'the student to whom Marie said that she would not come'

   b.*le livre qu' avait cru   que Jean écrirait
      the book that had   thought that Jean write-COND

---

[11] A similar argument can be made if *de* and *à* are analyzed as words: they would have to select a VP, but there is no VP for *à* to select in (23b) on a flat structure analysis.

> **mon éditeur parisien**
> my   publisher Parisian
> 'the book that my Parisian publisher thought that Jean would
> write'

(26) le livre que mon éditeur avait cru qu'écrirait **Jean**
     'the book my publisher believed that Jean would write'

Subject inversion is always acceptable with verbs taking a VP[*inf*] complement: inversion with a subject control verb is illustrated in (27a),
inversion with an object control verb is illustrated in (27b).

(27) a. le livre que voulait offrir à ma fille   **un libraire**
         the book that wanted offer to my daughter a   bookseller
         'the book that a bookseller wanted to offer to my daughter'

      b. le livre que m' a   convaincu d' offrir à ma fille
         the book that me has convinced DE offer to my daughter
         un libraire
         a   bookseller
         'the book that a bookseller convinced me to offer to my daugh-
         ter'

However, only subject control or raising verbs allow the problematic
order discussed above in 2.3.1 and illustrated again in (28a): the inverted
subject must follow the embedded complements when the higher verb is
an object control verb (28b).

(28) a. le rôle bénéfique que lui   semblait jouer **Pierre**
         the role favorable that to-him seemed   play Pierre
         dans ce   travail
         in   this work
         'the favorable role that Pierre seemed to play in this work to
         him'

      b.*le livre que m' a   convaincu d' offrir **mon libraire**
         the book that me has convinced DE offer my   bookseller
         à Marie
         to Marie
         'the book that my bookseller convinced me to offer to Marie'

We analyze these data in the following way: the sequence of the embedded V, the higher subject and the complement of the embedded V
indicates that all these items occur at the same level in the sentence's
word order domain. The slashed VP complement of a subject control
verb, but not that of an object control verb, may contribute its daughters
to a higher word order domain.

2.4.2 The treatment

Verb types. We distinguish between two HEAD *verb* values: *non-inv-vb* (noninverted verb) and *extr-inv-vb* (extraction inverted verb). While we do not constrain the former (e.g. its slash value may be empty or non-empty), we constrain the latter to have a non-empty slash value, a (canonical) accusative subject and no finite sentence complement. The following constraint holds for words.[12]

(29)
$$
\begin{bmatrix} word \\ \text{HEAD} \quad extr\text{-}inv\text{-}verb \end{bmatrix} \rightarrow \begin{bmatrix} \text{SUBJ} & \langle \text{NP}[acc] \rangle \\ \text{COMPS} & list([\text{HEAD } nonfin]) \\ \text{SLASH} & nelist \end{bmatrix}
$$

We rely on a lexicalized treatment of extraction (Sag 1997), whereby heads inherit the SLASH value of their arguments and pass it to their mother. Thus (29) allows subject inversion to occur whether the gap is local or inherited, while correctly excluding (25). To account for the contrast between subject and object control verbs (28), we force the VP complement of the latter to be *non-inv-vb* and leave the complement of the former unconstrained. The distinction between the verb subtypes is available for subcategorization since it is a HEAD value. Object control verbs are as follows:

(30)
$$
\begin{bmatrix} \text{ARG-ST} & \left\langle \text{NP, NP}_i, \begin{bmatrix} \text{HEAD} & \begin{bmatrix} non\text{-}inv\text{-}verb \\ \text{VFORM} & inf \end{bmatrix} \\ \text{SUBJ} & \langle \text{NP}_i \rangle \end{bmatrix} \right\rangle \end{bmatrix}
$$

Domain Union. Following Reape (1994), we assume that every phrase is associated with a word order domain (DOM), which is the locus of LP statements. DOM is a list of signs, and the PHON value of a phrase is obtained by concatenating the PHON values of the members of its DOM list, respecting order. A binary feature UN(ion) constrains the relation between phrase structure and order domains: a [UN−] phrase is inserted in its mother's domain as one item; on the other hand, the different items on a [UN+] phrase's DOM value are inserted into the mother's DOM instead of the phrase itself. In other words, the DOM value of a phrase is a list made of the [UN−] daughters and the elements of the DOM value of the [UN+] daughters.[13]

---

[12]We assume that the *finite/nonfinite* distinction applies uniformly to all head values. *list*([F *v*]) abbreviates a list of objects which all have the specification [F *v*].

[13]'○' notes the nondeterministic *shuffle* operation, which takes two lists and outputs a new list consisting of all their elements, preserving the order in the original lists. The DTRS feature, which is assumed here for brevity, shuffles the HD-DTR among

(31)

$$phrase \rightarrow \begin{bmatrix} \text{DTRS} & \boxed{0}list([\text{UN} -]) \bigcirc \left\langle \begin{bmatrix} \text{UN} & + \\ \text{DOM} & \boxed{1} \end{bmatrix}, \cdots, \begin{bmatrix} \text{UN} & + \\ \text{DOM} & \boxed{n} \end{bmatrix} \right\rangle \\ \text{DOM} & \boxed{0} \bigcirc \boxed{1} \bigcirc \cdots \bigcirc \boxed{n} \end{bmatrix}$$

We must now specify which phrases can be [UN+]. The inversion of a subject indicates that the VP is unioned. In addition, the occurrence of the higher subject between an embedded verb and its complement indicates that the downstairs VP is unioned into its mother (the VP). Thus, finite and infinitival VPs can union. Head-adjunct phrases can also union as shown by the acceptability of (23b), where the adjoined adverb is compatible with the order typical of VP[*inf*] union. On the other hand, finite sentences or head-filler phrases never union. These data follow from the following three constraints:

(32) a. *phrase* → [UN /−]

  b. $\begin{bmatrix} head\text{-}comps\text{-}ph \\ \text{HEAD} \quad extr\text{-}inv\text{-}vb \end{bmatrix} \rightarrow [\text{UN} +]$

  c. $\begin{bmatrix} head\text{-}adj\text{-}ph \\ \text{HEAD} \quad extr\text{-}inv\text{-}vb \\ \text{SUBJ} \quad nelist \end{bmatrix} \rightarrow [\text{UN} +]$

(32b–c) are the only types of phrases where an *extr–inv-vb* triggers union. We use a default value in (32a) to leave open the possibility that other grammatical constructions besides ETI may trigger domain union. The constraint such that the phrases triggering union are headed by an *extr-inv-vb* accounts for the long distance inversion effect along the extraction path (13). Even when the higher verb is a subject control verb, the characteristic ordering of the inverted subject preceding an embedded complement is only possible if the embedded verb is slashed.

(33) a. celui   à   qui avait promis   d' écrire à ce   sujet
      the-one to who had   promised DE write at this topic
      le directeur du   labo
      the boss   of-the lab
      'the person whom the boss of the lab promised to write about this topic'
    b.*celui à qui avait promis d'écrire **le directeur** à ce sujet

The analysis is illustrated in Figure 4, taking the example of (13a).

---

the NHD-DTRS. (31) differs slightly from Reape's domain principle in allowing head daughters to union; this is crucial to account for simple inversion sentences, where a head VP is unioned. Note that the data on VP marking in section 2.3.3 shows that both phrase structure and order domains are necessary for French; thus we do not follow Kathol 1995, which dispenses completely with phrase structure.

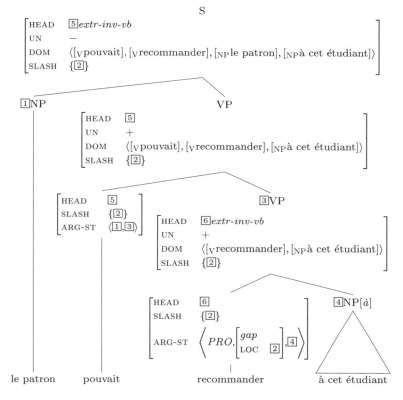

FIGURE 4   Domain union analysis of (13a)

LP statements. LP statements are constraints on DOM values. Two constraints are sufficient to account for the basic order pattern.

(34) a. $\begin{bmatrix} \textit{headed-phrase} \\ \text{HD-DTR} \quad \boxed{1}[\text{LEX } +] \end{bmatrix} \rightarrow \begin{bmatrix} \text{DOM} \quad \boxed{1} \prec [\quad] \end{bmatrix}$

b. $\textit{phrase} \rightarrow \begin{bmatrix} \text{DOM} \begin{bmatrix} \text{HEAD} \quad \textit{extr-inv-vb} \end{bmatrix} \prec \text{NP}[\textit{acc}] \end{bmatrix}$

Constraint (34a) accounts for the fact that the head verb comes first in any verb-headed phrase.[14]   Since it applies to DOM at all phrasal levels, (34a) also ensures that the verbs of unioned constituents come in the right order: each of them comes first in the lowest domain on which

---

[14]This is a simplification which does not take into account the distribution of adverbs and bare quantifiers (Abeillé and Godard 1997, 1998). For a fuller presentation and account of word order constraints in ETI, see Bonami and Godard to appear.

it occurs, which implies that it comes before the other members of this domain on higher domains too. For instance, in Figure 4, since *pouvoir* must precede *recommander* on the middle VP's DOM, it must precede it at higher nodes in the tree too.

Constraint (34b) accounts for the fact that the inverted subject must follow not only the verb selecting it, but any other inverted verb occurring on the same domain; this accounts for the contrast in grammaticality between (13b) and (35) below.

(35)*le livre que croyait **le patron du labo** pouvoir recommander à cet étudiant

2.5 Locative inversion

The analysis extends to French locative inversion (LI),a poorly studied construction, which looks like English LI, but turns out to be a subcase of PP topicalization.[15]

2.5.1 The inverted NP is a subject

The inverted NP in locative inversion, beginning with a locative or temporal PP, has the very same distribution of subject-like and object-like properties as the inverted NPs in ETI. It binds *se* (36a); it does not allow quantitative *en* (36b); it does not allow bare Qs lacking an accusative form (36c); it is not compatible with floating *beaucoup* (36d); finally, it exhibits the same person/number agreement pattern (36e).

(36) a. Dans le lac se reflétait **un château**.
      'In the lake was reflected a castle.'
   b.*Dans le salon en bavardaient **deux**.
      'In the lounge chattered two.'
   c.*Dans le salon bavardaient **quelques-uns**.
      'In the lounge some chattered (of men).'
   d.*Au mur étaient beaucoup accrochés **de tableaux**.
      'To the wall hung many pictures.'
   e. Près de l'église se trouvaient/*vous trouviez **Marie et toi**.
      'Near the church stood Marie and you.'

We thus conclude that if the inverted NP in ETI is an accusative subject, so is the inverted NP in LI.

---

[15] For reasons of space, we leave aside quotative inversion whose verb can also be shown to be an *extr-inv-vb*: there is a potential unbounded dependency between the verb of 'saying' and the higher verb, the subject can occur between the embedded V and and the embedded complement (*"Ce n'est pas de sa faute", semblait vouloir dire Marie aux policiers.* ' "He is not responsible", Marie seemed to want to say to the policemen').

2.5.2 Long-distance inversion

LI is possible in a context where a raising or even a control verb intervenes between the preposed PP and the verb selecting it. The subject is then realized on the right of the embedded verb.[16]

(37) a. Dans le jardin semblaient danser **des statues de pierre**.
          'In the garden seemed to be dancing statues of stone.'

      b. Du piano semblait vouloir s'échapper **un son métallique**.
          'From the piano, a metallic sound seemed to want to escape.'

As in ETI, the inverted subject of the main verb can be linearized between the constituents of an embedded VP, as (38) shows.

(38) Sur la place semblait se dresser **une cathédrale** avec majesté.
      'A cathedral appeared to stand majestically on the square.'

Moreover, the properties which are problematic for a flat structure analysis also hold in LI sentences: clitics stay on the downstairs verb (39a) and the verbal complement can be 'marked' (39b).

(39) a. A l'autre bout du pont semblait lui répondre **l'église de la Madeleine**.
          'On the other end of the bridge the church of la Madeleine seemed to match it.'

      b. Sur un côté de la place commence à se détacher **le futur opéra**.
          'On one side of the plazza the future opera house begins to emerge.'

We conclude that the position of the subject in ETI and in LI have the same source: in each case, the position of the subject is an effect of domain union. Since domain union can be licensed by extraction, we must examine whether LI is also an extraction construction.

2.5.3 The preposed PP is extracted

Regarding the initial PP, we are faced with two possibilities: either the PP is a filler, or the PP is not extracted; rather, it is a constituent of the VP, realized in initial position as an effect of domain union not triggered by extraction (Kathol and Levine 1993 provides such an analysis for English LI). We argue in favor of the first alternative.[17]

---

[16]English sentences parallel to (37a) have been taken as evidence that the initial PP in English LI is a subject (e.g., Bresnan 1994). This argument does not hold for French, given the possible occurrence of control verbs between the PP and the verb selecting it (37b). In addition, there is no case for subject PPs in French.

[17]The fact that the initial PP can be semantically either an argument or a modifier is not a counter-argument against an extraction analysis. In French, the two kinds of PPs do not contrast with respect to extraction (see Hukari and Levine 1995).

It is a fact that PP topicalization can trigger inversion (40a). This is true for locative PPs as well, independently of their argument (40b) or modifier (40c) status.[18]

(40) a. A ses fils, Paul pensait qu' était dévolue **la maison**.
           to his sons Paul thought that was allotted the house
           'Paul thought that the house was allotted to his sons.'

      b. Du   château, Paul croyait que sortirait **un**
          from-the castle   Paul believed that come-out-COND a
          groupe de soldats.
          group of soldiers
          'Paul believed that a group of soldiers would come out of the castle.'

      c. Dans la   cave,   Paul croyait que complotait **un**
          in   the basement Paul believed that conspired a
          groupe de terroristes.
          group of terrorists
          'Paul believed that a group of terrorists were conspiring in the basement.'

Therefore an extraction analysis for LI sentences is always available in the grammar of French. As there is no recognizable ambiguity in LI sentences, there is no case for an alternative syntactic analysis.

There appear to be some interpretive constraints on subject inversion, which we leave for further research. There certainly are some cases where inversion is obligatory, but these are found with non-locative (42) as well as locative (41) PPs.

(41) a. Dans le salon se trouvait **un groupe d' hommes**.
          In   the lounge SE stood   a   group   of men
          'A group of men stood in the lounge.'

      b.*Dans le salon, un groupe d'hommes se trouvait.

(42) a. Au   malheur   s' ajoute **la pauvreté**.
          to-the misfortune SE adds   the poverty
          'Poverty adds further to misfortune.'

      b.*Au malheur, la pauvreté s'ajoute.

We thus conclude that PP topicalization and LI are one and the same phenomenon, and that there is no specific locative inversion construction

---

[18]Note that extraction of PPs out of finite *wh-* clauses is possible in French (Godard 1988): *Dans le salon, pourquoi se saoulait **un groupe de soldats** ?* 'Why was a group of soldiers getting drunk in the lounge?'.

in French: purported LI sentences are just regular cases of extraction-triggered inversion.[19]

2.6 Conclusion

We have argued that the inverted NP in ETI constructions is best analyzed as a subject. After showing that both transformational and argument composition analyses fail, we provide a domain union analysis. This analysis extends to all cases of extraction, including locative inversion, which is shown to be an instance of PP topicalization in French. While domain union and argument composition may appear to be competing analyses for certain data, the comparison between NP subject inversion and causative constructions suggests that both mechanisms are necessary in a grammar of French. NP subject inversion may turn out to be the only family of constructions where domain union is required in a grammar of French. However, given the frequency of use of these constructions, NP subject inversion is a major feature of French discourse.

References

Abeillé, A. 1997. Fonction ou position objet? (ii et fin). *Le gré des langues* 12:8–34.

Abeillé, A. and D. Godard. 1997. The syntax of French negative adverbs. In D. Forget, P. Hirschbühler, F. Martineau, and M. Rivero, eds., *Negation and polarity*. Amsterdam: John Benjamins.

Abeillé, A. and D. Godard. 1998. A lexical account of quantifier floating. In G. Webelhuth, J.-P. Kœnig, and A. Kathol, eds., *Lexical and constructional aspects of linguistic explanation*. Stanford: CSLI Publications.

Abeillé, A., D. Godard, and I. Sag. 1998. Two kinds of argument composition. In E. Hinrichs, A. Kathol, and T. Nakazawa, eds., *Complex predicates*. New York: Academic Press.

Bonami, O. and D. Godard. to appear. Inversion du sujet, constituance et ordre des mots. In G. Lardreau, ed., *Cahier Jean-Claude Milner*. Paris: Verdier.

Bonami, O., D. Godard, and J.-M. Marandin. 1998. French subject inversion in extraction contexts. In G. Bouma, G.-J. M. Kruijff, and R. T. Oehrle, eds., *Proceedings of FHCG'98*, pages 101–112. Saarbrücken.

---

[19]This differs from the analysis we gave for LI in Bonami et al. 1998, of which this paper is a development and reappraisal.

Bresnan, J. 1994. Locative inversion and the architecture of universal grammar. *Language* 70:72–131.

Godard, D. 1988. *La syntaxe des relatives en français*. Paris: Ed. du CNRS.

Hinrichs, E. and T. Nakazawa. 1994. Linearizing AUXs in German verbal complexes. In J. Nerbonne, K. Netter, and C. Pollard, eds., *German in HPSG*, pages 11–37. Stanford: CSLI Publications.

Hukari, T. and R. D. Levine. 1995. Adjunct extraction. *Journal of Linguistics* 31:195–226.

Kathol, A. 1995. *Linearization-based German syntax*. Ph.D. thesis, Ohio State University.

Kathol, A. and R. D. Levine. 1993. Inversion as a linearization effect. In *Proceedings of NELS 23*, pages 207–221.

Kayne, R. S. 1972. Subject inversion in French interrogatives. In J. Casagrande and B. Saciuk, eds., *Generative studies in Romance languages*, pages 70–126. Rowley: Newbury House.

Kayne, R. S. and J.-Y. Pollock. 1978. Stylistic inversion, successive cyclicity and move NP in French. *Linguistic Inquiry* 9:595–621.

Lambrecht, K. and M. Polinsky. 1997. Typological variation in sentence-focus constructions. In *CLS 33*.

Le Bidois, R. 1950. *L'inversion du sujet dans la prose contemporaine*. Paris: Editions d'Artey.

Marandin, J.-M. 1997. Dans le titre se trouve le sujet. Mémoire d'habilitation, Université Paris 7.

Miller, P. 1992. *Clitics and constituents in phrase structure grammar*. New York: Garland.

Milner, J.-C. 1978. Cyclicité successive, comparatives et cross-over en français. *Linguistic Inquiry* 9:673–693.

Reape, M. 1994. Domain union and word-order variation in German. In J. Nerbonne, K. Netter, and C. Pollard, eds., *German in HPSG*, pages 151–197. Stanford: CSLI Publications.

Sag, I. A. 1997. English relative clause constructions. *Journal of Linguistics* 33:431–484.

de Wind, M. 1995. *Inversion in French*. Ph.D. thesis, Groningen University.

Zaenen, A. 1983. On syntactic binding. *Linguistic Inquiry* 14:469–504.

3

Morphosyntactic Paradoxa in Fox

Bertholds Crysmann

In this paper,[1] I shall discuss an apparent paradox in the morphology and syntax of Fox (Mesquakie)[2] complex verbs. In Fox, verbs can be modified by one or more of a variety of preverbs including modals, aspectuals, manner adverbials, numerals, quantifiers, as well as preverbs which increase the valence of the main verb (Dahlstrom, 1997a). While preverb and verb can be separated by words, phrases, or even embedded sentences, suggesting a status as syntactically independent words, inflection (Dahlstrom, 1997a) and derivation (Ackerman and LeSourd, 1994) appear to treat preverb-verb complexes as a single morphological unit. Following the basic assumptions of lexicalist syntax, I claim that Fox preverb-verb combinations are indeed morphologically derived, and that inflectional affixes are attached to complex morphological objects in the word-formation component already. In order to account for the syntactic effects, I propose an analysis in Linearization INSHead-driven Phrase Structure GrammarHPSG (Reape, 1994; Kathol, 1995), which builds on the assumption that Fox preverb-verb complexes introduce more than one domain object into syntax (cf. Kathol 1996 for German, Crysmann 1997, in preparation for European Portuguese). Further morphological material will then be distributed across preverb and verb by imposing partial morphological constraints on DOM-lists.

[1] This work has been financed by a scholarship from the Deutsche Forschungsgemeinschaft 'German Science Foundation' (DFG). I am gratefully indebted to Farrell Ackerman, Phil LeSourd, as well as to three anonymous reviewers for their helpful comments. I would also like to thank my colleagues at the University of the Saarland, and, in particular, Martine Grice and Wojciech Skut, for discussing various aspects of the approach presented here.

[2] Fox (Mesquakie) is an Algonquian language spoken in Iowa. The data cited in this paper are based on Dahlstrom 1996, 1997a,b, Goddard 1990a,b, and Ackerman and LeSourd 1994.

3.1 Introduction

Fox verbal morphology is characterized by an extremely rich set of inflectional paradigms (26 in total), which encode syntactic (i.e., matrix vs. embedded) and semantic (e.g. tense) information. Within these paradigms, verbs are inflected for both subject and object agreement. Although in most paradigms, agreement information is realized by suffixation alone, some paradigms, e.g., the INDEPENDENT INDICATIVE, exhibit prefixation in addition to suffixation, with person and number agreement information being split between prefix and suffix.

	SG	PL	
1	*ne-nowi*	*ne-nowi:-pena*	'I/we(excl) go out'
		ke-nowi:-pena	'we(incl) go out'
2	*ke-nowi*	*ke-nowi:-pwa*	'you go out'
3	*nowi:-wa*	*nowi:-waki*	(s)he/they go out

TABLE 1 The INDEPENDENT INDICATIVE paradigm

As the contrasts in Table 1 show, person information cannot always be determined on the basis of the prefix alone: 1st plural inclusive and 2nd plural forms can only be distinguished on the basis of the suffix. In morphological terms, this can be seen as an instance of multiple exponence.

When the main verb is modified by a preverb, the prefix obligatorily surfaces on the preverb, and realization on the main verb is blocked (Dahlstrom, 1997b). Similarly, the suffixal part of the person/number inflection can only appear on the main verb.

(1)   a.   i:tepi net- oči nowi: -pena

           there 1   from go out 1PL(EXCL)

           'We went out from there.'

   b.   * i:tepi oči ne- nowi: -pena

   c.   * i:tepi net- oči ne- nowi: -pena

Likewise, if the verb is modified by more then one preverb, the agreement prefix will only get realized on the first preverb with the suffix staying attached to the verb. As a first generalization, we may conclude that verbs in the INDEPENDENT INDICATIVE are sandwiched between pieces of inflectional material, regardless of whether the verb is simple or complex.

In contrast to the INDEPENDENT INDICATIVE, some inflectional paradigms in Fox are identified by a change of the first vowel in addition to suffixation. INITIAL CHANGE only affects short vowels, replacing /a/,/e/,/i/ with a long [e:], and short /o/ with [we:].

(2) a. mahkate:wi: -č -i
      fast   3 PLAIN CONJUNCT
      'He would fast.'

    b. me:hkate:wi: -č -i
      sc ic.fast   3 CHANGED CONJUNCT
      'when he fasted'

    c. me:hkate:wi: -č -ini
      sc ic.fast   3 ITERATIVE
      'whenever he fasted'

    d. a:kwi mahkate:wi: -č -ini
      not   fast   3 NEGATIVE
      'He didn't fast.'

If we have a closer look at the contrasts in (2), it becomes apparent that neither INITIAL CHANGE (glossed with sc ic) nor the mode suffix (-*i* vs. -*ini*) can be assigned a consistent interpretation on its own.

Again, in the context of preverb-verb combinations, INITIAL CHANGE affects the first vowel of the (first) preverb (3), parallel to the prefixes in the INDEPENDENT INDICATIVE (1).

(3) a. i:tepi we:či   nowi: -č -i
      there sc ic.from go out 3 CHANGED CONJUNCT
      'when he went out from there'

    b. * i:tepi oči nwe:wi: -č -i

    c. we:či   pwa:wi mawi nes -a:č -i
      sc ic.because not   go.to kill 3   3
      'why he didn't go to kill him'

A third piece of evidence pertaining to the observation that inflectional processes in Fox treat preverb-verb combinations as a single morphological unit is contributed by the 'proclitic' tense markers *e:h-* (AORIST) and *wi:h-* (FUTURE): with simple verbs, these markers are placed in a position immediately preceding the main verb, while in preverb-verb constructions they obligatorily have to precede the first preverb.

(4) a. e:h- mahkate:wi: -či
      AOR fast   3.AOR
      'that he fasted'

b.   e:h- pwa:wi =ke:hi =pi   mahkate:wi: -či
       AOR not   but   QUOT fast   3.AOR
       'But he didn't fast, it's said.'

c.   e:h- pwa:wi =ke:h =meko nahi ši:ša: -či
       AOR not   and   EMPH habit hunt 3.AOR
       'And he wasn't even in the habit of hunting.'

Turning now to the syntactic distribution of these elements, we find that preverb and verb can be separated by an arbitrary amount of other syntactic material, including multiple words (5a), or even phrases (5b). Dahlstrom (1997a) also presents an example in which an adjunct sentence intervenes between the preverb and the verb (5c). Although this sentence — due to the polysynthetic nature of the language — only consists of a finite verb, it is worth noting that it carries its own tense and agreement marking, a property which clearly sets the construction apart from ordinary verb clusters.

(5)   a.   ne- ki:ši   te:pi   tasenwi   kano:na:w
            1   PERFECT enough so many times speak to
            -a
            3/IND-IND
            'I have spoken to him enough times.'

       b.   e:h ki:ša:koči: -či: -meko na:hka [na:wi   -meko
            AOR extremely EXCLAM EMPH again   middle of EMPH
            nenoswahkiwe] sekiši -ki
            buffalo herd   lie   3.AOR
            'She was again lying in the middle of a buffalo herd.'

       c.   we:či   ni:miwa:čini   wa:wawa:wa:kahamowa:či
            because.sc ic dance.3p.ITER REDUP.whoop.3p-0.PART
            'why, whenever they dance, they whoop'

To conclude the description of the basic empirical pattern, it is safe to say that Fox confronts us with diverging evidence concerning the status of separable preverbs: under a morphological perspective, one is inclined to assume that preverb and verb constitute a single unit, while syntactic evidence suggests that preverb and verb should be conceived of as independent terminal nodes.

3.2   The lexical status of preverb-verb complexes

The evidence which I have summarized in support of a morphosyntactic paradox might still be found to be not fully conclusive, especially when adopting the WEAK LEXICALIST HYPOTHESIS, which assumes that inflection, as opposed to derivation, takes place in syntax.

Interestingly enough, it has been shown by Ackerman and LeSourd (1994) that preverb-verb combinations can also be input to derivational processes. While some preverbs can be combined with both verbs and nouns, adverbial and aspectual preverbs are restricted to verbal contexts. Despite the general syntactic incompatibility of adverbs and nouns, adverbial preverbs do cooccur with deverbal nominalizations, as evidenced in (6):

(6) a. menwi pema:tesiwa
         well   live.3SG

         'He lives well.'

     b. menwi pema:tesiweni
         well   live.NOM.INANIMATE-SG

         'good life'

If we assume, with Ackerman and LeSourd (1994), that the whole preverb-verb complex is nominalized, rather than just the main verb which carries the derivational morphology, no exceptionality has to be stipulated.

Further evidence in favour of the morphological derivation of preverb-verb complexes has been contributed by Goddard (1990a,b). First, with completive aspectual preverbs, some verbs are realized as a bound morpheme rather than as a separable word, while other stems, which do not possess such a bound allomorph, surface in the by now familiar separable preverb-verb construction.

(7) a. wi:seni -wa
         eat   3s

         '(s)he eats'

     b. ki:š- -isenye: -wa
         finish eat.suff 3s

         '(s)he has finished eating'

     c. meno -wa
         drink 3s

         '(s)he drinks'

     d. ki:ši meno -wa
         finish drink 3s

         '(s)he has finished drinking'

Thus, whether a given preverb-verb combination is realized analytically or synthetically, is partly a matter of lexical idiosyncrasy. The selection of a particular inseparable perfective stem instead of the separable stem used with other verbs can of course be related to the familiar phenomenon of morphological blocking: if a more specific lexical entry is available, application of a productive word-formation rule is typically illicit.

Second, Goddard discusses some cases where morphotactic constraints between certain preverbs determine analytic or synthetic realization: while *we:pi* 'start' and *pemi* 'along' exist as both bound and free forms, *pemi* always precedes *we:pi* when the two are combined. Furthermore, *we:pi* is realized as a bound morpheme in these cases. Obviously, surface order and boundedness disobey semantic scope here:

(8) a. pem- ose: -wa
    along walk 3s

    '(s)he walks along'

  b. pemi we:p- ose: -wa
    along begin walk 3s

    '(s)he begins to walk along'

  c. * we:pi pem- ose: -wa
    begin along walk 3s

Under the assumption that both separable and inseparable variants of a particular preverb are represented at the same level of grammatical description (i.e., morphology) the phenomena described above find a natural explanation.

The observation that (in)separability does not respect semantic scope is also illustrated by causatives:

(9) e:h- po:ni- mehtose:neniw -**iht** -o: -ye:kw -e
    AOR cease be.alive   CAUS THEME 2PL AOR
    ki:ya:wa:wi
    yourselves

    'that you make yourselves stop living'

In (9) the bound causative *-iht-* unambiguously has wide scope over both the main verb it attaches to and the separable preverb. Again, representing preverb, verb, and causative morpheme at the level of morphology enables us to impose the relevant scope restrictions in a simple and convenient way.

In addition to the evidence just described, recall that some Fox preverbs also serve the purpose of augmenting the main verb's argument structure. For lexicalist frameworks, this constitutes additional support for a morphological perspective on preverb-verb constructions.

3.3 The morphological status of Fox inflectional morphology

We have seen in the preceding section that there is ample support for the assumption that preverb-verb complexes, though separable in syntax, are represented as such at a morpholexical level already. In this section, I investigate more thoroughly the role of Fox verbal inflection with respect to its morphosyntactic status.

3.3.1 Syntactic approaches

Fox inflectional paradigms, as I have argued in section 3.1, display various instances of multiple exponence, lending support to a morphological rather than syntactic perspective on these entities. However, one might object that multiple encoding of a grammatical distinction (e.g., person/number specification) can, alternatively, be regarded as an instance of syntactic agreement. Halle and Marantz (1993) suggest that first and second person prefixes in Potawatomi, another language of the Algonquian family, should be conceived of as clitics rather than proper inflectional affixes. If this were indeed the case, they argue, then what appears as multiple exponence would better be analyzed as ordinary syntactic agreement between a first or second person pronominal and the main verb. However, they do not appear to provide any morphophonological evidence to substantiate the distinction between clitic and affixal status in that language.

If we investigate the properties of true postlexical clitics in Fox, we can observe that they behave quite differently from the prefixes under discussion: first, with the exception of the FUTURE and AORIST markers *e:h-* and *wi:h-*, clitics in Fox typically follow their host (Dahlstrom, 1996). Furthermore, enclitics, unlike suffixes, are separated from their hosts by a phonological word boundary: if a long vowel appears at a word boundary, it automatically undergoes shortening in Fox (*ne-na:kwa* 'I left'). However, if a (lexical) suffix is added, the stem-final vowel is long (*ne-na:kwa:-pena* 'We left.'). Adding an enclitic, however, does not affect word-final shortening at all (*ne-na:kwa=meko* 'I left indeed'). Thus, shortening applies as if the clitic was not there. According to Dahlstrom (1996, 1997b), similar restrictions can be observed at the beginning of a phonological word: while stem-initial short /e/ gets neutralized to [i] when occuring in word-initial position (*ine:wa* 'he said to him', derived from the verbal root *en* 'say'), a stem preceded by the inflectional affixes *ne-* is exempt from this alternation, surfacing as *net-ena:wa* 'I said to him'. This fact sets them clearly apart from the 'proclitic' FUTURE and AORIST markers which do not form a phonological word together with their host (*e:h-ina:či* 'that he said to him').

Turning now to the status of the 'proclitic' tense markers themselves, it is not clear whether an analysis as postlexical clitics makes the correct generalizations: to be sure, the existence of a phonological word boundary between the tense marker and its host appears to suggest a postlexical derivation. However, the markers *e:h-* and *wi:h-* display properties which nevertheless suggest a lexical derivation: first, unlike the postlexical clitics, they are highly selective for their host, precluding attachment to elements of any category other than (pre)verbs (Zwicky and Pullum, 1983). Second, if these markers cooccur with verbs in the INDEPENDENT INDICATIVE, inflectional prefixes are attached to them. In the case of *wi:h-*, the 1st and 2nd person prefixes select the truncated allomorph *ih:*, resulting in the fused forms *ni:h-* and *ki:h-*, respectively. Finally, phonological word boundaries are also found between preverbs and between the reduplicant and the base, with reduplication being an uncontroversial example of a lexical process. Thus, the putative 'proclitics' behave more or less like ordinary preverbs, further restricted to immediately precede another preverb or verb (Ackerman and Webelhuth, 1998).

Taking a second look at the data involving INITIAL CHANGE, it is clear that an analysis in terms of cliticization is unavailable there: neither is it the case that the abstract sc ic-morpheme comes with a fixed identifiable meaning, nor is it plausible to assume that such a tight phonological integration with a host can still be regarded as a syntactic or surface-phonological phenomenon. Given the high degree of similarity in the distribution of inflectional prefixes and 'Ablaut', it would be undesirable to locate them in entirely different modules of the grammar.

3.3.2 Arguments in favour of syntactically complex morphological objects

In order to resolve the kind of morphosyntactic paradox described here, it is conceivable[3] in lexicalist frameworks such as INSHead-driven Phrase Structure GrammarHPSG to assume that preverb and verb get inflected independently of each other by means of lexical rules, and to ensure the right distribution by means of subcategorization for preverbs of a particular lexical type or feature specification. Yet, such an approach misses a number of important generalizations which will be briefly outlined below:

---

[3]Cf., however, section 3.2 for some possible obstacles.

Uniqueness: Inflectional prefixes and suffixes are unique for every preverb-verb complex, e.g., no matter how many preverbs are added to a single main verb, in the INDEPENDENT INDICATIVE there is at most one prefix and one suffix for a particular grammatical function. If prefixes and main verb are inflected independently of each other, that uniqueness has to be stipulated. If we assume that the whole preverb-verb complex gets inflected as one unit, it is not surprising that only one instance of a particular morpheme can be found.

Peripheral realization: Inflectional prefixes in Fox are always positioned at the left-periphery, both locally, i.e., with respect to their morphological host, the verb or the preverb, and globally, i.e., they are always realized on the leftmost preverb, if any. Again, having preverbs and verbs in separate morphological domains misses this generalization. The same holds for the right-peripheral positioning of the inflectional suffixes.

Preverb-verb asymmetry: Fox inflectional morphology reveals an interesting asymmetry with respect to verbs and preverbs: while verbs can be inflected with both suffixes and prefixes, preverbs cannot be suffixed. Assuming verb and preverb to constitute a morphological complex headed by a verb, an explanation follows directly.

Multiple exponence: In the case of paradigms involving INITIAL CHANGE, one would either have to subcategorize for a [+IC] preverb, thereby violating the principle of "phonology-free" syntax (Pullum and Zwicky, 1988), or, alternatively, subcategorize for morphological categories like ITERATIVE, CHANGED CONJUNCT, CHANGED UNREAL and the like. As a drawback, however, INITIAL CHANGE (and the absence thereof) would introduce a high degree of ambiguity. This ambiguity can easily be avoided, provided that circumfixation to a preverb-verb complex is assumed.

Uniformity: The inflectional prefixes in Fox are always the same, regardless of where they are attached. Deriving them separately for main verbs and preverbs is bound to treat their uniformity as purely accidental. Under an approach which attaches one and the same prefix to a (syntactically complex) morphological entity, this property is a mere corollary.

Apart from its empirical shortcomings, an approach which separates prefixation and suffixation is uneconomical in that it triples the number of lexical rules or type constraints: one rule for suffixation to the verb, one rule for prefixation to a verb or preverb, and another one which introduces subcategorization for a prefixed preverb. Thus, this kind of analysis would lead to a proliferation of descriptive devices.

I therefore conclude that it is safe to assume that preverb and verb are best represented as a single unit at some level of morphology.

3.4 An account in linearization-based morphology

In the analysis that I am going to propose, I build on the assumption that Fox preverb-verb complexes constitute a single morphological object (i.e., word-level *sign*) which introduces more than one phenogrammatical object (*dom-obj*) into syntax. In the lexical component of the grammar, morphological constraints are formulated which distribute the appropriate inflectional material across preverb and verb.

3.4.1 German separable prefix verbs

Within recent work in INSHead-driven Phrase Structure GrammarHPSG (Reape, 1994; Kathol, 1995), it has been suggested, on the basis of data from "free word-order languages", to decouple generalizations about the linear order from immediate constituency, expressed in the DTRS attribute of INSHead-driven Phrase Structure GrammarHPSG phrasal signs. In Linearization INSHead-driven Phrase Structure GrammarHPSG, generalizations about word-order are instead stated over lists of domain objects (DOM) which in turn are constrained by the tectogrammatical (=constituent) structure: in particular, the DOM-lists of the daughters can be shuffled together into the DOM-list of the mother, thereby allowing phonological material from the daughter constituents to be interleaved. Thus, a strict view of constituency in terms of functor-argument structure can be maintained, while surface-oriented phenomena like linear order can operate across considerably larger domains.

Traditional INSHead-driven Phrase Structure GrammarHPSG has generally assumed a strict correspondance between syntactic atoms and morphological words. This entails that no syntactic constituent should ever be able to intervene between parts of a word. In Linearization INSHead-driven Phrase Structure GrammarHPSG, the effects of this assumption can be replicated by stipulating that the DOM-list of a word-level *sign* specify exactly one domain object.

In his approach to German separable prefix verbs, Kathol (1996), however, argues that these discontinuous lexical items can be analyzed in a straightforward way if one assumes that word-level signs can indeed introduce more than one phenogrammatical object into syntax.

(10) a. daß Heike auf- hört
         that Heike up- hears

         'that Heike stops'

b.   Hört Heike auf?
     hears Heike up

'Does Heike stop?'

German exhibits a large set of verbs consisting of a main verb and a particle which can be separated from each other by intervening syntactic material. Despite the (surface-)syntactic transparency, the meaning of the verb-particle combination cannot always be determined on compositional grounds (cf. (10)). Kathol (1996) proposes to represent separable prefix verbs as lexical items complete with their unpredictable semantic contribution. Separability, however, is captured by lexical specification of a DOM-list with two elements, one containing the particle, the other the (inflected) verb (see Figure 1).

$$
\begin{bmatrix}
\textit{word} \\
\text{VCOMPL} \quad \langle \rangle \\
\text{HEAD} \quad \boxed{1}\textit{verb} \\
\text{DOM} \quad \left\langle \begin{bmatrix} \text{PH} & \langle \text{hört} \rangle \\ \text{VCOMPL} & \langle \boxed{2} \rangle \\ \text{HEAD} & \boxed{1} \\ \text{INV} & \pm \end{bmatrix} \bigcirc \begin{bmatrix} \text{PH} & \langle \text{auf} \rangle \\ \text{SS} & \boxed{2}[\text{INV} \quad -] \end{bmatrix} \right\rangle
\end{bmatrix}
$$

FIGURE 1   German separable prefix verbs

With the main verb and the particle now having an independent representation for word order purposes, other syntactic material can be positioned between the two, in correspondance with the linearization constraints of the language. On the tectogrammatical side, however, prefix and verb still behave as one atomic lexical sign.

The lexical entry depicted in Figure 1 will also make correct predictions concerning inflectional morphology: if we assume that inflectional information is represented as a head feature, coindexation of the word's HEAD value with the HEAD value of the verbal domain object (indicated by $\boxed{1}$ in Figure 1) will determine that inflectional affixes be realized on the PHON-value of the verbal domain object only; a prediction, which is indeed borne out, as the following example of a participial form suggests: *auf-ge-hör-t* 'up-PART-hear-PART', and not **ge-auf-hör-t*.

3.4.2   Fox separable preverbs

As already noted above, German separable prefix verbs contrast with the Fox data under discussion in one important respect: while the former do not allow inflectional morphology to target the prefix-verb complex as a whole, treating the separable prefix as a mere "satellite", affixes in Fox get distributed over the separable preverb and the main verb. Thus, it is necessary to tie the introduction of domain objects to the morphological derivation, rather than just assuming them to be provided by fully specified lexical entries.

Before I turn to an analysis of the Fox data under discussion, I will briefly outline the assumptions about the organization of morphology underlying my proposal. As we have seen in section 3.1, inflectional morphology in Fox is not strictly agglutinative, involving syncretism and productive 'Ablaut'. Among morphologists, there is now general consent that the full range of non-concatenative processes in morphological systems strongly argues in favour of a realizational approach to morphology (cf. e.g., the arguments presented in Anderson 1992), a trend which is reflected by most proposals for an INSHead-driven Phrase Structure GrammarHPSG morphology component (Riehemann, 1994; Orgun, 1996). Consequently, in what follows, I will build on Riehemann's (1994) implementation of a realizational approach to morphology, couched in terms of generalizations over a hierarchy of lexical types. Due to its tight integration with the lexical type-hierarchy, Riehemann's system is quite well-equipped to integrate both exceptional and subregular formations with entirely regular and productive morphological processes.

$$
\begin{bmatrix}
\text{PH} & \boxed{1} \oplus \left\langle \text{able} \right\rangle \\[2ex]
\text{MORPH-B} & \left\langle \begin{bmatrix} \textit{trans-verb} \\ \text{PH} \quad \boxed{1} \\ \text{... VAL | COMPS} \quad \left\langle \text{NP}[\textit{acc}]\text{:}\boxed{2} \right\rangle \oplus \boxed{3} \end{bmatrix} \right\rangle \\[3ex]
\text{SS | LOC | CAT} & \begin{bmatrix} \text{HD} & \textit{adj} \\ \text{VAL} & \begin{bmatrix} \text{SUBJ} & \left\langle \text{NP:}\boxed{2} \right\rangle \\ \text{COMPS} & \boxed{3} \end{bmatrix} \end{bmatrix}
\end{bmatrix}
$$

FIGURE 2 Schema for regular -*able* affixation[4]

Morphological derivations are represented by means of 'schemata' which relate a (word-level) *sign* to its morphological base (the value of the MORPH-B feature in Figure 2): thus, generalizations such as the

---

[4]The schema for -*able* affixation has been modelled after Riehemann's (1994) entry for regular -*bar* '-able' derivation in German. For expository purposes, some information has been left out (e.g., semantics) and some of the paths have been shortened.

promotion of the transitive verb's direct object to the subject of the -*able* adjective can be stated as structure sharing between the valence information of the adjectival *sign* and the valence information of the transitive verb it is derived from (indicated by $\boxed{2}$ in Figure 2). In a sense, these 'schemata' are underspecified words, which can therefore be organized into a hierarchy on a par with fully specified lexical entries.

As in other realizational approaches (Anderson, 1992; Stump, 1993), affixal material is introduced syncategorematically on the PHON value of the derived sign, rather than enjoying an independent morphemic representation. Thus, non-concatenative morphological operations, such as zero-derivation and Ablaut, can easily be integrated without any commitment to the introduction of zero morphemes. However, the converse is not true: adopting a realizational view of morphology does not preclude the existence of bound morphs. Rather, it only denies concatenation operations their privileged status in morphology.

In order to model the morphosyntactic phenomena encountered in Fox, we will have to ensure that separable preverb(s) and verb are mapped onto the PHON values of separate domain objects, along with the appropriate inflectional material. To achieve this, it is crucial that the specification of DOM objects be closely linked to the morphological derivation: as we have seen in the discussion above, separability and linear order amongst the preverbs is, to a large extent, a matter of morphotactic constraints. I will therefore suggest to augment the elements on the M(ORPH-B) list with an ANC(HOR) feature which specifies whether a particular morph will contribute a separable domain object to surface syntax, or not. In a sense, this constitutes the key mechanism in generalizing Kathol's (1996) approach to German separable prefix verbs to the domain of Fox morphosyntax. Furthermore, I will assume that morphological representations in Fox are essentially flat, enabling us to capture interactions between (multiple) preverbs and verb in a convenient way: As we have seen in the previous section, stem linearization is sometimes subject to idiosyncratic ordering which does not always reflect relative scope properties (cf. (8)).[5] More generally, this assumption is supported by the rather traditional observation that morphology in polysynthetic languages is best described in terms of non-layered, templatic structure (Simpson and Withgott, 1986; Stump, 1993).

To start with, let us consider the morphological schema introducing a modifying preverb on a given Fox verb (cf. Fig. 3): apart from specifying a value for its contribution to the phonological string, it also introduces

---

[5] An analysis based on flat representations will also escape the ordering paradox observed by Dahlstrom (1997b, fn. 20) between reduplication and inflectional affixation (see Crysmann in preparation, for a treatment along the lines presented here).

$$\left[\begin{array}{l} \text{DOM} \quad list \bigcirc \boxed{2}\left[\text{PH}\left\langle\ \dots\ \boxed{1}\dots\right\rangle\right] \bigcirc \boxed{3}\left[\text{HD}\ \boxed{4}\right]\wedge \boxed{2}\prec\boxed{3} \\[4ex] \text{M} \quad list \bigcirc \left\langle\begin{bmatrix} sep\text{-}stem \\ \text{PH} \qquad \boxed{1}\left\langle\left\{o,\text{we:}\right\}\check{c}i\right\rangle \\ \text{ANC} \qquad \boxed{1} \\ \text{SS}\,|\,\text{LOC}\,|\,\text{CAT}\,|\,\text{SC}\ \boxed{5}\left\langle \text{XP}\left[loc\right]\right\rangle \end{bmatrix}\right\rangle \\[6ex] \text{SS}\,|\,\text{LOC}\,|\,\text{CAT}\begin{bmatrix} \text{HD} \quad verb\ \boxed{4} \\ \text{SC} \quad list\ \oplus\ \boxed{5} \end{bmatrix} \end{array}\right]$$

FIGURE 3 The preverb *oči*

an additional non-empty ANC(HOR)-feature ($\boxed{1}$) into the morphological structure. Furthermore, it specifies a constraint on the sign's DOM list, expressing the precedence relation between preverb ($\boxed{2}$) and verb ($\boxed{3}$). The syntacto-semantic effect of the compounding is captured in the modification to the SYNSEM value, basically adding a subcategorization requirement for a locative expression ($\boxed{5}$).

As we have seen in the preceding sections, inflectional affixes in Fox just attach to the left- and rightmost verbal element: using schemata, we can capture this fact quite naturally by combining their PHON values with the PHON value of some DOM object (cf. Figure 4). These objects are further constrained to appear peripherally.

$$\left[\begin{array}{l} \text{DOM} \quad \left\langle\left[\text{PH}\ \boxed{1}\oplus list\right]\right\rangle\oplus list\ \wedge\ list\ \oplus\left\langle\left[\text{PH}\quad list\ \oplus\ \boxed{2}\right]\right\rangle \\[4ex] \text{M} \quad list \bigcirc \begin{bmatrix} aff \\ \text{PH}\quad\boxed{1}\langle\text{ke}\rangle \\ \text{ANC}\ \langle\rangle \end{bmatrix}\bigcirc\begin{bmatrix} aff \\ \text{PH}\quad\boxed{2}\langle\text{pena}\rangle \\ \text{ANC}\ \langle\rangle \end{bmatrix} \\[6ex] \text{SS}\,|\,\text{LOC}\,|\,\text{CAT}\,|\,\text{SC}\ \left\langle \text{NP:}\begin{bmatrix} ppro \\ \text{PER}\quad\{1,2\} \\ \text{NUM}\quad\text{PL} \end{bmatrix}\right\rangle\oplus\ list \end{array}\right]$$

FIGURE 4 The 1st plural (incl) agreement circumfix

If this schema is instantiated to just a plain verb, specifying only a single element for DOM, both prefix and suffix will end up affixed to the same domain object. If, however, the DOM list is augmented by one (or more) preverb schemata, the suffix will obligatorily surface on the main verb, while the prefix will be attached to the first preverb.

Having shown how the general approach works for purely concatenative affixes, we can now proceed to formulate a treatment of the 'Ablaut' cases: as depicted in Figure 5, INITIAL CHANGE is not specified as a separate affix. Instead, it just constrains the PHON value of the left-most element on the DOM list to have a long vowel in the first V-slot.

$$
\begin{bmatrix} \text{DOM} & \left\langle \begin{bmatrix} \text{PH} & \textit{list} \wedge \left\langle (\text{C})\text{V}[+\text{LONG}]... \right\rangle \end{bmatrix} \right\rangle \oplus \textit{list} \wedge \textit{list} \oplus \left\langle \begin{bmatrix} \text{PH} & \textit{list} \oplus \boxed{1} \end{bmatrix} \right\rangle \\ \text{M} \quad \textit{list} \bigcirc \begin{bmatrix} \textit{aff} \\ \text{PH} & \boxed{1} \left\langle \text{ini} \right\rangle \\ \text{ANC} & \langle \rangle \end{bmatrix} \end{bmatrix}
$$

FIGURE 5   The ITERATIVE "circumfix"

Following common practice in Declarative Phonology (Bird, 1995; Scobbie, 1993), surface alternations are expressed as such in lexical representations. Thus, the first vowel of the preverb *oči* is specified as the alternant set {o,we:} (cf. Figure 3). Unification with an 'Ablaut' constraint like the one in Figure 5 selects the neutralized alternant [we:]. Similarly, in non-initial contexts, as well as in paradigms not exhibiting INITIAL CHANGE, the short vowel will be selected.

After having sketched how morphological schemata for both separable preverbs and inflectional affixes in Fox might look, we are in a position to examine the relationship between morphological structure and phenogrammatical objects in a more principled way. If we have another look at the morphological schema for the preverb *oči* (Figure 3), it becomes apparent that some of the information specified there is actually not specific to this particular preverb: as Fox preverbs always precede the head verb they modify, we can take advantage of the lexical type hierarchy by abstracting out the linearization constraint from the entry of *oči* and attach it instead as a lexical constraint on Fox verbs (Figure 6).

Another, more central, property that has been stipulated by the schema in Figure 3 is the relationship between the phonological representation of the separable stem, the ANC(HOR) feature and the phonology of the domain object the separable stem is mapped to. If we compare the schema for the introduction of a separable stem to those for the inflectional affixes in Figure 4, one might wonder whether the relationship between morphological boundedness and syntactic separability is not governed by some more general principle. Setting up a hierarchy of morphological types, we can again capture some fundamental general-

$$
\begin{bmatrix}
\text{DOM} & list \oplus \left\langle \left[\text{PH} \left\langle \ldots \boxed{1} \ldots \right\rangle \right] \right\rangle \\
\text{M} & \left\langle \ldots, \begin{bmatrix} sep\text{-}stem \\ \text{ANC} & \boxed{1} \\ \text{SS} \mid \text{LOC} \mid \text{CAT} \mid \text{HD} & \boxed{2} \end{bmatrix}, \ldots \right\rangle \\
\text{SS} \mid \text{LOC} \mid \text{CAT} \mid \text{HD} & \boxed{2}verb
\end{bmatrix}
$$

FIGURE 6 "Right-hand head rule"

izations: as depicted in Figure 7, morphs are primarily partitioned into stems and affixes, with the former having a SYNSEM feature in addition to PHON and ANC. This corresponds quite directly to the general observation that stems can form the base for a linguistic sign while true affixes cannot. Affixes, as prototypical bound elements, additionally constrain the ANC(HOR) feature to be the empty list. Stems, on the other hand, are further subclassified into separable stems and inseparable stems, reflecting the observation we have made concerning Fox morphology that (in)separability is partly governed by stem allomorphy. Thus, inseparable stems require their ANC feature to be the empty list, whereas separable stems specify a unary list, token-identical with their phonological contribution.

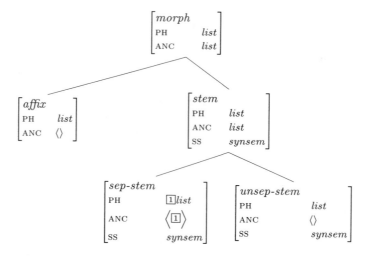

FIGURE 7 Hierarchy of morphological types

Given the underspecified format of the morphological schemata and the relatively high degree of interaction, it is now crucial that the correspondance between members on the MORPH-B and DOM lists be defined in a restrictive enough way. In principle, this boils down to the specification of two relations: first, how anchors are related to domain objects, and, second, how the phonological information contributed by some *morph* is reflected by the phonological representation of some DOM element. I shall therefore propose two general constraints to impose the necessary restrictions.

Let us briefly consider again the morphological schemata in Figures 3 and 4: a characteristic property of the way the phonological aspects of affixation and compounding are captured there is the specification of segmental material on radically underspecified "open" PHON lists. The assumption that morphological material be introduced in this particular fashion constitutes, of course, a fundamental prerequisite for the treatment of morphological productivity through interaction of multiple schemata, as these schemata have to operate on the same flat morphological representation. For the morphological anchoring of domain objects to be meaningful, i.e., for the relation between domain objects and separable stems to be deterministic, we will have to ensure that each *sep-stem* on MORPH-B corresponds to exactly one domain object, and that each domain object is anchored to exactly one *sep-stem*:

Definition 1 Morphosyntactic Anchoring:

i. For each lexical DOM object δ, there is exactly one MORPH-B element μ of type *sep-stem*, such that μ |ANC is token-identical with a sublist of δ |PHON.

ii. For each MORPH-B element μ of type *sep-stem*, there is exactly one DOM object δ, such that μ |ANC is token-identical with a sublist of δ |PHON.

In a similar way, we can also link the phonological contribution provided by the elements on the MORPH-B list to the PHON values of the domain objects. More specifically, I claim that the phonological material associated with the domain objects of a lexical *sign* is a function of its morphological makeup. So far, we have related the distinction between ordinary concatenative affixation and 'Ablaut' to the difference in the associated M(ORPH-B) list. In order to make this distinction explicit, we will appeal to a variant of the PRINCIPLE OF PHONOLOGICAL COMPOSITIONALITY (Bird and Klein, 1994):

Definition 2 Morphophonological Compositionality: The concatenation of the PHON values on a sign's DOM list is subsumed by a concatenation of the PHON values on the sign's M(ORPH-B) list.

In essence, morphophological compositionality asserts that phonological generalizations are both surface-true and surface-apparent, a basic tenet of Declarative Phonology.

Although space considerations preclude any more detailed discussion, I would briefly like to outline how some further aspects concerning Fox preverb-verb complexes can be accommodated under the current approach. The choice of a type-based approach to morphology in terms of underspecified morphological schemata lends itself quite naturally to an account of blocking phenomena like the one observed with *kišisenye:wa*. Under an open-world interpretation of the hierarchical lexicon (Koenig and Jurafsky, 1994), regular types can be dynamically inferred, with type inference being blocked by more specific subtypes. In addition to lexical idiosyncrasies, the type system can of course be used to relate morphological (stem vs. affix) and morphosyntactic (separability) information to prosodic constituents (such as the phonological word) in a principled way. Furthermore, the flat representation assumed for morphological structures not only provides a convenient basis for the fomulation of (regular and item-specific) morphotactic order constraints among stems or affixes in a template, it also facilitates the integration of the scope data presented in the paper: assuming an equally flat semantic representation (such as Minimal Recursion Semantics (Copestake et al., 1998)), scope relations within morphological complexes can directly be imposed by appropriate morphological schemata.

3.5   Implications for Lexical Integrity

Based on paradoxical morphosyntactic data from complex verb inflection in Fox, an analysis has been proposed which tries to reconcile diverging evidence by assuming that morphological objects can introduce more than one surface-syntactic atom (domain object). This raises the question as to whether such a move is not at odds with well-motivated assumptions about Lexical Integrity.

Lexical Integrity is generally assumed to prevent any syntactic operation from targeting parts of (morphologically derived) lexical words. In this sense, the present approach clearly violates the letter of morphological lexicalism. Yet, if we try to pin down the basic intuitions behind the formulation of the integrity hypothesis, we can identify three major factors. First, morphological and syntactic entities typically involve quite distinct principles of composition: while syntax is usually purely concatenative, morphology need not be. Second, morphological processes are often sensitive to the phonological shape of the participating elements, whereas syntax is assumed to be completely blind in this respect. Third, syntactic operations are usually considered to obey semantic compositionality. Morphology, as a lexical level, is subject to semantic idiosyncrasy, usually attributed to semantic drift of lexicalized material. Thus, it is undesirable to have morphological objects represented as legitimate syntactic signs.

The current approach, however, though it certainly relaxes the mapping from morphological to syntactic objects, does not include any of these side-effects. Morphological objects (e.g. stems, affixes and the like) never participate in syntactic operations. Rather, morphological material is assigned to surface-syntactic terminals (*dom-obj*) which fully obey morphological integrity. Furthermore, syntax can only target exactly those objects which are made available by the morphological component as domain objects. Likewise, the choice of using domain objects rather than fully-fledged signs enables us to hide undesirable semantic idiosyncrasies from the syntactic component. Encapsulation into syntactic objects implements one of the core ideas of lexicalist syntax, ensuring a clean modular organization of syntax and morphology.

References

Ackerman, F. and P. LeSourd. 1994. Preverbs and complex predicates: Dimensions of wordhood. In *Proceedings of the 12th Western Conference on Linguistics (WECOL), October 16–18, 1992, Tucson, AZ*.

Ackerman, F. and G. Webelhuth. 1998. *A Theory of Predicates*. Stanford: CSLI Publications.

Anderson, S. R. 1992. *A–Morphous Morphology*. Cambridge Studies in Linguistics. Cambridge: Cambridge University Press.

Bird, S. 1995. *Computational Phonology. A Constraint-based Approach*. Studies in Natural Language Processing. Cambridge: Cambridge University Press.

Bird, S. and E. Klein. 1994. Phonological analysis in typed feature systems. *Computational Linguistics* 20(3):455–491.

Copestake, A., D. Flickinger, and I. Sag. 1998. Minimal recursion semantics. An introduction. Course notes of ESSLLI 10, Saarbrücken.

Crysmann, B. 1997. Cliticization in European Portuguese using parallel morpho–syntactic constraints. In M. Butt and T. H. King, eds., *Proceedings of the LFG97 Conference*. Stanford: CSLI Publications.

Crysmann, B. in preparation. *Constraint-based Coanalysis*. Ph.D. thesis, Universität des Saarlandes, Saarbrücken.

Dahlstrom, A. 1996. Affixes vs. clitics in fox. *Contemporary Linguistics* 2:47–57.

Dahlstrom, A. 1997a. Discontinuity in morphology and syntax: Separable preverbs in Fox (Mesquakie). Paper presented at the 2nd Annual Conference on Lexical Functional Grammar (LFG97), University of Califonia at San Diego, CA.

Dahlstrom, A. 1997b. Fox reduplication. *International Journal of American Linguistics* 63(2):205–226.

Goddard, I. 1990a. Paradigmatic relationships. In *General Topics in American Indian Linguistics*. Berkeley, CA: Berkeley Linguistic Society.

Goddard, I. 1990b. Primary and secondary stem derivation in Algonquian. *International Journal of American Linguistics* 56(4).

Halle, M. and A. Marantz. 1993. Distributed morphology and the pieces of inflection. In K. Hale and S. J. Keyser, eds., *The View from Building 20. Essays in Linguistics in Honor of Sylvain Bromberger*, vol. 24 of *Current Studies in Linguistics*, pages 111–176. Cambridge, Massachusetts: The MIT Press.

Kathol, A. 1995. *Linearization-Based German Syntax*. Ph.D. thesis, Ohio State University.

Kathol, A. 1996. Discontinuous lexical entries. Manuscript, Paper presented at the Third International Conference on HPSG, Marseille.

Koenig, J.-P. and D. Jurafsky. 1994. Type underspecification and online type construction in the lexicon. In *West Coast Conference on Formal Linguistics*, vol. 13. Stanford University: CSLI Publications/SLA.

Orgun, C. O. 1996. *Sign-Based Morphology and Phonology (with special attention to Optimality Theory)*. Ph.D. thesis, University of California at Berkeley.

Pullum, G. and A. Zwicky. 1988. The syntax-phonology interface. In F. J. Newmeyer, ed., *Linguistics: The Cambridge Survey*, vol. 1, pages 255–280. New York: Cambridge University Press.

Reape, M. 1994. Domain union and word order variation in German. In J. Nerbonne, K. Netter, and C. Pollard, eds., *German in Head-Driven Phrase Structure Grammar*, no. 46 in Lecture Notes, pages 151–197. Stanford University: CSLI Publications.

Riehemann, S. 1994. Morphology and the hierarchical lexicon. Manuscript, CSLI, Stanford.

Scobbie, J. M. 1993. Constraint violation and conflict from the perspective of declarative phonology. *Canadian Journal of Linguistics* 38:155–167.

Simpson, J. and M. Withgott. 1986. Pronominal clitic clusters and templates. In H. Borer, ed., *The Syntax of Pronominal Clitics*, vol. 19 of *Syntax and Semantics*, pages 149–174. New York: Academic Press.

Stump, G. T. 1993. Position classes and morphological theory. In G. Booij and J. van Marle, eds., *Yearbook of Morphology 1992*, pages 129–180. Dordrecht: Kluwer.

Zwicky, A. and G. K. Pullum. 1983. Cliticization vs. inflection: English *n't*. *Language* 59:502–513.

4

VP Relatives in German

ERHARD W. HINRICHS AND TSUNEKO NAKAZAWA

4.1   Data Survey

Both German and English allow VPs to contain relative words (henceforth: VP relatives). For English such VP relatives seem to be limited
to subject VPs, cf. the contrast between (1) and (2), while German
allows both subject and non-subject VP relatives, as in (3) and (4),
respectively.

(1)   The elegant parties **to be admitted to one of which** was a
       privilege had usually been held at Delmonico's.
       (example due to Nanni and Stillings 1978).

(2)   * I attended the elegant parties **to be invited to one of which**
       I had tried for many years.

(3)   Das ist das Buch, **das**   **zu lesen** ein reines Vergnügen war.
       This is the book which to read   a   pure   pleasure   was
       'This is the book which was a real pleasure to read.'

(4)   Das ist das Buch, **das**   **zu lesen** er seine Frau überredet
       This is the book which to read   he his   wife persuaded
       hat.
       has
       'This is the book which he persuaded his wife to read.'

A second difference between VP relatives in the two languages concerns
the position of the relative pronoun inside the VP. In English, relative
pronouns may occur *in situ* in complex relativized phrases such as *to be
admitted to one of which* in (1). By contrast, relative words in German

Constraints and Resources in Natural Language Syntax and Semantics.
Gosse Bouma, Erhard W. Hinrichs, Geert-Jan M. Kruijff, and Richard T. Oehrle.
Copyright © 1999, Stanford University.

have to appear at the left periphery of the relativized phrase, as in (5), and may not be realized *in situ*, as the ungrammatical (6) shows.[1]

(5) Das ist das Buch, **das   Peter zu überreden _ zu lesen** er
     that is the book which Peter to persuade   to read   he
     sich geweigert hat.
     self refused   has
     'This is the book which he refused to persuade Peter to read.'

(6) * Das ist das Buch, **Peter zu überreden das zu lesen** er
     that is the book Peter to persuade which to read   he
     sich geweigert hat.
     self refused   has

     '(intended) This is the book which he refused to persuade Peter to read.'

The requirement that the relative pronoun appear at the left periphery of the relativized phrase is not restricted to relativized VPs in German. It holds for complex relativized NPs as well, as the contrast between (7) and (8) shows.

(7) Peter suchte   den Jungen, **dessen Schwester** er kennt.
     Peter searched the boy   whose sister   he knows
     'Peter was looking for the boy whose sister he knows.'

(8) * Peter suchte   den Jungen, **die Schwester von dem** er
     Peter searched the boy   the sister   of whom he
     kennt.
     knows
     'Peter was looking for the boy the sister of whom he knows.'

Another property that relativized NPs and VPs share is the fact that the distance between the relativized phrase and the head which

---

[1]In examples (5) and (6) the relative word appears as the leftmost word in the relative clause. However, if the relative word forms part of a PP, as in (i)

(i) Das ist das Buch über dessen Autor nichts bekannt ist.
     That is the book about whose author nothing known ist.
     'This is the book whose author nothing is known about.'

the preposition, e.g., *über* in (i), must precede the relative word, e.g., *dessen* in (i), since stranding of the preposition is prohibited in German relative clauses. Since the present paper focuses on VP relativization, rather than on relativized PPs, we will leave the precise characterization of what it means that the relative word has to appear at the left periphery to future research. However, see Müller (1999) for further details.

subcategorizes for this phrase is in principle unbounded. This is shown in (9) and (10) for relativized NPs and VPs, respectively.

(9)   a.   Peter suchte   das Buch, **das**   Uwe behauptete _ zu
Peter searched the book which Uwe claimed   to
lesen.
read.

'Peter looked for the book which Uwe claimed to read.'

      b.   Peter suchte   das Buch, **das**   Uwe behauptete Maria
Peter searched the book which Uwe claimed   Maria
überzeugt zu haben _ zu lesen.
convinced to have to read.

'Peter looked for the book which Uwe claimed to have convinced Maria to read.'

(10) a.   Das ist das Buch, **das**   **zu lesen** er sich weigerte seiner
That is the book which to read he self refused his
Frau _ zu versprechen.
wife   to promise.

'That is the book which he refused to promise his wife to read.'

      b.   Das ist das Buch, **das**   **zu lesen** er sich weigerte zu
That is the book which to read he self refused to
versuchen seiner Frau _ zu versprechen.
try   his   wife to promise

'That is the book which he refused to try to promise his wife to read.'

As (10a) and (10b) show, the VP relative can be governed by a control verb that is embedded under an arbitrary number of other control verbs. VP relatives also exhibit a second type of unboundedness that pertains to the relativized VP itself.

(11) a.   Das ist das Buch, **das**   **Peter zu überreden** _ **zu**
that is the book which Peter to persuade   to
lesen er sich geweigert hat.
read he self refused has

'This is the book which he refused to persuade Peter to read.'

b.   Das ist das Buch, **das**   **Maria zu versprechen Peter**
     that is the book which Maria to promise   Peter

    zu überreden _ zu lesen er sich geweigert hat.
    to persuade   to read he self refused   has

    'This is the book which he refused to promise Maria to persuade Peter to read.'

The examples in (11) are meant to illustrate that the relative word *das* can be licensed by a verb that can appear at an arbitrary level of embedding under one or more control verbs within the relativized VP such as *überreden* in (11a), or *überreden* and *versprechen* in (11b).

At the same time, not all verbs that govern verbal complements allow VP relativization. Raising verbs such as *pflegen* or auxiliaries such as *können* do not license this construction, as (12) and (13) show.

(12)   * Das ist das Buch, **das**   **zu lesen** er pflegte.
       that is the book which to read he used to

     '(intended) That is the book which he used to read.'

(13)   * Das ist das Buch, **das**   **lesen** er kann.
       that is the book which read he can

     '(intended) That is the book which he can read.'

In the following sections we will provide an HPSG analysis that will account for the range of facts that we have just outlined.

4.2   Subcategorization Frames for Different Verb Classes

Our analysis of German VP relatives is based on the constituent structures proposed by Hinrichs and Nakazawa (1998) for verbs of German that govern verbal complements. In this earlier work we assume that among verbs which govern the *zu*-infinitive, some, e.g. *sich weigern*, subcategorize for VPs, as shown in the lexical entry (14), while others, e.g. *pflegen* do not. Instead, as shown in lexical entry (15), verbs such as *pflegen* raise the arguments of the *zu*-infinitive it governs by the operation of *argument composition* .

(14) $\begin{bmatrix} word \\ \text{PHON} < weigerte > \\ \text{SYNSEM} \mid \text{LOC} \mid \text{CAT} \begin{bmatrix} \text{HEAD } verb \\ \text{VAL} \mid \text{COMPS} \langle \text{ NP, NP, VP} \rangle \end{bmatrix} \end{bmatrix}$

(15)
$$
\begin{bmatrix}
word \\
\text{PHON } <pflegte > \\
\text{SYNSEM} \mid \text{LOC} \mid \text{CAT}
\begin{bmatrix}
\text{HEAD } verb \\
\text{VAL} \mid \text{COMPS } (\langle NP \rangle \oplus \boxed{1} \oplus \\
\qquad \langle \begin{bmatrix} \text{LOC} \mid \text{CAT} \begin{bmatrix} \text{HEAD } verb \\ \text{VAL} \mid \text{COMPS } \boxed{1} \end{bmatrix} \end{bmatrix} \rangle)
\end{bmatrix}
\end{bmatrix}
$$

As a result, *sich weigern* takes a VP complement such as *das Buch zu lesen* in (16). A verb like *pflegen*, on the other hand, forms a verbal complex with *zu lesen*, as shown in (17), while the NP complement *das Buch* is raised outside this verbal complex.[2]

(16) daß er [das Buch zu lesen] sich weigerte.
      that he the   book to read   self refused

      '... that he refused to read the book.'

(17) daß er das Buch [zu lesen pflegte].
      that he the book to   read used to

      '... that he used to read the book.'

As we discussed in the previous section, the two classes of verbs that govern verbal complements also show characteristically different behavior with respect to VP relativization.

(18) Das ist das Buch, **das**   **zu lesen** er sich weigerte.
      That is the book which to read he self refused

      'That is the book which he refused to promise his wife to read.'

(19) * Das ist das Buch, **das**   **zu lesen** er pflegte.
      that is the book which to read he used to

      '(intended) That is the book which he used to read.'

The ungrammaticality of (19) provides independent evidence for the constituent structures assumed by Hinrichs and Nakazawa (1998), since *das zu lesen* does not form a VP. In fact, as Bech (1955) was the first to point out, whether or not a particular verb can license VP relatives correlates with a number of other syntactic properties such as VP extraposition, auxiliary fronting, and scrambling.

---

[2]The alert reader may wonder whether the structure in (17) is the only one admitted. It appears that nothing in the lexical entry in (15) requires that argument raising is obligatory. The obligatory nature of argument raising can be enforced by the interaction between the feature NPCOMP, which signals whether a verbal element has combined with any of its (nominal) complements and which marks the verbal complements of auxiliaries, and the ID rule that licenses the verbal complex. We refer interested readers to Hinrichs and Nakazawa (1994a, 1998) for further details.

4.3   VP Relatives: Extraction or Scrambling

Previous analyses of VP relativization in the GB framework have assumed either a movement analysis of this construction (Riemsdijk, 1985; Grewendorf, 1986, 1989) or have tried to account for the relevant data in terms of scrambling (Haider, 1985). In Haider's account, the VP relative *das zu lesen* in (20) is ordered as the leftmost element among all the complements of *weigern*.

(20)   Das ist das Buch, **das   zu lesen** er sich weigerte.
       That is the book which to read   he self refused

       'That is the book which he refused to read.'

As already noted by Grewendorf, a scrambling analysis cannot adequately account for the full range of data. In particular it fails with respect to examples such as (21) in which a VP is relativized that is embedded inside the VP complement of a control verb such as *sich weigern*.

(21)   Das ist das Buch, **das   zu lesen** er sich weigerte seiner
       That is the book which to read   he self refused   his
       Frau _ zu versprechen.
       wife   to promise.

       'That is the book which he refused to promise his wife to read.'

(21) offers strong evidence against a scrambling analysis of VP relatives proposed by Haider (1985). (21) demonstrates that VP relatives instead involve genuine extraction. Coordination data, although not the most reliable test for constituenthood, provide additional support that the relative clause forms a constituent without a relativized VP, i.e., a fact which could not be accounted for if the relativized VP were not extracted out of the clause. The following example is taken from Grewendorf (1986).

(22)   ein Mann, **mit dem zu argumentieren** Peter versuchte
       a   man   with whom to argue   Peter tried
       und Hans ablehnte
       and Hans refused

       'a man with whom Peter tried to argue and Hans refused (to argue)'

Our analysis of German VP relatives will posit two filler-head rules: the Filler-Head Relative Clause ID Rule, which licenses extraction of relative phrases as such, and the Filler-Head Relative VP ID Rule, which is responsible for the internal extraction of relative pronouns within relativized VPs.[3] The interaction between these two ID-rules, which we will introduce shortly, is illustrated in the tree for example (5) shown in Figure 1.[4]

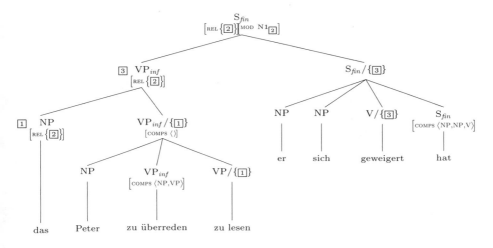

FIGURE 1 tree for relative clause in (5)

In Figure 2 the relative pronoun *das* is licensed within the VP as a filler by the Filler-Head Relative VP ID rule shown in Figure 3. The VP complement of *geweigert* is extracted and licensed by the Filler-Head Relative Clause ID Rule shown in Figure 2.[5]

The feature REL on the filler is specified as a singleton set. We assume that at the word level non-empty REL sets are introduced only by relative pronouns . Thus, the filler has to contain exactly one relative pronoun, while the head clause contains none as indicated by the empty REL value. In order to prevent the value of the non-local feature SLASH

---

[3] Just before this volume went to press, we became aware of an HPSG analysis of the same construction by De Kuthy (1999), which was developed independently of the account presented here. De Kuthy also argues for a double-extraction account and sketches how such an account can be rendered in the construction-type approach to the syntax of relative clauses proposed by Sag (1997).

[4] We assume that the possible values for the feature VFORM for German include *bse*, *inf*, and *psp*. They are meant to differentiate among bare infinitives such as *kaufen*, infinitives marked by *zu* such as *zu kaufen*, and past participles such as *gekauft*, respectively. The three values also correspond to the three types of verbal STATUS identified by Bech (1955).

[5] The rule in Figure 2 is modeled after the relative clause rule proposed for English by Sag (1997).

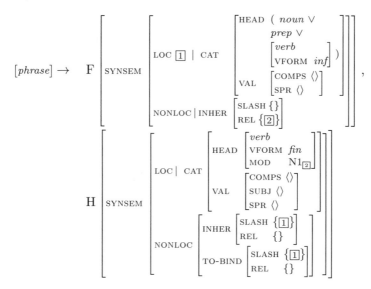

FIGURE 2 Filler-Head Relative Clause ID Rule

from percolating to the mother category of the rule, the value has to appear under the feature TO-BIND of the head. The Nonlocal Feature Principle of Pollard and Sag (1994) will then ensure that the SLASH value on the mother category is the empty set. The empty specification of the SLASH value disallows extraction out of relative clauses, as in the ungrammatical example (23).

(23)   * Wen ist das das Buch, **das   zu lesen** er _ _ überredet hat?
         who is this the book which to read   he   persuaded has

In addition, the rule in Figure 2 restricts the head to projections of finite verbs which carry the feature MOD. Following Sag (1997) we assume that lexical heads of relative clauses carry the feature MOD which specifies the syntactic category that the relative clause modifies. Reentrancy $\boxed{2}$ ensures that the REL and MOD value share the same index. Since REL is a non-local feature and MOD is a head feature, this index will also be instantiated on the REL and MOD values of the mother category of any local tree licensed by the rule.

The syntactic category of the filler is restricted to NPs, PPs and infinitival VPs. The set of categories that can appear as fillers in a relative clause is, of course, language specific. For German infinitival VPs have to be included, while for English we assume, following Bresnan (1976) and Sag (1997), that relative clause fillers are restricted to NPs and PPs.

The second filler-head rule that is presupposed in the tree in Figure 1 is given in Figure 3 and licenses a relativized VP. Either an NP or a PP is extracted inside of a relativized infinitival VPs, as the relative pronoun *das* is extracted out of *Peter zu überreden zu lesen* in the tree in Figure 1.

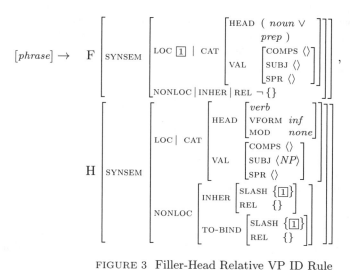

FIGURE 3 Filler-Head Relative VP ID Rule

Note that the restriction of the HEAD in Figure 3 to non-finite VPs is crucial to prevent undesirable interactions with the Filler-Head Relative Clause ID Rule in Figure 2. Due to the restriction to non-finite verbal head in Figure 3, the rule can only apply to the filler phrase in Figure 2, but crucially not to the verbal head of Figure 2. Conversely, the ID rule in Figure 2 cannot apply to the phrasal head in Figure 3 since their VFORM specifications clash. Therefore, the only purpose that the ID rule in Figure 3 can serve is to extract an NP or a PP within a relativized VP. The *none* value of MOD on the head, and hence on the mother, indicates that the relativized VP alone cannot modify a head noun unless it is embedded as a filler in a relative clause headed by a finite verb.[6] Thus, the *none* value of MOD can successfully block ungrammatical sentences such as (24).

(24) * Das ist das Buch, das   zu lesen.
        that is the book which to read

---

[6] We are indebted to an anonymous referee for this idea.

As is the case for the other filler-head ID rule in Figure 2, the REL value of the filler is specified to be non-empty in the Filler-Head Relative VP ID Rule in Figure 3. Unlike the previous rule, however, this REL value is not bound by the head. Due to the Nonlocal Feature Principle, the REL value of the filler will be identified with that of the mother, thus marking the entire infinitival VP with a non-empty REL value.

Finally, we need to introduce one more ID rule that lets us expand filler and head of the relative clause. The Head-Complement ID Rule that we will adopt for this purpose is taken from Hinrichs and Nakazawa (1994b) and is slightly modified in Figure 4.

$$\left[\text{SYNSEM} \left[\text{LOC} \mid \text{CAT} \left[\begin{array}{l} \text{HEAD } verb \\ \text{VAL} \mid \text{COMPS } \langle\rangle \end{array} \right] \right] \atop \text{NONLOC} \mid \text{INHER} \mid \text{REL } \{\} \right] \rightarrow \text{C*}, \text{H}_{word}$$

FIGURE 4 Head-Complement ID Rule

The ID rule discharges all of the complements of a verbal head in a flat structure. Since the rule does not require a particular value for VFORM, the rule is meant to be used for finite and non-finite verbal phrases alike. The empty REL value of the mother has the effect of disallowing a relativized phrase to remain *in situ* in finite clauses and a relative pronoun to remain unextracted within a fronted infinitival VP.

(25) * Das ist das Buch, Peter zu überreden **das   zu lesen** er sich
         that is the book Peter to persuade which to read he self
         geweigert hat.
         refused   has

         '(intended) This is the book which he refused to persuade Peter
         to read.'

Ungrammatical sentences such as (25) can be ruled out since the un-extracted VP *das zu lesen* contains a relative word and hence has to be dominated by a phrasal node whose REL value is non-empty. The Head-Complement ID Rule is therefore not applicable, and the sentence is successfully blocked.

It might seem that the analysis presented above introduces a structural ambiguity when a relative pronoun is not an embedded object, as is the case in Figure 1, but rather the highest object NP of the relativized VP such as *das zu lesen* in example (4). Although the linear order of the relativized VP may be generated with or without extraction of the relative pronoun, there is no independent syntactic or semantic motivation to support such an ambiguity. Instead, the ID rules proposed above analyze the relative clause in (4) as a case of double extraction and assign an unambiguous structure similar to that in Figure 1, schematically given in (26).

(26)   [das [_ zu lesen]] er seine Frau _ überredet hat

If the relativized VP *das zu lesen* were licensed without extraction of *das* within the VP, it would have to be licensed by the Head-Complement ID Rule in Figure 4 rather than by the Filler-Head Relative VP ID Rule in Figure 3. However, the Head-Complement ID Rule requires the REL value of the licensed constituent to be empty, i.e., specifies the constituent to contain no relative words. Hence, this requirement would clash with the fact that a non-empty REL value would have to percolate from *das* to the node that dominates the relativized VP.

To complete the analysis, we introduce the Head-Adjunct ID Rule in Figure 5 which allows us to combine relative clauses with the nominal heads they modify.

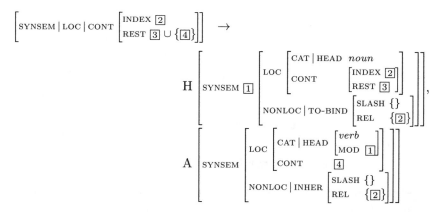

FIGURE 5   Head-Adjunct ID Rule

Although the analysis of head-adjunct constructions is fairly disjoint with the analysis of the internal structure of relative clauses themselves, a few points merit mentioning. As is the case in the Head-Adjunct ID Rule proposed in Pollard and Sag (1994), our Head-Adjunct ID Rule ensures that the INDEX value of the nominal head is identical to that of the MOD value of the adjunct, i.e., a relative clause. This interaction between the values for MOD and INDEX is illustrated in the tree in Figure 6 for example (18) by tag [2]. Furthermore, the index of the MOD value is required to be identical to the REL value of the adjunct. Since this REL value originates from the relative pronoun contained in the adjunct, the nominal head and the relative pronoun must share the same INDEX value, as shown in Figure 6. Finally, the REL value of the adjunct is bound by the TO-BIND feature of the head so that it cannot percolate up beyond the scope of the relative clause.

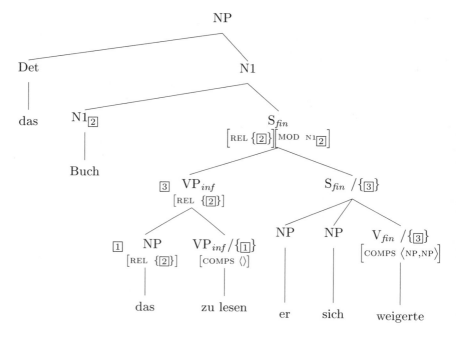

FIGURE 6 tree for relative clause in (18)

Following Sag (1997), our Head-Adjunct ID Rule further stipulates that the CONT value of the relative clause is included as an additional member in the RESTRICTION set of the mother. This stipulation makes it possible to treat the CONT value of the relative clause in the same way as the semantics of other verbal projections. It also marks the main difference to the relative clause analysis by Pollard and Sag (1994), who introduce an empty relativizer which assimilated the CONT of the relative clause to the CONT specification appropriate for nominal projections.

Since neither Sag's analysis for English, nor the one we propose for German employs an empty relativizer, which incorporates the CONT of the relative clause into the CONT specification of the nominal head, the Head-Adjunct ID Rule has to take over this task. This has the further consequence that we cannot adopt the Semantics Principle of

Pollard and Sag (1994), which states that the semantic head, i.e., the relative clause in this case, has to share its CONT value with that of the mother. However, since the definition of semantic head in the Semantics Principle of Pollard and Sag (1994) is highly disjunctive to begin with, having to stipulate semantic composition on each ID-rule seems a much lower cost to pay than having to adopt an empty relativizer whose only purpose is to assimilate the semantics of relative clauses to a nominal-type semantics.[7]

4.4 Subject Relatives

So far we have only considered the structures that our account assigns to VP relatives that are subcategorized objects. We will now return to relativized subject VPs, as in (3), repeated below as (27).

(27) Das ist das Buch, **das zu lesen** ein reines Vergnügen war.
       This is the book which to read a   pure   pleasure   was
       'This is the book which was a real pleasure to read.'

As we discussed in section 3, the distance between a relativized object VP and the head which subcategorizes for this phrase is in principle unbounded. This unboundedness then leads us to propose an extraction analysis of VP relatives. However, the question arises whether subject VP relatives also require extraction, or whether they should be licensed *in situ* by the Head-Complement ID Rule. Such an *in-situ* analysis of subject VP relatives has been proposed for English by Sag (1997) to account for the subject/object asymmetry that we noted in section 1 (cf. examples 1 and 2). Sag assumes that relative clauses in which a non-subject phrase is relativized involve extraction while subject relatives do not. Following Bresnan (1976), Sag limits extraction of relativized constituents to NPs and PPs. Thus, non-subject VP relatives are ruled out, while VP subject relatives are admitted because only the former involves extraction. Since German allows non-subject VP relatives, the language-specific restriction for English which limits fillers to NPs and PPs cannot be upheld for German. However, the question remains whether an *in-situ* analysis of subject VP relatives can be adopted for German as well.

Crucial evidence against an *in-situ* analysis of relativized subject VPs can be derived from scrambling data. In German, complement

---

[7]One way to maintain some version of the Semantics Principle and at the same time adopt an analysis in which relative clauses are assigned CONT specifications that are appropriate for verbal projections, is to adopt a Bach-Cooper-style analysis of relative clauses (Bach and Cooper, 1978). In their analysis, relative clauses modify NPs rather than N1s, and the NP functions as the semantic head.

phrases, including subjects, which precede verbal elements in a clause may be reordered among themselves due to various pragmatic factors (see, e.g., Uszkoreit (1987) for details). The relativized subject phrase, however, may not participate in this type of complement scrambling, as (28), which is taken from Grewendorf (1989), shows. (28a) is an example where the embedded object of the subject VP *das zu beleidigen* is relativized.

(28)   a.   ein Mädchen, **das**   **zu beleidigen** Hans gestört   hat
           a   girl   whom to offend   Hans bothered has

          'a girl whom to offend bothered Hans'

      b. * ein Mädchen, **das**   Hans **zu beleidigen** gestört   hat
           a   girl   whom Hans to offend   bothered has

If it were merely the relative pronoun which is extracted while the subject VP remains in the clause, then nothing would prevent the rest of the subject VP from being scrambled with other complements, as shown in (28b). The ungrammaticality of (28b) thus provides strong evidence for an extraction analysis of subject VP relatives.

In our characterization of (28) we have tacitly assumed that the relative pronoun *das* is extracted within the relativized subject VP. That such VP-internal extraction is, in fact, required, is due to the unbounded distance between relative pronouns and their subcategorizing heads which subject VPs exhibit in the same way as object VPs, cf. (29a) and (29b), respectively.

(29)   a. Das ist das Buch, **das**   **Peter zu empfehlen** _ **zu lesen**
         that is the book which Peter to recommend to read
         ein Vergnügen war.
         a   pleasure   was

         'This is the book which was a pleasure to recommend to Peter to read.'

      b. Das ist das Buch, **das**   **Peter zu überreden** _ **zu lesen**
         that is the book which Peter to persuade   to read
         er sich geweigert hat.
         he self refused   has

         'This is the book which he refused to persuade Peter to read.'

Thus, subject VP relatives require extraction of the entire VP and VP-internal extraction of the relative pronoun in the same way as object VP relatives. In fact, the ID rules that we have introduced in the previous sections interact in such a way that this two-fold extraction is applicable to subject relatives as well. The extraction of subjects and objects is licensed by the Complement Extraction Lexical Rule in Figure 7 which eliminates a member of the COMPS list and places it on a SLASH set.

$$\left[\text{SYNSEM}\left[\text{LOC}\begin{bmatrix}\text{CAT} \mid \text{VAL} \mid \text{COMPS}\ \langle\ \ldots\ ,\ \boxed{1}\ [\textit{phrase}],\ \ldots\ \rangle \\ \text{NONLOC} \mid \text{INHER} \mid \text{SLASH}\ \boxed{2}\end{bmatrix}\right]\right]\ \mapsto$$

$$\left[\text{SYNSEM}\left[\text{LOC}\begin{bmatrix}\text{CAT} \mid \text{VAL} \mid \text{COMPS}\ \langle\ \ldots\ \rangle \\ \text{NONLOC} \mid \text{INHER} \mid \text{SLASH}\ \boxed{2}\ \cup\ \{\boxed{1}\}\end{bmatrix}\right]\right]$$

FIGURE 7 Complement Extraction Lexical Rule

Following Borsley (1987), the COMPS list is assumed to include all non-subject complements of infinitival verbs while it also contains the subject if the input to the lexical rule is a finite verb. Therefore the same extraction lexical rule suffices both for extraction of a subject and an object. It is also this lexical rule which is responsible for the extraction of a relative pronoun within the relativized infinitival VP. It should be noted that this extraction lexical rule is independently motivated in previous analyses of German such as Pollard (1996), Nerbonne (1994), and Hinrichs and Nakazawa (1994b) for the topicalization construction, i.e., verb-second clauses, where either a subject or an object is fronted to the left of a finite verb.

The Complement Extraction Lexical Rule together with the ID rules given before assigns the constituent structure in Figure 8 to the subject relative in (28a). The subject VP *das zu beleiigen* is extracted and the relative pronoun *das* is also extracted within the subject VP.

The top local tree is licensed by the Filler-Head Relative Clause ID Rule in Figure 2; the filler VP is licensed by the Filler-Head Relative VP ID Rule in Figure 3; and the head of the clause is licensed by the Head-Complement ID Rule in Figure 4. The structure is similar to the one for the object relative in Figure 1. The only difference is that the object VP is relativized in Figure 1 while it is the subject VP that is relativized in Figure 8. The REL specifications of the ID rules prevent structural ambiguity of subject relatives in a similar fashion to that of object relatives. If the relativized subject VP remained *in situ* in the clause, the clause would have to be licensed by the Head-Complement ID Rule in Figure 4 rather than by the Filler-Head Relative Clause ID Rule in Figure 2. However, such a subject contains a relative pronoun, regardless of whether this pronoun is fronted within the subject, and is marked by a non-empty REL value, resulting in a conflict with the empty REL specification of the mother of the ID rule. If the relative pronoun

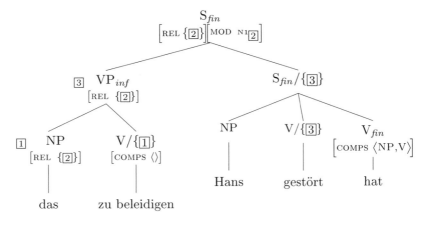

FIGURE 8 tree for relative clause in (28a)

were not extracted within the subject VP, the subject VP would have to be licensed by the Head-Complement ID Rule in Figure 4 instead of the Filler-Head Relative VP ID Rule in Figure 3. This would result in a similar REL value clash since the subject VP contains a relative pronoun.

4.5   Further Issues

In Section 1.3, we demonstrated that our Head-Complement ID Rule does not allow the possibility of an unmotivated structure in which a relative pronoun is not extracted within a relativized VP. Instead, the relative pronoun is forced to be extracted even when it is the leftmost NP within the relativized VP as schematically shown in (26).

However, there is another source of structural ambiguity. Namely, if a subject or object VP is realized as the leftmost constituent in the Mittelfeld, then either the entire VP can be extracted, or only a relative pronoun can be extracted from this VP. For example, for the relative clause in (28a), repeated below as (30), our analysis admits the double-extraction structure shown in the tree in Figure 8 above, but in addition also the structure in Figure 9.

(30)   ein Mädchen, **das**   **zu beleidigen** Hans gestört   hat
        a   girl   whom to offend   Hans bothered has
        'a girl whom to offend bothered Hans'

In Figure 9 the relative pronoun has been extracted out of the lower finite clause, i.e., the lower S$_{fin}$, instead of the VP *zu beleidigen*. This

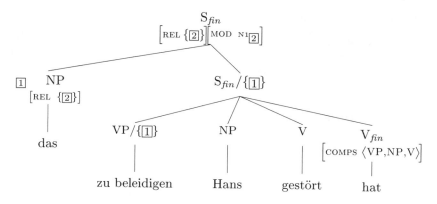

FIGURE 9 alternative tree for the relative clause in (30)

structure is possible since the Complement Extraction Lexical Rule in Figure 7 can extract the embedded object of the subject VP, and this object can be licensed as a filler by the Filler-Head Relative Clause ID Rule in Figure 2.

Since the two syntactic structures do not correlate with distinct semantic interpretations, there is no independent, semantic evidence in favor of two distinct syntactic analyses. Rather, the licensing of the two structures is a reflection of two possible realizations of relative phrases in German: as a VP or as an NP as demonstrated in (9) and (10) respectively. However, where extraction of an NP or a VP results in no difference of linear order of strings, as in (30), we are not aware of any syntactic evidence that would favor one structure or the other.

4.6   Conclusion

In this paper we have argued that VP relatives in German involve two types of extraction: extraction of the entire relativized VP and extraction of the relative pronoun within the extracted VP. Accordingly, our analysis of German VP relatives posits two filler-head rules: the Filler-Head Relative Clause ID Rule, which licenses extraction of relativized VPs, and the Filler-Head Relative VP ID Rule, which is responsible for the internal extraction of relative pronouns within the VP. We have demonstrated that subject VP relatives require double extraction in the same way object VP relatives do and that the proposed filler-head ID rules are applicable to both types of VP relatives.

Acknowledgments

The research reported in this paper is part of the Sonderforschungsbereich 340 *Theoretical Foundations of Computational Linguistics* funded by the Deutsche Forschungsgemeinschaft. We wish to thank Gosse Bouma, Kordula De Kuthy, Stefan Müller, Frank Richter, Ivan Sag, two anonymous referees for the present volume as well as three anonymous referees of the 1997 conference on Head-Driven Phrase Structure Grammar for their comments on earlier versions of this paper. Special thanks also to Detmar Meurers, who helped us enormously with many LaTeX formatting issues.

References

Bach, E. and R. Cooper. 1978. The NP-S-analysis of relatives and compositional semantics. *Linguistics & Philosophy* 2:145–150.

Bech, G. 1955. *Studien über das deutsche verbum infinitum*. Historisk-filologiske Meddelelser udgivet af Det Kongelige Danske Videnskabernes Selskab. Bind 35, no. 2, 1955; Bind 36, no. 6, 1957; Kopenhagen. Reprinted 1983, Tübingen: Max Niemeyer Verlag.

Borsley, R. 1987. Subjects and complements in HPSG. CSLI Report 87-107, Stanford University, Stanford.

Bresnan, J. 1976. On the form and function of transformations. *Linguistic Inquiry* 7:3–40.

Grewendorf, G. 1986. Relativsätze im Deutschen: Die Rattenfänger-Konstruktion. *Linguistische Berichte* 105:409–434.

Grewendorf, G. 1989. *Ergativity in German*, vol. 35 of *Studies in Generative Grammar*. Dordrecht: Foris.

Haider, H. 1985. Der Rattenfängerei muß ein Ende gemacht werden. *Wiener Linguistische Gazette* 35/36:27–50.

Hinrichs, E. and T. Nakazawa. 1994a. Linearizing AUXs in German verbal complexes. In J. Nerbonne, K. Netter, and C. Pollard, eds., *German in Head-Driven Phrase Structure Grammar*, no. 46 in Lecture Notes, pages 11–38. Stanford: CSLI Publications.

Hinrichs, E. and T. Nakazawa. 1994b. Topicalization in German - an HPSG analysis. In E. Hinrichs, D. Meurers, and T. Nakazawa, eds., *Partial-VP and Split-NP Topicalization in German – An HPSG Analysis and its Implementation*, no. 58 in Arbeitsberichte des Sonderforschungsbereich 340, pages 1–46. Tübingen: Seminar für Sprachwissenschaft.

Hinrichs, E. and T. Nakazawa. 1998. Third construction and VP extraposition in German: An HPSG analysis. In *Complex Predicates in Nonderivational Syntax*, vol. 30 of *Syntax and Semantics*, pages 115–157. Academic Press.

De Kuthy, K. 1999. German pied-piped infinitives. In G. Webelhuth, J.-P. Koenig, and A. Kathol, eds., *Lexical and Constructional Aspects of Linguistic Explanation*, pages 97–112. Stanford: CSLI Publications.

Müller, S. 1999. *Deutsche Syntax deklarativ. Head-Driven Phrase Structure Grammar für das Deutsche.* Tübingen: Max Niemeyer Verlag.

Nanni, D. and J. T. Stillings. 1978. Three remarks on pied piping. *Linguistic Inquiry* 9:310–318.

Nerbonne, J. 1994. Partial verb phrases and spurious ambiguities. In J. Nerbonne, K. Netter, and C. Pollard, eds., *German Grammar in Head-Driven Phrase Structure Grammar*, no. 46 in Lecture Notes, pages 109–150. Stanford: CSLI Publications.

Pollard, C. 1996. On head non-movement. In H. Bunt and A. van Horck, eds., *Discontinuous Constituency*, pages 279–305. Berlin/New York: Mouton de Gruyter. (Published version of a ms. dated January 1990).

Pollard, C. and I. Sag. 1994. *Head-Driven Phrase Structure Grammar.* Chicago: University of Chicago Press and Stanford: CSLI Publications.

Riemsdijk, H. v. 1985. Der Rattenfängereffekt bei Infinitiven in deutschen Relativsätzen. In W. Abraham, ed., *Erklärende Syntax des Deutschen.* Tübingen: Max Niemeyer Verlag.

Sag, I. A. 1997. English relative clause constructions. *Journal of Linguistics* 33(2):431–483.

Uszkoreit, H. 1987. *Word Order and Constituent Structure in German.* Stanford: CSLI.

5

Restrictive Modification and Polycategorial NPs in English

Andreas Kathol

5.1 $\overline{\text{X}}$-syntax and modification

The received wisdom of most, if not all, current syntactic theories which incorporate some version of $\overline{\text{X}}$-Theory is that modification and specification map into different structural configurations. In the nominal domain, this usually means that modifiers attach at the $\overline{\text{N}}$-level and are dominated by another $\overline{\text{N}}$ node, whereas specifiers combine with $\overline{\text{N}}$ constituents giving rise to a maximal nominal projection (i.e., NP).[1] The view of NP-internal restrictive modifiers as combining with $\overline{\text{N}}$ categories usually extends to both prenominal and postnominal occurrences. A typical structure of this sort is given in (1).

(1)
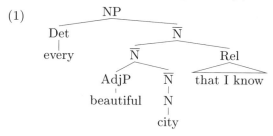

In this paper I undertake a critical assessment of the way that $\overline{\text{X}}$-theory has commonly been implemented in a theory such as HPSG in which bar-level typically is not treated as a syntactic primitive, but rather in terms of valence properties. It will be shown that the facts

---

[1]In theories that adopt a DP-based view of nominals, specification also involves a change in category type (i.e., D).

Constraints and Resources in Natural Language Syntax and Semantics.
Gosse Bouma, Erhard W. Hinrichs, Geert-Jan M. Kruijff, and Richard T. Oehrle.

appear to favor an analysis in which postnominal modification involves attachment to NP-structures. Based on a reconsideration of the notion of $\overline{\text{N}}$ in prenominal modification, I argue for dissolving the "classical" distinction between NP vs. DP in favor of a polycategorial analysis which treats both categories as subtypes of *nominal*. Among other advantages, this proposal offers an elegant solution to the longstanding problem of the interaction between modification and specification.

5.2 Postnominal modification

While the structural difference between modification and specification straightforwardly translates into a positional difference in the prenominal case, the issue is not as clear in postnominal structures. Thus, as far as the placement of specifiers and modifiers is concerned, the NP *every beautiful city that I know* is equally compatible with an alternative analysis along the lines given in (2):

(2)

```
                      NP
              _____/_____
             NP                 Rel
       _____/_____       _____/\_____
    every beautiful city    that I know
```

5.2.1 Postnominal modification and semantic construal

Apart from the desirability of having a uniform combinatorics for all modifiers, the main motivation for preferring (1) over (2) appears to stem from semantic considerations. From the perspective of model-theoretic semantics, the function of a modifier is to restrict the $\overline{\text{N}}$-denotation, usually by intersection. It is this restricted set, rather than the original $\overline{\text{N}}$-denotation, that the determiner takes as an argument, giving rise to a generalized quantifier. As a result, treating postnominal modifers as NP-modifiers would require a very different semantic type from that for prenominal modifiers.[2]

5.2.2 Postnominal modification and quantifier retrieval

However, in a theory like HPSG, in which the semantic construal is based primarily on representation and only indirectly on denotation, this prob-

---

[2]An implicit argument for the $\overline{\text{N}}$-modification analyis lies in the fact that it gives rised to a structural distinction between restrictive and nonrestrictive modification. However, as the following example demonstrates, attributive adjectives can also be construed in these two manners, arguably without a corresponding structural distinction:

(i) **The affluent Parisians** buy expensive jewelry.
    'Only those Parisians who are affluent buy expensive jewelry.'
    'Parisians are affluent and buy expensive jewelry.'

lem disappears. This is so because of the split between quantificational information (mediated by quantifier storage and retrieval) and information about "referential" identity (i.e., *index*). Quantifier retrieval is standardly assumed to only occur with those categories that have relational semantics such as verbs.[3] As a result, the CONTENT specification of N̄ and NP categories in standard HPSG is identical in type (*nom-obj*). The addition of a determiner to an N̄-projection merely changes the content of the quantifier store (Q-STORE), but leaves the CONTENT of the nominal unaffected. This means, however, that whether we choose the structure in (1) or the one in (2), the result will be exactly identical; both yield the representation in (3). The unscoped quantifier can be taken out of storage once the whole NP combines as an argument of a scope-determining category such as a complement-taking verb.

$$(3) \quad \begin{bmatrix} \text{Q-STORE} & \left\{ \begin{bmatrix} \text{DET } forall \\ \text{RESTIND } \boxed{1} \end{bmatrix} \right\} \\ \text{CONT } \boxed{1} & \begin{bmatrix} nom\text{-}obj \\ \text{IND } i \\ \text{RESTR } \{city(i),\ beautiful(i),\ know(I,\ i)\} \end{bmatrix} \end{bmatrix}$$

This being the case, we may now revisit the benefits and costs of an N̄-based view of postnominal modification. As it turns out, independent empirical evidence for this position is rather weak.

5.2.3 Coordination evidence

One supporting piece of evidence has been the coordinationability of N̄ constituents with relative clauses (cf. McCawley 1988:368):

(4) [Those [[linguists who wear sweatshirts] and [philosophers who wear suits and ties]]] are having another argument.

Yet, the strength of this argument is far from clear. Coordination-based arguments for constituent status are notoriously unreliable because it is known independently that not all conjoinable sequences are bona fide constituents. Among the best known exceptions are nonconstituent coordination constructions of the kind seen in (5):

(5) Kim gave [a record] [to Sandy] and [a book] [to Dana].

Therefore, the ability to occur in coordination structures does not immediately allow the conclusion that the sequences in question have constituent status.[4]

---

[3]Cf. Pollard and Sag's (1994) CONTENT PRINCIPLE (p. 322).

[4]Incidentally, the situation is different in the other direction, i.e., all other things being equal, failure to coordinate can generally be relied on as a strong diagnostic for the **lack** of constituent status.

5.2.4   Postnominal modifiers and pronouns/proper nouns

Second, it is generally assumed that the $\overline{\text{N}}$-based view of modification immediately accounts for the lack of restrictive relative clauses with proper nouns or personal pronouns:[5]

(6) a.*Kim that I know rather well
  b.*she that I saw last night

But again, the force of the argument is questionable once one takes into account the fact that in order for a restrictive relative clause to work, it has to combine with a nominal that provides a domain of reference which could be effectively restricted by the relative clause. The referents of proper names and pronouns are usually fixed by world knowledge or conversational context. Therefore these categories do not typically give rise to a referential domain that a restrictive relative clause could restrict in a nonvacuous fashion. Hence, it appears that no appeal to syntax is necessary to explain why the combinations in (6) are unacceptable.

5.2.5   Restrictive modification in cross-linguistic comparison

Inasmuch as $\overline{\text{X}}$-syntax is thought to make claims about cross-linguistic-ally available patterns, the assumption of (universal applicability of) restrictive $\overline{\text{N}}$-modification is further challenged by languages in which determiners can intervene between the nominal and the restrictive rel-ative clause. Korean constitutes an instance of this kind in which the nominal is phrase-final, whereas Urhobo exemplifies the mirror image with phrase-initial occurrence of the nominal:

(7) a. Rel+Det+Nom
    [nae-ka an-un]   **ku** salam
    I-NOM know-REL that man
    'that man whom I know' (Korean)
  b. Nom+Det+Rel
    oshale **ne** [l-aye   na teye o]
    man   the that-woman the hit him
    'the man that the woman hit' (Urhobo)

---

[5]As was pointed out to me by an anonymous reviewer, this latter claim does not seem to be factually true. Acceptable instances of restrictively modified pronouns do exist, as for instance in:

(i) a.   You who have already finished may leave.
  b.   He who comes early will get a table.

Such cases are perfectly consistent with the view espoused here, namely that the modification of pronouns by relative clauses is not an issue of projection level ($\overline{\text{N}}$ vs. NP), but rather of the availability of a suitable restrictable domain of reference. Thus, the pronouns in (i) seem to be construed more like (contextually restricted) indefinite pronouns, rather than anaphoric element with specific referents.

Unless one adopts an analysis that treats the placement of the NP parts as derived by movement from an $\overline{\text{X}}$-compliant underlying structure, facts like these strongly suggest that restrictive modification of NP structures is at least an available option in the world's languages.

5.2.6 Restrictive NP modification in HPSG

The idea that not all instances of restrictive relative clause modification involve $\overline{\text{N}}$-structures has recently been adopted by Sag (1997). Sag's analysis rests on a fine-grained construction-based approach to relative clauses. The major distinction among relative clause constructions is between those with an overt filler (*wh*-relative clauses, including those with initial *that*) and those without (*that*-less relative clauses). Sag assumes that this distinction in internal syntax is correlated with a difference in modificational properties. In particular, only *that*-less relative clauses modify $\overline{\text{N}}$-structures, whereas *wh*-relative clauses combine with NPs. As evidence for this proposal Sag cites the difference between (8) and (9). In (9), there is no $\overline{\text{N}}$-node that the relative clause could attach to, hence the ungrammaticality.

(8) a. Who [that you like] does Sandy also like?

 b. All [who lost money in the scam] are eligible for the program.

(9)*Who [you like] does Sandy also like?

Sag's proposal for NP-modification by a subset of restrictive relative clauses straightforwardly extends to indefinite pronouns as in (10), which arguably have NP status by themselves.

(10) somebody [who Kim talked to]

Importantly, indefinite pronouns of this kind can also be modified by *that*-less relative clauses, as shown in (11).

(11) somebody [Kim talked to]

Such examples obviously present a problem for any analysis based on $\overline{\text{N}}$-attachment. Sag's suggestion for (11a) is to analyze *somebody* as *some+body*, giving rise to structures such as the following (cf. also McCawley 1988:424)

(12)
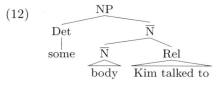

An analysis of this kind, however, raises significant questions about semantic compositionality and the proper interplay between syntactic generality and idiosyncracy. In particular, what ensures that it is only in combination with *some* that *body* can (but does not have to) mean 'person'? Moreover, what is the nature of the bonding between *some* and *body* in the idiomatic case (and only then) that prevents any attributive modifiers from intervening between *some* and *body* (cf. *some nice body* vs. *somebody nice*)? It seems that the analysis in (12) creates far more problems than it solves. By contrast, none of these issues arises if indefinite pronouns such as *somebody* are simply treated as syntactic NPs without syntactically visible internal organization. As a result, relative clauses of all kinds, not just those of the *wh* variety, would have to be treated as NP-modifiers. Moreover, as the data in (13) suggest, this idea would have to also extend to other kinds of postnominal restrictive modifiers, such as reduced relatives of different kinds:

(13) a. [$_{NP}$ [$_{NP}$ somebody] [in the garden]]
      b. [$_{NP}$ [$_{NP}$ somebody] [lying on the floor]]
      c. [$_{NP}$ [$_{NP}$ somebody] [proud of Pee Wee Herman]]

If this analysis is adopted, it becomes clear that the prohibition against *that*-less relative clauses as modifiers of *wh* pronouns is not reducible to a failure to produce a structure of the appropriate projection level. Instead it must be assumed that *that*-less relative clauses are sensitive to the kind of NP that they attach to, *wh*-phrases obviously not being eligible modifiees.[6]

5.2.7 Noun-less nominals

As shown in (14), precisely the same range of possibilities of postnominal modification can be observed with NPs that appear to lack an overt head noun:

(14) a. those [Kim talked to]
      b. those [in the garden]
      c. those [lying on the floor]
      d. those [proud of Pee Wee Herman]

It is a well-known fact (most recently brought to broader attention by Hudson (Forthcoming)), that there exists a quite systematic relationship between determiners that occur either in combination with a common noun or by themselves, as for instance in (15b) and (16b).[7]

(15) a. Kim bought **some broccoli** yesterday.

---

[6] It seems plausible to assume that the prohibition at work in (9) may be motivated by the garden path effects. Such effects seem to arise in such structures due to the *wh*-phrase being construed as a filler for the following relative clause.

[7] Exceptions to this regularity are *the*, *a*, and *every*.

    b. Kim bought **some** yesterday.

(16) a. She read **that book** this morning.

    b. She read **that** this morning.

5.2.8 Arguments against the null-head analysis

The absence of a common noun in the (b) examples above as well as in (14) may of course be attributable to to an empty element occupying that position, as has been proposed in the constraint-based literature, for instance by Nerbonne et al. (1989). However, apart from the general undesirability of positing inaudibilia of this sort, such an analysis faces a number of explanatory challenges. For one thing it is not clear how to rule out the combination of determiners such as *the* with the empty noun head, cf. (17b).

(17) a. She read the book.

    b.*She read the ∅.

Moreover, additional stipulations have to be made to prevent the occurrence of the empty head in the presence of prenominal attributive modification even with those determiners that ordinarily would seem to allow that empty element:

(18) a. He saw those green shoes.

    b.*He saw those green ∅.

Such problems simply become a nonissue if we instead assume that in the noun-less cases in (15b) and (16b), determiners such as *some* and *that* have full phrasal status by themselves. Since prenominal modifiers can only combine at the $\overline{\text{N}}$-level, there is no eligible node to attach to in (18). At the same time, if postnominal modification involves combination at the maximal phrasal level, as argued in the preceding section for indefinite pronouns, then the status of such noun-less constituents as maximal projections does not render them ineligible for postnominal modification, as was seen in (14). Furthermore, the unacceptability of (17) then straightforwardly follows from the assumption that for a subset of determiners such as *the*, a corresponding phrasal version does not exist.[8]

---

[8] An anonymous reviewer raises the issue of ambiguities arising with postnominal modifiers with scopal behavior similar to prenominal *fake* or *former*. While it is not obvious to me whether clear cases of this kind exist, the current proposal predicts their non-existence only if the required scopal relations are derivative of phrase structure configurationality. In contrast, no such prediction would follow with a theory such as Minimal Recursion Semantics (MRS, Copestake et al. 1997). Since MRS has been shown to be able to handle scope distinctions involving sublexical scoping possibilities, there does not seem to be any principled reason why this approach could

In the next section, we turn to the issue of the categorial type of noun-less nominals.

5.3 Categorial status of noun-less nominals

If noun-less constituents are analyzed as having maximal phrasal status by virtue of their lexical properties, rather than as a result of combining with an inaudible head, one issue to be resolved is whether in such "independent" uses, determiners are of category *noun* or *determiner*. The former would be the natural choice on the basis of their external distribution, whereas the latter would ensure categorial uniformity with respect to their dependent occurrences as specifiers of nouns. Stating the possibilities in this exclusive fashion is standard practice,[9] but, as will become clearer below, these distinctions may very well turn out to be less categorical than is usually assumed.

5.3.1 The DP analysis

If noun-less structures are headed by determiners, we obtain a DP analysis for those cases. In much of the transformational literature since Abney (1987), the assumption of structures headed by determiners has been taken to argue for the uniform reanalysis of **all** NP structures as DPs. However, there is no logical necessity for such a conclusion. In fact, the proposals by Netter (1994, 1996) and more recently by Hudson (Forthcoming) have specifically embraced the possibility that nominal structures may be "polycategorial", i.e., that DP structures exist alongside the familiar NPs. By contrast, as Hudson shows convincingly, the uniform DP approach to all nominal categories has a number of undesirable consequences, for instance the postulation of strange invisible determiners to account for the DP status of unadorned proper nouns such as *Sandy*.

5.3.2 A polycategorial approach

In a theory such as HPSG, which provides a rather fine-grained categorial space, it is straightforward to allow for different nominal structures to be headed either by typical nouns or determiners without danger of missing a generalization. For instance, if we assume that rather than picking out a single, rather homogeneous lexical class (i.e., N), *nominal* is the common supertype of a range of categories which (minimally) contains

---

not be extended to account for scope ambiguities even if a uniform attachment site for postnominal modifiers is assumed.

[9]Note, for instance, that transformational grammar commonly assumes a categorial dichotomy between "functional" categories such as D, Infl, etc. and "lexical" categories such as N, V, etc.

common/mass nouns and determiners, as indicated in (19), then the parallelism in external distribution is straightforwardly accounted for.

(19)   *nominal*

common/mass   determiner

Specifically, selection of an "NP", i.e., a category satisfying the description in (20) is indeterminate with respect to the particular subtype that instantiates the category *nominal*. Yet, what unites all instances of NP/DPs is there must not be any unsaturated specifier requirements, hence the empty list as the value of the SP(ECIFIE)R feature.

(20)
$$\text{NP} = \begin{bmatrix} \text{HEAD } nominal \\ \text{SPR } \langle\rangle \\ \text{COMPS } \langle\rangle \end{bmatrix}$$

As we will see in the next section, the polycategorial NP approach idea provides the basis for the solution to a longstanding puzzle in in constraint-based approaches to the syntax of English nominal expressions.

5.4   Prenominal modification reconsidered

In the valence-based encoding of $\overline{\text{X}}$-syntax proposed, for instance, in Pollard and Sag (1994), $\overline{\text{N}}$ has been described as $\begin{bmatrix} \text{SPR } \langle\text{DETP}\rangle \end{bmatrix}$. This specification indicates that the nominal still requires a determiner (phrase) in order to become complete. Accordingly, attributive adjectives such as *hot* combine with nominal categories of this sort, as in (21).

(21)   a. the hot stove

b.

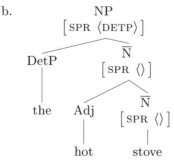

5.4.1   Problems with the SPR-based approach

An analysis of this kind faces a problem when we try to extend it to cases of missing determiners, such as with bare plurals or mass nouns such as *water* in (22a). If we reject a null determiner analysis, the straightforward solution is to assume that such nominals are lexically specified as being saturated with respect to the SPR feature: $[\text{SPR} \langle\rangle]$. Concomitantly this would mean that attributive adjectives now have to be able to combine with nominals of this kind too. But then it is no longer obvious how to distinguish between lexically SPR-saturated nominals like bare plurals and mass nouns and those that are saturated due to their combination with determiners. Consequently, the combination in (22b) is falsely predicted to be acceptable.

(22) a. hot water
      b.*hot the stove

The solution that suggests itself in a polycategorial NP approach is rather straightforward. The operative constraint is that restrictive adjectives can only modify nominals whose HEAD value is *common/mass noun*, without any reference to the level of SPR-saturation. A nominal projection containing a determiner is headed by the latter; therefore the HEAD value is not of the type that would allow for prenominal modification, rendering combinations as in (22b) impossible. Note also that on the basis of what we said earlier, the situation is the opposite for postnominal modification. Here, it is precisely the SPR-saturated status which ensures that the modified nominal is of the kind that is appropriate for postnominal modification.

5.4.2   Adjectival NP modifiers

Once we abandon the idea that SPR-saturation determines whether prenominal modification is possible, we may also reconsider the occurrence of adjectives in other prenominal environments. In particular, let us briefly consider attributive adjectives modifying full NPs, as in (23):

(23) a. poor Sandy
      b. poor him

While standard $\overline{\text{X}}$-theory would have nothing to say about such cases, the proposal made here provides the basis for an analysis.

Attributive adjectives that can occur as modifiers of proper nouns sometimes exhibit differences in meaning that coincide with their status as restrictive or nonrestrictive modifiers. For instance, *poor* with the meaning 'without means' can only act as a restrictive modifier and combine with common nouns. With the interpretation 'unfortunate', it acts as a nonrestrictive modifier and can also combine with proper nouns (23a) and, to a certain degree, with accusative personal pronouns (23b). An ambiguity arises in the case of common nouns, cf. (24).

(24) the poor man
    'the pennyless man'
    'the unfortunate man'

Yet, nonrestrictive uses of prenominal adjectives are never possible when the phrase is headed by a determiner—even if the phrase as a whole has the status of a name, cf. (25).

(25)   a. poor Elvis; beautiful Austria
     b.*poor The King; *beautiful The Alps

Hence prenominal modification of this kind too is sensitive to whether or not the phrase is headed by a determiner.

5.5   An HPSG analysis

The preceding sections have made a case for treating determiners as heads, either when they cooccur with nouns or when they constitute a nominal phrase by themselves. In present section, I will explore the technical ramifications of this idea.

5.5.1   Revised hiearchy of nominal types

To reconcile the head status of determiners in (15) and (16) with the category of **nominal** phrase, I propose that the partial hierarchy in (19) be revised and expanded along the lines given in (26), which resembles Hudson's proposal for a "unified analysis" quite closely. The major division between the different kinds of *noun* is between those that canonically have referential properties of their own—common, mass, and proper nouns—and those which either are highly dependent in their referential properties on context or may not have referential properties at all—pronouns and what I will call *para-nominals*, that is, "dependent" determiners cooccurring with a noun.[10]

(26)

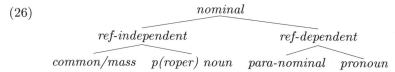

5.5.2   Alternative combinatorics of Det-N structures

In order to allow for determiners to act as syntactic heads of nominal constituents two major changes of the HPSG theory of nominal specifi-

---

[10] As Dick Hudson (p.c.) has pointed out to me, the distinction between *para-nominal* and *pronoun* assumed here may not actually be necessary in terms of defining irreducibly distinct word classes. That is, nouns of type *para-nominal* could simply seen as *pronouns* with a nonempty SPEC value as suggested by Hudson (Forthcoming).

cation are suggested:

First, SPEC is treated as a list-valued valence feature with a concomitant combinatorial schema, outlined in (27).

(27) **Specification schema**

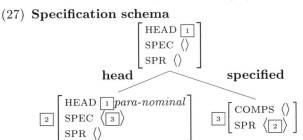

Second, I require that determiner-noun constructions may only be built by means of the schema in (27), but not of the SPECIFIER-HEAD SCHEMA of Pollard and Sag (1994). That is to say, while common nouns still record their specifiers via SPR, the empty SPR value of the phrasal mother in (27) should not be thought of as the result of discharging the noun's SPR value. Instead it follows from the specification of the determiner head in the schema in (27) as $\left[\text{SPR } \langle \rangle \right]$. This assumption guarantees that determiner+noun combinations are always headed by the determiner.

The proposed change in the relations involved does not interfere with the way in which standard HPSG captures similarities between specifiers and subjects, which was one of the inspirations behind Abney's DP analysis. Both specifiers and subjects are lexically selected by the noun via the features SPEC and SUBJ, respectively. If we take the values of these features to be less oblique than anything on the COMPS list, the commonality of subjects and specifiers as potential binders is straightforwardly captured. Since proper binding relations in HPSG for the most part boil down to well-formedness conditions on lexical valence structures, the fact that the noun part in Det-N structures is now a syntactic nonhead is therefore immaterial for binding and other purposes. Similarly, the present proposal should carry over directly to the treatment of specifiers and subjects in various gerund constructions as proposed by Malouf (1998).

A concrete example of how the schema in (27) can be used to license combinations of specifiers and nouns is provided in somewhat simplified form in (28):

(28)

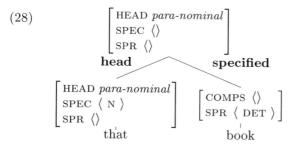

As in Pollard and Sag (1994), (singular) count and mass nouns (and bare plurals) continue to be distinguished in terms of their obligatory vs. optional SPR marking:

(29)   a.   **Count noun**   b.   **Mass noun**

$$\begin{bmatrix} \text{HEAD } common/mass \\ \text{SPR } \langle [\ ] \rangle \end{bmatrix}$$ $$\begin{bmatrix} \text{HEAD } common/mass \\ \text{SPR } \langle ([\ ]) \rangle \end{bmatrix}$$

Furthermore, determiners that also double as pronouns such as the demonstrative *that* are lexically underspecified in terms of their nominal subtype. The two different instantiations are listed in (30b,c). In contrast, determiners that cannot make a phrase of their own in English (such as the definite article *the*) only have a lexical description corresponding to (30b).

(30)   a.   *that*

$$\begin{bmatrix} \text{HEAD } ref\text{-}dependent \\ \text{SUBJ } \langle \rangle \\ \text{SPR } \langle \rangle \\ \text{COMPS } \langle \rangle \end{bmatrix}$$

   b.   **as a determiner**   c.   **as a pronoun**

$$\boxed{1}\begin{bmatrix} \text{HEAD } para\text{-}nominal \\ \text{SPEC } \langle \text{N}[\text{SPR } \langle \boxed{1} \rangle] \rangle \end{bmatrix}$$ $$\begin{bmatrix} \text{HEAD } pronoun \\ \text{SPEC } \langle \rangle \end{bmatrix}$$

In contrast with Hudson (Forthcoming), I do not assume that the two environments of occurrence are a result of the determiner's nominal "complement" being merely optional. This conclusion is motivated on the one hand by their different semantic type of pronouns vs. para-nominal determiners in HPSG (restricted index and quantifier, respectively) and on the other hand by subtle but important lexical semantic differences, as Hudson himself acknowledges, cf. (31), as well as morphological distinctions exhibited by certain determiners, cf. (32).

(31)   a.   I'm married to that woman.
       b.#I'm married to that.

(32)   a.   **Para-nominal:** my, her, our, your, their, no

    b. **Pronoun:** mine, hers, ours, yours, theirs, none

Moreover, in maintaining a distinction between the HEAD values of dependent (*para-nominal*) and independent (*pronoun*) occurrences of determiners, we can account for important differences between these categories with regard to the capacity to occur in possessive phrases.

Common accounts of the possessive constructions, such as Pollard and Sag's (1994) analysis of *'s* as a "transitive" determiner, fail to account for the selectivity with respect to pronominal status exhibited by this possessive marker. Thus while all of the examples in (33a) are grammatical, none of the ones in (33b) are.[11]

(33) a. Sandy's coat; some people's concerns; this dog's tail
      b.*she's coat; *some's concerns; *this's tail

This is accounted for straightforwardly if we assume that the possessive marker attaches to NPs which must not be headed by a pronoun.[12]

Furthermore, the present analysis retains the mutual dependency between determiners and nouns proposed by Pollard and Sag (1994). This makes it possible to treat all obligatory cooccurrences entirely as valence properties: a determiner such as *the* requires an accompanying common noun because of its SPEC specification, whereas a singular count noun such as *stove* does not qualify as a complete NP because of its nonempty SPR value. This treatment is in contrast to Hudson's account[13] which makes reference to dependency relations unavailable in standard HPSG. The closest analogue within HPSG would be in terms of configurational relations, that is, by reference to phrase structure encoded via DTR-features. However, such solutions are generally disfavored in that they do not readily provide the notion of syntactic locality which can be captured by restricting the amount of information which syntactic de-

---

[11]As an anonymous reviewer points out, the present account of the unacceptability of *this's tail* appears not to carry over to equally unacceptable constructions such as *a/the tail of this*. However, constructions of this kind are not universally unacceptable as is shown in (ia).

  (i) a. One of the consequences of this/that is that ...
      b.*One of this's/that's consequences is that ...

Note, however, that even in cases where the postnominal PP is possible, the corresponding possessive construction does not seem to be available, as is seen in (ib).

[12]Moreover, what are usually considered indefinite pronouns seem to be generally exempt from this constraint, as seen in (i).

  (i) someone's coat; whose (= who's) concerns

I will not try here to properly characterize those pronominals that can occur with a possessive marker. One solution that suggests itself is to introduce additional distinctions among pronominals in terms of subtypes of *pronoun*.

[13]"[A] singular countable common noun must have a pronoun as its parent" (p. 18).

pendencies can be sensitive to (cf. the use of SYNSEM or LOCAL in the description of various dependencies in current HPSG). Therefore, inasmuch as HPSG's valence features afford such a lexically-based notion of syntactic locality, reference to phrase structure would be dispreferred.

5.6 Specification schema and semantic headedness

One aspect of (27) that requires more discussion is the construction of semantic representations within the NP, in particular the issue of semantic headedness. Since syntactic headedness by default also correlates with the status as semantic head, it would be natural to adopt that position for our proposal as well. Since the content of determiner-less NPs is commonly assumed to be of type *nom-obj* while that of determiners is *quantifier*, a direct implementation of that idea would result in an undesirable semantic type dichotomy among the different kinds of NPs.

Alternatively we could leave the CONTENT value of the determiner underspecified and instead structure-share it with the CONTENT specification of the nominal, cf. the schematic feature description in (34):

$$(34) \quad \begin{bmatrix} \text{HEAD } para\text{-}nominal \\ \text{SPEC } \langle \text{N:}\boxed{2}\rangle \\ \text{CONT } \boxed{2} \\ \text{Q-STORE } \left\{ \begin{bmatrix} \text{DET ...} \\ \text{REST-IND } \boxed{2} \end{bmatrix} \right\} \end{bmatrix}$$

The advantage of this solution is that it allows us to have a single type for both the paranominal and the pronominal occurrences of determiners, viz. *nom-obj*.

At the same time, however, this proposal poses a severe problem for the current treatment of NP-internal binding phenomena. Structure sharing with the nominal in CONTENT entails that the determiner's index value is identical with that of the nominal. That being so, we are immediately faced with violations of Principle A in examples such as (35), where *that* is less oblique than *himself* within the valence of *picture*.

(35) that picture of himself

According to the binding theory of Pollard and Sag (1994), *that* does not count as an o-commander since its CONTENT specification is not that of a referential NP. Therefore, *himself* is an exempt anaphor in this context, allowing for well-formed examples such as *John doesn't like that picture of himself*. However, if the content of *that* is token-identical with the referential nominal it specifies (*picture of himself*), it takes on the status of an o-commander and hence *himself* is no longer an exempt anaphor, contrary to fact.

It therefore follows that the determiner, being the syntactic head of the schema in (27), must nevertheless count as a semantic nonhead. Thus, as with the HPSG treatment of adjunction, specification must be seen as an instance of a mismatch between syntactic and semantic headedness.[14]

5.7 Summary and conclusion

The two central claims of this paper are: (1) *pace* long-standing assumptions of $\overline{\text{X}}$-theory, pre- and postnominal restrictive modification in English map onto different structural configurations; and (2) the head properties of English NPs depend on what constructions are involved in building the phrase.

With respect to the second part a brief comparison may be in order with Netter (1994), who develops a theory of German NPs which is superficially rather similar to Hudson's polycategorial NP proposal and its adaptation advocated here. Instead of relying on a common supertype for nominals of different kinds, Netter accounts for the commonality in the external distribution by positing a feature FCOMPL which indicates whether a given category is "functionally complete". A negative value indicates that a determiner is still missing a noun to achieve functional completeness whereas a positive value correlates with fully phrasal status.

On Netter's own admission, the concept of functional completeness is a primitive in the system without any relation to other properties in the grammar. In our system—as in Pollard and Sag's (1994) original formulation—on the other hand, no such primitive is needed because prenominal specifiers are selected by common nouns (cf. (29a)). This not only allows us to describe NP-internal binding relations in the same fashion as in the case of clauses. More significantly for the issues at hand, the nominal's valence properties are sufficient to distinguish between fully saturated, maximal projections and nonmaximal occurrences of nominals.[15] We conclude, therefore, that despite superficial similarities

---

[14] For an alternative approach to nominal semantics see Allegranza 1998.

[15] Note further that, as Netter (1994, p. 322) concedes, the FCOMPL feature alone is not sufficient to provide a satisfactory solution to the modification vs. specification problem pointed out above in the discussion of (21). Rather, in order to prevent the generation of ill-formed examples such as (22b), he has to stipulate another binary head feature (SPEC, not to be confused with the category-valued feature SPEC used here and in Pollard and Sag 1994) that signals whether or not the current nominal category contains a determiner. But as has been shown here, a feature that only records the presence/absence of a determiner is completely superfluous if we make more fine-grained distinctions among different nominal head types to which

with Netter's proposal, the current adaptation of the polycategorial NP approach is clearly to be preferred.

The current proposal is an instance of a growing number of analyses that break down the strict categorial boundary between "lexical" or "substantive" and "functional" categories. Another instance of this line of investigation is Sag's (1997) idea of subsuming both verbs and complementizers under the single category *verbal*. Underlying this move is HPSG's type system which affords the expression of rather fine-grained lexical distinctions and relationships.

Acknowledgments

I would like to thank Dick Hudson, John Nerbonne, and five anonymous reviewers for comments and Paul Kay for extensive discussion. The usual disclaimers apply.

References

Abney, S. 1987. *The English Noun Phrase in its Sentential Aspect*. Ph.D. thesis, MIT.

Allegranza, V. 1998. Determination and quantification. In F. van Eynde and P. Schmidt, eds., *Linguistic Specifications for Typed Feature Structure Formalisms*, vol. 10 of *Studies in Machine Translation and Natural Language Processing*, pages 281–314. Luxembourg: European Commission.

Copestake, A., D. Flickinger, and I. Sag. 1997. Minimal recursion semantics: an introduction. Unpubl. ms., Stanford University.

Hudson, R. Forthcoming. Syntax without functional categories. In R. D. Borsley, ed., *Syntactic Categories*, vol. 31 of *Syntax and Semantics*. New York: Academic Press.

Malouf, R. 1998. *Mixed Categories in the Hierarchical Lexicon*. Ph.D. thesis, Stanford University.

McCawley, J. 1988. *The Syntactic Constructions of English*. University of Chicago Press.

Nerbonne, J., M. Iida, and W. Ladusaw. 1989. Running on empty: null heads in head-driven grammar. In J. Fee and K. Hunt, eds., *Proceedings of the Eighth West Coast Conference on Formal Linguistics*, pages 276–288. Stanford University: CSLI Publications/SLA.

Netter, K. 1994. Towards a theory of functional heads: German nominal phrases. In J. Nerbonne, K. Netter, and C. J. Pollard, eds., *German in Head-Driven Phrase Structure Grammar*, pages 297–340. Stanford: CSLI Publications.

---

prenominal modification is sensitive.

Netter, K. 1996. *Functional Categories in an HPSG for German*. Ph.D. thesis, University of Saarland.

Pollard, C. J. and I. A. Sag. 1994. *Head-Driven Phrase Structure Grammar*. Chicago, IL: University of Chicago Press and Stanford: CSLI Publications.

Sag, I. A. 1997. English relative clause constructions. *Journal of Linguistics* 33(2):431–484.

6

The Syntactic Structure of Romanian Auxiliary (and Modal) Verbs

PAOLA MONACHESI

6.1   Introduction

Romanian auxiliary verbs exhibit certain peculiar properties that set
them aside from other Romance counterparts. It will be suggested that
the differences between Romanian auxiliaries and French and Italian
auxiliaries can be accounted for in terms of different syntactic structures. While in French and in Italian the auxiliary verb, the nonfinite
one and the complements combine in a flat structure, in Romanian, the
auxiliary and the lexical verb form a compound structure. If this structure is assumed, it is possible to account for the properties of Romanian
auxiliaries and for the fact that they can be placed after the verbal
complement, in certain registers.

Furthermore, it will be shown that the Romanian data argue in favor
of a monoclausal auxiliary structure and against the biclausal configuration proposed in Dobrovie-Sorin (1994). She assumes that auxiliaries
should be analyzed as adjoined to a CP/IP category and that the Infl
node and the NP subject position of the main clause are lacking. However, the fact that no element can intervene between the auxiliary and
the verbal complement and the distribution of clitics seem to support a
monoclausal configuration.

Auxiliary verbs differ from modal verbs like *a putea* ('can') in certain
respects. It will be shown that these differences can be accounted for if
the modal verb is associated with a flat structure. On the other hand,
the similarities with respect to the distribution of clitics follow as conse-

Constraints and Resources in Natural Language Syntax and Semantics.
Gosse Bouma, Erhard W. Hinrichs, Geert-Jan M. Kruijff, and Richard T. Oehrle.

	1 Sg	2 Sg	3 Sg	1 Pl	2 Pl	3 Pl	
Aux Psp.	am	ai	a	am	aţi	au	past participle
Aux Cond.	aş	ai	ar	am	aţi	ar	bare infinitive
Aux Fut.	voi	vei	va	vom	veţi	vor	bare infinitive

TABLE 1 Different forms of the auxiliaries

quence of *argument composition*. This is a lexical mechanism according to which the auxiliary inherits the complements of the embedded verb, including those ones which might be realized as clitics.

6.2   Basic properties of Romanian auxiliaries

Romanian auxiliaries can be found in the present perfect, conditional and future paradigms. In the case of the present perfect, the auxiliary combines with a past participle, while in the other two cases it combines with a bare infinitive, that is an infinitive without the particle *a*. Table 1 summarizes the different forms of auxiliaries. A crucial property of these auxiliaries is that they are strictly adjacent to the lexical verb. Thus, unlike in French and in Italian, adverbs cannot separate them from the verbal complement:

(1) a. * Am   adesea văzut filme bune.
            have often   seen   good films

     b.   Am   văzut adesea filme bune.
            have seen   often   good films

        'I have often seen good films.'

The only exception to this is constituted by a group of five monosyllabic intensifiers which have clitic status.[1]

Similarly, quantifiers cannot intervene between the auxiliary and the verb as shown in the following example from Dobrovie-Sorin (1994):

(2) a. * Elevii   tăi   au   toţi citit un poem de Verlaine.
            students yours have all   read a poem by Verlaine

     b.   Elevii   tăi   au   citit toţi un poem de Verlaine.
            students yours have read all   a poem by Verlaine

        'Your students have all read a poem by Verlaine.'

In Romanian, subjects can be found in different positions. They can occur before the verb (3a), between the verb and the direct object (3b)

---

[1]These intensifiers have a peculiar distribution since they are the only elements which can occur between pronominal clitics and the verb. I refer to Monachesi 1999b for an analysis which is compatible with the treatment of auxiliaries proposed here.

and after the direct object (3c):

(3) a. Mama a   făcut o prăjitură.
     mum   has made a cake
     'Mum has made a cake.'

     b. A făcut mama o prăjitură.
        has made mum   a cake

     c. A făcut o prăjitură mama.
        has made a cake   mum

However, the subject cannot intervene between the auxiliary and the lexical verb:

(4) * A   mama făcut o prăjitură.
       has mum made a cake
     (intended) 'Mum has made a cake.'

The situation is different in French where subject clitics can occur between the auxiliary and the lexical verb and in Italian where in certain cases this order is possible:

(5) Avendo Martina deciso   di partire, possiamo usare la sua
     having Martina decided to leave,   can   use   the her
     stanza.
     room
     'Martina having decided to leave, we can use her room .'

However, as noticed by Dobrovie-Sorin (1994), Romanian does not present any construction in which the subject can intervene between the auxiliary and the lexical verb.

Furthermore, complements cannot occur between the two verbs:

(6) * Am filme bune văzut.
       have good films seen
     (intended) 'I have seen good films.'

The data presented above suggest that the auxiliary and the lexical verb form a unit which cannot be separated by other elements and argue thus in favor of a monoclausal configuration and against the biclausal one proposed by Dobrovie-Sorin (1994).

6.3 The syntactic structure of auxiliary verbs

Two possible structures can be suggested in order to account for the properties of auxiliaries discussed in the previous section. One in which the nonfinite verb and its complements are sisters of the auxiliary verb in a flat structure (7) and one in which the auxiliary and the nonfinite verb constitute a complex verb (8):

(7)   Flat structure   (8)   Compound structure

Given that the auxiliary and the lexical verb form a unit which cannot be separated by other elements, it seems that the compound structure in (8) is the most appropriate to capture this intuition. If the flat structure is adopted, it would be necessary to formulate special linearization constraints in order to account for the fact that it is not possible for subjects, adverbs, quantifiers and complements to intervene between the two verbs. On the other hand, the flat structure in (7) has been adopted for French (Abeillé and Godard, 1994) and Italian (Monachesi, 1996) auxiliaries. Given this structure, it is possible to account for the fact that, differently from Romanian, (clitic) subjects and adverbs can occur between the auxiliary and the nonfinite verb, both in French and in Italian.

A third possible representation in which the auxiliary takes a VP complement has not been taken into consideration:

(9)   Hierarchical structure

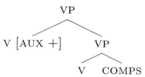

This hierarchical structure does not seem plausible in view of the fact that Romanian auxiliaries can be optionally placed after the verbal complement:[2]

---

[2]In Monachesi 1999b I suggest that auxiliaries have word status unlike pronominal clitics which I claim have affixal status. The fact that auxiliaries can occur before and after the verb seems to argue against their affixal status. Romanian pronominal clitics can also exhibit this alternation but different forms surface depending on whether they are proclitic or enclitic while this is not the case with the auxiliaries. Furthermore, in the case of pronominal clitics, the morphosyntactic features of the verb determine their attachment, while auxiliaries are not sensitive to this information. They can precede or follow the verb regardless of its form.

(10) a. Văzut-am.
         seen have
         'I have seen.'

      b. Mira-m-aş.
         wondered-CL.ACC would
         'I would wonder.'

      c. Pleca-voi.
         leave shall
         'I shall leave.'

These data, which are discussed at length in Dobrovie-Sorin (1994) and in Rivero (1994), are limited to certain registers and are not triggered by illocutionary factors, as Rivero claims. In fact, this kind of inversion is only possible in some dialects, in poetry and in curse expressions. If the two verbs belong to the same domain, as in the compound configuration, one can account for the inversion data by means of simple linearization principles. This is not feasible if a hierarchical structure is assumed since the two verbs would belong to different domains.

In order to account for the inversion data, an approach similar to the one proposed by Pollard and Sag (1994) for English can be assumed.[3] It relies on the use of the feature [INV]. Auxiliaries which cannot occur after the verb, such as the passive auxiliary, are specified as [INV −], while auxiliaries which optionally invert have [INV *boolean*] as their value. This applies to the future and the present perfect auxiliaries. The following LP constraints account for the relevant orders:

- Auxiliaries which are marked [INV −] must precede the verb.
- Auxiliaries which are marked [INV +] must follow the verb.

Given this analysis, it is quite straightforward to deal with the fact that in the case of conditionals, inversion is possible only if clitics are present, as shown in (10b). The auxiliary cannot occur after the verb if there are no clitics:

(11) * Mînca aş.
         eat   would
         (intended) 'I would eat.'

This is accounted for by having conditional auxiliaries, which have combined with clitics, marked [INV *boolean*]. They can thus occur both

---

[3]Given the relatively simple Romanian inversion data, it seems more economical to assume an analysis as in Pollard and Sag 1994 than a linearization approach as in Kathol 1995.

before and after the lexical verb. Conditional auxiliaries which have not combined with clitics are marked [INV −], so that they can only occur before the lexical verb.

It should be mentioned that the compound structure proposed for Romanian auxiliaries requires an appropriate schema to license it; the underlying assumption is that this kind of compounding occurs in syntax and not in morphology. The schema suggested for the German verbal complex in Hinrichs and Nakazawa (1994) could also be adopted for this case:

(12) $\left[\text{SS} \mid \text{L} \mid \text{C} \mid \text{HEAD } verb\right] \rightarrow \text{H } word , \text{C} \left[\text{SS} \mid \text{C} \mid \text{HEAD } verb\right]$

The schema allows for the auxiliary and the lexical verb to combine together before any non-verbal complements are added. This structure thus accounts for the fact that no element can intervene between the two verbs, which is the desired result.

6.4 Auxiliary verbs and the distribution of clitics

Additional support in favor of a monoclausal auxiliary structure (and against the biclausal one proposed by Dobrovie-Sorin (1994)) comes from the distribution of clitics. If an auxiliary verb is present, the pronominal clitic, which is an argument of the embedded verb, must precede the auxiliary and cannot attach to the lower verb. The two verbs act thus as a unit:

(13) Le   am   văzut.
     CL.ACC have seen
     'I have seen them.'

It is possible to account for the position of the clitic if an analysis in terms of *argument composition* (Hinrichs and Nakazawa, 1990) along the lines of that proposed for French (Abeillé and Godard, 1994) and Italian (Monachesi, 1996) is adopted. This means that the auxiliary *am* in (13) has the lexical entry shown in Figure 6.4 associated with it: The complements of the auxiliary verb are identified with those of the embedded verb through the operation of argument composition. This is reflected by the fact that the tag ② is present both in the COMPS list of the auxiliary verb and in that of the embedded verb. The abbreviation *w-ss* stands for *word synsem* and it is employed to distinguish words from phrases. Alternatively the attribute [LEX +/−] could be used.

Therefore, in the case of (13), the auxiliary inherits from the past participle the direct object, which will be realized as a clitic.

$$
\begin{bmatrix}
\text{PHON } \langle am \rangle \\[2ex]
\text{SS} \mid \text{L} \mid \text{C}
\begin{bmatrix}
\text{HEAD}
\begin{bmatrix}
verb \\
\text{AUX} +
\end{bmatrix} \\[3ex]
\text{VAL}
\begin{bmatrix}
\text{SUBJ } \langle \boxed{1}\text{NP} \rangle \\[3ex]
\text{COMPS }
\left\langle
\begin{bmatrix}
w\text{-}ss \\
\text{HEAD } verb \\
\text{VAL}
\begin{bmatrix}
\text{SUBJ } \langle \boxed{1}\text{NP} \rangle \\
\text{COMPS } \boxed{2}
\end{bmatrix}
\end{bmatrix}
\right\rangle \oplus \boxed{2}
\end{bmatrix}
\end{bmatrix}
\end{bmatrix}
$$

FIGURE 1 Lexical entry for the auxiliary *am* in (13).

6.4.1 A lexical analysis of Romanian cliticization

I assume a lexical approach to cliticization which treats Romanian pronominal clitics as affixes (cf. also Miller and Sag 1997 for French and Monachesi 1996 for Italian). There are several arguments which support this view. The order of pronominal clitics is fixed; Romanian has only accusative and dative object clitics and they occur in the order *dative-accusative*. There is thus a similarity between clitics and affixes which also exhibit rigid order. Furthermore, Romanian pronominal clitics do not have wide scope over coordination, but they must be repeated in front of each conjunct, a property they share with affixes. They also present arbitrary gaps in their combinations, as in certain inflectional paradigms. In addition, under certain conditions, they can cooccur with full complements behaving virtually as agreement markers:

(14) Ion m-a   văzut pe mine.
      Ion CL.ACC-has seen   PE me

      'Ion saw me.'

They also present morphophonological idiosyncrasies, such as vowel deletion, which occurs in the case of the clitics *mă, vă* and *se* before verbs that begin with *a* or *o*. This process does not seem to be explainable in terms of productive phonological rules: different allomorphs should be postulated.[4]

---

[4] A potential problem with treating Romanian pronominal clitics as affixes is that they can (phonologically) attach not only to verbs, but also to negation, complementizers, wh-elements and to the subject. See Monachesi 1998 for a possible solution which is compatible with the analysis presented here.

Therefore, three classes of pronominal clitics can be distinguished in Romanian: those that occur in front of any verbs, those that occur before verbs that begin with *a* or *o* and those that occur as enclitics.

Given the affixal status of clitics, they will not be considered lexical items, that is *signs*, but featural information which is provided in the lexicon and used in morphophonology for the realization of the cliticized verb form. I assume that cliticization is a lexical operation which has both a syntactic/semantic and a morphophonological effect (cf. also Monachesi 1996, Miller and Sag 1997). The former is reflected in the fact that clitics satisfy the subcategorization requirements of the verb of which they are an argument. Within HPSG, a lexical rule can be proposed to achieve this effect; it relates two sets of words:[5]

(15)   Complement Cliticization Lexical Rule (CCLR)

$$\begin{bmatrix} word \\ \text{HEAD} \quad verb \\ \text{VAL} \mid \text{COMPS} \quad \boxed{1} \bigcirc \boxed{2} \\ \text{CLTS} \quad elist \end{bmatrix} \Rightarrow \begin{bmatrix} \text{VAL} \mid \text{COMPS} \quad \boxed{1} \\ \text{CLTS} \quad \boxed{2} \end{bmatrix}$$

The rule relates verbs which subcategorize for certain complements to other ones with the same properties except that their subcategorization list is reduced. In other words, the effect of the rule is that some complements which are in the COMPS list are removed and added as members of the CLTS list.[6] This list contains syntactic and semantic information about those complements which will be realized as clitics.[7] Verbs which have undergone cliticization are enriched with the relevant featural information, which is used for the morphophonological realization of the cliticized verb form. The crucial issue is then how this information can

---

[5]I will assume an interpretation of lexical rules as in Meurers and Minnen 1997 which views them as descriptions relating *word* objects. Note that in the lexical rule, the input and output descriptions are connected via "⇒", while in the case of the implicational constraints "→" is used. In the lexical rule, ◯ is the shuffle operator defined in Reape 1994.

[6]The rule does not account for cases of clitic doubling exemplified in (14) which are outside of the scope of this paper. However, it is possible to extend the analysis by assuming that those complements that satisfy the semantic and pragmatic conditions of doubling should remain on the COMPS list. An additional requirement is that the pronominal clitic and the doubled complement should share agreement and case information.

[7]The approach presented here differs in certain respects from that in Miller and Sag 1997. They propose constraints on types in order to deal with French cliticization. This leads to a distinction of (morphosyntactic) words in plain and cliticized ones. However, in the case of cliticization, the crucial opposition seems to be between cliticized verbs and non cliticized ones and this property can be naturally captured by means of a lexical rule.

be used in order to spell out the cliticized verb form in phonology. I suggest that appropriate constraints should relate the information contained in the CLTS list to the phonological realization of the clitic.

The realization of the clitics Before presenting the relevant constraints, I will introduce the signature assumed, which shares similarities with that proposed by Bird and Klein (1994). In particular, I suggest that the type *word* has MORPH as an additional appropriate attribute, with value *morph*. Furthermore, the type *morph* should be partitioned into two subtypes, which are *complex-morph* and *basic-morph*. The type *complex-morph* is relevant in the treatment of inflection and of morphologically complex forms and it thus plays a role in the analysis of cliticization developed here. In addition, the attribute STEM is defined as appropriate for *morph* and it is inherited by both of its subtypes, while the attribute AFFIX is appropriate only for *complex-morph*:

(16)

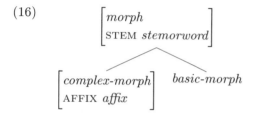

The value of STEM is *stemorword* which is a subtype of *sign*:

(17)

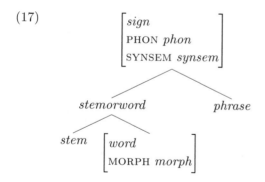

In the case of inflection, the attribute STEM has *stem* as value, while in the case of cliticization its value is *word*. The same apparatus can be employed to account both for inflection and for cliticization. This is a desirable result, given the similarities between the two.

The type *affix* is further partitioned in order to distinguish *prefixes* from *suffixes*:

(18)   *affix*

      prefix   *suffix*

In addition, it should be mentioned that the only appropriate attribute for *affix* is PHON:

(19) $\begin{bmatrix} \textit{affix} \\ \text{PHON } \textit{phon} \end{bmatrix}$

Following Bird and Klein (1994), I assume that *phon* has certain appropriate features which are necessary to distinguish the segmental structure:

(20) $\begin{bmatrix} \textit{phon} \\ \text{SKEL } \textit{list of segments} \\ \text{CONS } \textit{list of consonants} \\ \text{VOW } \textit{list of vowels} \end{bmatrix}$

Since affixes (and pronominal clitics) have only phonological information associated with them, it follows that they are not considered *signs*. This approach thus shares insights with realizational approaches to morphology such as those of Anderson (1992) or Stump (1992) that assume that morphemes do not exist as lexical entries, but only as the realization of certain morphosyntactic properties of the host. However, a crucial difference between the approach presented here and realizational analyses is that the latter assume a function in order to spell out the relevant morphemes. On the other hand, I have suggested that morphemes have a PHON feature associated with them which allows for an appropriate treatment of their phonological properties.

On the basis of the signature proposed, it is possible to formulate appropriate constraints which relate the featural information present on verbs to the actual phonological realization of the clitics. They are sensitive to the phonological structure (and the morphosyntactic form) of the verb. In the case of (13), the following constraint is relevant:

(21) $\begin{bmatrix} \textit{word} \\ \text{MORPH} \mid \text{STEM} \mid \text{SS} \mid \text{L} \mid \text{C} \mid \text{CLTS} \left\langle \text{NP}\big[\textit{acc}\big]_{3fpl} \right\rangle \end{bmatrix} \rightarrow$
$\begin{bmatrix} \text{AFFIX} \begin{bmatrix} \textit{prefix} \\ \text{PHON} \mid \text{SKEL} \left\langle \ \textit{le} \ \right\rangle \end{bmatrix} \end{bmatrix}$

It states that if a verb contains an accusative, third plural feminine element in its CLTS list (which encodes the information about those elements that will be realized as clitics), the clitic *le* must also be present in the structure.

It is through the interaction of the lexical rule and the constraint presented above that a cliticized verb form like *le am*, which occurs in example (13), is licensed:

(22)

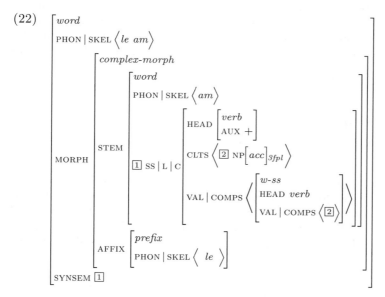

The description above states that the auxiliary has inherited the complement of the embedded verb which is realized as a clitic. The information about the complement is thus contained in the CLTS list which triggers its spell out as the clitic *le*.[8]

6.4.2 Clitic climbing

Romanian constitutes an exception to the generalization which holds across Romance languages that object clitics must precede the auxiliary verb. Unlike the other clitics, the third person singular feminine clitic *o* must attach to the embedded verb (23a) and cannot precede the auxiliary (23b):

---

[8]An additional constraint, which I have not mentioned here, accounts for the position of the clitic with respect to the host. I refer to Monachesi 1998 for a comprehensive analysis of the morphophonological properties of Romanian cliticization.

(23) a. Am văzut-o.
          have seen-CL.ACC
          'I have seen her.'

    b. * O-am   văzut
          CL.ACC-have seen

The reason for this fact seems to be of phonological nature: the clitic *o* cannot precede an auxiliary which begins with a vowel. Evidence for this hypothesis comes from the observation that in the future paradigm, the auxiliary begins with a consonant (e.g., *voi*) and in this case the clitic *o* can occur either after the infinitive (24a) or in front of the auxiliary (24b):

(24) a. Voi vedea-o.
          will see-CL.ACC
          'I will see her.'

    b. O   voi vedea.
          CL.ACC will see

In order to account for these peculiar facts, past participles and bare infinitives should be excluded as possible hosts for pronominal clitics. They can only be hosts for the clitic *o*. Additional conditions should be added to the constraints responsible for the realization of the clitics. For example, the one in (21) should be modified in the following way:

$$
(25) \quad
\begin{bmatrix}
word \\
\text{MORPH} \mid \text{STEM} \mid \text{SS} \mid \text{L} \mid \text{C} \mid \text{CLTS} \left\langle \text{NP} \big[acc \big]_{3fpl} \right\rangle
\end{bmatrix}
\rightarrow
$$

$$
\begin{bmatrix}
\begin{bmatrix}
complex\text{-}morph \\
\text{STEM} \begin{bmatrix} \text{SS} \mid \text{L} \mid \text{C} \mid \text{HEAD} \begin{bmatrix} \text{VFORM} \neg (psp \lor bare\text{-}inf) \end{bmatrix} \end{bmatrix} \\
\text{MORPH} \quad \\
\text{AFFIX} \begin{bmatrix} prefix \\ \text{PHON} \mid \text{SKEL} \left\langle le \right\rangle \end{bmatrix}
\end{bmatrix}
\end{bmatrix}
$$

The additional condition states that the VFORM of the host must be different from past participle or from bare infinitive. It is thus possible to account for obligatory clitic climbing in the general case.[9] On the other hand, this condition will not be present in the constraint that is

---

[9]In this respect, Romanian is similar to French and different from Italian. In Italian, pronominal clitics can combine with a past participle, in certain configurations, while in French this is never the case.

responsible for the realization of the clitic *o*. It is therefore possible to deal with example (23a), where the clitic combines with a past participle. However, it is necessary to exclude those cases in which the clitic *o* attaches to the auxiliary, exemplified by (23b). This can be achieved by adding further conditions to the constraint that accounts for the realization of the clitic *o*:

(26)

$$
\begin{bmatrix} word \\ \text{MORPH} \mid \text{ST} \mid \text{SS} \mid \text{L} \mid \text{C} \mid \text{CLTS} \left\langle \text{NP}\left[acc\right]_{3fsg} \right\rangle \end{bmatrix} \rightarrow
$$

$$
\begin{bmatrix} \begin{bmatrix} complex\text{-}morph \\ \text{MORPH} \begin{bmatrix} \text{STEM} \neg \begin{bmatrix} word \\ \text{PHON} \begin{bmatrix} \text{VOW} \left\langle \boxed{1} \right\rangle \oplus \boxed{2} \\ \text{SKEL} \left\langle \boxed{1} \right\rangle \oplus \boxed{3} \end{bmatrix} \\ \text{SS} \mid \text{L} \mid \text{C} \begin{bmatrix} \text{HEAD} \begin{bmatrix} verb \\ \text{AUX} + \end{bmatrix} \end{bmatrix} \end{bmatrix} \\ \text{AFFIX} \begin{bmatrix} prefix \\ \text{PHON} \mid \text{SKEL} \left\langle o \right\rangle \end{bmatrix} \end{bmatrix} \end{bmatrix} \end{bmatrix}
$$

The constraint states that if a STEM contains an accusative, third singular feminine element in its CLTS list, the clitic *o* must also be present in the structure and the verb is not an auxiliary which begins with a vowel. Recall that the clitic *o* can combine with auxiliaries that begin with a consonant, as shown by the example (24b).

6.5 Modal verbs

Romanian does not exhibit many environments in which clitic climbing is allowed. This might be due to the fact that the use of bare infinitives is disappearing in this language. Therefore, raising and control verbs are generally followed by a subjunctive. However, the clitic distribution shown in (13) can also occur if the modal verb *a putea* ('can/may') is present:

(27) O   pot vedea.
     CL.ACC can see

     'I can see her.'

An analysis in terms of argument composition can be assumed in this case as well. The following lexical entry is associated with the modal verb:

$$
(28) \quad \begin{bmatrix} \text{HEAD } verb \\ \text{VAL} \begin{bmatrix} \text{SUBJ } \left\langle \boxed{1}\text{NP} \right\rangle \\ \text{COMPS} \left\langle \begin{bmatrix} w\text{-}ss \\ \text{HEAD } verb \\ \text{CLTS } elist \\ \text{VAL} \begin{bmatrix} \text{SUBJ } \left\langle \boxed{1}\text{NP} \right\rangle \\ \text{COMPS } \boxed{2} \end{bmatrix} \end{bmatrix} \right\rangle \oplus \boxed{2} \end{bmatrix} \end{bmatrix}
$$

It should be noticed that the fact that the clitic *o* does not attach to the embedded verb but to the modal constitutes further support for the phonological explanation of the impossibility of (23b). The modal begins with a consonant, so that *o* can attach to it, while this is not the case in (23b) where the auxiliary begins with a vowel. Furthermore, the condition CLTS *elist* excludes the possibility of the clitic *o* being attached to the bare infinitive:[10]

(29) * Pot vedea-o.
       can see-CL.ACC

       (intended) 'I can see her.'

Thus, clitic climbing is obligatory with the verb *a putea*, it is not possible to have any type of clitic attached to the infinitival:

(30) * Pot vedea le.
       can see   CL.ACC

       (intended) 'I can see them.'

This provides further support for the constraint in (25) which excludes bare infinitives as possible hosts for clitics. Therefore, the sentence above is correctly ruled out.

The analysis of the modal *a putea* interacts in the appropriate way with that of the auxiliaries presented in the previous sections. If both

---

[10]This feature is dispensed with in Miller and Sag 1997. However, they introduce new types to achieve the same result: *basic verbs* to which noncliticized verb forms belong and *reduced verbs*, which include cliticized verbs. In their approach, the information that we have a cliticized verb form thus is encoded twice: in the subtyping of *word* and in that of *verb*.

the modal and an auxiliary verb are present, the clitic attaches to the former and not to the latter:[11]

(31)   a.   Am putut-o   vedea.
           have can-CL.ACC see
           'I have been able to see her.'

       b. * O-am   putut vedea.
           CL.ACC-have can   see

These data constitute additional evidence for the constraint in (26), which allows the clitic *o* to combine with a past participle. Recall that the condition [VFORM ¬ *psp*] is not present in this case. On the other hand, the constraint states that the clitic cannot combine with an auxiliary which begins with a vowel, thus accounting for the sentences in (31).

There are certain additional differences between the modal verb *a putea* and the auxiliaries. For example, a pronominal subject (32a) or an adverb (32b) can separate the modal from the infinitival:

(32)   a. Putem noi închipui.
         can   we imagine
         'We can imagine.'

       b. Se   putea uneori   pierde.
          CL.REFL can   sometimes lose
         'He could sometimes lose himself.'

These differences can be accounted for if the modal verb is associated with a flat structure like the one in (7) since this configuration allows elements to intervene between the two verbs. The linearization constraints proposed for Italian modals (Monachesi, 1999a) are assumed to be operative also in this case.

The proposed analysis thus accounts for the differences between the Romanian auxiliaries and the modal *a putea* by assuming a slightly different constituent structure while the similarities, such as the distribution of the clitics, follow as consequence of the lexical operation of argument composition. It should be noted that the modal has the same structure as the Italian and French auxiliaries, with which it shares several properties.

6.6   Conclusions

Romanian auxiliaries differ from French and Italian auxiliaries in several respects. These differences are accounted for by assuming that in

---

[11] Thanks to a reviewer for bringing these data to my attention.

Romanian the auxiliary and the verbal complement form a compound structure. Given this configuration it is possible to deal with the fact that no elements can intervene between the two verbs. This is not the case in French and Italian, where the auxiliary verb, the nonfinite one and the complements combine in a flat structure. On the other hand, there are some crucial similarities across these Romance languages with respect to the distribution of the clitics in the presence of auxiliary (and modal) verbs, it is shown that they follow as consequence of the lexical mechanism of argument composition.

Acknowledgments

I would like to thank the audience of the EUROLAN summer school in Tusnad for comments and suggestions. Many thanks to all the people who helped me with the data: Ana Maria Barbu, Agnes Bende Farkas, Emil Ionescu, Alexandra Popescu, Amalia Todiraşcu and Diana Zaiu. I would also like to thank Detmar Meurers for discussing aspects of the formalization with me and Michael Moortgat for his comments on an earlier draft of this paper. Thanks to the two anonymous reviewers for useful suggestions. This work was partially supported by a grant from the *Netherlands Organization for Scientific Research* (NWO).

References

Abeillé, A. and D. Godard. 1994. The complementation of French Auxiliaries. In *Proceedings of the Thirteenth West Coast Conference on Formal Linguistics*, pages 157–173. Stanford: CSLI Publications.

Anderson, S. 1992. *A-Morphous Morphology*. Cambridge: Cambridge University Press.

Bird, S. and E. Klein. 1994. Phonological analysis in typed feature systems. *Computational Linguistics* 20(3):455–491.

Dobrovie-Sorin, C. 1994. *The syntax of Romanian. Comparative studies in Romance*. Berlin: Mouton de Gruyter.

Hinrichs, E. and T. Nakazawa. 1990. Subcategorization and VP structure in German. In S. Hughes and Salmons, eds., *Proceedings of the Third Symposium on Germanic Linguistics*. Amsterdam: John Benjamins.

Hinrichs, E. and T. Nakazawa. 1994. Linearizing finite AUX in German verbal complexes. In K. Netter, J. Nerbonne and C. Pollard, eds., *German in Head-driven Phrase Structure Grammar*, pages 11–38. Stanford: CSLI Publications.

Kathol, A. 1995. *Linearization-based German syntax*. Ph.D. Thesis, Ohio State University.

Meurers, D. and G. Minnen. 1997. Computational Treatment of Lexical Rules in HPSG as Covariation in Lexical Entries. *Computational Linguistics* 23(4):543–568.

Miller, P. and I. Sag. 1997. French clitic movement without clitics or movement. *Natural Language and Linguistic Theory* 15(3):573–639.

Monachesi, P. 1996. *A grammar of Italian clitics*. Ph.D. Thesis, Tilburg University.

Monachesi, P. 1998. The morphosyntax of Romanian cliticization. In P.-A. Coppen, H. van Halteren, and L. Teunissen, eds., *Proceedings of Computational Linguistics in The Netherlands 1997*, pages 99–118. Amsterdam-Atlanta: Rodopi.

Monachesi, P. 1999a. *A lexical approach to Italian cliticization*. Stanford: CSLI publications.

Monachesi, P. 1999b. Linearization properties of the Romanian verbal complex. In *Proceedings of WECOL 98*. Tempe.

Pollard, C. and I. Sag. 1994. *Head-driven Phrase Structure Grammar*. Chicago and London: University of Chicago Press and CSLI publications.

Reape, M. 1994. Domain Union and Word order variation in German. In K. Netter, J. Nerbonne and C. Pollard, eds., *German in Head-driven Phrase Structure Grammar*, pages 151–198. Stanford: CSLI Publications.

Rivero, M. L. 1994. Clause structure and V-movement in the languages of the Balkans. *Natural Language and Linguistic Theory* 12:63–120.

Stump, G. 1992. On the theoretical status of position class restrictions on Inflectional affixes. In G. Booij and J. van Marle, eds., *Yearbook of Morphology*, pages 211–241. Dordrecht: Kluwer Academic Press.

7

A Generalized-Domain-Based Approach to Serbo-Croatian Second Position Clitic Placement

GERALD PENN

7.1 Introduction

This paper has three main purposes. The first is to generalize the work by Reape (1994), Kathol (1995) and others on domain-based treatments of free verb-phrase-level and clause-level word order to a framework that can express the embedding of word-order domains inside larger domains, and that can deal with multiple kinds of word-order domains in the same grammar. The second is to provide a different formalization of word-order domains in the logic of typed feature structures that allows them to account not only for cases of word order that are under-determined by syntactic principles, but also for cases where principles from different levels of linguistic structure interact mutually to constrain the surface realization of a grammatical string. Such is the case in Serbo-Croatian where prosodic constituency plays a role on a par with syntactic constituency in determining the allowable placements of second-position (2P) clitics. The third is to sketch a formal theory of Serbo-Croatian 2P clitic placement using generalized word-order domains in RSRL (Richter et al., 1999; Richter, forthcoming), a relational extension of feature logic for expressing linguistic principles on the feature structures that license utterances, to provide the first analysis of a construction in HPSG that integrates both prosodic and syntactic knowledge.

Constraints and Resources in Natural Language Syntax and Semantics.
Gosse Bouma, Erhard W. Hinrichs, Geert-Jan M. Kruijff, and Richard T. Oehrle.
Copyright © 1999, Stanford University.

7.2 Clitic placement in Serbo-Croatian

Serbo-Croatian is often called a free word-order language; but it is not entirely free. Phrasal constituents generally have a fixed, contiguous order that they must adhere to for a sentence to be grammatical; and the catalog of exceptions, e.g., the free ordering of daughters of verbal projections, the dislocation of prosodically heavy post-modifiers, is, for the most part, unsurprising.

One very interesting exception is the distribution of a class of enclitic particles known as *second-position* (2P) clitics. These clitics attach to a word or phrase at the beginning of their clause. What the host word or words (the "first" position) can be is constrained by several prosodic and syntactic factors, the net effect of which is frequently classified in the literature, e.g., Browne (1974), Zec and Inkelas (1990), Halpern (1995), as one of either *2D placement* (to use Halpern 1995's terminology), where the first element is a syntactic daughter of the clitic's clause, or *2W placement*, where the first element is a prosodic word, possibly disrupting the contiguity of a syntactic constituent:

(1) a. Taj čovek je   video Mariju.   (2D)
         that man   cl.3s saw   Marija-ACC
         That man saw Mary.

     b. Taj je čovek video Mariju. (2W)

In (1a), the clitic *je* is placed after the first syntactic daughter, *Taj čovek*, which is the subject of the sentence. That NP consists of two prosodic words, *Taj* and *čovek*, so that the 2W placement in (1b) makes the NP discontinuous. All 2P clitics in Serbo-Croatian are capable of both placements, in spite of the fact that some are auxiliaries, some are personal pronouns, and one (*li*) is an interrogative particle. When two or more 2P clitics occur in the same clause, they occur in a cluster in a fixed order, as noted by Browne (1974).

(2) a. Taj pesnik mi   je   napisao knjigu.   (2D)
         that poet   cl.1S.DAT cl.3s wrote   book-ACC
         That poet wrote me a book.

     b.*Taj pesnik je mi napisao knjigu.

     c. Taj mi je pesnik napisao knjigu. (2W)

     d.*Taj je mi pesnik napisao knjigu.

The general order is (1) *li*, then (2) the auxiliaries except the third singular *je*, (3) dative pronominals, (4) genitive pronominals, (5) accusative pronominals and the reflexive *se*, and (6) auxiliary *je*. There are no nominative pronominal clitics; Serbo-Croatian is a pro-drop language.

The binary classification of 2P clitic placement is widely accepted by Slavicists as a workable idealization. What is not as widely accepted is the precise role of syntax and prosody in determining placement, even with respect to this classification. Much of the transformational work on this subject has predictably been devoted to determining the position of these clitics at surface structure, which is non-trivial, given sentences such as (3b):

(3) a. U lepi   grad je   stigao. (2D)
     in beautiful city   cl.3s arrived
     He has arrived in the beautiful city.

   b. U lepi je grad stigao. (2W)

Serbo-Croatian has another class of clitics which are prepositions proclitic to the first word of their NP objects. In (3), *u* is such a prepositional proclitic. It attaches to *lepi*, so that *u lepi* is the first prosodic word, although it is not traditionally regarded as a syntactic constituent.

There is now at least a general agreement that prosody does in fact play some role in 2W placement. It is, nevertheless, often assumed or concluded, notably by Halpern (1995), which reviews all of the major proposals up to 1995, that the surface position of Serbo-Croatian 2P clitics must be either Comp or a distinguished clitic position adjacent to Comp, such as left-adjoined to IP, with 2W placement being achieved in sentences like (3b) by a prosodic repair operation that dislocates the clitic to its surface-realized position. Several recent papers, e.g., Ćavar (1997), Penn (1998), Penn (1999a), have argued against the adequacy of post-syntactic repair by prosody. The last two have done so along the way to making a more general point about the need for a separate, linear level of constituency that can mediate the interaction of the different kinds of constituency or structure at work in determining the linear realization of a phonological string. This point echoes earlier misgivings about analyzing syntactic structure with only a single flavor of constituency, e.g., Zwicky (1986), Blevins (1994), Dowty (1996), and ultimately dates back to Curry (1961)'s call for a distinction between *tectogrammatical* structure, where semantic interpretations are constructed compositionally, and *phenogrammatical* structure, which is concerned with the overt, linear realization of words in a string.

That call is also what has inspired recent work in HPSG, most notably Kathol (1995), on combining lists of domain objects, abstractions of linear substrings, with topological fields, abstract classes of linear order relative to linearly defined regions, to account for word-order phenomena such as scrambling and verb position in German clauses. In that research program, however, topological fields and domain lists were used to state principles on a syntactically under-determined problem (hence the relatively free order witnessed in German), in a more elegant way than traditional syntactic tree structures plus movement could provide.

The claim pursued here is that Curry's (1961) level of phenogrammatical structure, of which domain lists and topological fields constitute one reasonable formalization, can also serve as the mediating level of structure in which prosodic, syntactic and other constraints must be reconciled in order for a string to be grammatical. In simpler terms, the domain objects of Kathol (1995) and the assignment of topological fields to them can be constrained by principles from not only tectogrammar but also prosodic structure and discourse structure. Grammatical strings must have an assignment of domain objects and topological fields that is simultaneously consistent with the principles from each of these sources, although each source can have its own additional abstract representation of structure, such as *synsem* structures in the case of syntax.

This application of domain lists is particularly useful in making sense of the cases where the 2W vs. 2D classification of clitic placement breaks down. There are certain syntactically defined combinations of words in which clitics cannot intervene, called *fortresses* by Halpern (1995), even if that position would be 2W, i.e., immediately following the first prosodic word. One of them is postnominal genitive modifiers:[1]

(4) a. Roditelji uspešnih   studenata   su   se   razišli.
        parents   successful-GEN students-GEN cl.3P cl.REFL dispersed
        The parents of the successful students dispersed.
     b.*Roditelji su se uspešnih studenata razišli.

Roditelji is the first prosodic word; but the clitic cluster, *su se* cannot intervene between it and its genitive plural postmodifier, *uspešnih studenata*.

Another case is the grammatical placement of a clitic within the daughter of a verbal projection in a position other than 2W:[2]

(5) a. Na čiji   povratak iz   Afrike je   Ivan čekao? (2D)
        on whose return   from Africa cl.3s Ivan waited
        On whose return from Africa was Ivan waiting?
     b. Na čiji je povratak iz Afrike Ivan čekao? (2W)
     c. Na čiji povratak je iz Afrike Ivan čekao?

(5c) is grammatical, even though *iz Afrike* modifies *Na čiji povratak*.[3] 2P clitics, however, cannot cause discontinuities within the modifier phrases.

---

[1] The example is taken from Progovac 1996.

[2] The example was provided by Damir Ćavar, p.c.

[3] Halpern 1995 claims that similar examples of 2P clitics separating nouns from their PP post-modifiers are ungrammatical, but cites only adjunct PPs. These

(6) a. U radnji u lepom   gradu je   kupio čamac. (2D)
       in shop   in beautiful city   cl.3s bought boat
       He bought the boat in (a) shop in (the) beautiful city.

   b. U radnji je u lepom gradu kupio čamac. (2W)

   c.*U radnji u lepom je gradu kupio čamac.

A more accurate generalization of the distribution of 2P clitics is a restriction on interrupting prosodic words plus a syntactic "one-level-deep rule,"[4] that clitics may only intervene one phrasal level deep within the daughters of verbal projections. That, of course, prompts the question as to what the precise phrasal structure of these daughters is; and the answer is not entirely straightforward. For example, with a related discontinuous construction, it does not appear that sequences of prenominal adjectives behave as though nested in separate NP or N̄ projections in this respect.[5] For the purposes of this paper, however, it will suffice to accept this generalization at face value.

7.3   Assumptions about prosody

For expository reasons, I assume that signs have the feature geometry shown in Figure 1. They have an extra feature, PROSODY, appropriate

$$
\begin{bmatrix}
\text{sign} & \\
\text{SYNSEM} & \begin{bmatrix} \text{synsem} \\ \text{LOCAL} \quad \text{local} \\ \text{NONLOCAL} \quad \text{nonlocal} \end{bmatrix} \\
\text{QSTORE} & \text{set(quantifier)} \\
\text{QRETR} & \text{list(quantifier)} \\
\text{DTRS} & \text{con\_struc} \\
\text{DOM} & \text{list(dom\_obj)} \\
\text{PROSODY} & \text{list(prosodic\_word)}
\end{bmatrix}
$$

FIGURE 1 Part of the structure of *sign*.

to a list of prosodic words, which represent basic prosodic constituency. For every syntactic sign, the value of this feature contains the prosodic words that correspond to the yield of that sign. Because I assume that all prosodic constituents can ultimately be derived from subconstituents that are no larger than syntactic words, this list is well-defined, i.e., it is always possible to find constituents small enough to cover the yield

---

are often awkward because of an attachment ambiguity, not because of a syntactic prohibition.

[4]Wayles Browne, p.c.

[5]Zlatić 1997, Penn 1998 and Penn 1999a discuss this discontinuous construction in more detail.

of the current syntactic sign exactly. I will not delve any further into prosody here than the level of syntactic words themselves.

While it is clearly outside the scope of this paper to formulate an entire theory of prosodic structure, a few points deserve to be made about it here. First, it is entirely unsatisfying to represent prosodic structure as a disconnected list of prosodic words to be carried around in an otherwise syntactic derivation. Ultimately, the notion of sign in HPSG must be changed to allow parallel derivations of prosody, syntax and discourse that mutually constrain each other through a common DOM list. This would involve, among other things, adding respective DTRS features for each derivation, with appropriate *constituent-structure* objects containing not more signs, but independent syntactic, i.e., *synsem*, or prosodic structures, respectively.[6] The representation of prosodic structure here is only adopted for the purposes of illustrating a more general point.

Second, I follow Inkelas (1989) in assuming that clitics are characterized by their possession of prosodic subcategorization requirements. Within *prosodic_word*, I therefore assume the existence of a PSUBCAT feature, whose value is a list of suitable frames of prosodic information that satisfy these requirements. The only contribution to a theory of prosody that I am, at present, prepared to provide is a Prosodic Subcategorization Principle that discharges these requirements to form larger prosodic words,[7] in the case of Serbo-Croatian clitics, or prosodic phrases in some other languages, much like its syntactic counterpart. A *prosodic_word* will also need to bear a domain list of its own, PDOM.

Third, there must be a principle that requires the list of domain objects in the DOM feature of the sign itself to be the result of appending the lists of domain objects in the list of prosodic words. The fact that these are the same is what requires the results of prosodic and syntactic constraints on a grammatical utterance to be consistent.

7.4 The structure of domain lists

To control the freedom of word-order variation, Reape (1994) and Kathol (1995) use *compaction*, the combination of domain objects into a single domain object whose phonology has a fixed order and must be contiguously realized in the domain lists of mother signs. Compaction is

---

[6]This will mean that signs themselves are not recursive structures. With certain subordinate clauses, one could perhaps make a case for treating them as embedded signs, as in the case of German *denn* clauses and verb-second *weil* clauses (Frank Richter, p.c.); but it is not at all beyond question that a theory of "sub-utterance events" is warranted in the general case.

[7]Inkelas 1989 also claims that Serbo-Croatian clitics, in contrast to those of some other languages, subcategorize for prosodic words to create new prosodic words, not prosodic phrases.

also used in the present analysis to enforce contiguity among the daughters of verbal projections, and, as a special case of that, to control the placement of 2P clitics within a clause.

Reape (1994) and Kathol (1995) use a representation of domain lists in which compaction is encoded by placing a *sign* or *dom(ain)_obj(ect)* on the list that contains a list of compacted structures from a daughter instead of the structures themselves. Daughter domain lists and mother domain lists are constrained by relations that enforce the appropriate compaction or shuffling of structures. Extending this to a formulation that allows prosodic and syntactic constraints to interact is no easy matter. Figure 2, for example, shows potential syntactic and prosodic

$$\langle[\text{u lepi}],\text{grad}]\rangle$$
Prosody: prosodic words compact
$$\langle[\text{u}],[\text{lepi grad}]\rangle$$
Syntax: non-initial NPs compact

FIGURE 2 A prosodic and syntactic compaction on a non-initial PP.

compaction requirements on a non-sentence-initial PP that must combine. A non-initial NP normally must compact; but, on the other hand, the preposition *u* is a proclitic, and so it compacts with the adjective, *lepi*, to form a prosodic word. Unfortunately, the two resulting lists are inconsistent in feature logic if the compacted intervals are represented as single feature structures of any kind, including those of Reape (1994) and Kathol (1995), so many more relations would be necessary. In order not only to compact, but to merge compactions from different sources in a convenient way, we need a different representation.

One representation is shown in Figure 3. The type *rf* is a topological field marker, and will be introduced shortly. Here, the domain list contains one domain object for each word, but compaction is represented by the structure-sharing of a C(OMPACTION) feature. Using this distributed representation of phenogrammatical constituency, the process of adding compaction information to a list of domain objects becomes monotonic. In this case, a consistent domain list would compact the entire non-initial PP, as shown in the figure.

Every *dom_obj* has a PHON(OLOGY), to represent the phonological realization of its word. The order in which several phonological strings are realized is determined by the order in which their domain objects occur in the list itself. To enforce compaction, there is a principle on every domain list that no two domain objects with the same C value can have a domain object between them with a different C value (see the topolog-

$$\left\langle \begin{bmatrix} \text{dom\_obj} \\ \text{PHON} \quad \text{u} \\ \text{C} \quad \boxed{0} \text{ rf} \end{bmatrix}, \begin{bmatrix} \text{dom\_obj} \\ \text{PHON} \quad \text{lepi} \\ \text{C} \quad \boxed{0} \end{bmatrix}, \begin{bmatrix} \text{dom\_obj} \\ \text{PHON} \quad \text{grad} \\ \text{C} \quad \text{rf} \end{bmatrix} \right\rangle$$

Prosody: prosodic words compact

$$\left\langle \begin{bmatrix} \text{dom\_obj} \\ \text{PHON} \quad \text{u} \\ \text{C} \quad \text{rf} \end{bmatrix}, \begin{bmatrix} \text{dom\_obj} \\ \text{PHON} \quad \text{lepi} \\ \text{C} \quad \boxed{0} \text{ rf} \end{bmatrix}, \begin{bmatrix} \text{dom\_obj} \\ \text{PHON} \quad \text{grad} \\ \text{C} \quad \boxed{0} \end{bmatrix} \right\rangle$$

Syntax: non-initial NPs compact

$$\left\langle \begin{bmatrix} \text{dom\_obj} \\ \text{PHON} \quad \text{u} \\ \text{C} \quad \boxed{0} \text{ rf} \end{bmatrix}, \begin{bmatrix} \text{dom\_obj} \\ \text{PHON} \quad \text{lepi} \\ \text{C} \quad \boxed{0} \end{bmatrix}, \begin{bmatrix} \text{dom\_obj} \\ \text{PHON} \quad \text{grad} \\ \text{C} \quad \boxed{0} \end{bmatrix} \right\rangle$$

Consistent domain list

FIGURE 3 A distributed representation of compaction.

ical principle, Planarity, below). The equivalent of Reape (1994)'s and Kathol (1995)'s compacted domain objects is now a sequence of domain objects with a shared feature, which cannot, and should not, bear *sign*- or *synsem*-typed values, because phenogrammatical constituents in this account sometimes correspond to prosodic words that cannot be assigned syntactic categories or certain other syntactic properties in a meaningful way. Penn (1999a) argues for the elimination of this information from domain objects at more length.

Using this representation, an example of the distribution of different domain lists in a sign is given in Figure 4. Normal syntactic constituency

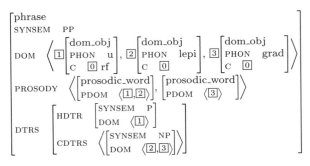

FIGURE 4 A *sign* object with distributed compaction.

is indicated in the DTRS value; prosodic constituency is indicated in the PROSODY value. All of the different representations use the same domain objects to express constraints on word order. The combination of those constraints is, thus, reflected in the DOM list of a *sign*.

7.5 Topological fields

Following Kathol (1995), I also assume the existence of *topological fields*. Topological fields are often defined as classes of domain objects over which linear precedence constraints are stated. This is not quite correct. They are classes of domain objects within a particular *region* over which linear precedence constraints are stated for that region. The ones that Kathol (1995) uses are for the region of a clause consisting of a verb and its complements and adjuncts. To illustrate how multiple regions interact, we shall consider this one plus the region of 2P clitics, with the topology given by Browne (1974). One would need yet another set of topological fields, for example, to describe the order of domain objects inside an NP. When regions are embedded inside other regions, as with the clitic region, NPs, PPs or embedded clauses in the verbal case, a new assignment of fields must be considered. By convention, membership in one of these classes is indicated with a TOPO attribute on domain objects appropriate to one of a language-specific collection of topological field objects for a particular region. Often, these regions are defined syntactically, but that does not need to be the case in general.

In the case of Kathol's (1995) treatment of compaction, the compacting relation can assign a new field to the compacted structure in a higher region, if it requires one. For the distributed representation used here, a simple change of "assignment" is not possible because the same domain objects (as feature structures) are used in every region.

In the present analysis, instead of using another attribute, we can use the C attribute itself, with structure-sharing indicating compaction as before, and with the type of the C value bearing the topological field, such as *rf* in Figure 3. We can also explicitly represent the region in which the topological field is defined so that the field itself may persist in the domain object. To do this, every topological field except one must have an appropriate feature, R(EGION), which is also appropriate to a topological field. The one exception is the topological field, *matrix*, which has no appropriate features. In theory, one could use topological fields to order sentences within a larger discourse-defined region, in which case *matrix* would also have an R feature. As a result, every domain object has a string of topological field assignments along a path of R features, ending in *matrix*. For every sentence, there is only one matrix region, so this *matrix* object occurs on every C/R path of every domain object in a sentence (see the topological principle, Matrix Compaction, below). Figure 5 shows the domain list for (7).

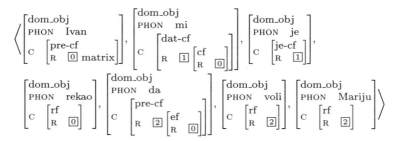

FIGURE 5 A simple sentence with an embedded clause.

(7) Ivan mi   je   rekao da   voli Mariju.
    Ivan cl.1S.DAT cl.3S told that loves Marija-ACC
    Ivan told me that he loves Mary.

The topological fields themselves will be introduced shortly. For clarity, we can represent these structures as graphs, as shown in Figure 6. These

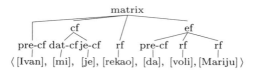

FIGURE 6 A graphical representation of a domain list.

look like trees; and they are. C values encode the derivations of linear, phenogrammatical constituents, just as phrase structure trees encode the derivations of syntactic constituents.

We need one more definition to state linear precedence constraints with topological fields. The natural question when stating linear precedence constraints is which topological field in the string of fields for a domain object should be used. Again, this does not have an absolute answer, because topological fields do not necessarily specify absolute positions or orderings in a domain list. Given two objects on a domain list, D_1 and D_2, the *relative topological fields* of D_1 and D_2 are the types of the deepest non-identical structures in their C values whose R values are identical. If their C values themselves are the same object, then their relative topological fields are the type of that object, i.e., the same field. Of course, we may also speak of the topological field of an object relative to a region. This is its topological field assignment relative to the other objects of that region.

Linear precedence is then enforced by requiring every D_1 and D_2 to be ordered in accordance with the ordering of their relative topological fields. In Figure 5 or 6, the relative topological fields of *da* and *voli* are *pre-cf* and *rf*, respectively. As will be seen shortly, *pre-cf* objects must appear before *rf* objects; so *da* must precede *voli*. The relative topological fields of *rekao* and *da* are *rf* and *ef*, respectively. *rf* objects precede *ef* objects; so *rekao* precedes *da*. Note that if we had used *da*'s *pre-cf* assignment, the reverse would have been predicted.

In the graph notation, the relative topological fields of domain objects are the highest projections of those domain objects that are distinct and have an identical parent, or, if their C values are the same, their common pre-terminal field. Viewed in this way, it can easily be seen that the topological fields plus compaction of Kathol (1995) are just a different way of writing an ID/LP grammar over phenogrammatical constituents. Because every domain object in Kathol (1995) has a SYNSEM value, they are also equivalent to a liberation-style ID/LP grammar over tectogrammatical constituents where intermediate verbal projections are liberated. With partial compaction, they are strictly stronger than ID/LP with liberation, even over phenogrammatical constituents, because one daughter can liberate while the rest of the local tree stays intact.

In general, this device is more powerful than classical ID/LP in terms of strong generative capacity, relative to the same set of topological field assignments. If one were to add different regions with their own topologies, then it would be possible to encode linear precedence principles relative only to a particular region. In classical ID/LP, on the other hand, every linear precedence rule applies to every immediate dominance rule. Of course, one can always expand the set of categories in an ID/LP grammar to compensate for this.

In the present analysis, the use of topological fields is also equivalent to a phenogrammatical ID/LP grammar; but the correspondence with tectogrammatical ID/LP does not exist because some phenogrammatical constituents are formed not on the basis of tectogrammatical compaction, but rather on the basis of prosodic compaction.

The structure of domain objects given here is proposed as a language-universal construct. The language-specific components of linear precedence are the specification of regions, each with a topology, the assignment of topological fields, and the compaction constraints that form phenogrammatical constituents. In more configurational languages, compaction occurs so prolifically among syntactic constituents that, when we restrict our attention to these languages, we see a much more direct correspondence between syntactic constituents and domain objects. This is why, in the case of German and English, domain objects with *synsem*- or *sign*-typed substructures have worked to the extent that they do.

The two regions considered in this paper for Serbo-Croatian, one for clauses, and one for 2P clitic clusters, are shown in Tables 1 and 2. These regions predict the placement of second-position clitics and embedded clauses within clauses, and the relative positions of clitics in clitic clusters, as described on p. 120. Each table shows the possible names for

Compacts to	matrix $\vee$ ef				
Field	pre-cf	cf	post-cf	rf	ef
Occupancy	1	≤ 1	≤ 1	—	≤ 1

TABLE 1   Topology for clauses.

Compacts to	cf					
Field	li-cf	aux-cf	dat-cf	gen-cf	acc-cf	je-cf
Occupancy	≤ 1	≤ 1	≤ 1	≤ 1	≤ 1	≤ 1

TABLE 2   Topology for clitic clusters.

the region within larger regions, i.e., what the appropriate R(EGION) values are for the topological field types, the names of the topological fields for the region, and what the occupancy requirements (per instance of region) are for each field, if any. Some fields, such as *pre-cf* are required to have exactly one object. This requirement on *pre-cf* is what makes 2P clitics "second-position." Others can require at most one or at least one object. Note that these are not requirements on the number of words that can occur in a field, but on the number of actual structures of the type corresponding to that field within a given region. The *pre-cf* field, for example, can be filled by two words, such as *u lepi*, but because they compact, the C values of the *dom_obj* objects for *u* and *lepi* are the same *pre-cf* object, which is unique for that region. *cf* can be filled by a cluster of clitics, but those clitics belong to a single *cf* region; so there is at most one *cf*-typed structure in the next higher clause region.

The topological fields defined for these regions are, for the most part, self-explanatory. The field, *post-cf*, is necessary to hold the remnant of a syntactic constituent that has been made discontinuous by 2W clitic placement. When a 2P clitic is placed after the first prosodic word, the rest of the syntactic constituent to which the first prosodic word belongs is constrained to occur either immediately after the 2P clitic(s), i.e., in the position marked by *post-cf*, or in certain other locations whose significance and availability are not completely understood. The other locations are, therefore, omitted from the present analysis.[8] *ef* is for embedded clauses. Note that embedded clauses can contain embedded clauses, so the clausal region is potentially recursive. The field, *rf*, is the remainder field, for everything else.

The parochial principles governing the clausal topological fields and their assignment are formalized in RSRL in the appendix, assuming the definitions of some basic relations:

- **topo_field**(d,r,f): the relative topological field of domain object, d, with respect to region, r, is f.
- **region**(ds,r): r is the smallest region that contains the domain objects on the domain list, ds.
- **topo_order**(ds,r): the domain list, ds, respects the topological ordering defined on region, r.
- **exist**(x,y): y is a component of x.[9]

The formal definitions of these can be found in Penn (1999b).

The principles, Matrix Compaction, Planarity and Relevance, ensure the integrity of the C values. Matrix Compaction guarantees the acyclicity of R paths, since *matrix* has no appropriate features,[10] and their convergence on a single object per utterance. Without Planarity, constituents in a multiply-fillable topological field (such as *rf*) could be made discontinuous by other occupants of that field. It is what also allows us to draw C values as planar graphs, as in Figure 6. Relevance is the price of using a constraint-based rather than deductive approach: without it, the other constraints would not preclude the existence of arbitrarily long R paths whose structures did not correspond to any particular region, since some of them, such as clauses, are necessarily recursive. The Relevance principle is also open to modification whenever new regions are added because those new regions may then license the existence of new structures. As it stands, it says that topological field structures are licensed either by the lexicon, by embedded clause compaction, by a clitic cluster (*cf* structures), or by an unembedded sign (*matrix* structures).

The other principles essentially encode the information presented in Tables 1 and 2. They do not constrain the internal structure of NPs or

---

[8]Some other locations are briefly discussed in Ćavar 1997. Seemingly the most common one, clause-final position, has been discussed at much greater length, e.g., Halpern 1995, Ćavar 1997, Zlatić 1997, Penn 1999a.

[9]There is no known, single method of expressing this over an arbitrary RSRL signature. It can, however, be defined for the necessary cases within the fixed signature of this analysis.

[10]If discourse-level regions are added on top of *matrix*, then *matrix* would have an R feature, and another field would need to take its place in this constraint.

PPs, nor, crucially, the compaction of prepositional proclitics to the first prosodic word of their hosts. We eventually need to define topological regions for NPs and PPs in order to account for those facts. One also needs the usual extensions to the ID Schemata that shuffle domain lists of daughters together.

7.6 Putting it together: a small example

Figure 7 shows a syntactic derivation for (3b), along with its compaction

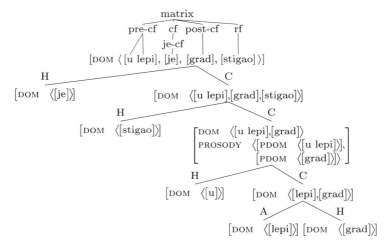

FIGURE 7 A derivation of (3b).

tree at the top. For brevity, only the DOM and, where significant, PROSODY values are shown. In domain lists, compaction is depicted in the more traditional way with bracketings for convenience. Of course, in reality, C values are used everywhere, and a compaction on two objects is visible in every list where both of those domain objects occur. As with all linearization-based analyses, the yield of the syntactic tree is not the phonology of the utterance. That information is only available from the DOM list. Here, the PP itself does not compact in our regions; but the PP's region requires a prosodic compaction in the clausal region.

7.7 Appendix: topological principles

In the principles formulated here, conjunction has tighter precedence than disjunction, quantification has tighter precedence than conjunction, and implication has tighter precedence than quantification. $x\exists y.p$ means that y is a component of x, i.e., accessible from x by a (finite) path. It is a shorthand for $\exists y.(exist(x,y)\ \&\ p)$, where $\exists$ is RSRL's component quantification operator (Richter et al., 1999). $x\forall y.p$ abbreviates $\neg(x\exists y.\neg p)$. $x \sim \tau$ is a type description. : denotes the object that a constraint describes.

1. **Topological Order:** In any domain list, domain objects are ordered by relative topological field in the order shown in Tables 1 and 2.
$nelist(dom\text{-}obj) \rightarrow \exists r.(region(:,r)\ \&\ topo\_order(:,r))$

2. **Field Existence:** Among the relative topological fields of every complete clause's domain list, there is at least one feature structure of type *pre-cf.*
$(unembedded\text{-}sign \vee \text{DTRS}:head\text{-}mark\text{-}struc) \rightarrow$
$\quad \exists ds.\exists r.(\text{DOM}:ds\ \&\ region(ds,r)\ \&$
$\quad\quad ds\exists d.\exists f.(topo\_field(d,r,f)\ \&\ f \sim pre\text{-}cf))$

3. **Field Uniqueness:** Among the relative topological fields of every complete clause's domain list, there is at most one feature structure of type *pre-cf.*[11]
$(unembedded\text{-}sign \vee \text{DTRS}:head\text{-}mark\text{-}struc) \rightarrow$
$\quad \exists ds.\exists r.(\text{DOM}:ds\ \&\ region(ds,r)\ \&$
$\quad\quad ds\forall d_1.ds\forall d_2.\forall f_1.\forall f_2.$
$\quad\quad\quad (d_1 \neq d_2\ \&\ topo\_field(d_1,r,f_1)\ \&$
$\quad\quad\quad topo\_field(d_2,r,f_2)\ \&\ f_1 \sim pre\text{-}cf\ \&\ f_2 \sim pre\text{-}cf)$
$\quad\quad\quad \rightarrow f_1 = f_2)$

4. **2P Clitic Compaction:** In the domain list of any prosodic word, its initial domain object cannot have a field *cf*, relative to any clause; and if there is a domain object with field *cf* relative to a clause, then it compacts in the next higher region with the preceding *pre-cf* object, relative to that clause.
$prosodic\text{-}word \rightarrow$
$\quad \exists ds.\exists c_1.(\text{PDOM}:ds\ \&\ ds\text{FIRST}:\text{C}:c_1\ \&$
$\quad\quad c_1\forall f_1 \sim topo\_field.\neg(f_1 \sim cf)\ \&$
$\quad\quad \exists dsrest.(ds\text{REST}:dsrest\ \&$
$\quad\quad\quad dsrest\forall d \sim dom\_obj.\exists c.(d\text{C}:c\ \&$
$\quad\quad\quad\quad c\forall f.f \sim cf \rightarrow c_1\exists f_1'.(f_1' \sim pre\text{-}cf\ \&\ f_1'\text{R}= f\text{R}))))$

---

[11]Likewise for *cf, post-cf, ef, li-cf, aux-cf, dat-cf, gen-cf, acc-cf*, and *je-cf.* The formalizations for these are obtained by replacing occurrences of *pre-cf* in the one provided here with each of these fields in turn.

5. **Embedded Clause Compaction:** In the domain list of any head-marker phrase, there is a unique object of type *ef* that is the R value of the relative topological fields of every pair of domain objects in that domain list.

DTRS:*head-mark-struc* $\rightarrow$ $\exists ds.$(DOM:*ds* & $\exists r \sim$ *ef.region*(ds, r))

6. **NP/PP Compaction:** For every NP and PP, either it compacts in its clause to *rf* (non-initial), compacts in its clause to *pre-cf* (2D placement), or does not compact, with its first prosodic word compacting to *pre-cf* and the rest compacting to *post-cf* (2W placement).

SYNSEM:LOCAL:CAT:(HEAD:(*noun* $\vee$ *prep*) & SUBCAT:$\langle\rangle$) $\rightarrow$
$\quad \exists ds.\exists r.$(DOM:*ds* & *region*$(ds, r)$ &
$\quad\quad (r \sim$ *pre-cf*
$\quad\quad \vee r \sim$ *rf*
$\quad\quad \vee (r \sim$ *ef* $\vee r \sim$ *matrix*) &
$\quad\quad\quad \exists ps.\exists pr.\exists r.$(PROSODY:FIRST:PDOM:*ps* &
$\quad\quad\quad\quad region(ps, pr)$ & $pr \sim$ *pre-cf* & prR:r &
$\quad\quad\quad\quad \exists restr.(restr \sim$ *post-cf* & $restr$R:r &
$\quad\quad\quad\quad\quad ds\forall d \sim$ *dom_obj.*$(ps\forall d'.d' \neq d) \rightarrow exist(d, restr)))))$

7. **Matrix Compaction:** There is a unique *matrix* object that appears in every C value of every domain object in any domain list.

dom-obj $\rightarrow$ $\exists y.y \sim$ *matrix*
unembedded-sign $\rightarrow$ $\forall y\forall z.(y \sim$ *matrix* & $z \sim$ *matrix*$) \rightarrow y = z$

8. **Planarity:** Given three domain objects on a domain list, the shortest R path at whose value the first (by order in the list) has a substructure of the second's C value must be a (not necessarily proper) prefix of the shortest path at whose value the first has a substructure of the third's, i.e., the graphical representations as in Figure 6 must be planar.

$\forall d_1.\forall d_2.\forall d_3.\forall r.\forall f.$
$\quad (nelist(dom\text{-}obj)$ & FIRST:d_1 & REST:FIRST:d_2 &
$\quad\quad$ REST:REST:FIRST:d_3 & $region(:, r)$ & $topo\_field(d_1, r, f)$ &
$\quad\quad topo\_field(d_3, r, f))$
$\quad \rightarrow topo\_field(d_2, r, f)$

9. **Relevance:** In every domain list, for every domain object in that list, for every object, X, in its C value, there is another domain object such that their relative topological fields' R values are both X.

$sign \rightarrow$
$\quad \forall f \sim field.(\exists s \sim word.s \exists d \sim dom\_obj.\text{DC}:f$
$\quad \quad \vee \exists s \sim phrase.\exists ds.(\text{SDTRS} \sim head\text{-}mark\text{-}struc \ \&$
$\quad \quad \quad s\text{DOM}:ds \ \& \ region(ds, f) \ \&$
$\quad \quad \quad \forall d.\exists c.(\text{DC}:c \ \& \ (c \exists f'.f' = f) \rightarrow ds \exists d'.d' = d))$
$\quad \quad \vee f \sim cf$
$\quad \quad \vee f \sim matrix)$

References

Blevins, J. 1994. Derived constituent order in unbounded dependency constructions. *Journal of Linguistics* 30:349–409.

Browne, W. 1974. On the problem of enclitic placement in Serbo-Croatian. In R. Brecht and C. Chvany, eds., *Slavic Transformational Syntax*, Michigan Slavic Materials 10. Ann Arbor: Department of Slavic Languages and Literatures, University of Michigan.

Ćavar, D. 1997. On cliticization in Croatian: Syntax or prosody? In *Proceedings of the Workshop on the Syntax, Morphology and Phonology of Clitics. ZAS Papers in Linguistics, 6 (October)*, pages 51–65. Universität Potsdam.

Curry, H. B. 1961. Some logical aspects of grammatical structure. In *Structure of Language and its Mathematical Aspects: Proceedings of the Twelfth Symposium in Applied Mathematics*, pages 56–68. American Mathematical Society.

Dowty, D. 1996. Toward a minimalist theory of syntactic structure. In H. Bunt and A. van Horck, eds., *Discontinuous Constituency*. Walter de Gruyter.

Halpern, A. 1995. *On the Placement and Morphology of Clitics*. Stanford: CSLI.

Inkelas, S. 1989. *Prosodic Constituency in the Lexicon*. Ph.D. thesis, Stanford University.

Kathol, A. 1995. *Linearization-Based German Syntax*. Ph.D. thesis, Ohio State University.

Penn, G. 1998. On the plausibility of purely structural multiple WH-fronting. In *Proceedings of the Second European Conference on Formal Description of Slavic Languages*. Slavica Publishers.

Penn, G. 1999a. Linearization and WH-extraction in HPSG: Evidence from Serbo-Croatian. In R. Borsley and A. Przepiórkowski, eds., *Slavic in HPSG*, pages 149–182. Palo Alto: CSLI Publications.

Penn, G. 1999b. An RSRL formalization of Serbo-Croatian second position clitic placement. In V. Kordoni, ed., *Tübingen Studies in HPSG*. Arbeitspapier des SFB 340, Nr. 132.

Progovac, L. 1996. Clitics in Serbian/Croatian: Comp as the second position. In A. Halpern and A. Zwicky, eds., *Approaching Second: Second Position Clitics and Related Phenomena*. Stanford: CSLI Publications.

Reape, M. 1994. Domain union and word order variation in German. In J. Nerbonne, K. Netter, and C. Pollard, eds., *German in Head-Driven Phrase Structure Grammar*, CSLI Lecture Notes. CSLI Publications.

Richter, F. forthcoming. *A Mathematical Formalism for Linguistic Theories with an Application in Head-Driven Phrase Structure Grammar and a Fragment of German*. Ph.D. thesis, Universität Tübingen. Working Title. Version: February 9th, 1998.

Richter, F., M. Sailer, and G. Penn. 1999. A formal interpretation of relations and quantification in HPSG. In G. Bouma, E. Hinrichs, G.-J. M. Kruijff, and R. T. Oehrle, eds., *Constraints and Resources in Natural Language Syntax and Semantics*.

Zec, D. and S. Inkelas. 1990. Prosodically constrained syntax. In S. Inkelas and D. Zec, eds., *The Phonology-Syntax Connection*. Chicago: University of Chicago Press.

Zlatić, L. 1997. *The Structure of the Serbian Noun Phrase*. Ph.D. thesis, University of Texas at Austin.

Zwicky, A. 1986. Concatenation and liberation. In *Papers from the 22nd Regional Meeting of the Chicago Linguistic Society*, pages 65–74. Chicago Linguistic Society.

8

Major and Minor Pronouns in Dutch

Frank Van Eynde

8.1 Introduction

Many languages have two paradigms of personal pronouns. French, for instance, has both tonic pronouns, such as *moi* and *toi*, and clitic pronouns, such as *me* and *te*. In Dutch most of the personal pronouns also come in two variants. Table 1 provides a summary of the data in (Haeseryn et al., 1997, 237-242).

pers	number	gender	full nom	full oblique	reduced nom	reduced oblique
1st	sing	m/f	*ik, ikke*	*mij*	*'k*	*me*
	plur	m/f	*wij*	*ons*	*we*	
2nd	sing	m/f	*jij*	*jou*	*je*	*je*
	sg/pl	m/f	*gij*	*u*	*ge*	
	plur	m/f	*jullie*	*jullie*		
3rd	sing	masc	*hij*	*hem*	*ie*	*'m*
	sing	neut			*het, 't*	*het, 't*
	sg/pl	fem	*zij*	*haar*	*ze*	*ze, d'r, 'r*
	plur	m/f/n	*zij*	*hen, hun*	*ze*	*ze*

TABLE 1 Two paradigms for personal pronouns in Dutch

There are some forms without reduced counterpart (*ons, u* and *jullie*), and there is one form which lacks a full counterpart, i.e. the singular neuter *het* ('it').[1] For the other pronouns there is at least one full form

---

[1]Diachronically, it is the reduced counterpart of the demonstrative *dat* ('that').

Constraints and Resources in Natural Language Syntax and Semantics.
Gosse Bouma, Erhard W. Hinrichs, Geert-Jan M. Kruijff, and Richard T. Oehrle.
Copyright © 1999, Stanford University.

and one reduced form. Most of the reduced forms consist of the schwa and one or two consonants; the exceptions are the singular masculine *ie* ('he') and the non-syllabic variants of *'k* ('I') and *'t* ('it').[2] For obvious reasons, the non-syllabic forms lack phonological autonomy: they form a phonological unit with the immediately preceding (enclitic) or following (proclitic) word. Somewhat less obviously, this also holds for *ie*, which is invariably enclitic: it is not possible to start a sentence with *ie*. Apart from these three, which I will henceforth call the clitics, the reduced forms are autonomous phonological words.

The purpose of this paper is to identify the main syntactic and semantic differences between the full and the reduced pronouns and to propose a way of capturing them in terms of the formal apparatus of Head-driven Phrase Structure Grammar. Within that framework, the reduced pronouns of Dutch raise a double challenge. One concerns their syntactic properties (section 2), the other concerns the relation between syntax and semantics (section 3).

8.2 On the syntax of the reduced pronouns

8.2.1 Major and minor pronouns

A salient syntactic difference between the full pronouns and their reduced counterparts is that the former can take various types of adjuncts, such as prepositional modifiers, relative clauses and appositions, whereas the latter cannot.

(1) Jij/*Je met je   eeuwige gezeur.
    you   with your eternal   complaining
    'You with your endless complaints.'

(2) Zij/*Ze die gaan sterven groeten u.
    they   who go   die   greet   you
    'Those who are about to die greet you.'

(3) Wij/*We, Albert, Koning der   Belgen,   ...
    we   Albert King   of-the Belgians ...
    'We, Albert, King of the Belgians, ... '

The same contrast can be observed in French. While the tonic pronouns can take an adjectival modifier or a relative clause, their clitic counterparts cannot.

Notice that the French clitic *il* ('he' or 'it') also derives from a demonstrative, cf. the Latin *ille* ('that').

[2] The other truncated forms (*'m*, *'r* and *d'r*) are always syllabic.

(4) Moi/*Je seule connais mon appétit.
     I   alone know   my   appetite
     'I alone know my appetite.'

(5) Lui/*Il qui était perdu est retrouvé.
     he   who was lost   is   retrieved
     'He who was lost has been retrieved.'

As a consequence, since pronouns do not take any other kinds of dependents, such as complements, subjects, markers or fillers, it can be concluded—in more general terms—that the full or tonic pronouns can take syntactic dependents, whereas the reduced or clitic ones cannot. Another way of stating this is that the former can be the head of a non-vacuous phrasal projection (NP), whereas the latter cannot.[3] As for the French clitics, the standard HPSG treatment not only recognizes their lack of a phrasal projection, it also claims that they do not even qualify as syntactic atoms. More specifically, employing the criteria which have been proposed for distinguishing between words and affixes in Zwicky and Pullum (1983), Miller (1992) argues that the French clitics are inflectional affixes of verbs, and Monachesi (1995) reaches the same conclusion for the Italian ones.

In terms of this dichotomy, the reduced pronouns of Dutch take an intermediate position, for, on the one hand, they lack a (non-vacuous) phrasal projection, but, on the other hand, they do qualify as syntactic atoms. To see this it suffices to apply the criteria of Zwicky and Pullum (1983). First, affixes tend to be rather selective with respect to the category of their host. The French and Italian clitics, for instance, behave as affixes since they invariably combine with verbs. The reduced pronouns of Dutch, however, combine equally well with verbs, prepositions and adjectives.[4]

(6) Heb jij [ze/het gezien]?
     have you [her/it seen]
     'Did you see her/it?'

(7) Ze heeft vannacht [van me/je] gedroomd.
     she has   tonight   [of me/you] dreamt
     'She has dreamt of me/you tonight.'

---

[3] The addition of *non-vacuous* is relevant, since it is always possible to postulate a vacuous projection, also for elements which never take any syntactic dependents.

[4] *Waard* belongs to a small class of predicative adjectives with a preceding NP complement; some other members of this class are *beu* ('fed up with') and *moe* ('tired of'). For a full list, see (Haeseryn et al., 1997, 398).

(8) Zij is [het waard].
    she is [it   worth]
    'She is worth it.'

Second, affixes are adjacent to the stem. The French and Italian clitics, for instance, cannot be separated from the verb by other words or phrases. For the reduced pronouns of Dutch this constraint does not hold. In the following sentence the oblique pronoun (*me* or *je*) is separated from the verb *betalen* by the adjuncts *morgen* and *eindelijk*.

(9) ... dat ze me/je morgen eindelijk betalen.
    ... that they me/you tomorrow finally pay

    '... that they will finally pay me/you tomorrow.'

Third, unlike the affixes and the French clitics, the reduced pronouns can have scope over coordination.

(10) Hij heeft het gelezen en goedgekeurd.
     he has it read   and approved

     'He has read and approved it.'

Even the three Dutch clitics do not behave like affixes: the nominative *ie* ('he') and *'k* ('I') attach to finite verbs, complementizers and conjunctions, and the non-syllabic *'t* ('it'), which can also be oblique, attaches to almost anything, including another clitic, as in ... *of ie 't al weet* ('... whether he already knows it'). It can also have scope over coordination, as in *Heb je 't gekookt of gebakken?* ('Have you cooked or baked it?').

In sum, the Dutch reduced pronouns are syntactic atoms, but at the same time they cannot have a non-vacuous phrasal projection. At first sight, this combination of properties may not seem particularly unusual, but in the framework of contemporary phrase structure grammar (GPSG and HPSG) it does raise a problem.

Taking a lead from the GPSG distinction between major and minor categories, HPSG makes the distinction between the words which can head a phrasal projection and those which cannot, in terms of the parts of speech to which they belong. More specifically, of the six parts of speech which are distinguished in Pollard and Sag (1994), there is one which contains all words which cannot have a phrasal projection, i.e., *marker*.

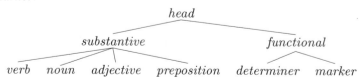

The markers include a.o. the complementizers and the coordinating conjunctions. The other words belong to parts of speech which have a phrasal projection (VP, NP, AP, PP, DetP).

The problem now with the reduced pronouns of Dutch, is that they do not fit into this classification. For if they are nouns, just like their full or tonic counterparts, they are allowed to have a phrasal projection (NP), and if they are grouped with the words which cannot have a phrasal projection, they are included in a class of words with which they have nothing in common, such as the complementizers and the conjunctions.

In order to resolve this conflict, I propose to apply the *major-minor* distinction to the objects of type *category* rather than to the parts of speech.

As before, all objects of type *category* have a HEAD feature, but the novelty is that only the major ones can select dependents and therefore have the appropriate features to model this selection (ARG-ST and VALENCE). The HEAD feature takes an object of type *head* as its value, and the subtypes of this value correspond to the traditional parts of speech. There is no separate value for elements which lack a (non-vacuous) phrasal projection.[5]

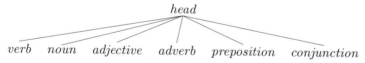

As usual, nouns have a CASE feature, verbs a VFORM feature, etc.

Making use of these partitions and declarations, the distinction between the full and reduced pronouns can be captured as follows.

$$
\begin{bmatrix}
major \\
\text{HEAD} \quad \begin{bmatrix} noun \\ \text{CASE} \quad case \end{bmatrix} \\
\text{VALENCE} \quad valence \\
\text{ARG-ST} \quad \langle\,\rangle
\end{bmatrix}
$$

---

[5] The complementizers are treated as minor prepositions (*for* and *to*) or as minor adverbs (*that*), see Van Eynde (1998).

$$
\begin{bmatrix}
minor \\
\text{HEAD} \quad \begin{bmatrix} noun \\ \text{CASE} \quad case \end{bmatrix}
\end{bmatrix}
$$

Both types of pronouns are nominal and specified for case, but their CATEGORY values are different.

Since the *major/minor* distinction is now orthogonal to the part of speech classification, it is predicted to apply not only to nouns but also to prepositions, adjectives and other parts of speech. This obviously raises the question of how the minor signs can be identified; this is the topic of the next paragraph.

8.2.2 Criteria for identifying minor signs

As a background for the discussion I use the typology of phrase types in (Sag, 1997, 439).

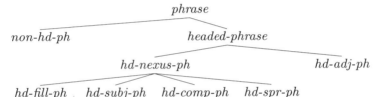

Since the signs of minor categories are—by definition—signs which lack a phrasal projection, it follows that phrasal signs must be major.

$$phrase \longrightarrow [\text{SYNSEM|LOC|CAT} \quad major\,]$$

Another constraint which follows from the definition itself is that minor signs cannot be used as heads, and that head daughters must hence be major.

$$headed\text{-}phrase \longrightarrow [\text{HEAD-DTR|SYNSEM|LOC|CAT} \quad major\,]$$

The other types of daughters in headed phrases are not constrained in this general manner, but they can be subject to more specific constraints. The nominative pronouns, for instance, may be minor when they are the subject of a finite clause, but not when they are the subject of a non-finite or verbless clause.

(11) Wij/*We gediskwalificeerd? Kom nou!
       we   disqualified   come now
       'We disqualified? You must be kidding!'

(12) Zij/*Ze alleen naar China? Daar is ze te jong voor.
       she   alone to   China   there is she too young for

'She alone to China? But she's too young for that.'

Similarly, the oblique pronouns may be minor when they are used as complements, but there are some exceptions. The preposition *volgens*, for instance, requires a major complement, cf. *volgens mij/*me* ('according to me').[6]

Another—more general—constraint on the oblique pronouns is that only their full forms may be topicalized.

(13) Mij/*Me hebben ze   niets   gevraagd.
      me   have   they nothing asked

'To me they did not ask anything.'

Turning to the nonheaded phrases, we find some further general constraints. In coordinate phrases, for instance, the conjunct daughters must all be major.

(14) Ze   twijfelen nog tussen   Mark en jou/*je.
      they hesitate still between Mark and you

'They are still hesitating between Mark and you.'

(15) We zullen onderhandelen met hen/*ze en hun   aanhangers.
      we shall negotiate   with them   and their allies

'We shall negotiate with them and their allies.'

Interestingly, this constraint need not be stipulated, since it follows from the interaction of the present treatment with the COORDINATION PRINCIPLE, as defined in (Pollard and Sag, 1994, 203).

> *In a coordinate structure, the* CATEGORY *and* NONLO-CAL *value of each conjunct daughter is subsumed by (is an extension of) that of the mother.*

Since coordinate structures are by definition phrasal, they have CATEGORY values of type *major*, and given the principle this implies that the conjunct daughters cannot be minor.

Generalizing over the constraints which have been mentioned so far, it turns out that a phrase has to contain at least one major daughter, i.e. the head daughter in headed phrases or the conjunct daughters in coordinate phrases. Further evidence for this generalization is provided by the fact that elliptical clauses have to contain at least one major word; they may not consist of a single minor word.

---

[6]In French, this constraint applies to all prepositions, cf. *pour moi/*me* ('for me') and *avec lui/*le* ('with him').

(16) Wie heeft het gedaan? Zij/*Ze.
      who has it done   she

      'Who did it? She did.'

(17) Hij heeft meer gereisd dan zij/*ze.
      he has   more traveled than she

      'He has traveled more than she has.'

Summing up, minor signs are words which do not take any dependents, which cannot be topicalized or conjoined, and which cannot be the only constituent of a clause.

These criteria are sufficiently general to be applicable to other languages as well, but this should not be expected to mean that the results will be identical across languages. The English pronoun *it*, for instance, is the translational equivalent of the Dutch *het*, but in contrast to the latter, it does not qualify as minor, for it can take dependents and it can be conjoined.

(18) a. The history of culture is in great part the story of a protracted struggle between pictorial and linguistic signs, each claiming for itself certain property rights on a 'nature' to which [only it] has access.   (W.J.T. Mitchell)

      b. You might be tempted to read [it and it alone], fanatically, the rest of your days.   (P. Hanrahan on D. Delillo's *Underworld*)

      c. Recently speculation has been growing that [it and the Roman Catholic Church] will reunite. (TIME, May 5th, 1997, p. 47)

      d. I have leaned over backwards to keep the balance between [it and the North] in these fearful and unsettled times.   (John Updike, *Memories of the Ford Administration*, p. 315)

In none of these examples can *it* be translated as *het*, in spite of the fact that they are semantically equivalent. This discrepancy between the Dutch minor *het* and the English major *it* clearly demonstrates that the distinction is syntactic rather than semantic, for in the latter case one would expect the criteria to give the same result in both languages.

The criteria are also sufficiently general to be applicable to other classes of words, as will be demonstrated in the next paragraph.

8.2.3 Application to other types of pronouns

A contrast which resembles the one between the personal pronoun *het* ('it') and the demonstrative *dat* ('that'), is the one between *er* and *daar* ('there'). They belong to a paradigm which also includes *hier* ('here'), *waar* ('where'), *ergens* ('somewhere'), *nergens* ('nowhere') and *overal* ('everywhere'), also known as the [+R] pronouns (Van Riemsdijk, 1978, 36–45). Like their English counterparts, they can be used as locative adjuncts or complements.

(19)   Hij woont daar/er/hier al   jaren.
       he lives   there/–/here already years

       'He has been living there/here for years.'

In addition, they have acquired a second use: When combined with a preposition, various pronouns must be replaced by a [+R] counterpart, especially when their referent is non-human.

P + pronoun	example	[+R] + P	example
P + Personal (3rd)	* *op het*	er + P	*erop*
P + Demonstrative (Prox)	* *op dit/deze*	hier + P	*hierop*
P + Demonstrative (Dist)	* *op dat/die*	daar + P	*daarop*
P + Relative	* *op dat/die*	waar + P	*waarop*
P + Interrogative	* *op wat*	waar + P	*waarop*

TABLE 2   [+R] rponouns in Dutch

The [+R] pronoun must precede the preposition, and in spite of what the orthography suggests, it does not necessarily lose its syntactic autonomy in this combination, since the two parts of the prepositional phrase can be separated by other constituents, such as the adverbs *liever* and *niet* in

(20)   We hadden daar/er/hier liever niet op gewacht.
       we had   there/–/here rather not for waited

       'We had rather not waited for that/it/this.'

The interesting fact now, in the present context, is the contrast between *er* and the other [+R] pronouns. Applying the tests of adjunction, topicalization, conjunction and ellipsis, it turns out that the latter all qualify as major whereas the former does not.

(21)   We zijn precies   daar/*er waar de Greenwich lijn de
       we are precisely there   where the Greenwich line the
       evenaar kruist.
       equator crosses

       'We are exactly there where the Greenwich line crosses the equator.'

(22) Daar/*Er had ze niet aan gedacht.
      there   had she not of thought
      'Of that she had not thought.'

(23) Wil je liever hier of daar/*er zitten ?
      want you rather here or there   sit
      'Would you rather sit here or there?'

(24) Ik zit liever hier dan daar/*er.
      I sit rather here than there
      'I'd rather sit here than there.'

As is clear from the glosses, English does not have a contrast which is comparable to the one between *er* and *daar*: the closest translational equivalent in both cases is the major *there*.

The *major/minor* dichotomy is also relevant for the Dutch reflexive pronouns. The two forms of the third person reflexive, for instance, which are *zich* and *zichzelf*, can be differentiated in terms of the same distinction. While *zichzelf* can be modified, topicalized, conjoined and used as the only constituent of a clause, *zich* cannot.

(25) Hij heeft alleen zichzelf/*zich bedrogen.
      he has only himself   cheated
      'He has cheated only himself.'

(26) Zichzelf/*zich heeft hij nog niet geschoren.
      himself   has he yet not shaved
      'Himself he has not shaved yet.'

(27) Ze hebben zichzelf/*zich en hun families verdedigd.
      they have   themselves and their families defended
      'They have defended themselves and their families.'

(28) Ze heeft niemand meer lief dan zichzelf/*zich.
      she has nobody more love than herself
      'She does not love anybody more than herself.'

Once again, there is a similar contrast in French (*se* vs. *soi-même*), but not in English: the English third person reflexives (*himself/herself/ itself/themselves*) are all major.

Summing up, the minor signs not only include the reduced forms of the personal pronouns, but also the [+R] pronoun *er* and the reflexive *zich*. This list can further be extended with words from other parts of speech. Van Eynde (1997), for instance, identifies a number of minor determiners on the basis of the same four criteria, and Van Eynde

(1998) argues that the complementizers qualify as minor prepositions or adverbs.

8.3 On the semantics of the reduced pronouns

There is often assumed to be a correlation between syntactic and semantic 'lightness'. Words which cannot have a phrasal projection are expected to carry little or no autonomous content. In terms of HPSG: "markers tend to be semantically vacuous, or else their semantic contributions are of a logical nature." (Pollard and Sag, 1994, 364). The purpose of this section is to investigate whether this also holds for the minor pronouns.

8.3.1 Referential and expletive pronouns

A nominal is nonreferential or expletive if it is not assigned any semantic role. The English pronouns *it* and *there*, for instance, are referential in (29), but not in (30).

(29) I'll put it there.

(30) It bothers her that there are no napkins on the table.

A quick-and-easy test to distinguish a referential nominal from an expletive one is that the former can be replaced by another referential nominal, whereas the latter cannot. Further tests are provided in Postal and Pullum (1988).

Now, if there were a correlation between syntactic and semantic lightness, one would expect the minor pronouns to be expletive, but this is not the case. Instead, they can all be used referentially, and given the fact that their full counterparts are somewhat emphatic, they are even more commonly used than the major ones, also in argument positions.

At the same time, it should be added that the *major/minor* distinction is not entirely unrelated to the *referential/expletive* one, for there is some evidence that the major pronouns must be referential. In terms of the HPSG sort hierarchy this can be expressed as follows.[7]

$$\begin{bmatrix} local \\ \text{CATEGORY} & major \\ \text{CONTENT} & pronoun \end{bmatrix} \longrightarrow \begin{bmatrix} \text{INDEX} & referential \end{bmatrix}$$

---

[7]In Pollard and Sag (1994) *pronoun* is the CONTENT value of the personal and anaphoric pronouns; it contrasts with *nonpronoun*, which stands for the CONTENT values of all other nominal objects, such as the ones of proper nouns and common nouns.

As a corollary, the expletive pronouns must be either minor words or affixes.

As far as Dutch is concerned, this constraint appears to be valid. The anticipatory pronoun in a sentence with an extraposed clausal complement, for instance, must be either *het* ('it') or *er* ('there').

(31) Het schijnt dat ze   niet komt.
       it   seems that she not comes
       'It seems that she does not come.'

(32) We rekenen er   niet op dat ze   komt.
       we count   there not on that she comes
       'We do not count on it that she comes.'

Similarly, the subject of a weather verb must be *het* ('it'), and the subject of an existential clause must be *er* ('there'). The constraint also applies to the reflexive pronouns. In the case of inherently reflexive verbs, such as *zich vergissen* ('to err') and *zich schamen* ('to be ashamed'), the reflexive pronoun is expletive, since it cannot be replaced by a referential NP, and must—hence—be minor.

(33) Hij heeft zich/*zichzelf vergist.
       he has   –/himself   erred
       'He has erred.'

(34) Ze   schamen zich/*zichzelf niet.
       they shame   –/themselves not
       'They are not ashamed.'

Expletive uses of non-3rd person pronouns are rare, but do occur. A relevant example is the use of the first person singular *me* as an ethical dative. In that use it does not express a semantic role of the predicate, but rather some kind of emotional involvement of the speaker (Haeseryn et al., 1997, 254). Its expletive nature is clear from the fact that it cannot be replaced with any other NP, and the fact that it has to be minor is clear from the fact that it cannot be replaced by its major counterpart *mij*.

(35) Wat zeg je   me/*mij/*ons/*hem daarvan?
       what say you –/me/us/him   there-of
       'What do you say of that?'

On the whole then it turns out that the Dutch expletive pronouns must indeed be minor.

Whether the constraint also holds for English is less obvious. At first sight, it does not, for the most commonly used expletives in English, *it* and *there*, have both been argued to be major in the previous section. However, taking a closer look at those examples, it turns out that they all concern referential uses of the pronouns. In examples with expletive uses, the typical properties of major pronouns are lost: The addition of adjuncts or of appositions leads to ungrammaticality, and topicalization and conjunction turn out to be impossible.

(36) a. * It alone bothers me that she snores.

   b. * It, that she snores, bothers me.

   c. * It I take that you will leave.

   d. * It and there were/was respectively proved to be raining and claimed to be floods in the valley.

In (Postal and Pullum, 1988, 636), from which the last example is taken, the non-conjoinability is even treated as one of the diagnostic properties of expletives. It appears then that the expletives *it* and *there* are minor, even if their referential counterparts are not.

In sum, it turns out that while the minor pronouns have got both referential and expletive uses, their major counterparts have only got the referential ones. In a sense, this is exactly the opposite of the initial hypothesis: instead of being semantically deficient, the minor pronouns turn out to be more versatile. This will be further substantiated in the next paragraph.

8.3.2 Constraints on anchoring

Pronouns often impose specific constraints on their referents. A second person singular pronoun, for instance, standardly refers to the addressee. In HPSG, this is expressed as a constraint on the anchor of the index (Pollard and Sag, 1994, 77)

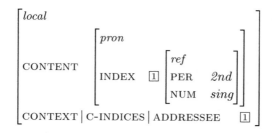

What is interesting now is that this constraint holds for the major pronouns, but not for the minor ones. In Dutch, *jij* and *jou* must refer to the addressee, but their minor counterpart *je* can also have generic reference, as in

(37) Je zou   niet zeggen dat ze   zwanger is.
      you would not tell   that she pregnant is
      'One would not tell she is pregnant.'

A similar remark applies to the first person plural. Whereas the major *wij* has to include the speaker in its reference, the minor *we* need not. As a consequence, if the pronoun's reference is not meant to include the speaker, one has to use the reduced form.

(38) Nu gaan we/*wij slapen.
      now go   –/we   sleep
      'We are going to bed now.'

(39) ... zoals we/*wij in het vorige   hoofdstuk al   zagen.
      ... as   –/we   in the previous chapter   already saw
      '... as we saw in the previous chapter.'

The first sentence can be used to tell a child to go to bed, without implying that also the speaker goes to bed, and the second sentence can be used by an author who takes the perspective of the readers.

The contrast can also be observed in the third person plural pronouns: whereas the major *zij*, *haar*, *hen* and *hun* all require a human or—at least—an animate referent, the minor *ze* can refer to any kind of aggregate.

In sum, also in their modes of anchoring, the minor pronouns turn out to be less constrained than the major ones.

8.4 Conclusion

Like French and Italian, Dutch has two paradigms of personal pronouns, the full or tonic ones and the reduced ones. In contrast to the Romance clitics, the Dutch reduced pronouns are syntactic atoms, but at the same time they cannot head an NP. As such, they are problematic for syntactic frameworks in which all words without phrasal projection are required to belong to a small set of minor categories (GPSG) or to a special part of speech (HPSG's markers). As a solution, I propose to treat the *major/minor* distinction as orthogonal to the part of speech classification, thus predicting that all parts of speech may contain words which can never head a phrase. In order to identify such words I have presented four criteria: minor signs are words which do not take any dependents, which cannot be topicalized, which cannot be conjoined, and which cannot be the only constituent of a clause. To demonstrate the generality of these criteria they have also been applied to other Dutch and English pronouns.[8]

In the second part of the paper, I have provided evidence that the distinction between major and minor pronouns is also semantically relevant. More specifically, it has been demonstrated that the expletive pronouns must be minor, both in Dutch and in English, but that the converse does not hold: minor pronouns may be referential as well. As a consequence, the pronouns which are semantically more constrained are the major ones, i.e., those which are syntactically less restricted. This is confirmed by the constraints on their modes of anchoring: in that respect as well, the major pronouns are more constrained than the minor ones.

The wider significance of this analysis of the reduced pronouns of Dutch can be summed up as follows: (1) there are words which lack a (non-vacuous) phrasal projection; (2) such words can belong to any part of speech; (3) semantically, those words tend to be less restricted than their major counterparts.

References

Haeseryn, W., K. Romijn, G. Geerts, J. De Rooij, and M. Van den Toorn. 1997. *Algemene Nederlandse Spraakkunst*. Groningen/Deurne: Martinus Nijhoff Uitgevers / Wolters Plantyn.

Miller, P. 1992. *Clitics and Constituents in Phrase Structure Grammar*. New York: Garland.

Monachesi, P. 1995. *A Grammar of Italian Clitics*. Ph.D. thesis, Tilburg University.

Pollard, C. and I. Sag. 1994. *Head-driven Phrase Structure Grammar*. Stanford/Chicago: CSLI and University of Chicago Press.

Postal, P. and G. Pullum. 1988. Expletive Noun Phrases in Subcategorized Positions. *Linguistic Inquiry* 19:635–670.

Sag, I. 1997. English Relative Clause Constructions. *Journal of Linguistics* 33:431–484.

Van Eynde, F. 1997. On the notion 'Minor category'. In J. Landsbergen, J. Odijk, K. van Deemter, and G. Veldhuijzen van Zanten, eds., *CLIN VII. Papers from the Seventh CLIN meeting*, pages 191–206. IPO, University of Eindhoven.

Van Eynde, F. 1998. Functional projections and Dutch complementizers. In T. Kiss and D. Meurers, eds., *Current topics in constraint-based*

---

[8]They have also been applied to determiners, prepositions and adverbs in Van Eynde (1997) and Van Eynde (1998).

theories of Germanic syntax. ESSLLI-10, University of Saarbrücken, 149-164.

Van Riemsdijk, H. 1978. *A case study in syntactic markedness*. Peter de Ridder Press.

Zwicky, A. and G. Pullum. 1983. Cliticization vs. inflection: English *n't*. *Language* 59:502–513.

Part II

Resource-Sensitive Approaches

9

Contour and Structure: A Categorial Account of Alignment

HERMAN HENDRIKS

In this paper it is argued that within the proof-theoretic sign-based categorial analysis of intonation presented in Hendriks (1999), the problem of alignment, which has been characterized as 'one of the earliest and most intractable problems in prosodic phonology', does not even arise. The alignment of pitch accents with the prosodically strongest syllable of their domain is a problem for prosodic phonology, because a level of 'accentual phrase' cannot be defined for English. This impossibility can be attributed to the fact that the relevant 'accentual phrase' may either be considerably bigger or substantially smaller than a prosodic word. However, on the natural and straightforward assumption that lexical items have themselves prosodically headed phonological forms, the observed indifference of English pitch accent assignment to phonological levels follows without any further stipulation in the proof-theoretic sign-based grammar formalism, due to the fact that the resulting system accommodates a completely uniform account of lexical and phrasal prosodic headedness.

9.1 Alignment

In the paper 'Alignment and Prosodic Heads' (Pierrehumbert 1994), pitch accent assignment in English is characterized as '[o]ne of the earliest and most intractable problems in prosodic phonology'. (Pierrehumbert 1994: 273–274.)

> Intonation contours in English consist of one or more pitch
> accents plus boundary tones marking phrasal edges. Each
> pitch accent is aligned with the most prominent syllable of

Constraints and Resources in Natural Language Syntax and Semantics.
Gosse Bouma, Erhard W. Hinrichs, Geert-Jan M. Kruijff, and Richard T. Oehrle.
Copyright © 1999, Stanford University.

> its domain. [...] That is, the head of the pitch accent is aligned with the prosodic head of the associated text. (Pierrehumbert 1994: 278.)

However,

> [p]itch accent assignment in English is a prosodic problem because [...] pitch accents are aligned with the prosodically strongest syllable of their domain. (The position of boundary tones is also prosodically determined, but by grouping rather than prominence.) The main difference between pitch accent assignment and what are considered to be standard examples of prosodic phonology is that standard examples involve lexical processes, while pitch accent is post-lexical; the well-formedness of the accent placement is determined with respect to the intonation phrase, a prosodic unit which can only be formed after words are combined into sentences. (Pierrehumbert 1994: 278.)

It is primarily the latter aspect that causes the trouble:

> The problem has been intractable because the major regularities governing accent placement have proved difficult to express in several successive versions of autosegmental and metrical phonology. (Pierrehumbert 1994: 278.)

More in particular:

> Pitch accent assignment in English presents what is perhaps the worst outstanding problem for the level-ordering hypothesis of Selkirk (1984), Nespor and Vogel (1986) and Beckman (1986). Although a level of 'accentual phrase' can be defined in some other languages such as Japanese (see e.g. Poser 1985, Beckman 1986, Pierrehumbert and Beckman 1988), it is impossible to do so for English. The difficulty arises because the accentual phrase can either be bigger than a prosodic word or smaller than a prosodic word. (Pierrehumbert 1994: 279.)

The problem can be illustrated as follows. According to the pragmatic focus/ground approach, sentences can consist of a focus and a ground. The *focus* is the informative part of the sentence, the part that (the speaker believes) expresses 'new' information in that it makes some contribution to the hearer's mental state. The *ground* is the non-informative part of the sentence, the part that expresses 'old' information and anchors the sentence to what is already established or under discussion in (the speaker's picture of) the hearer's mental state. Although sentences may lack a ground altogether, sentences without focus do not exist.

Now, if an English sentence only expresses new information—for example because it answers the question *What's up?*—, it will typically contain a single focal pitch accent which is aligned with its prosodic head, that is, with the prosodically most prominent syllable of the sentence. Thus, in a transitive all-focus sentence such as (1), it is the direct object noun phrase of the verb *likes* that will be accented:

(1) Kim likes JIM.

Following Pierrehumbert (1980), we will take tune, or intonation contour, to be a sequence of low (L) and high (H) tones, made up from pitch accents, phrase accents and boundary tones. Beckman and Pierrehumbert (1986) and Pierrehumbert and Hirschberg (1990) distinguish six pitch accents: two simple tones, H* and L*, and four complex ones, L*+H, L+H*, H*+L, H+L*, where the '*' indicates that the tone is aligned with a stressed syllable.

Tune meaning is assumed to be built up compositionally, and 'intonation contour is used to convey information to the hearer about how the propositional content of the [...] utterance is to be used to modify what the hearer believes to be mutually believed'. (Pierrehumbert and Hirschberg 1990: 289.) Thus in English, H* pitch accent is associated with the focus of the sentence, while L+H* pitch accent serves to mark topics (which will be discussed below).

We will use SMALL CAPS for expressions that bear H* pitch accents, and **boldface** for expressions that bear L+H* pitch accents. (H* accent and L+H* accent are called A accent and B accent, respectively, in Jackendoff 1972.)[1]

The prosodic head of the sentence may also be embedded more deeply. Observe that if the direct object of the transitive verb of an all-focus sentence is a compound noun phrase such as *the boss*, it is the common noun of the noun phrase, rather than the determiner, that supplies the most prominent syllable of the sentence:

(2) Eve fears the BOSS.

The examples (1) and (2) illustrate the fact that pitch accent assignment is indeed post-lexical, as was noted above, in the sense that accent

---

[1]The system of the present paper restricts itself to the distribution of H* and L+H* pitch accents. A grammar that exhausts the full gamut of intonation contours studied in Pierrehumbert and Hirschberg 1990 may retain the elegance of the restricted system proposed here by actually *decomposing* Pierrehumbert and Hirschberg's grammar of intonation (something which is suggested in Hobbs 1990).

placement is determined with respect to prosodic units which can only be considered after words have been combined into sentences.

Still, pitch accent assignment is not an entirely post-lexical matter. While (1) and (2) show that the relevant prosodic unit can be considerably bigger than a prosodic word, it is equally obvious that units which are substantially smaller than a prosodic word have a crucial role to play as well. It is, for example, the lexical prosodic structure of the word *broccoli* which is responsible for the fact that the focal pitch accent in the all-focus sentence (3) is aligned with the first syllable of the direct object:

(3)   Pam loves BROCcoli.

In addition to this, moreover, it can be observed that pitch accent assignment always involves the most prominent syllable of its domain, quite independent of the type of pitch accent that is involved.

Thus the pragmatic topic/comment approach splits the set of subexpressions of a sentence into a *topic*, the—typically sentence-initial—part that expresses what the sentence is about, and a *comment*, the part that expresses what is said about the topic. Topics are points of departure for what the sentence conveys, they link it to previous discourse. (We will not go further into the interpretation of topic and focus. The interested reader might wish to consult Hendriks 1998 and Rooth 1992.)

Sentences may be topicless: so-called 'presentational' or 'news' sentences such as the above examples (1–3) consist entirely of a comment. But if an English transitive sentence such as *Jim knows Pam* contains a topical subject—for example because it answers the question *What about Jim?*—, it will not only contain a focal H* pitch accent which is aligned with its prosodic head, that is, the direct object noun phrase of the transitive verb, but also an additional topical L+H* pitch accent aligned with the subject of the sentence:

(4)   **Jim** knows PAM

Within its domain—the subject of the sentence—, the alignment of this topical L+H* pitch accent observes the same regularities as the alignment of the focal H* pitch accent, in that this pitch accent also attaches to the prosodically most prominent syllable. In other words: both types of pitch accent exploit the same notion of prosodic head.

This is illustrated by the examples (5) and (6). So, if the topical subject of the sentence is a compound noun phrase such as *the boss*, it is the common noun of the noun phrase, rather than the determiner, that supplies the most prominent syllable of the topic.

(5)   The **boss** wants EVE.

And, again, it is the lexical prosodic structure of the word *broccoli* which is responsible for the fact that the L+H* pitch accent in the topical subject of (6) is aligned with the first syllable of that word:

(6)   **Broc**coli haunts Kim.

Below we will argue that the sign-based categorial grammar that was presented in Hendriks (1999) is capable of elegantly handling both the phrasal and the lexical alignment of pitch accents with the prosodically strongest syllable of their domain.

In Section 9.2, the basic system for focal H* pitch accent assignment will be presented, as well as its treatment of the post-lexical all-focus examples (1) and (2). In Section 9.3, the system is extended with the means for assigning topical L+H* pitch accents. These means are employed in an analysis of the topic-focus post-lexical examples (4) and (5).

Finally, Section 4 departs from the proposals of Hendriks (1999) in that it will propose a straightforward minor modification of the way in which the grammar is applied, which builds on the fully natural assumption that lexical items themselves have prosodically headed phonological forms as well.

As a result of this modification, the grammar accommodates a completely uniform account of lexical and phrasal prosodic headedness. As shown by the analyses of the lexical all-focus and topic-focus examples (3) and (6), the observed indifference of English pitch accent assignment to phonological levels follows without any further stipulation in the resulting system.

9.2   Focal pitch accent

In this section we will present the basic system for focal H* pitch accent assignment that was introduced in Hendriks (1999), and show how it applies to the examples (1) and (2). Basically, the formalism is a both intonationally/syntactically and semantically/informationally interpreted version of an extension of the non-associative calculus of Lambek (1961). The signs, the grammatical resources of this formalism, are Saussurian form-meaning units which reflect the fact that the dimensions of linguistic form and meaning contribute to well-formedness in an essentially parallel way:

(7)   intonational term ◁ category ▷ informational term

The calculus **D** that functions as the proof-theoretic categorial engine of the grammar represents sequents as composed of such multidimensional signs. It instantiates a minimal 'base logic', which makes no assumptions at all about structural aspects of grammatical resource management, since the formalism is based on a—'dependency'; cf. Moortgat and Morrill (1991)—doubling of the non-associative Lambek (1961) calculus **NL**, the 'pure logic of residuation'. In this double system, the phonological head/non-head opposition is captured by decomposing the product into a left-dominant and a right-dominant variant and obtaining residuation duality for both variants.

First, focusing on the categories, we define a *sequent* as an expression $\Gamma \Rightarrow C$, where Γ, the *antecedent* of the sequent, is a structured term, and C, the *consequent* or *goal* of the sequent, is a category. The set CAT of categories is based on some finite set ATOM of atomic categories and is defined as the smallest set such that:

(8) $\qquad$ ATOM $\subseteq$ CAT; and
$\qquad$ if $A \in$ CAT and $B \in$ CAT, then
$\qquad (B\backslash_* A) \in$ CAT, $(A \overset{*}{/} B) \in$ CAT, $(A^* {\bullet} B) \in$ CAT and
$\qquad (B \overset{*}{\backslash} A) \in$ CAT, $(A/_* B) \in$ CAT, $(A {\bullet}^* B) \in$ CAT.

The set TERM of structured terms is defined as the smallest set such that:

(9) $\qquad$ CAT $\subseteq$ TERM; and
$\qquad$ if $\Gamma \in$ TERM and $\Delta \in$ TERM, then
$\qquad [\Gamma, \Delta] \in$ TERM and $[\Gamma \, ' \, \Delta] \in$ TERM.

The categories $(B\backslash_* A)$, $(A \overset{*}{/} B)$ and $(A^* {\bullet} B)$ are associated with structures $[\Gamma, \Delta]$ that have their prosodic head in their left-hand side, and the categories $(B \overset{*}{\backslash} A)$, $(A/_* B)$ and $(A {\bullet}^* B)$ are associated with structures $[\Gamma \, ' \, \Delta]$ that have their prosodic head in their right-hand side.[2] More precisely: structured terms Δ of category $(B\backslash_* A)$ combine with structured terms Γ of category B on their left-hand side to form prosodically left-dominant structured terms $[\Gamma, \Delta]$ of category A; structured terms Γ of category $(A \overset{*}{/} B)$ combine with structured terms Δ of category B on their right-hand side to form prosodically left-dominant structured terms $[\Gamma, \Delta]$ of category A; and the category $(A^* {\bullet} B)$ represents prosodically left-dominant structured terms $[\Gamma, \Delta]$ in which Γ and Δ are of category A and B, respectively. Likewise, structured terms Δ of category $(B \overset{*}{\backslash} A)$ combine with structured terms Γ of category B on their left-hand side to form prosodically right-dominant structured terms $[\Gamma \, ' \, \Delta]$ of category A; structured terms Γ of category $(A/_* B)$ combine with structured term Δ of

---

[2]Thus ' and , 'embrace' their prosodic heads in the structured terms, while the relative position of $*$ with respect to $\backslash$, $/$ and $\bullet$ indicates the direction of prosodic dominance in the category operators.

category B on their right-hand side to form prosodically right-dominant structured terms $[\Gamma`\Delta]$ of category $A$; and the category $(A\bullet^\cdot B)$ represents prosodically right-dominant structured terms $[\Gamma`\Delta]$ in which Γ and Δ are of category A and B, respectively.

These characterizations are reflected in the calculus **D**, which has the axioms and inference rules specified in (10) through (16) below (where A, B, C denote categories, Γ and Δ structured terms, and $\Gamma\{\Delta\}$ represents a structured term Γ containing a distinguished occurrence of the structured subterm Δ):

(10) $$\frac{}{A \Rightarrow A}\ [Ax] \qquad\qquad \frac{\Delta \Rightarrow A \quad \Gamma\{A\} \Rightarrow C}{\Gamma\{\Delta\} \Rightarrow C}\ [Cut]$$

(11) $$\frac{\Delta \Rightarrow B \quad \Gamma\{A\} \Rightarrow C}{\Gamma\{[\Delta\,,B\backslash A]\} \Rightarrow C}\ [\backslash L] \qquad \frac{[B\,,\Gamma] \Rightarrow A}{\Gamma \Rightarrow B\backslash A}\ [\backslash R]$$

(12) $$\frac{\Delta \Rightarrow B \quad \Gamma\{A\} \Rightarrow C}{\Gamma\{[\Delta`B\backslash A]\} \Rightarrow C}\ [\backslash L] \qquad \frac{[B`\Gamma] \Rightarrow A}{\Gamma \Rightarrow B\backslash A}\ [\backslash R]$$

(13) $$\frac{\Delta \Rightarrow B \quad \Gamma\{A\} \Rightarrow C}{\Gamma\{[A/B\,,\Delta]\} \Rightarrow C}\ [/L] \qquad \frac{[\Gamma\,,B] \Rightarrow A}{\Gamma \Rightarrow A/B}\ [/R]$$

(14) $$\frac{\Delta \Rightarrow B \quad \Gamma\{A\} \Rightarrow C}{\Gamma\{[A/B`\Delta]\} \Rightarrow C}\ [/L] \qquad \frac{[\Gamma`B] \Rightarrow A}{\Gamma \Rightarrow A/B}\ [/R]$$

(15) $$\frac{\Gamma\{[A\,,B]\} \Rightarrow C}{\Gamma\{A\bullet B\} \Rightarrow C}\ [\bullet L] \qquad \frac{\Gamma \Rightarrow A \quad \Delta \Rightarrow B}{[\Gamma\,,\Delta] \Rightarrow A\bullet B}\ [\bullet R]$$

(16) $$\frac{\Gamma\{[A`B]\} \Rightarrow C}{\Gamma\{A\bullet^\cdot B\} \Rightarrow C}\ [\bullet L] \qquad \frac{\Gamma \Rightarrow A \quad \Delta \Rightarrow B}{[\Gamma`\Delta] \Rightarrow A\bullet^\cdot B}\ [\bullet R]$$

Observe that the calculus **D** is indeed a doubling of the non-associative Lambek calculus: both (10), (11), (13), (15) and (10), (12), (14), (16) constitute an isomorphic copy of **NL**.

As noted above, the calculus **D** is used in a so-called sign-based set-up. That is: the calculus functions as the proof-theoretic engine of a grammar that represents sequents as composed of multidimensional *signs*. More formally, SIGN, the set of signs, is the following set:

(17) $\{\varphi \triangleleft C \triangleright \gamma \mid \varphi \in \text{PROS and } C \in \text{CAT and } \gamma \in \text{SEM}\}$

The sets PROS and CAT are defined in (21) below and (8) above, respectively, and SEM is the set of simply-typed lambda terms built up from variables and (possibly) constants using abstraction, application, projection and pairing. Based on (17), the sign-based set TERM of structured terms is now defined as the smallest set such that:

(18)   SIGN $\subseteq$ TERM; and
if $\Gamma \in$ TERM and $\Delta \in$ TERM, then
$[\Gamma, \Delta] \in$ TERM and $[\Gamma \, ' \, \Delta] \in$ TERM.

For a structured term Γ, the sequence $s(\Gamma)$ of signs of Γ is defined as follows:

(19) $s(\alpha \triangleleft C \triangleright \tau) = \alpha \triangleleft C \triangleright \tau$; and
$s([\Gamma, \Delta]) = s([\Gamma \, ' \, \Delta]) = s(\Gamma), s(\Delta)$.

The sign-based grammar derives sequents $\Gamma \Rightarrow S$, where Γ is a structured term (as defined in (18) above) and S is a sign (see (17) above). Its axioms and rules are listed in (22) through (35) below. Observe that apart from the respective assignments $\varphi \triangleleft$ and $\triangleright \gamma$ of prosodic (intonational) and semantic (informational) terms to categories, this system is identical to the calculus **D** specified in (10) through (16) above. We will pay no attention to the—standard—assignment of semantic terms. The assignment of prosodic terms proceeds in an analogous—though type-free—fashion. First, the set of simple prosodic terms is defined as the union of some (possibly empty) set CON of prosodic constants and an infinite set VAR of prosodic variables:

(20)   VAR $= \{f_i \mid i \in \mathbb{N}\}$

Next, the set PROS of prosodic terms is defined as the smallest set satisfying the following:

(21)   VAR $\cup$ CON $\subseteq$ PROS;
$\langle \varphi, \psi \rangle \in$ PROS if $\varphi \in$ PROS and $\psi \in$ PROS (*head left*); and
$\langle \varphi \, ' \, \psi \rangle \in$ PROS if $\varphi \in$ PROS and $\psi \in$ PROS (*head right*).

Head-left prosodic terms $\langle \varphi, \psi \rangle$ and head-right prosodic terms $\langle \varphi \, ' \, \psi \rangle$ will have their prosodic head in their left-hand side subterm φ and their right-hand side subterm ψ, respectively.

Furthermore, every category occurrence in a derivable sequent $\Gamma \Rightarrow S$ is assigned a prosodic term: the categories in the antecedent term Γ are assigned distinct prosodic variables, and the single category in the consequent sign S is assigned a possibly complex prosodic term. In (22) through (35) below, the expressions φ and ψ denote arbitrary prosodic terms, and f, g and h represent prosodic variables. In the prosodic domain, we let the expression $\varphi[\psi \to \chi]$ denote the result of replacing all occurrences of the subterm ψ in φ by occurrences of the term χ. This may involve more than mere substitution for prosodic variables. Thus, prosodically, in (22) through (35) below, axioms amount to identity (assignment of f to antecedent and goal category), the rules *Cut* and $\backslash L, /L$

and $\backslash L, /L$ to substitution ($\varphi[f \to \psi]$ and $\varphi[f \to \langle \psi, g \rangle]$ and $\varphi[f \to \langle \psi \, ' g \rangle]$), the rules $\backslash R, /R$ and $\backslash R, /R$ to taking a subterm (φ, of $\langle f, \varphi \rangle$ and $\langle f \, ' \varphi \rangle$), and the rules $^*\bullet R$ and $\bullet^* R$ to the construction of a head-left and head-right term ($\langle \varphi, \psi \rangle$ and $\langle \varphi \, ' \psi \rangle$), respectively, but the rules $^*\bullet L$ and $\bullet^* L$ involve the replacement of the occurrences of complex prosodic terms $\langle f, g \rangle$ and $\langle f \, ' g \rangle$ in φ by occurrences of a prosodic variable h.

In the context of a proof, we will assume that all prosodic variables f, g and h assigned to an axiom instance or introduced in the conclusion of a $\backslash L, \backslash L, /L, /L, ^*\bullet L$ or $\bullet^* L$ inference are different. This has the same consequences as the parallel assumption concerning semantic variables: the prosodic variables $f_1, \dots f_n$ assigned to the antecedent categories of a sequent $\Gamma \Rightarrow S$ are all different, they make up the variables of the prosodic term φ assigned to the consequent category, and they occur exactly once in φ.

$$(22) \quad \overline{f \triangleleft A \triangleright u \Rightarrow f \triangleleft A \triangleright u} \; [Ax]$$

$$(23) \quad \frac{\Delta \Rightarrow \psi \triangleleft A \triangleright \alpha \quad \Gamma\{f \triangleleft A \triangleright u\} \Rightarrow \varphi \triangleleft C \triangleright \gamma}{\Gamma\{\Delta\} \Rightarrow \varphi[f \to \psi] \triangleleft C \triangleright \gamma[u \to \alpha]} \; [Cut]$$

$$(24) \quad \frac{\Delta \Rightarrow \psi \triangleleft B \triangleright \beta \quad \Gamma\{f \triangleleft A \triangleright u\} \Rightarrow \varphi \triangleleft C \triangleright \gamma}{\Gamma\{[\Delta, g \triangleleft B \backslash A \triangleright x]\} \Rightarrow \varphi[f \to \langle \psi, g \rangle] \triangleleft C \triangleright \gamma[u \to x(\beta)]} \; [\backslash L]$$

$$(25) \quad \frac{\Delta \Rightarrow \psi \triangleleft B \triangleright \beta \quad \Gamma\{f \triangleleft A \triangleright u\} \Rightarrow \varphi \triangleleft C \triangleright \gamma}{\Gamma\{[\Delta \, ' g \triangleleft B \backslash A \triangleright x]\} \Rightarrow \varphi[f \to \langle \psi \, ' g \rangle] \triangleleft C \triangleright \gamma[u \to x(\beta)]} \; [\backslash L]$$

$$(26) \quad \frac{\Delta \Rightarrow \psi \triangleleft B \triangleright \beta \quad \Gamma\{f \triangleleft A \triangleright u\} \Rightarrow \varphi \triangleleft C \triangleright \gamma}{\Gamma\{[g \triangleleft A /B \triangleright x, \Delta]\} \Rightarrow \varphi[f \to \langle g, \psi \rangle] \triangleleft C \triangleright \gamma[u \to x(\beta)]} \; [/L]$$

$$(27) \quad \frac{\Delta \Rightarrow \psi \triangleleft B \triangleright \beta \quad \Gamma\{f \triangleleft A \triangleright u\} \Rightarrow \varphi \triangleleft C \triangleright \gamma}{\Gamma\{[g \triangleleft A /B \triangleright x \, ' \Delta]\} \Rightarrow \varphi[f \to \langle g \, ' \psi \rangle] \triangleleft C \triangleright \gamma[u \to x(\beta)]} \; [/L]$$

$$(28) \quad \frac{[f \triangleleft B \triangleright v, \Gamma] \Rightarrow \langle f, \varphi \rangle \triangleleft A \triangleright \alpha}{\Gamma \Rightarrow \varphi \triangleleft B \backslash A \triangleright \lambda v. \alpha} \; [\backslash R]$$

$$(29) \quad \frac{[f \triangleleft B \triangleright v \, ' \Gamma] \Rightarrow \langle f \, ' \varphi \rangle \triangleleft A \triangleright \alpha}{\Gamma \Rightarrow \varphi \triangleleft B \backslash A \triangleright \lambda v. \alpha} \; [\backslash R]$$

$$(30) \quad \frac{[\Gamma, f \triangleleft B \triangleright v] \Rightarrow \langle \varphi, f \rangle \triangleleft A \triangleright \alpha}{\Gamma \Rightarrow \varphi \triangleleft A /B \triangleright \lambda v. \alpha} \; [/R]$$

$$(31) \quad \frac{[\Gamma \, ' f \triangleleft B \triangleright v] \Rightarrow \langle \varphi \, ' f \rangle \triangleleft A \triangleright \alpha}{\Gamma \Rightarrow \varphi \triangleleft A /B \triangleright \lambda v. \alpha} \; [/R]$$

$$(32) \quad \frac{\Gamma\{[f \triangleleft A \triangleright u, g \triangleleft B \triangleright v]\} \Rightarrow \varphi \triangleleft C \triangleright \gamma}{\Gamma\{h \triangleleft A^* \bullet B \triangleright y\} \Rightarrow \varphi[\langle f, g \rangle \to h] \triangleleft C \triangleright \gamma[u \to (y)_0, v \to (y)_1]} \; [^*\bullet L]$$

$$(33) \quad \frac{\Gamma\{[f \lhd A \rhd u \, {}^{\backprime} g \lhd B \rhd v]\} \Rightarrow \varphi \lhd C \rhd \gamma}{\Gamma\{h \lhd A \bullet {}^{\cdot} B \rhd y\} \Rightarrow \varphi[\langle f \, {}^{\backprime} g \rangle \!\to\! h] \lhd C \rhd \gamma[u \!\to\! (y)_0, v \!\to\! (y)_1]} \quad [\bullet {}^{\cdot} L]$$

$$(34) \quad \frac{\Gamma \Rightarrow \varphi \lhd A \rhd \alpha \quad \Delta \Rightarrow \psi \lhd B \rhd \beta}{[\Gamma, \Delta] \Rightarrow \langle \varphi, \psi \rangle \lhd A {}^{\cdot} \bullet B \rhd \alpha \star \beta} \quad [{}^{\cdot} \bullet R]$$

$$(35) \quad \frac{\Gamma \Rightarrow \varphi \lhd A \rhd \alpha \quad \Delta \Rightarrow \psi \lhd B \rhd \beta}{[\Gamma {}^{\backprime} \Delta] \Rightarrow \langle \varphi {}^{\backprime} \psi \rangle \lhd A \bullet {}^{\cdot} B \rhd \alpha \star \beta} \quad [\bullet {}^{\cdot} R]$$

In keeping with the set-up outlined above, we will assume that the lexicon is a collection of lexical signs $\varphi \lhd C \rhd \gamma$, where φ is a prosodic term, C is syntactic category, and γ is a semantic term of type TYPE(C).

Given a lexicon L, we will say that a (possibly compound) sign $\varphi' \lhd C \rhd \gamma'$ is in the language of L if and only if for some derivable sequent $\Gamma \Rightarrow \varphi \lhd C \rhd \gamma$ such that $s(\Gamma) = f_1 \lhd C_1 \rhd v_1, \ldots, f_n \lhd C_n \rhd v_n$, there are lexical signs $\varphi_1 \lhd C_1 \rhd \gamma_1 \in L, \ldots, \varphi_n \lhd C_n \rhd \gamma_n \in L$ such that $\varphi\{f_1 \!\to\! \varphi_1, \ldots, f_n \!\to\! \varphi_n\} = \varphi'$ and $\gamma[v_1 \!\to\! \gamma_1, \ldots, v_n \!\to\! \gamma_n] = \gamma'$.

Observe that the sequence $s(\Gamma)$ of signs of a structured term Γ has been defined in (19) above. The expression $\gamma[v_1 \!\to\! \gamma_1, \ldots, v_n \!\to\! \gamma_n]$ standardly denotes the result of simultaneously and respectively substituting $v_1, \ldots, v_n$ by $\gamma_1, \ldots, \gamma_n$ in γ, and the expression $\varphi\{f_1 \!\to\! \varphi_1, \ldots, f_n \!\to\! \varphi_n\}$ refers to the result of performing the following prosodic substitution:

$$(36) \quad \begin{aligned} \langle \varphi, \psi \rangle \{ \vec{s} \} &= \varphi \{ \vec{s} \} \, \psi \{ \vec{s} \} \\ \langle \varphi {}^{\backprime} \psi \rangle \{ \vec{s} \} &= \varphi \{ \vec{s} \} \, \psi \{ \vec{s} \} \\ f \{ \vec{s}, f \!\to\! term, \vec{s}\,' \} &= \text{TERM} \\ \langle \varphi, \psi \rangle \{\!\!\{ \vec{s} \}\!\!\} &= \varphi \{\!\!\{ \vec{s} \}\!\!\} \, \psi \{\!\!\{ \vec{s} \}\!\!\} \\ \langle \varphi {}^{\backprime} \psi \rangle \{\!\!\{ \vec{s} \}\!\!\} &= \varphi \{\!\!\{ \vec{s} \}\!\!\} \, \psi \{\!\!\{ \vec{s} \}\!\!\} \\ f \{\!\!\{ \vec{s}, f \!\to\! term, \vec{s}\,' \}\!\!\} &= term \end{aligned}$$

The prosodic substitution defined in (36) is a 'forgetful mapping' that takes care of the assignment of focal H* pitch accent to the prosodic terms which are substituted for the prosodic variables in the initial prosodic term. In the process, there is an important difference between the two substitution modes $\{ \ldots \}$ and $\{\!\!\{ \ldots \}\!\!\}$: performing a substitution $\varphi\{ \vec{s} \}$ will result in an expression that contains a single H* pitch accent, while executing $\varphi\{\!\!\{ \vec{s} \}\!\!\}$ will yield an expression that lacks H* pitch accents. Note that the assignment of focal H* pitch accent proceeds in such a way that the accent is always aligned with the prosodically most prominent subexpression of a given structure, since it consistently follows its path down via prosodic heads.[3]

---

[3] As a consequence of this architecture, we have that performing a prosodic substitution in different prosodic terms may result in one and the same string, some-

We are now in a position to provide the analyses of the examples (1) and (2).[4]

(37) Kim likes Jim $\lhd s \rhd$ LIKE$(j)(k)$

First, as regards example (1), Kim likes Jim, it can be observed that the sign (37) belongs to the language of the lexicon $L = \{Kim \lhd n \rhd k, \, likes \lhd (n \overset{*}{\backslash} s) / n \rhd \text{LIKE}, \, Jim \lhd n \rhd j\}$, in view of the fact that $[f \lhd n \rhd x \, ' \, [g \lhd (n \overset{*}{\backslash} s) / n \rhd y \, ' \, h \lhd n \rhd z]] \Rightarrow \langle f \, ' \, \langle g \, ' \, h \rangle \rangle \lhd s \rhd y(z)(x)$ is a derivable sequent: the type-logical part of its derivation is given in (38), and the prosodic and semantic interpretation of (38) are specified in (39) and (40), respectively:

(38)
$$\frac{n \Rightarrow n \quad \dfrac{n \Rightarrow n \quad s \Rightarrow s}{[n \, ' \, n \backslash s] \Rightarrow s} \, [\backslash L]}{[n \, ' \, [(n \overset{*}{\backslash} s) / n \, ' \, n]] \Rightarrow s} \, [/ L]$$

(39)
$$\frac{f \Rightarrow f \quad \dfrac{f \Rightarrow f \quad g'' \Rightarrow g''}{[f \, ' \, g'] \Rightarrow \langle f \, ' \, g' \rangle}}{[f \, ' \, [g \, ' \, h]] \Rightarrow \langle f \, ' \, \langle g \, ' \, h \rangle \rangle}$$

(40)
$$\frac{x \Rightarrow x \quad \dfrac{x \Rightarrow x \quad y'' \Rightarrow y''}{[x \, ' \, y'] \Rightarrow y'(x)}}{[x \, ' \, [y \, ' \, z]] \Rightarrow y(z)(x)}$$

The process of prosodic substitution is displayed in (41), while (42) presents the result of performing the required semantic substitution:

(41) $\langle f \, ' \, \langle g \, ' \, h \rangle \rangle \{ \, f{\to}Kim, g{\to}likes, h{\to}Jim \, \} \, =$
$f \{ \, f{\to}Kim, g{\to}likes, h{\to}Jim \, \} \, \langle g \, ' \, h \rangle \{ \, f{\to}Kim, g{\to}likes, h{\to}Jim \, \} \, =$
Kim $\langle g \, ' \, h \rangle \{ \, f{\to}Kim, g{\to}likes, h{\to}Jim \, \} \, =$
Kim $g \{ \, f{\to}Kim, g{\to}likes, h{\to}Jim \, \} \, h \{ \, f{\to}Kim, g{\to}likes, h{\to}Jim \, \} \, =$
Kim likes $h \{ \, f{\to}Kim, g{\to}likes, h{\to}Jim \, \} \, =$
Kim likes Jim

thing which holds by virtue of the possibility that $\varphi \{ \, f_1{\to}\varphi_1, \ldots, f_n{\to}\varphi_n \, \} = \varphi' \{ \, f_1{\to}\varphi_1, \ldots, f_n{\to}\varphi_n \, \}$. This can be exploited in an account of what is known as *focus projection*, that is: the fact that a single prosodic form such as *Kim likes* Jim can correspond to different information packagings, for example [F *Kim likes* Jim] (in answer to the question *What's new?*), *Kim* [F *likes* Jim] (in answer to the question *What about Kim?*) and *Kim likes* [F Jim] (in answer to the question *Who does Kim like?*). Discussion of this phenomenon will have to be resumed on another occassion.

[4]On the informational side, we will assume that proper names such as *Kim* and *Jim* are assigned individual constants k and j, while verbs, determiners and nouns such as *likes*, *the* and *boss* are represented as logical constants LIKE, THE and BOSS of appropriate types that will not be analyzed further here. The latter also holds for the constant TOPIC that figures in the translation $\lambda R \lambda y \lambda x.[\text{TOPIC}(x) \wedge R(y)(x)]$ of the abstract defocusing operator ϵ to be discussed below. A proposal concerning its analysis is offered in Hendriks (1998).

(42) $\quad y(z)(x)[x\to k, y\to \text{LIKE}, z\to j] = \text{LIKE}(j)(k)$

We now turn to the analysis of example (2), Eve fears the BOSS:

(43) $\quad$ Eve fears the BOSS $\lhd\, s\,\rhd$ FEAR(THE(BOSS))(e)

The sign (43) can be shown to belong to the language of the lexicon L = $\{Eve \lhd n \rhd e, fears \lhd (n\backslash s)/_\ast n \rhd \text{FEAR}, the \lhd n/_\ast c \rhd \text{THE}, boss \lhd c \rhd \text{BOSS}\}$, because the sequent $[f \lhd n \rhd x\,{}^\backprime\,[g \lhd n\backslash^\ast(s/_\ast n) \rhd y\,{}^\backprime\,[h \lhd n/_\ast c \rhd z\,{}^\backprime\,k \lhd c \rhd w]]] \Rightarrow$ $\langle f\,{}^\backprime\,\langle g\,{}^\backprime\,\langle h\,{}^\backprime\,k\rangle\rangle\rangle \lhd s \rhd y(z(w))(x)$ is a derivable sequent: (44) represents the type-logical part of its derivation; the prosodic and semantic interpretation of (44) appear in (45) and (46), respectively; and the results of performing the relevant prosodic and semantic substitutions are listed in (47) and (48), respectively.

(44) $\quad \dfrac{\dfrac{c \Rightarrow c \quad n \Rightarrow n}{[n/_\ast c\,{}^\backprime\,c] \Rightarrow n}\,[/_\ast L] \quad \dfrac{n \Rightarrow n \quad s \Rightarrow s}{[n\,{}^\backprime\,n\backslash^\ast s] \Rightarrow s}\,[\backslash^\ast L]}{[n\,{}^\backprime\,[(n\backslash^\ast s)/_\ast n\,{}^\backprime\,[n/_\ast c\,{}^\backprime\,c]]] \Rightarrow s}\,[/_\ast L]$

(45) $\quad \dfrac{\dfrac{k \Rightarrow k \quad h' \Rightarrow h'}{[h\,{}^\backprime\,k] \Rightarrow \langle h\,{}^\backprime\,k\rangle} \quad \dfrac{f \Rightarrow f \quad g'' \Rightarrow g''}{[f\,{}^\backprime\,g'] \Rightarrow \langle f\,{}^\backprime\,g'\rangle}}{[f\,{}^\backprime\,[g\,{}^\backprime\,[h\,{}^\backprime\,k]]] \Rightarrow \langle f\,{}^\backprime\,\langle g\,{}^\backprime\,\langle h\,{}^\backprime\,k\rangle\rangle\rangle}$

(46) $\quad \dfrac{\dfrac{w \Rightarrow w \quad z' \Rightarrow z'}{[z\,{}^\backprime\,w] \Rightarrow z(w)} \quad \dfrac{x \Rightarrow x \quad y'' \Rightarrow y''}{[x\,{}^\backprime\,y'] \Rightarrow y'(x)}}{[x\,{}^\backprime\,[y\,{}^\backprime\,[z\,{}^\backprime\,w]]] \Rightarrow y(z(w))(x)}$

(47) $\quad \langle f\,{}^\backprime\,\langle g\,{}^\backprime\,\langle h\,{}^\backprime\,k\rangle\rangle\rangle\{\,f\to Eve, g\to fears, h\to the, k\to boss\,\} =$
$\qquad$ Eve fears the BOSS

(48) $\quad y(z(w))(x)[x\to e, y\to \text{FEAR}, z\to \text{THE}, w\to \text{BOSS}] =$
$\qquad$ FEAR(THE(BOSS))(e)

9.3 Topical pitch accent

In the minimal system of the previous section, each expression is assigned exactly one focal H* pitch. However, we saw above that if an English transitive sentence contains a topical subject, then it may not only contain a focal H* pitch accent aligned with its prosodic head, that is: the direct object noun phrase of the transitive verb, but also an additional L+H* pitch accent aligned with the subject of the sentence. Within the domain of the subject of the sentence, the alignment of this L+H* pitch accent observes the same regularities as the alignment of H* pitch accent, in that it attaches to the prosodically most prominent syllable in that domain.

In order to account for the occurrence of L+H* pitch accents in English, the double pure logic of residuation of Section 9.2 will now be enriched with the minimal logical rules of the unary modal operators $\Diamond$ and $\boxdot$ which can be found in Moortgat (1996) (where $\boxdot$ denotes Moortgat's $\Box^{\downarrow}$).[5] It may be noted that these operators are used in a pure, basic way as well: they do not figure in structural postulates, but are associated with unary brackets which serve to demarcate specific phonological domains (something which is also suggested in Morrill 1994), within which special pitch accents are assigned in the process of prosodic substitution. The type-logical rules for these operators are given in (49) and (50), and sign-based versions appear in (51–54):

(49) $\quad \dfrac{\Gamma\{A\} \Rightarrow B}{\Gamma\{[\boxdot A]\} \Rightarrow B}\ [\boxdot L] \qquad\qquad \dfrac{[\Gamma] \Rightarrow A}{\Gamma \Rightarrow \boxdot A}\ [\boxdot R]$

(50) $\quad \dfrac{\Gamma\{[A]\} \Rightarrow B}{\Gamma\{\Diamond A\} \Rightarrow B}\ [\Diamond L] \qquad\qquad \dfrac{\Gamma \Rightarrow A}{[\Gamma] \Rightarrow \Diamond A}\ [\Diamond R]$

(51) $\quad \dfrac{\Gamma\{f \triangleleft A \triangleright u\} \Rightarrow \psi \triangleleft B \triangleright \beta}{\Gamma\{[f \triangleleft \boxdot A \triangleright u]\} \Rightarrow \psi[f \to \langle f \rangle] \triangleleft B \triangleright \beta}\ [\boxdot L]$

(52) $\quad \dfrac{[\Gamma] \Rightarrow \langle \varphi \rangle \triangleleft A \triangleright \alpha}{\Gamma \Rightarrow \varphi \triangleleft \boxdot A \triangleright \alpha}\ [\boxdot R]$

(53) $\quad \dfrac{\Gamma\{[f \triangleleft A \triangleright u]\} \Rightarrow \psi \triangleleft B \triangleright \beta}{\Gamma\{f \triangleleft \Diamond A \triangleright u\} \Rightarrow \psi[\langle f \rangle \to f] \triangleleft B \triangleright \beta}\ [\Diamond L]$

(54) $\quad \dfrac{\Gamma \Rightarrow \varphi \triangleleft A \triangleright \alpha}{[\Gamma] \Rightarrow \langle \varphi \rangle \triangleleft \Diamond A \triangleright \alpha}\ [\Diamond R]$

Because (51–54) introduce unary brackets, which constitute a new type of prosodic structure, we will now provide an extension of the definition of prosodic substitution $\varphi\{ f_1 \to \varphi_1, \ldots, f_n \to \varphi_n \}$ that was given in (36):

---

[5] Slightly different rules for unary modal operators were initially introduced by Morrill (1992) against the background of the class of so-called *functional* models, where the unary and binary operators are interpreted in terms of unary and binary functions, respectively. In the larger class of so-called *relational* models which is assumed by Moortgat (1996), on the other hand, the unary and binary operators are interpreted in terms of binary and ternary relations, respectively.

$$
\begin{aligned}
\langle \varphi , \psi \rangle \{\, \vec{s}\, \} &= \varphi \{\, \vec{s}\, \}\ \psi \{\, \vec{s}\, \} \\
\langle \varphi \,{}^{\backprime}\, \psi \rangle \{\, \vec{s}\, \} &= \varphi \{\, \vec{s}\, \}\ \psi \{\, \vec{s}\, \} \\
\langle \varphi \rangle \{\, \vec{s}\, \} &= \varphi \{\, \vec{s}\, \} \\
f \{\, \vec{s}, f \to term, \vec{s}'\, \} &= \text{TERM} \\
\langle \varphi , \psi \rangle \{\!\!\!|\; \vec{s}\; |\!\!\!\} &= \varphi \{\!\!\!|\; \vec{s}\; |\!\!\!\}\ \psi \{\!\!\!|\; \vec{s}\; |\!\!\!\} \\
\langle \varphi \,{}^{\backprime}\, \psi \rangle \{\!\!\!|\; \vec{s}\; |\!\!\!\} &= \varphi \{\!\!\!|\; \vec{s}\; |\!\!\!\}\ \psi \{\!\!\!|\; \vec{s}\; |\!\!\!\} \\
\langle \varphi \rangle \{\!\!\!|\; \vec{s}\; |\!\!\!\} &= \varphi \{\!\!\!|\; \vec{s}\; |\!\!\!\} \\
f \{\!\!\!|\; \vec{s}, f \to term, \vec{s}'\; |\!\!\!\} &= term \\
\langle \varphi , \psi \rangle \{\!\!\!|\; \vec{s}\; |\!\!\!|\} &= \varphi \{\!\!\!|\; \vec{s}\; |\!\!\!|\}\ \psi \{\!\!\!|\; \vec{s}\; |\!\!\!|\} \\
\langle \varphi \,{}^{\backprime}\, \psi \rangle \{\!\!\!|\; \vec{s}\; |\!\!\!|\} &= \varphi \{\!\!\!|\; \vec{s}\; |\!\!\!|\}\ \psi \{\!\!\!|\; \vec{s}\; |\!\!\!|\} \\
\langle \varphi \rangle \{\!\!\!|\; \vec{s}\; |\!\!\!|\} &= \varphi \{\!\!\!|\; \vec{s}\; |\!\!\!|\} \\
f \{\!\!\!|\; \vec{s}, f \to term, \vec{s}'\; |\!\!\!|\} &= \mathbf{term}
\end{aligned}
$$

As above, the substitution $\varphi \{\, \vec{s}\, \}$ produces an expression that contains a single focal H* pitch accent, and the substitution $\varphi \{\!\!|\, \vec{s}\, |\!\!\}$ generates an expression in which no H* pitch accent is assigned. In addition, we now have that carrying out a substitution $\varphi \{\!\!|\, \vec{s}\, |\!\!|\}$ will lead to an expression which carries a topical L+H* pitch accent. Note that this assignment of L+H* pitch accent indeed proceeds in such a way that it is always aligned with the prosodically most prominent subexpression of a given structure inside its domain, which is demarcated by the unary brackets that come with the operator $\lozenge$, since just as the assignment of H* pitch accents, the assignment of L+H* pitch accent consistently follows its path down via prosodic heads.

We will now provide analyses of the examples (4), **Jim** knows PAM, and (5), The **boss** wants EVE, in which we will assume that the topichood of the subjects is taken care of by an 'abstract' defocusing operator, the lexical sign $\epsilon \lhd ((\lozenge n \backslash s)/n)/((n \backslash s)/n) \rhd \lambda R \lambda y \lambda x.[\text{TOPIC}(x) \wedge R(y)(x)]$, where ϵ denotes the empty string. This operator is a higher-order functor that combines with the transitive verb and affects the intonational and informational interpretation of the sentence in which it occurs in the required way (cf. Hendriks 1999).

(56) **Jim** knows PAM $\lhd s \rhd [\text{TOPIC}(j) \wedge \text{KNOW}(p)(j)]$

The sign (56) belongs to the language of the lexicon $L = \{ Jim \lhd n \rhd j, \epsilon \lhd ((\lozenge n \backslash s)/n)/((n \backslash s)/n) \rhd \lambda R \lambda y \lambda x.[\text{TOPIC}(x) \wedge R(y)(x)], knows \lhd (n \backslash s)/n \rhd$ KNOW, $Pam \lhd n \rhd p \}$, since $[[f \lhd n \rhd x]\,{}^{\backprime}\,[[g \lhd ((\lozenge n \backslash s)/n)/((n \backslash s)/n) \rhd y\,{}^{\backprime}\, h \lhd (n \backslash s)/n \rhd z]\,{}^{\backprime}\, k \lhd n \rhd w]] \Rightarrow \langle \langle f \rangle \,{}^{\backprime}\, \langle \langle g \,{}^{\backprime}\, h \rangle \,{}^{\backprime}\, k \rangle \rangle \lhd s \rhd y(z)(w)(x)$ is a derivable sequent: the type-logical part of its derivation is given in (57); the prosodic and semantic interpretation of (57) are specified in (58) and (59), respectively; and the results of performing the relevant prosodic and semantic substitutions can be found in (60) and (61).

(57)
$$\frac{(n\backslash^{*}s)/_{*}n \Rightarrow (n\backslash^{*}s)/_{*}n \qquad \dfrac{n\Rightarrow n \qquad \dfrac{\dfrac{\dfrac{n\Rightarrow n}{[n]\Rightarrow\Diamond n}[\Diamond R] \qquad s\Rightarrow s}{[[n]\,{}^{\backprime}\Diamond n\backslash^{*}s]\Rightarrow s}[\backslash^{*}L]}{[[n]\,{}^{\backprime}[(\Diamond n\backslash^{*}s)/_{*}n\,{}^{\backprime}n]]\Rightarrow s}[/_{*}L]}{[[n]\,{}^{\backprime}[[((\Diamond n\backslash^{*}s)/_{*}n)/_{*}((n\backslash^{*}s)/_{*}n)\,{}^{\backprime}(n\backslash^{*}s)/_{*}n]\,{}^{\backprime}n]]\Rightarrow s}[/_{*}L]}{}$$

(58)
$$\frac{h\Rightarrow h \qquad \dfrac{k\Rightarrow k \qquad \dfrac{\dfrac{f\Rightarrow f}{[f]\Rightarrow\langle f\rangle} \qquad g'''\Rightarrow g'''}{[[f]\,{}^{\backprime}g'']\Rightarrow\langle\langle f\rangle\,{}^{\backprime}g''\rangle}}{[[f]\,{}^{\backprime}[g'\,{}^{\backprime}k]]\Rightarrow\langle\langle f\rangle\,{}^{\backprime}\langle g'\,{}^{\backprime}k\rangle\rangle}}{[[f]\,{}^{\backprime}[[g\,{}^{\backprime}h]\,{}^{\backprime}k]]\Rightarrow\langle\langle f\rangle\,{}^{\backprime}\langle\langle g\,{}^{\backprime}h\rangle\,{}^{\backprime}k\rangle\rangle}$$

(59)
$$\frac{z\Rightarrow z \qquad \dfrac{w\Rightarrow w \qquad \dfrac{\dfrac{x\Rightarrow x}{[x]\Rightarrow x} \qquad y'''\Rightarrow y'''}{[[x]\,{}^{\backprime}y'']\Rightarrow y''(x)}}{[[x]\,{}^{\backprime}[y'\,{}^{\backprime}w]]\Rightarrow y'(w)(x)}}{[[x]\,{}^{\backprime}[[y\,{}^{\backprime}z]\,{}^{\backprime}w]]\Rightarrow y(z)(w)(x)}$$

(60) $\quad \langle\langle f\rangle\,{}^{\backprime}\langle\langle g\,{}^{\backprime}h\rangle\,{}^{\backprime}k\rangle\rangle\{\,f\rightarrow Jim, g\rightarrow\epsilon, h\rightarrow knows, k\rightarrow Pam\,\} =$
$\qquad\qquad$ **Jim** knows PAM

(61) $\quad y(z)(w)(x)[x\rightarrow j, y\rightarrow\lambda R\lambda y\lambda x.[\text{TOPIC}(x) \wedge R(y)(x)],$
$\qquad\qquad z\rightarrow\text{KNOW}, w\rightarrow p] = [\text{TOPIC}(j) \wedge \text{KNOW}(p)(j)]$

Example (5) is analyzed as follows:

(62) $\quad$ The **boss** wants EVE $\triangleleft s \triangleright$ [TOPIC(THE(BOSS)) $\wedge$
$\qquad\qquad$ WANT(e)(THE(BOSS))]

The sign (62) is in the language of $L = \{the \triangleleft n/_{*}c \triangleright$ THE, $boss \triangleleft c \triangleright$ BOSS, $\epsilon \triangleleft ((\Diamond n\backslash^{*}s)/_{*}n)/_{*}((n\backslash^{*}s)/_{*}n) \triangleright \lambda R\lambda y\lambda x.[\text{TOPIC}(x) \wedge R(y)(x)], wants \triangleleft (n\backslash^{*}s)/_{*}n \triangleright$ WANT, $Eve \triangleleft n \triangleright e\}$, on account of the fact that $[[[f \triangleleft n/_{*}c \triangleright x\,{}^{\backprime}g \triangleleft c \triangleright y]]\,{}^{\backprime}[[h \triangleleft ((\Diamond n\backslash^{*}s)/_{*}n)/_{*}((n\backslash^{*}s)/_{*}n) \triangleright z\,{}^{\backprime}k \triangleleft (n\backslash^{*}s)/_{*}n \triangleright v]\,{}^{\backprime}l \triangleleft n \triangleright w]] \Rightarrow \langle\langle\langle f\,{}^{\backprime}g\rangle\,{}^{\backprime}\langle\langle g\,{}^{\backprime}h\rangle\,{}^{\backprime}k\rangle\rangle \triangleleft s \triangleright y(z)(w)(x)$ is a derivable sequent, as shown by derivation (63) and its respective prosodic and semantic interpretations in (64) and (65). The results of performing the relevant prosodic and semantic substitutions are listed in (66) and (67), respectively:

(63)
$$\frac{(n\backslash^{*}s)/_{*}n \Rightarrow (n\backslash^{*}s)/_{*}n \qquad \dfrac{n\Rightarrow n \qquad \dfrac{\dfrac{\dfrac{\dfrac{c\Rightarrow c \qquad n\Rightarrow n}{[n/_{*}c\,{}^{\backprime}c]\Rightarrow n}[/_{*}L]}{[[n/_{*}c\,{}^{\backprime}c]]\Rightarrow\Diamond n}[\Diamond R] \qquad s\Rightarrow s}{[[[n/_{*}c\,{}^{\backprime}c]]\,{}^{\backprime}\Diamond n\backslash^{*}s]\Rightarrow s}[\backslash^{*}L]}{[[[n/_{*}c\,{}^{\backprime}c]]\,{}^{\backprime}[(\Diamond n\backslash^{*}s)/_{*}n\,{}^{\backprime}n]]\Rightarrow s}[/_{*}L]}{[[[n/_{*}c\,{}^{\backprime}c]]\,{}^{\backprime}[[((\Diamond n\backslash^{*}s)/_{*}n)/_{*}((n\backslash^{*}s)/_{*}n)\,{}^{\backprime}(n\backslash^{*}s)/_{*}n]\,{}^{\backprime}n]]\Rightarrow s}[/_{*}L]}{}$$

(64)
$$\frac{\displaystyle \frac{\displaystyle \frac{\displaystyle \frac{\displaystyle \frac{g \Rightarrow g \quad f' \Rightarrow f'}{[f`g] \Rightarrow \langle f`g \rangle}}{[[f`g]] \Rightarrow \langle \langle f`g \rangle \rangle \quad h''' \Rightarrow h'''}}{l \Rightarrow l \quad [[[f`g]]`h''] \Rightarrow \langle \langle \langle f`g \rangle \rangle`h'' \rangle}}{k \Rightarrow k \quad [[[f`g]]`[h'`l]] \Rightarrow \langle \langle \langle f`g \rangle \rangle`\langle h'`l \rangle \rangle}}{[[[f`g]]`[[h`k]`l]] \Rightarrow \langle \langle \langle f`g \rangle \rangle`\langle \langle h`k \rangle`l \rangle \rangle}$$

(65)
$$\frac{\displaystyle \frac{\displaystyle \frac{\displaystyle \frac{\displaystyle \frac{y \Rightarrow y \quad x' \Rightarrow x'}{[x`y] \Rightarrow x(y)}}{[[x`y]] \Rightarrow x(y) \quad z''' \Rightarrow z'''}}{w \Rightarrow w \quad [[[x`y]]`z''] \Rightarrow z''(x(y))}}{v \Rightarrow v \quad [[[x`y]]`[z'`w]] \Rightarrow z'(w)(x(y))}}{[[[x`y]]`[[z`v]`w]] \Rightarrow z(v)(w)(x(y))}$$

(66) $\langle \langle \langle f`g \rangle \rangle`\langle \langle h`k \rangle`l \rangle \rangle \{\, f \rightarrow the, g \rightarrow boss,$
$\qquad h \rightarrow \epsilon, k \rightarrow wants, l \rightarrow Eve \,\} =$
$\qquad$ The **boss** wants EVE

(67) $\qquad z(v)(w)(x(y))[x \rightarrow \text{THE}, y \rightarrow boss,$
$\qquad z \rightarrow \lambda R \lambda y \lambda x.[\text{TOPIC}(x) \wedge R(y)(x)], v \rightarrow \text{WANT}, w \rightarrow e] =$
$\qquad [\text{TOPIC}(\text{THE}(\text{BOSS})) \wedge \text{WANT}(e)(\text{THE}(\text{BOSS}))]$

9.4 Sublexical pitch accent

In order to account for the sublexical cases of pitch accent assignment, we will continue to assume that the lexicon is a collection of lexical signs $\varphi \lhd C \rhd \gamma$, where φ is a prosodic term, C is syntactic category, and γ is a semantic term of type TYPE(C). However, the lexical assignment of prosodic terms φ will involve more than mere constants, since also complex prosodic terms may be asssigned.

In addition to this, we will now say that given a lexicon L, a (possibly compound) sign $\varphi' \lhd C \rhd \gamma'$ is in the language of L if and only if for some derivable sequent $\Gamma \Rightarrow \varphi \lhd C \rhd \gamma$ such that $s(\Gamma) = f_1 \lhd C_1 \rhd v_1, \ldots, f_n \lhd C_n \rhd v_n$, there are lexical signs $\varphi_1 \lhd C_1 \rhd \gamma_1 \in L, \ldots, \varphi_n \lhd C_n \rhd \gamma_n \in L$ such that $\{\, \varphi[f_1 \rightarrow \varphi_1, \ldots, f_n \rightarrow \varphi_n] \,\} = \varphi'$ and $\gamma[v_1 \rightarrow \gamma_1, \ldots, v_n \rightarrow \gamma_n] = \gamma'$.

The sequence $s(\Gamma)$ of signs of a structured term Γ is a notion that was defined in (19) above. Note that the phrase '$\{\, \varphi[f_1 \rightarrow \varphi_1, \ldots, f_n \rightarrow \varphi_n] \,\}$' has come to replace the phrase '$\varphi\{\, f_1 \rightarrow \varphi_1, \ldots, f_n \rightarrow \varphi_n \,\}$' that figured in the corresponding definition in the previous section. The subexpression $\varphi[f_1 \rightarrow \varphi_1, \ldots, f_n \rightarrow \varphi_n]$ of this phrase standardly denotes the result of simultaneously and respectively substituting $f_1, \ldots, f_n$ by $\varphi_1, \ldots, \varphi_n$

in φ, just as the expression $\gamma[v_1 \to \gamma_1, \ldots, v_n \to \gamma_n]$ denotes the result of simultaneously and respectively substituting $v_1, \ldots, v_n$ by $\gamma_1, \ldots, \gamma_n$ in γ. But, importantly, instead of having the prosodic substitution that was defined in (36) and extended in (55), we will now assume that $\{\varphi\}$ is defined by the structurally fully parallel rewrite relation given in (68) below:

(68)
$$
\begin{aligned}
\{\langle \varphi, \psi \rangle\} &= \{\varphi\}\{\psi\} \\
\{\langle \varphi \, ' \, \psi \rangle\} &= \{\varphi\}\{\psi\} \\
\{\langle \varphi \rangle\} &= \{\varphi\} \\
\{constant\} &= \text{CONSTANT} \\
\{\langle \varphi, \psi \rangle\} &= \{\varphi\}\{\psi\} \\
\{\langle \varphi \, ' \, \psi \rangle\} &= \{\varphi\}\{\psi\} \\
\{\langle \varphi \rangle\} &= \{\varphi\} \\
\{constant\} &= \text{constant} \\
\{\langle \varphi, \psi \rangle\} &= \{\varphi\}\{\psi\} \\
\{\langle \varphi \, ' \, \psi \rangle\} &= \{\varphi\}\{\psi\} \\
\{\langle \varphi \rangle\} &= \{\varphi\} \\
\{constant\} &= \textbf{constant}
\end{aligned}
$$

Since $\{\varphi[f_1 \to \varphi_1, \ldots, f_n \to \varphi_n]\} = \varphi'$ according to definition (68) whenever $\varphi' = \varphi\{f_1 \to \varphi_1, \ldots, f_n \to \varphi_n\}$ on account of definition (55), the prosodic results of the previous sections are all preserved. Besides, we are now in a position to provide the analyses of the examples (3), Pam loves BROCcoli, and (6), **Broc**coli haunts KIM.

(69)   Pam loves BROCcoli $\lhd s \rhd$ LOVE$(b)(p)$

First, it can be observed that the sign (69) belongs to the language of the lexicon $L = \{Pam \lhd n \rhd p, loves \lhd (n \backslash s) /_* n \rhd \text{LOVE}, \langle\langle broc, co\rangle, li\rangle \lhd n \rhd b\}$, because the sequent $[f \lhd n \rhd x \, ' \, [g \lhd (n \backslash s)/_* n \rhd y \, ' \, h \lhd n \rhd z]] \Rightarrow \langle f \, ' \langle g \, ' h\rangle\rangle \lhd s \rhd y(z)(x)$ is derivable: its derivation is identical to that of the sign (37), of which the type-logical part was given in (38), while the prosodic and semantic interpretation of (38) were specified in (39) and (40), respectively. The results of performing the relevant prosodic and semantic substitutions are listed in (70) and (71), respectively:

(70) $\langle f \, ' \langle g \, ' h\rangle\rangle[f \to Pam, g \to loves, h \to \langle\langle broc, co\rangle, li\rangle] =$
$\langle Pam \, ' \langle loves \, ' \langle\langle broc, co\rangle, li\rangle\rangle\rangle$

(71) $y(z)(x)[x \to p, y \to \text{LOVE}, z \to b] = \text{LOVE}(b)(p)$

Rewriting the prosodic term in (70) results in (72):

(72) $\{\langle Pam \, ' \langle loves \, ' \langle\langle broc, co\rangle, li\rangle\rangle\rangle\} = $ Pam loves BROCcoli

Finally, we present the analysis of example (6):

(73) **Broc**coli haunts K$_{\text{IM}}$ $\vartriangleleft s \vartriangleright$ [TOPIC(b) $\wedge$ HAUNT(k)(b)]

Note that the sign (73) belongs to the language of $L = \{\langle\langle broc\,, co\rangle\,, li\rangle\vartriangleleft$ $n \vartriangleright b, \epsilon \vartriangleleft ((\Diamond n\backslash^{*}\!s)/_{*}n)/_{*}((n\backslash^{*}\!s)/_{*}n)\vartriangleright \lambda R\lambda y\lambda x.[\text{TOPIC}(x) \wedge R(y)(x)], haunts \vartriangleleft$ $(n\backslash^{*}\!s)/_{*}n\vartriangleright\text{HAUNT}, Kim\vartriangleleft n\vartriangleright k\}$, as $[[f \vartriangleleft n\vartriangleright x]\,{}^{\backprime}\,[[g\vartriangleleft((\Diamond n\backslash^{*}\!s)/_{*}n)/_{*}((n\backslash^{*}\!s)/_{*}n)\vartriangleright$ $y\,{}^{\backprime}\,h \vartriangleleft (n\backslash^{*}\!s)/_{*}n \vartriangleright z]\,{}^{\backprime}\,k \vartriangleleft n \vartriangleright w]] \Rightarrow \langle\langle f\rangle\,{}^{\backprime}\,\langle\langle g\,{}^{\backprime}\,h\rangle\,{}^{\backprime}\,k\rangle\rangle \vartriangleleft s \vartriangleright y(z)(w)(x)$ is a derivable sequent: the derivation of this sign is identical to that of (56), of which the type-logical part was presented in (57), while the prosodic and semantic interpretation of (57) were given in (58) and (59), respectively. The results of performing the relevant prosodic and semantic substitutions are listed in (74) and (75), respectively:

(74) $\langle\langle f\rangle\,{}^{\backprime}\,\langle\langle g\,{}^{\backprime}\,h\rangle\,{}^{\backprime}\,k\rangle\rangle[f \to \langle\langle broc\,, co\rangle\,, li\rangle, g \to \epsilon, h \to haunts,$
 $k \to Kim] = \langle\langle\langle\langle broc\,, co\rangle\,, li\rangle\rangle\,{}^{\backprime}\,\langle\langle\epsilon\,{}^{\backprime}\,haunts\rangle\,{}^{\backprime}\,Kim\rangle\rangle$

(75) $y(z)(w)(x)[x \to b, y \to \lambda R\lambda y\lambda x.[\text{TOPIC}(x) \wedge R(y)(x)],$
 $z \to \text{HAUNT}, w \to k] = [\text{TOPIC}(b) \wedge \text{HAUNT}(k)(b)]$

And rewriting the prosodic term in (74) results in (76):

(76) $\{\langle\langle\langle\langle broc\,, co\rangle\,, li\rangle\rangle\,{}^{\backprime}\,\langle\langle\epsilon\,{}^{\backprime}\,haunts\rangle\,{}^{\backprime}\,Kim\rangle\rangle\} =$
 Broccoli haunts K$_{\text{IM}}$

9.5 Conclusion

By way of conclusion, then, we observe that the completely uniform analysis of lexical and phrasal prosodic headedness provided by the present proof-theoretic sign-based categorial approach is the key to an account of the observed indifference of English pitch accent assignment to phonological levels, since it is this fully general and abstract notion of prosodic head that is exploited by the various pitch accents, quite independent of the particular type of pitch accent involved, in the sense that all pitch accents are invariably aligned with the prosodically strongest syllable of their domain.

References

Beckman, M. 1986. *Stress and Nonstress Accent*. Dordrecht: Foris.

Beckman, M. and J. Pierrehumbert. 1986. Intonational Structure in Japanese and English. *Phonological Yearbook* 3:15–70.

Hendriks, H. 1998. L+H* Accent and Non-Monotonic Anaphora. In R. Kager and W. Zonneveld, eds., *Phrasal Phonology*. Dordrecht: Foris.

Hendriks, H. 1999. The Logic of Tune. A Proof-Theoretic Account of Intonation. In A. Lecomte, ed., *Logical Aspects of Computational Linguistics*. New York: Springer.

Hobbs, J. 1990. The Pierrehumbert and Hirschberg Theory of Intonation Made Simple: Comments on Pierrehumbert and Hirschberg. In P. Cohen, J. Morgan and M. Pollack, eds., *Intentions in Communication*. Cambridge (Mass.): MIT Press.

Jackendoff, R. 1972. *Semantic Interpretation in Generative Grammar*. Cambridge (Mass.): MIT Press.

Lambek, J. 1961. On the Calculus of Syntactic Types. In R. Jakobson, ed., *Structure of Language and its Mathematical Aspects*. Providence: American Mathematical Society.

Moortgat, M. 1996. Multimodal Linguistic Inference. *Journal of Logic, Language and Information* 5:349–385.

Moortgat, M. and G. Morrill. 1991. *Heads and Phrases: Type Calculus for Dependency and Constituent Structure*. OTS Research Paper. University of Utrecht: Research Institute for Language and Speech.

Morrill, G. 1992. *Categorial Formalisation of Relativisation: Pied Piping, Islands, and Extraction Sites*. Report de Recerca. Universitat Politècnica de Catalunya: Departament de Llenguatges i Sistemes Informàtics.

Morrill, G. 1994. *Type Logical Grammar: Categorial Logic of Signs*. Dordrecht: Kluwer.

Nespor, M. and I. Vogel. 1986. *Prosodic Morphology*. Dordrecht: Foris.

Pierrehumbert, J. 1980. *The Phonology and Phonetics of English Intonation*. Cambridge (Mass.): Ph.D. Dissertation MIT.

Pierrehumbert, J. 1994. Alignment and Prosodic Heads. In *Proceedings of the Eastern States Conference on Formal Linguistics*. Cornell: Graduate Student Association.

Pierrehumbert, J. and M. Beckman. 1988. *Japanese Tone Structure*. Cambridge (Mass.): MIT Press.

Pierrehumbert, J. and J. Hirschberg. 1990. The Meaning of Intonational Contours in the Interpretation of Discourse. In P. Cohen, J. Morgan and M. Pollack, eds., *Intentions in Communication*. Cambridge (Mass.): MIT Press.

Poser, W. 1985. *The Phonetics and Phonology of Tone and Intonation in Tokyo Japanese*. Cambridge (Mass.): Ph.D. Dissertation MIT.

Rooth, M. 1992. A Theory of Focus Interpretation. *Natural Language Semantics* 1:75–116.

Selkirk, E. 1984. *Phonology and Syntax: The Relation Between Sound and Structure*. Cambridge (Mass.): MIT Press.

10

Topic and Focus Structures: The Dynamics of Tree Growth

RUTH KEMPSON AND WILFRIED MEYER-VIOL

10.1 Introduction

Despite a considerable amount of work on the semantics of focus, the relation between topic and focus is not often addressed in formal terms.[1] In this paper, we address the relatively modest goal of modelling the on-line process of interpreting the family of 'dislocation' structures which includes Clitic Left-Dislocation, Topicalization and Scrambling, for which we present a cross-linguistic typology.[2] These structures are associated with different restrictions, and hence assumed to require quite different characterizations. Pragmatically, despite widespread assumption to the contrary, as Prince (1995) demonstrates in detail, none of the structures corresponds to but a single form of processing and constructing structural explanations for each form leads to multiplication of structural possibilities well beyond what is realised in any natural language. We shall argue that these structures are nevertheless to be explained in terms of the dynamics of language processing, by showing how the different cross-language effects arising from the interaction of long-distance dependency and anaphora resolution can be explained in terms of a model based on the step by step, left to right, processing of the structures in question. The explanation is in terms of an entirely general characterization of pronoun construal, without a grammar-specific characterization of resumptive (or any other sub-type of) pronouns. We shall take this

---

[1]cf. Porter & Yabushita 1998 for a model-theoretic account of topic, and Erteschik-Shir 1997 for an account of topic and focus structures in terms of 'files'.

[2]The work on this project has been partly funded by EPSRC projects GR/K68776, GR/K67397

Constraints and Resources in Natural Language Syntax and Semantics.
Gosse Bouma, Erhard W. Hinrichs, Geert-Jan M. Kruijff, and Richard T. Oehrle.

to be indicative of the general perspective adopted - that a natural language grammar *is* a schematic parser integrating the articulation of the structural basis of natural language with pragmatic processes such as anaphora resolution.

The background framework is a formal model of the incremental process of natural language (NL) parsing, where this is defined as the progressive building up of a logical form corresponding to a possible interpretation of the string. The centrepin of the interpretation process is the concept of tree growth. Using a modal tree-description language (*LOFT* - Blackburn & Meyer-Viol 1994), we model the interpretation process for a sentence as the successive setting up of nodes in a tree representation of a logical form for that string. Each node comes into being with some set of *requirements* (for annotations on that node), which must then be progressively satisfied by annotations supplied by the string. Only those trees in which the requirements associated with all nodes are satisfied the moment the string has been completely traversed, can correspond to logical forms for a given string. We propose that the interpretive effects associated with Clitic Left Dislocation and Topicalization structures result from discrete ways of building up a logical form from the various strings, an explanation which (partly) turns on this requirement/annotation distinction.

10.2   The LDS_{NL} framework

The overall process of interpretation is modelled as a goal-driven, incremental, structure-building operation: the goal is to establish the logical form of the NL string, a logical formula of truth value type t, by setting up an annotated tree structure reflecting its combinatorial structure. In this paper the logical form of an NL string will be represented by a *labelled* formula of the lambda calculus. A formula of the lambda calculus can be represented by an annotated binary tree as follows. The sentence **John read a book**, represented by the formula **read(john, some(x,book(x)))**, can be seen as resulting from the term

$$\text{APL}(\text{APL}(\lambda x \lambda y \mathbf{read}(y)(x), \text{APL}(\lambda P(\mathbf{some}P), (x, \mathbf{book}x))), \mathbf{john})$$

by β-reduction. The obvious tree structure of this term we will exhibit in the form of a *bracketed formula*:

$$[_0[_0\mathbf{John}]\ [_1[_1\lambda x \lambda y \mathbf{read}(\mathbf{y})(\mathbf{x})]\ [_0[_1\lambda P(\mathbf{some}P)]\ [_0(x, \mathbf{book}x)\ ]]]]$$

where 0 represents the argument- and 1 the function daughter. Tree and decorations can be considered independently by pulling them apart (see Figure 1).

$$[_0[_0 \ ] \ [_1[_1 \ ] \ [_0 \ [_0 \ ] \ [_1 \ ]]]]$$

$$\underbrace{}_{Tree}$$

$$\underbrace{\{00\text{:}\textbf{john}, \ 011\text{:}\lambda x\lambda y\textbf{read}(y)(x), \ 0111\text{:}\lambda P(\textbf{some}P), \ 0110\text{:}(x, \textbf{book}x)\}.}_{Decorations}$$

FIGURE 1   A term as a labelled tree

This we do in order to deal with the partial information arising during the construction of a logical form. By representing them as decorated trees we can describe objects which are not themselves lambda terms but which can be extended, or completed, to them. By pulling term structure and term content apart, we can consider terms to be partial, or underspecified, both in structure and in content. In our set-up, the annotations at a node of the tree are formulated in $LOFT$, a propositional modal language of finite trees (cf. Blackburn & Meyer-Viol 1994).

The atomic propositions of the language express that certain *label-* and *formula*-predicates have some value. The values of the Fo ($Formula$) predicate are the expressions of the lambda calculus under consideration. The set of label predicates includes the type predicate Ty, and predicates for other syntactic features.

The modalities of (our version of) the language $LOFT$ for describing tree relations are interpreted on *linked binary trees*. These are structures of the form $\langle T, \prec_i, \rangle_{i \in I}$, for $I = \{0, 1, \downarrow, *, L, D\}$, where the domain T is the union of some finite number k of disjoint sets, $T = \bigcup_{i<k} T_i$, such that each $\langle T_i, \prec_0, \prec_1, \prec_\downarrow, \prec_* \rangle$ is a binary tree with $\prec_0$ the left daughter relation, $\prec_1$, the right daughter relation, $\prec_\downarrow$ the immediate dominance relation ($\prec_\downarrow = \prec_0 \cup \prec_1$), and $\prec_*$ is the dominance relation, i.e., the reflexive and transitive closure of $\prec_\downarrow$. Now, $\prec_L \subseteq T \times T$ is the *link* relation which connects the node of some tree $T_i \subseteq T$ to the root node of a second, disjoint, tree $T_j \subseteq T$. This relation will connect (representations of) linguistic 'islands'. The relation $\prec_D \subseteq T \times T$, finally, is the reflexive and transitive closure of $\prec_* \cup \prec_L$.

The modalities of the language of finite trees, $LOFT$, include $\langle 0 \rangle$ (interpreted over the left daughter relation $\prec_0$), $\langle 1 \rangle$ (over right daughter $\prec_1$), $\langle \downarrow \rangle$ (over the immediate dominance relation $\prec_\downarrow$), and $\langle * \rangle$ (over the dominance relation $\prec_*$), $\langle L \rangle$ (interpreted over the *link* relation), and $\langle D \rangle$ (over the dominance-plus-link relation). So we have the interpretations: $\langle 0 \rangle \phi$:"ϕ holds on the first daughter"), $\langle 1 \rangle \phi$ ("ϕ holds on the second daughter", $\langle \downarrow \rangle \phi$:"ϕ holds on some daughter", $\langle * \rangle \phi$:"ϕ holds here or somewhere below", $\langle L \rangle \phi$: "ϕ holds at a linked node", and $\langle D \rangle \phi$: "ϕ holds somewhere along $\prec_j$ for $j \in I^*$ (that is, j is a finite non-nil sequence of elements from I).[3]

Note that in a linked binary tree we have,

$$\prec_0, \prec_1 \; \subseteq \; \prec_\downarrow \; \subseteq \; \prec_* \; \subseteq \; \prec_D \, .$$

The *local* tree of a node a consists of the set of all nodes b connected to a by a sequence of $\prec_{i_j}$ transitions, where for all j, $i_j \neq L$ and $i_j \neq D$. By the *global* tree of a we will mean all nodes b connected to a by a sequence of $\prec_{i_j}$ transitions where for each j, $\prec_{i_j}$ is an arbitrary $LOFT$ tree relation. A linked binary tree may consist of a (finite) number of trees related by the link relation. The individual trees in this structure are the *local* trees, the entire structure is the *global* tree.

By means of tree descriptions with operators '$*$' and 'D' we define tree relations such as dominance which underspecify a given sequence of node relations. These weakly specified tree relations we use to characterise long-distance dependencies.

10.2.1 The dynamics of tree growth

The growth of information accumulated during the parsing process is defined by a set of rules licensing transitions between descriptions of *partial trees*. A partial tree is a structure of the signature of linked binary trees that can be $LOFT$-*homomorphically* mapped into to some linked binary tree. That is, if $a \prec_i b$ holds at a certain partial tree ($i \in I$), and f homomorphically maps this partial tree to a linked binary tree, then $f(a) \prec_i f(b)$. Notice that this may involve narrowing down of $a \prec_D b$ to $a \prec_0 b$ via $a \prec_* b$ and $a \prec_\downarrow b$. In a partial tree, the tree relations may be *underspecified*, for instance, in a partial tree $a \prec_* b$ need not (yet) imply that there is a finite $\prec_\downarrow$ sequence connecting a and b.

Each node in a partial tree will be associated with two finite lists of $LOFT$ formulae: a list of *requirements*, the $TODO$ list, and a list of *annotations*, the $DONE$ list. Individual transitions developing tree structure may move formulae from the $TODO$ to the $DONE$ list. The emphasis of our parsing model is on the partial nature of information available at any point in the tree development, where tree nodes may yet have non-empty $TODO$ lists and may as yet have merely $\prec_\downarrow, \prec_*$, or $\prec_D$ predecessors (that is, it may as yet have no fully determined position on the (subterm) tree).

Wellformedness for a sentence-string s is defined as the availability of a set of transitions from the *axiom* as starting point for the first word of s, to the *goal* as the result of processing the last word of s. The axiom

---

[3]The converses of these modalities are also of use. We will only mention $\langle \uparrow \rangle$ as the converse of $\langle \downarrow \rangle$.

is a partial tree consisting of a single (root) node with empty $DONE$ list and $TODO$ list $\{Ty(t)\}$, The goal is a a tree representation of a logical formula, that is, the root node has $Ty(t)$ on the $DONE$ list and all $TODO$ lists are empty. The partial tree structures arising successively by processing the string left to right starting from the axiom are $LOFT$ homomorphically related. Every move from one partial tree to the next one is guided by a *transition rule*.

Transition rules

The transition rules mapping the initial partial tree, the axiom, eventually to a full-blown linked binary tree, representing the logical form of a string, are formulated in terms of *descriptions* of nodes and trees.

Tree nodes are represented by *ordered pairs of $DONE/TODO$ lists* for a given node positioner n:

$$[_n DONE \bullet TODO].$$

For instance, the *axiom* as defined above, is represented by $[_a \bullet Ty(t)\,]$ for some arbitrary a. A finite partial linked tree is represented by a *nested set of node representations* where the node positioner gives the relation of the embedded to the embedding node. Node positioners are the constants 0 (left daughter), 1 (right daughter), $\downarrow$ (daughter, immediate dominance), $*$ (dominance), L (Link), D (any combination of dominance and/or Link relations), and the variables n, m ranging over any of these. The transition rules are defined over finite partial linked trees formulated in terms of nested node representations.

Transitions between partial trees are (essentially) induced by the words in an NL string and may involve, for instance, creation of tree structure and compilation of annotations. No transition removes tree structure or elements from the $DONE$ list of a node. In the statement of the rules we will employ the following conventions to represent tree *patterns*. In the node representations we let the variables X, Y and Z range over (possibly empty) contexts of $LOFT$ formulae and the variables A, B and C over (possibly empty) contexts of nested node representations. So, in the representation

$$[_n \; \bullet X, Ty(t)]$$

no $LOFT$ formulae occur in the $DONE$ list where the $TODO$ list contains the atomic proposition $Ty(t)$ and possibly some other formulae as well. Whenever the $TODO$ list of a node is empty, we will leave out the bullet '$\bullet$' and display only the $DONE$ list (and the node positioner). [4]

---

[4]Some conventions concerning nested node representations: if a node A is embedded in some node B at *arbitrary depth* we write $B = [_n \; Y \ldots A \ldots \bullet \; X]$ or

Transition rules are of two kinds. The first kind reflects operations on partial linked trees that are independent of the words of a string. These rules deal with general structural aspects of the natural language under consideration. The second kind of rule is captured under the name of *Scanning*. Each Scanning rule reflects the transitions induced by an individual (category of) word(s) of the language. In general, a word projects an "IF Σ THEN α ELSE α'" statement. The set Σ, the *condition* of the lexical item, consist of a finite number of *LOFT* facts and *LOFT* requirements. If these hold on the tree node currently in focus, then action α is executed; if some proposition or requirement in Σ does not hold on that node, then α' is executed.

Examples of the first kind of rules are the following:

Elimination   Introduction

$$\frac{[_m \ldots [_n \ \langle 0 \rangle \psi, \langle 1 \rangle \phi, Y \bullet X] \ldots]}{[_m \ldots [_n \ \langle 0 \rangle \psi, \langle 1 \rangle \phi), \chi, Y \bullet X] \ldots]} \qquad \frac{[_m \ldots [_n \ Y \bullet \chi, X] \ldots]}{[_m \ldots [_n \ Y \bullet \chi, \langle 0 \rangle \psi, \langle 1 \rangle \phi, X], \ldots]}$$

provided that (ψ, ϕ) reduces to χ in our rewrite system (in the Lambda calculus: $\mathtt{APL}(\psi, \phi) \triangleright_\beta \chi$). For instance, by Introduction, $[_0 \ \bullet \ Ty(t)]$ may be developed into $[_0 \ \bullet \ Ty(t), \langle 0 \rangle Ty(e), \langle 1 \rangle Ty(e \to t)]$, a requirement for a type e and type $e \to t$. The information developed by Introduction may be exploited by the righthand rule of the following pair.

Completion   Prediction

$$\frac{[_m \ldots [_n \ Y \ [_i \phi]] \ldots]}{[_m \ldots \ [_n Y, \langle i \rangle \phi, [_i \phi]] \ldots]} \qquad \frac{[_m \ldots [_n \ Y \bullet \langle i \rangle \phi, X] \ldots]}{[_m \ldots [_n \ Y \bullet \langle i \rangle \phi, X, [_i \ \bullet \ \phi]] \ldots]}$$

where $i \in \{0, 1, L, *, D\}$ where $i \in \{0, 1, L\}$

Notice that the rules are not completely symmetric. The creation of new nodes, by the Prediction rule, is restricted to ones connected by the basic tree relations to the spawning node. The evaluation of information on existing nodes, however, as happens in the Completion rule, is completely free.[5] Now, $[_0 \ \bullet \ Ty(t), \langle 0 \rangle Ty(e), \langle 1 \rangle Ty(e \to t)]$ may spawn $[_0 \ \emptyset \bullet \ Ty(t), \langle 0 \rangle Ty(e), \langle 1 \rangle Ty(e \to t), [_0 \ \bullet \ Ty(e)], [_1 \ \bullet \ Ty(e \to t)]]$; the root node grows into a tree with root, left daughter and right daughter. In this way the requirements generate extensions of partial trees. These

---

$B = [_n \ Y \bullet \ldots A \ldots X]$, depending on whether all elements in the context A have an empty $TODO$ list (and thus are represented without a bullet) or some have a non-empty $TODO$ list, respectively. The notion of arbitrary depth includes the case that this depth is zero. If we leave out the dots '$\ldots$', then we mean *immediate* embedding. Finally, the *order* in which sisters occur within nested representations is irrelevant (their positioners, of course, are not).

[5]After all, the soundness of the Completion rule is guaranteed by the semantics of the tree logic: if $a \prec_i b$ and node b satisfies ϕ, then a satisfies $\langle i \rangle \phi$.

rules reflect directly the structure of terms in a language with a binary operation APL. Analogous rules accompany the other operators one may consider.

A rule called *Thinning* allows us to remove a formula from the *TODO* list of the node currently in focus if that formula also is a member of the *DONE* list. This removal of formulae from the *TODO* list is essential to reach the overall goal of constructing a linked binary tree where all nodes are without requirements.

In this paper we will also use a substitution rule for pronominal elements. This rule is of the form

$$\frac{[_m \cdots [_n Fo(\mathbf{he}_i), X \bullet Y\,]\ldots]}{[_m \cdots [_n Fo(\mathsf{John}_i), X \bullet Y\,]\ldots]}$$

subject to appropriate *locality restrictions*.[6]

$\lfloor_m \bullet Ty(t)]$	Axiom
$\lfloor_m \bullet Ty(t), \langle 0\rangle Ty(e), \langle 1\rangle Ty(e \to t)]$	Intr'n
$\lfloor_m \bullet Ty(t), X, [_0 \bullet Ty(e)], [_1 \bullet Ty(e \to t)]]$	Pred'n
$\lfloor_m \bullet Ty(t), X, [_0 Fo(\mathsf{John}), Ty(e) \bullet Ty(e)], [_1 \bullet Ty(e \to t)]]$	John
$\lfloor_m \bullet Ty(t), X, [_0 Fo(\mathsf{John}), Ty(e)], [\underline{_1} \bullet Ty(e \to t)]]$	Thinn'g
$\lfloor_m \bullet Ty(t), X, Tens(PR), [_0 Y], [_1 \bullet Z, \langle 0\rangle Ty(e),$	
$\qquad\qquad [_1 Fo(\mathsf{admire}), Ty(e \to (e \to t))]]]$	*admires*
$\lfloor_m \bullet Ty(t), X, [_0 Y], [_1 \bullet Z, [_0 \bullet Ty(e)],$	
$\qquad\qquad [_1 Fo(\mathsf{admire}), Ty(e \to (e \to t))]]]$	Pred'n
$\lfloor_m \bullet Ty(t), X, [_0 Y], [_1 \bullet Z, [_0 Fo(\mathsf{Nadia}), Ty(e) \bullet Ty(e)], [_1 V]]]$	*Nadia*
$\lfloor_m \bullet Ty(t), X, [_0 Y], [\underline{_1} \bullet Z, [_0 Fo(\mathsf{Nadia}), Ty(e)], [_1 V]]]$	Thinn'g
$\lfloor_m \bullet Ty(t), X, [_0 Y], [\underline{_1} \langle 0\rangle (Fo(\mathsf{Nadia}), Ty(e)),$	
$\quad \langle 1\rangle (Fo(\mathsf{admire}), Ty(e \to (e \to t)) \bullet Ty(e \to t), [_0 Z], [_1 V]]]$	Compl'n
$\lfloor_m \bullet Ty(t), X, [_0 Y], [\underline{_1} Z, Fo(\mathsf{admire(Nadia)}),$	
$\qquad\qquad Ty(e \to t) \bullet Ty(e \to t), [_0 V], [_1 U]]]$	Elim'n
$\lfloor_{\underline{m}} \bullet Ty(t), X, [_0 Y], [_1 Z Fo(\mathsf{admire(Nadia)}),$	
$\qquad\qquad Ty(e \to t), [_0 V], [_1 U]]]$	Thinn'g
$\lfloor_{\underline{m}} \langle 0\rangle (Fo(\mathsf{John}), Ty(e)), \langle 1\rangle (Fo(\mathsf{admire(John)}),$	
$\qquad\qquad Ty(e \to t)) \bullet Ty(t), [_0 Y], [_1 , [_0 Z], [_1 V]]]$	Compl'n
$\lfloor_{\underline{m}} Fo(\mathsf{admire(Nadia)(John)}), Ty(t) \bullet Ty(t), [_0 Y],$	
$\qquad\qquad [_1 , [_0 Z], [_1 V]]]$	Elim'n
$\lfloor_{\underline{m}} Fo(\mathsf{admire(Nadia)(John)}), Ty(t), [_0 Y], [_1 , [_0 Z], [_1 V]]]$	Thinn'g

FIGURE 2 Parsing **John admires Nadia**.

---

[6]For a full set of rules, see Meyer-Viol 1997, Kempson Meyer-Viol & Gabbay, and Kempson & Meyer-Viol forthcoming.

Example

The various stages arising during the parse of the sentence **John admires Nadia** displayed in Figure 2 are annotated by either the rule used in generating the next stage, or by the word which creates the next stage through scanning. The transition rules are formulated with respect to a pointer located at some node in the tree structure created up to that point (in Figure 2 the pointer is indicated by the underlined node positioner). The NP **John** (or **Nadia**) is associated with the scanning rule:

IF $Ty(e)$ occurs to the right of the bullet,

THEN   add $Fo(\mathtt{John})$, (or $Fo(\mathtt{Nadia})$), and $Ty(e)$ to the left of the bullet,

ELSE   abort.

The actions associated with the word **admires** are more complex.[7]

IF $Ty(e \rightarrow t)$ occurs to the right of the bullet,

THEN   create a function daughter and annotate this
with $Fo(\mathtt{admire})$, and $Ty(e \rightarrow (e \rightarrow t))$,
add $\langle 0 \rangle Ty(e)$ to the right of the bullet at the current node,
add $Tens(PR)$ to the left of the bullet at the top node,

ELSE   abort

The actions undertaken by scanning this word involve three nodes. A new node is created with an annotation in $DONE$, the $TODO$ of the current node is extended by a requirement for object to the verb (a 'subcategorization' statement) and the proposition $Tens(PR)$ (indicating present tense) is added to $DONE$ of the top node.

Once the last word (**Nadia**) has been processed (by scanning **Nadia** and getting rid of $Ty(e)$ as $TODO$ by Thinning), a tree will have been constructed, in which all terminal nodes will have empty $TODO$ lists. This tree represents an unreduced lambda term. Now the information from the terminal nodes is propagated upwards by the Completion rule all the way to the top. By Elimination and Thinning, the $TODO$ lists at the internal nodes are emptied.

10.2.2   Dislocation

In the remainder of this paper we will concentrate on the rules dealing with dislocation in its various "focus" and "topic" guises. They are all rules that develop the tree description independent of the words of the

---

[7]We give here the characterization of tense as part of the lexical entry by way of illustration, though, arguably, such regular morphological inflexion should be given a separate lexical characterization.

string. Each case of left dislocation involves a node description for the dislocated constituent which does not fully specify the contribution made by the dislocated expression to the final tree, an initial underspecification of its relation to other constituent nodes of the tree which is updated at a subsequent step in the interpretation process.

Star Adjunction

This rule will be used for *Focus* constructions.[8] It prepares for the interpretation of a clause initial left-dislocated NP.

$$\frac{[_m \cdots [_n \ \bullet \ Ty(t), X] \dots]}{[_m \cdots [_n \ \bullet \ Ty(t), X, [_* \ \bullet \ Ty(e)]] \dots]}$$

This rule licenses the adjunction of an unfixed node — a node which is only constrained to occur at some node in the local tree under construction. The condition Σ of the action projected by an NP like **John** wants $Ty(e)$ on $TODO$ list of the node under construction; its actions then contribute the propositions $Fo(\text{John})$ and $Ty(e)$ to the $DONE$ list of that node. Thus, processing a left-dislocated NP **John** may result in the structure

$$[_m \cdots [_n \ [_* Fo(\text{John}), Ty(e) \ \bullet \ Ty(e)] \ \bullet \ Ty(t)]] \dots].$$

The rule *Thinning* now allows the removal of '$Ty(e)$' to the right of the bullet.

Link Adjunction rules

The concept of *linked* tree structures was introduced to characterise the construal of relative clauses and their relation to the nominal 'head'. The incremental projection of such linked structures involves *Link Adjunction* rules. A Link Adjunction rule adjoins the root node of a fresh tree to a 'head' node and ensures that this head and some node in the adjoined tree share a common formula. It does this by decorating the new root node with a modal requirement dictating that an occurrence of the formula annotating the head be constructed within this tree. It turns out that these rule are also the appropriate ones to deal with *Topic* constructions (involving resumptive pronouns), as in the English example **As for John, he likes me.**

$$\frac{[_m \cdots [_n \ Fo(\alpha), Ty(X) \ \bullet \ ] \dots]}{[_m \cdots [_n \ Fo(\alpha), Ty(X) \ \bullet \ [_L \ \bullet \ Ty(t), \langle z \rangle (Fo(\alpha) \wedge Ty(X))]] \dots]}$$
$$z \in \{*, D\}$$

---

[8]Confusingly, the term in recent syntactic literature for what is here dubbed a 'Focus' structure is *Topicalization*.

The rule applies to a node with empty $TODO$ list of any type giving rise to an ordered pair of trees.[9] Thus processing a clause initial topicalised **as for John,** results in the structure

$$[_n \; Fo(\text{John}), Ty(e) \; \bullet \; [_L \; \bullet \; Ty(t), \langle D \rangle (Fo(\text{John}) \wedge Ty(e))]].$$

The instantiations of the rule vary according to whether the information from the head is shared with the *local* or with the *global* linked tree.[10]

Unification

When we have constructed a tree with an unfixed node, that is, a node with an underspecified positioner, e.g. $[_*$, these nodes have to be *unified* with fixed nodes.

$$\frac{[_{m_1} \cdots [_{m_2} [_{m_3} \; X_1 \; \bullet \; Y_1 \;], \; [_* \; X_2 \; \bullet \; Y_2], A] \cdots]}{[_{m_1} \cdots [_{m_2} [_{m_3} \; X_1, X_2 \; \bullet \; Y_1, Y_2], A] \cdots]}$$

This rule licenses the unification of a node with underspecified position with a more specified tree position (cf. Meyer-Viol (1997)). Depending on the instantiations of X and Y different cases are covered by this rule. In the following specific example we let $X_2 = Y_1 = 0$ and $Y_2 = Ty(e)$. Unification then has the form

$$\frac{[_m \cdots [_n \; [_l \; \bullet \; Ty(e)], \; [_* \; Fo(\alpha), Ty(e) \; \bullet \;]] \cdots]}{[_m \cdots \; [_n \; [_l Fo(\alpha), Ty(e) \; \bullet \; Ty(e)]] \cdots]}$$
$$\overline{[_m \cdots [_n \; [_l \; Fo(\alpha), Ty(e)]] \cdots]}$$

in the last step $Ty(e)$ has been removed from the $TODO$ list by the Thinning rule. This covers the cases where a *gap* occurs in an NL string: a constituent of type e is required, but the NL string does not supply it (at the right moment). The unfixed node then provides what the string does not.

For $Y_1 = X_2 = Fo(\alpha), Ty(e)$ and $Y_2 = X_1 = 0$, Unification (followed by Thinning) looks like

$$\frac{[_m \cdots [_n [_* \; \bullet \; Fo(\alpha), Ty(e) \;], [_l \; Fo(\alpha), Ty(e)]] \cdots]}{[_m \cdots [_n [_l \; Fo(\alpha), Ty(e) \; \bullet \; Fo(\alpha), Ty(e)]] \cdots]}$$
$$\overline{[_m \cdots [_n [_l \; Fo(\alpha), Ty(e) \; \bullet \;]] \cdots]}$$

This covers the cases where the dislocated constituent is interpreted as identical to some subsequent pronominal. For arbitrary X, Y, the Uni-

---

[9]Link Adjunction rules may be paired with a rule of $LINK$ completion which applies only when all $TODO$ lists of the linked structure are empty, which has the effect of absorbing the formula established in the linked structure into the head to which the linked tree is adjoined (Kempson & Meyer-Viol, forthcoming).

[10]This variation on where in the *linked* tree the shared formula should occur is also observed in relative clauses.

fication rule may result in an unsuccessful parse sequence by producing tree nodes with a *TODO* list that cannot be emptied or an inconsistent *DONE* list.

10.3 The analysis

The analysis makes use of two primary properties of the model. First, annotations of nodes may occur on the *TODO*- or on the *DONE*-list. Second, we may have pairs of linked trees with transfer of information from one tree to another, the transferred information constraining the subsequent development of the second tree. All languages make use of these possibilities, though they may do so subject to different locality restrictions. This gives us a number of options for expressing the relation between a dislocated structure and its environment.

On the one hand, left-dislocated expressions ('Focus' constructions, with no resumptive pronoun) induce the projection within a tree structure of a node annotated with a formula as *DONE* but which lacks a fixed tree position (*Star Adjunction*). This internal tree relation has subsequently to be identified (by *Unification*), so that an interpretation of the whole string can be built up which is identical to that of the non-dislocated normal form. (This process is characteristically available at any depth of embedding.) The explanation thus ensures that the following have the same resulting interpretation:

(1) Nadia, John admires.

(2) John admires Nadia.

The parse of the first sentence is displayed in Figure 3.

Clitic left dislocation on the other hand (with a resumptive pronoun), involves the projection of the formula associated with the dislocated expression as a requirement (*TODO*). Since however, such dislocated expressions may be indefinitely complex, and their associated formula accordingly constructed by a tree-building process, the imposition of the necessary formula as a requirement has to be a consequence of having first built a tree whose root node is annotated with the formula in question. Hence clitic left dislocation structures are interpreted through the process of *Link Adjunction*, with the formula of the root node of the first tree (projected from the dislocated expression) transferred as a requirement on the root node of the second tree for a copy of that transferred formula somewhere within the second tree. To supply this copy is the task of the (resumptive) pronoun. The result is that a clitic left dislocation structure will share with simple clausal sequences and with left dislocation structures the projection of a propositional structure, differing from them both in that the dislocated constituent is projected

$[_m \bullet Ty(t)]$ — Axiom

$[_m \bullet Ty(t), [_* \bullet Ty(e)]]$ — *-adj'n

$[_m \bullet Ty(t), [_* Fo(\text{Nadia}), Ty(e)]]$ — *Nadia*

$[_m \bullet Ty(t), \langle 0 \rangle Ty(e), \langle 1 \rangle Ty(e \to t), [_* W]]$ — Intr'n

$[_m \bullet Ty(t), X, [_0 \bullet Ty(e)], [_1 \bullet Ty(e \to t)], [_* W]]$ — Pred'n

$[_m \bullet Ty(t), X, [_0 Fo(\text{John}), Ty(e) \bullet Ty(e)], [_1 \bullet Ty(e \to t)], [_* W]]$ — *John*

$[_m \bullet Ty(t), X, [_0 Fo(\text{John}), Ty(e)], [_{\underline{1}} \bullet Ty(e \to t)], [_* W]]$ — Thinn'g

$[_m \bullet Ty(t), X, Tens(PR), [_0 Y], [_{\underline{1}} \bullet Z, \langle 0 \rangle Ty(e),$

$[_1 Fo(\text{admire}), Ty(e \to (e \to t))], [_* W]]]$ — *admires*

$[_m \bullet Ty(t), X, [_0 Y], [_1 \bullet Z, [_{\underline{0}} \bullet Ty(e)],$

$[_1 U], [_* Fo(\text{Nadia}), Ty(e)]]]$ — Pred'n

$[_m \bullet Ty(t), X, [_0 Y], [_1 \bullet Z, [_{\underline{0}} Fo(\text{Nadia}), Ty(e) \bullet Ty(e)], [_1 U]]]$ — Unif'n, $* = 0$

$\vdots$ — see Fig. 2

$[_m Fo(\text{admire}(\text{Nadia})(\text{John})), Ty(t), [_0 Y], [_1 \ , [_0 Z], [_1 U]]]$ — Thinn'g

FIGURE 3 Parsing **Nadia, John admires**.

also separately. A further potential for variation in clitic left dislocation structures lies in whether the node to be built within the linked tree has to be within the local tree induced from the root node of this newly initiated tree, or whether it merely needs to be constructed somewhere in the global tree under development.

This leads us to expect two different types of language depending on whether the resumptively construed pronoun in a clitic left-dislocation structure is or is not restricted to occurring within the same local tree as that on which the requirement is imposed. This is what we find. First we have the Romance case, which like English has left dislocation with no resumptive pronoun, but which has in addition a process of clitic left dislocation ($CLLD$), in which fronted noun phrases are paired with resumptive pronominals:

(3) GIANNI ho cercato, non Piero.
    'Gianni I looked for, not Piero.'

(4) Gianni l'ho cercato.
    'As for Gianni, I looked for him.'

$CLLD$ in Italian is restricted. The pairing of clitic and dislocated constituent can be separated across the so-called "weak" islands, *eg* involving an intervening *wh* expression, but cannot be used across strong islands such as a relative clause barrier,

(5) Mario, non so perche lo abbiano invitato.
    'Mario, I don't know why they invited him.'

(6)*A Carlo$_i$ ti parlero solo delle persone che gli$_i$ piacciono .. (Italian)
to Carlo I will talk to you only about the people that appeal to
him.

This pattern is characterisable through the use of * *Adjunction* for
the cases without any resumptive pronoun, and the more stringent variant of the *Link Adjunction* rule for the cases with resumptive pronoun:[11]

"*Focus*" $[_m...[_n[_* Fo(\alpha), Ty(e)] \bullet Ty(t)]...]$

"*Topic*" $[_m...[_n Fo(\alpha), Ty(e) [_L \bullet Ty(t), \langle * \rangle (Fo(\alpha), Ty(e))]]...]$

The occurrence of the resumptive pronoun in the linked tree will have
the effect of satisfying the modal requirement imposed on the root node
of that tree only if the formula assigned as the value of the pronominal
is taken to be that projected by the left-dislocated expression. Hence
the obligatory interpretation of the pronoun as identical to that of the
left-dislocated expression. Notice how it is the constraints on the un-
folding tree structure that guarantee that the otherwise freely available
pragmatic process of anaphora resolution leads in these sequences to a
fixed result.

The less stringent form of requirement on the introduction of a linked
tree is displayed by regular resumptive pronoun languages such as Arabic. Arabic differentiates between *wh* structures (in questions) and other
dislocation structures (including referentially construed *wh* forms), in
that while the former are associated with a gap in the clausal sequence,
the latter are invariably (except in subject position) associated with a resumptive pronoun, without any restriction as to where in the subsequent
string that pronoun should occur:[12]

(7) (Lebanese Arabic)
hal-kteeb   smeʕt   ʔenno l-wallad ʕalee
this-the-book heard-1s that   the boy wrote on-it
'I heard that the boy wrote on this book.'

(8) hal-kteeb   hkiit   maʕ l-wallad yalli katab ʕalee
this-the-book talked-2s with the-boy who wrote on-it
'I heard that you talked with the boy who wrote on this book.'

---

[11]These characterizations match the processes of Topicalization and Clitic Left
Dislocation (*CLLD*) distinguished by Cinque (1990), from whom the Italian data
are taken.

[12]Some forms of Arabic dialects allow the full range of NPs in the initial dislocated
position without any subsequent resumptive pronoun, eg some dialects of Moroccan
Arabic, presumably under the influence of French.

The resumptive pronominal clitic, if duly identified with the formula annotating the head, will, as in the Romance case, have the effect of satisfying the requirement that some node in the $LINK$ tree must display a copy of this formula. Furthermore, despite the fact that no resumptive pronoun normally ever occurs in subject position, no additional statement is needed to cover these cases, since Arabic projects a pronominal-type formula for the subject position in the tree directly from the predicate, which satisfies the imposed requirement by being identified anaphorically as though the pronoun had been morphologically expressed:

(9) hal-wallad   smeʕt   ʔenno ʕalee l-kteeb
    this-the-boy heard-1SG that   wrote on the book
    'I heard that this boy wrote on the book.'

The pattern (with variation across the different forms of Arabic as to the need of any additional specification distinguishing non-referential *wh* question forms) is:

"*Focus*" $[_m...[_n [_* \, Fo(\alpha), Ty(e)] \quad \bullet \, Ty(t) \,]...]$

"*Topic*" $[_m...[_n \, Fo(\alpha), Ty(e)[_L \quad \bullet Ty(t), \langle D \rangle (Fo(\alpha), Ty(e)) \,]]...]$

Japanese (and other verb-final languages) might seem to provide evidence for parametric variation in the application of *Unification*, in parallel with *Link Adjunction*, since it displays left-dislocation structures in which the dislocated expression, if marked with the topic marking suffix *wa*, need have no resumptive pronoun but nevertheless may be interpreted in clear violation of any island constraints (eg across a relative-clause boundary):

(10) Ano hon-wa$_i$ Hanako-ga e_j t_i katta   hito$_j$
     that book-TOPIC Hanako-NOM   bought person-ACC
     sagasite iru rasii
     looking-for seem
     'It seems that Hanako is looking for the person who bought that book.'

If this were correct, we would expect a four-way distinction with a further type of language that displays an unrestricted *Focus* construction and a locally-restricted *Topic* construction. However, as it turns out, the pattern set out above for Arabic applies equally to Japanese, despite the superficially different behaviour of pronominal elements in the two languages. Japanese is a verb-final language with free "*pro*-drop" phenomena for all argument positions - there is no obligatory resumptive use of pronominals. Reflecting this, verbs can be defined to project a propositional template, with tree nodes not only for the predicate but also with nodes for its arguments filled with place-holding pronominal-like formulae. This characterization of information projected by predicates in Japanese allows a left-dislocated expression (marked with *wa*) to be interpreted as providing the annotation for some node in a tree structure without any explicit resumptive use of a lexical pronoun. As in Arabic, the left-dislocated expression is taken to project a formula of type e for the root node of some tree, which then imposes a requirement on the root node of the linked tree that this new tree contain a copy of this formula. This requirement is then met by identifying some abstract pronominal element within the linked tree with the formula projected directly by the *wa*-marked expression, exactly as in Arabic.[13] There is however one restriction over and above that associated with inducing linked tree structures in Arabic. It seems that the *wa*-marked expressions can only project such a $LINK$ structure at the absolute root node. This, a common restriction across languages, is straightforwardly expressible, by specifying that the containing context is node 0.

$$\text{``}Topic\text{''} \quad [_0 ... [_n \; Fo(\alpha), Ty(e)[_L \; \bullet Ty(t), \langle D \rangle (Fo(\alpha), Ty(e))\;]]...]$$

This structure is distinguished from that involving "scrambling" of case-marked noun phrases, which requires that the position of the node projected from the dislocated expression be subsequently identified as fixed within the local tree (cf. Saito 1985):

---

[13]Though there are cases in which the topic-marked -*wa* constituent is not explicitly associated with any internal clausal position, all such constructions involve an 'aboutness' relation between the expressions constituting the clause and the *wa*-marked expression, suggesting that a copy of the *wa*-marked expression is projected as a sub-formula of the whole in the resulting logical form, the presence of which may be guaranteed through some intervening step of inference, much as with anaphora resolution (cf. Kempson Meyer-Viol & Gabbay):

  (i)   sono   sakura-no   ki-wa   hana-ga   titta.
        the   cherry tree-GEN   tree-TOP   flower-NOM   has fallen
        'As for the cherry tree, its flowers have fallen.'

  (ii)   sono   itiba-wa,   sakana-ga   warui.
        the   market-TOP   fish-NOM   bad
        'As for the market, the fish there is bad.'

  (iii) hana-wa   sakura-ga   ii.
        flower-TOP   cherry blossoms-NOM   good.
        'As for flowers, cherry blossoms are good.'

(11)*Ano hon-o$_i$ Hanako-ga e_j t_i katta   hito$_j$
     that book-ACC Hanako-NOM   bought person-ACC
     sagasite iru rasii
     looking-for seem
     'It seems that John is looking for the person who bought that
     book.'

Such case-marked dislocated expressions are analysed as triggering instances of *Adjunction*, with case-marking defined as dictating the relative position within the tree for the unfixed node (accusative case for example defined as imposing the modal requirement that the node so decorated have as a mother a node of type $e \rightarrow t$). Notice that such case-marked NPs could not be analysed as $LINK$ structures, since on that analysis, projecting a formula for the root node of the first tree in a pair of $LINK$ structures, their case requirement would never be met. There are, then 'Focus' and 'Topic' structures exactly as in Arabic, the primary difference in left-dislocation structures in the two types of language stemming from the information projected by the predicate in the two languages.

10.4   Crossover and related phenomena

This might seem the extent of the interaction between anaphora resolution and left-dislocation processes. But further variation is predictable, explaining two further phenomena. Up to this point anaphora resolution has been taken to fulfil some requirement on a fixed tree node, playing no part in fixing a tree position for some unfixed node. However, nothing precludes *Unification* applying to the pair of an unfixed node with empty $TODO$ and a pronoun construed as identical to the formula of that node; and this provides a basis for explaining the strong crossover restriction debarring the sequence of a dislocated constituent of type e, a pronominal construed as identical to it, and a following gap:

(12)*Sue$_i$, I know she$_i$'s worrying e_i is sick, because she keeps talking
     about it.

In our account, it is the formula projected by the pronoun **she**$_i$, realised by $[_x \, Fo(\mathsf{Sue}), Ty(e)]$ in (12) that unifies with the (projection of the) dislocated constituent $[_* \, Fo(\mathsf{Sue}), Ty(e)]$ through *Unification*, and not the gap e_i left by an unfilled node $[_y \, \bullet \, Ty(e)]$. Consequently, no subject is assigned to the predicate 'is sick' (and there is no possibility, English not being a "*pro*-drop" language, of projecting a subject directly from the predicate). Thus the formula $Ty(e)$ on the $TODO$-list of the node associated with the gap will not be removed by information supplied by the string and the parse cannot finish successfully. The

Unification rule shows the problem clearly:

$$\frac{[_k...[_m\ [_*\ Fo(\mathtt{Sue}_i),Ty(e)\bullet\ ]\quad X\quad [_n\ Fo(\mathtt{she}_i),Ty(e)\ \bullet\ ]]...]}{[_k...[_m\ [_*\ Fo(\mathtt{Sue}_i),Ty(e)\bullet\ ]\quad X\quad [_n\ Fo(\mathtt{Sue}_i),Ty(e)\ \bullet\ ]]...]}$$

$$[_k...[_m\ X\ [_n\ Fo(\mathtt{Sue}_i,Ty(e))\ \bullet\ ]]]$$

$$\vdots$$

$$\overline{\qquad[_k...[_m\ X\ [_n\ Fo(\mathtt{Sue}_i,Ty(e))\ \bullet\ ]\quad [_l\ \bullet\ Ty(e)]]\ ...]\qquad}$$

Here the first transition substitutes the pronoun, the second applies Unification. At the arrival of the gap, node l, no fulfilment of the requirement for a type e objects is possible without an appropriate expression projected from the string (at the right moment). The *Unification* rule again shows why the acceptable order, antecedent ... gap ... pronominal, may lead to successful parses:[14]

$$\frac{[_k...[_m\ [_*\ Fo(\mathtt{Sue}_i),Ty(e)]\quad X\quad [_n\ \bullet\ Ty(e)]...]...]}{[_k...[_m\ [_n\ Fo(\mathtt{Sue}_i),Ty(e)]\ ...\ ]}$$

$$\vdots$$

$$\frac{[_k...\ [_n\ Fo(\mathtt{Sue}_i),Ty(e)]\ ...\ [_l\ Fo(\mathtt{she}_i),Ty(e)]...]}{[_k...\ [_n\ Fo(\mathtt{Sue}_i),Ty(e)]\ ...\ [_l\ Fo(\mathtt{Sue}_i),Ty(e)]...]}$$

Anaphora may also be used to project an annotated unfixed node which is at later stage unified with some fixed tree position. In particular, when the root node of a linked structure has a requirement on its *TODO* list for a copy of the formula ϕ, projected by the head, merely as occurring somewhere in the *global* tree under construction (that is, the requirement is of the form $\langle D\rangle\phi$) instead of the in the *local* tree (i.e., a requirement of the form $\langle *\rangle\phi$), then anaphora resolution may fulfil that requirement by supplying the formula as annotation on some locally unfixed node. Such a process explains the surprising phenomenon whereby a resumptive pronoun can be "moved" to a higher clause yielding the order antecedent .... pronominal .... gap, all construed identically, without inducing a crossover violation (cf. Demirdache 1991):

---

[14]This account leads us to expect that the string will be acceptable if pronouns are used throughout:

(i)　?Sue$_i$ I know SHE$_i$'s worrying she$_i$ is sick, because she$_i$ keeps talking about it. But not Ruth. She seems to be refusing to recognise the problem.

Cf. Edwards Kempson & Meyer-Viol for detailed justification of this account of strong crossover, and for a demonstration of how the pragmatic constraint of optimal relevance invariably leads to reduced acceptability of resumptive pronouns unless they are used for a specific pragmatic effect not otherwise attainable.

(13) Shalom$_i$, ʔani xošev še   ʔamarta še   ʔalav$_i$ sara katva
     Shalom$_i$, I   think that said-you that about him$_i$ sara wrote
     šir e_i
     poem
     'Shalom$_i$, I think that you said that Sara wrote a poem about
     him$_i$.'

(14) Shalom$_i$, ʔani xošev še   ʔalav$_i$ ʔamarta še   sara katva
     Shalom$_i$, I   think that about-him$_i$ said-you that sara wrote
     šir e_i
     poem

(15) Shalom$_i$, ʔalav$_i$ ʔani xošev še   ʔamarta še   sara katva
     Shalom$_i$, about him$_i$ I   think that said-you that sara wrote
     šir e_i
     poem

The transition from the imposition of a requirement on the root node
of the tree to a fixed node of the required form involves two steps. The
first is the provision of a value for the formula projected by the pronoun
(following a step of *Adjunction*). The second is a Unification step:[15]

$$\frac{[_0 Fo(\text{Shalom}_i), Ty(e) \ [_L \ ... \ [_* \ Fo(\text{him}_i), Ty(e)]... \bullet \ Ty(t), \langle D\rangle(Fo(\text{Shalom}_i)))]]}{[_0 Fo(\text{Shalom}_i), Ty(e) \ [_L \ ... \ [_* Fo(\text{Shalom}_i), Ty(e) \ ] \ ... \bullet Ty(t)]]}$$

$$\vdots$$

$$\frac{[_0 Fo(\text{Shalom}_i), Ty(e) \ [_L \ ... \ [_* Fo(\text{Shalom}_i), Ty(e) \ ] \ Y \ [_n \ \bullet Ty(e)]... \bullet Ty(t)]]}{[_0 Fo(\text{Shalom}_i).Ty(e) \ [_L \ ...[_n \ Fo(\text{Shalom}_i), Ty(e)] \ ... \bullet \ Ty(t)]]}$$

$$\vdots$$

Note that the update transitions in the tree description are LOFT-
homomorphisms.

This process of so-called *Contrastive Dislocation* is, as we would expect, available in other languages, as witness Dutch (cf. Zaenen 1997;
Vat 1997)

---

[15]For these purposes we assume for simplicity that *alav* is of type *e* (with some
distinguishing feature reflecting the specific preposition) rather than projecting complex internal structure. Should the complex structure turn out to be the preferred
analysis, the initially unfixed node would be of type $(e \to t) \to (e \to t)$ containing a
subtree of root node type *e*. The monotonic nature of the update relation would be
unaltered by this additional complication.

(16) Jan,   DIE   denk ik niet dat we hier nog   dikwijls zullen
John, that-one think I not that we here again often   will
zien.
see
'John, I don't think we will see that one here again often.'

10.5   Conclusion

This paper has introduced an analysis of long-distance dependency in terms of a process of tree update, in which 'dislocated' constituents are assigned initially weak tree descriptions which are subsequently updated. The account has been set in a model of language understanding with interpretation defined as a process of progressively building up a logical form on a left-right basis. A typology of long-distance dependency effects has been shown to emerge, with the added bonus of providing accounts of crossover and partial left dislocation (Hebrew), without additional stipulation. The account succeeds in formally differentiating a range of left-dislocation phenomena while preserving the insight that the semantic content of these types of structure is identical to the counterpart in which each constituent expression is in its expected position. It also respects Prince's observations, by leaving open the possibility of there being different pragmatic uses to which these structures might be put, depending on other forms of contrast available in the individual languages. The significance of this account is that it provides a natural basis for describing the interaction between anaphora resolution and long-distance dependency, while preserving the generality both of anaphora resolution and the characterization of how initially unfixed nodes come to be assigned a fixed position in the resultant tree. Its success in capturing the semantic property of dislocation structures and their cross-linguistic diversity confirms the LDS_{NL} perspective on natural language - that a natural-language grammar should be defined in intrinsically dynamic terms, characterising possible sequences of transitions for a left-to-right parser.

References

Blackburn, P. and Meyer-Viol, W. 1994. Linguistics, logic and finite trees, *Bulletin of IGPL* 2: 2-39.

Cinque, G. 1990. *Types of A' Dependencies*. MIT Press.

Demirdache, H. 1991. *Resumptive Chains in Restrictive Relatives, Appositives and Dislocation Structures*. MIT. Ph.D.

Edwards, M., Kempson, R. and Meyer-Viol, W. forthcoming. Resumptive Pronouns in English and Arabic. In Ouhalla,J. and Perrett,D. (eds.), *Proceedings of 4th Afro-Asiatic Conference*.

Erteschik-Shir, N. 1997. *The Dynamics of Focus Structure*. Cambridge University Press.

Kempson, R. and Meyer-Viol, W. forthcoming. Syntactic Computation as Labelled Deduction: WH a case study. in Borsley, R. and Roberts, I. (eds.), *Syntactic Categories*. Academic Press. New York.

Kempson, R, Meyer-Viol, W. and Gabbay, D. 1997. On representationalism in semantics: a dynamic account of WH. Dekker, P. et al (eds.), *Proceedings of 11th Amsterdam colloquium* 193-8.

Kempson, R. Meyer-Viol, W. and Gabbay, D. forthcoming. VP ellipsis: towards a dynamic structural account. In Lappin, S. & Benmamoun, I. (eds), *Fragments: Studies in Ellipsis and Gapping*. Oxford University Press, Oxford.

Meyer-Viol, W. 1997. Parsing as tree construction. Dekker, P. et al (eds.), *Proceedings of 11th Amsterdam Colloquium* 229-34.

Portner, P and Yabushita, K. 1998. The semantics and pragmatics of topic phrases. *Linguistics and Philosophy* 21, 117-57.

Prince, E. 1995. On the limits of syntax, with reference to Left-Dislocation and Topicalization. ms.

Saito, M. 1985. *Some Asymmetries in Japanese and their Theoretical Implications*. Ph.D. MIT.

Vat, J. 1997. Left dislocation, connectedness and reconstruction. In Anagnostopolou, E., van Riemsdijk, H., Zwarts, F. (eds.) *Materials on Left Dislocation*, 67-92. John Benjamins, Amsterdam.

Zaenen, A. 1997. Contrastic dislocation in Dutch and Icelandic. In Anagnostopolou, E., van Riemsdijk, H., Zwarts, F. (eds.) *Materials on Left Dislocation*, 119-50. John Benjamins, Amsterdam.

11

Constants of Grammatical Reasoning

Michael Moortgat

11.1 Cognition = computation, grammar = logic

Within current linguistic frameworks a rich variety of principles has been put forward to account for the properties of local and unbounded dependencies. Valency requirements of lexical items are checked by subcategorization principles in HPSG, principles of coherence and completeness in LFG, the theta criterion in GB. These are supplemented by, and interacting with, principles governing non-local dependencies: movement and empty category principles, slash feature percolation principles, *e tutti quanti*.

It is tempting to consider the formulation of such principles as the ultimate goal of grammatical theorizing. But we could also see them as the starting point for a more far-reaching enterprise. Suppose, following the slogan 'Cognition=Computation', we model the cognitive abilities underlying knowledge and use of language as a 'logic of grammar' — a specialized deductive system, attuned to the task of reasoning about the composition of grammatical form and meaning. Rather than using a general purpose logic (say FOL) to 'formalize' certain aspects of linguistic theory, we are interested in capturing the appropriate laws of inference for the 'computational system' of grammar. The logic of grammar, so conceived, would provide an *explanation* for the grammaticality principles mentioned above, and thus remove the need to state them as irreducible primitives.

To work out this concept of a logic of grammar, the following issues have to be addressed.

- What are the CONSTANTS of grammatical reasoning? Can we pro-

Constraints and Resources in Natural Language Syntax and Semantics.
Gosse Bouma, Erhard W. Hinrichs, Geert-Jan M. Kruijff, and Richard T. Oehrle.

vide an explanation for the *uniformity* of the form/meaning correspondence across languages in terms of this vocabulary of logical constants, together with the deductive principles governing their use?

- How can we reconcile the idea of 'constants of grammatical reasoning' with the differences between languages, that is, with STRUCTURAL VARIATION in the realization of the form/meaning correspondence?

Some progress has been made on these questions recently, through a combination of ideas from two research traditions: linear logic and categorial grammar.

Linear logic is a well-studied representative of what is known as a *resource-sensitive* system of inference. In linear logic, assumptions have the status of finite, 'material' *resources*, and the rules of inference keep track of the production and consumption of these resources: free multiplication ('cloning') or waste of assumptions is not allowed. Technically, resource-sensitivity is obtained by removing the rules of Contraction and Weakening as 'hard-wired' components of the inference machinery. The resource-sensitive style of inference is more fine-grained than the 'classical' style, in the sense that more logical constants become distinguishable. Specifically, it becomes possible to identify logical constants (the so-called modalities) for the explicit *control* over resource multiplicity: constants that license multiplication or waste of assumptions, on the condition that these assumptions are modally marked. The linear style of inference, in other words, is more discriminating, but thanks to the modalities, not less expressive, than its classical relative.

The second line of research has grown out of the work of Lambek. In a linguistic setting, the resources under consideration are natural language expressions: elementary form/meaning units ('words') and composite form/meaning configurations built out of these. Well-formedness, in this case, is determined not just by the multiplicity of the grammatical material, but also by its *structure*. The tradition of categorial type logics further refines the linear vocabulary, and introduces logical constants that are sensitive to linguistically relevant structural dimensions such as precedence (word order), dominance (constituency) and dependency. And parallel to the linear modalities controlling resource multiplicity, the categorial vocabulary can be enriched with control features providing deductive instruments for the fine-tuning of these structural aspects of grammatical resource management.[1]

---

[1]Needless to say, our presentation here is not historical: the concept of a logic 'without structural rules' as introduced in Lambek's 1958 and 1961 papers antedates

The developments sketched here have changed the 'categorial' perspective rather drastically. These changes have been well documented on the technical level — see Moortgat (1997) for an up-to-date presentation. The purpose of the present contribution is to present the motivation underlying this line of research in a non-technical way, so as to facilitate a fruitful exchange of ideas with related linguistic frameworks. One can think here of resource-logical themes within LFG and HPSG. Perhaps more surprisingly, one can find non-trivial convergences on the theme of structural control with ideas that are currently developed in 'derivational' versions of the minimalist program.[2]

The paper is organized as follows. In §11.1.1, we show that the concept of resource-sensitivity provides the logical core of fundamental grammaticality principles underlying both local and non-local dependencies. The interplay between logical and structural aspects of grammatical composition, and the need for structural control, are discussed in §11.1.2. In §11.2, we illustrate the approach with a laboratory exercise, contrasting relativization in English and Dutch. We show that significant clusterings of empirical phenomena that differentiate between these two languages arise naturally from logical choices in the fine-tuning of structural resource management.

11.1.1 Grammatical resources

The starred examples below show two ways of violating a fundamental grammaticality principle. Compare (1a) and (1b) in a setting where the context cannot provide additional information — for example, at the opening of a chapter. Example (1a) fails to be a well-formed sentence because there is *not enough* grammatical material: the verb 'offer' requires a subject, a direct and an indirect object. In (1b) these three arguments are supplied, but in (1a) only one of them, leaving the sentence incomplete. The opposite is true when one compares (1c) and (1d). Here, (1c) is illformed because of a *surplus* of grammatical material: there is no way for a direct and an indirect object to enter into grammatical composition with the intransitive verb 'grin' which just requires a subject.

(1) a.*the Mad Hatter offered

    b. the Mad Hatter offered Alice a cup of tea

    c.*the Cheshire Cat grinned Alice a cup of tea

---

the introduction of linear logic by more than a quarter of a century. But the original Lambek systems had fixed resource management regimes: they lacked the vocabulary for structural *control*. The logical framework for structural control features is developed in Moortgat (1996); Kurtonina & Moortgat (1997).

[2]See Stabler (1997) for a computational interpretation of Chomsky (1995), and for example Cornell (1997) for the connection with resource-logical principles.

d. the Cheshire Cat grinned

As noted in the introduction, different linguistic theories have formulated a variety of principles to account for these basic facts of grammatical (in)completeness: the Subcategorization Principle in HPSG, the Theta Criterion in GB, the principles of Coherence and Completeness in LFG, to mention a few.[3] These principles, each stated in the theoretical vocabulary of the grammatical framework in question, have in common that they can be traced back to valency requirements of a *local* nature, stateable within the subcategorizational domain of lexical items.

Comparing (1) with the examples in (2), one sees that dependencies of a potentially unbounded nature exhibit the same pattern of grammatical incompleteness and overcompleteness. In (2a) there is a correlation between the presence of the relative pronoun 'which' and the *absence* of an overtly realized direct object in the relative clause body: addition of the underlined phrase makes (2b) overcomplete, just like (1c). But now, as the examples (2c) and (2d) show, there is no guarantee that the relative pronoun which pre-empts the direct object slot can be found in the local subcategorizational domain of the verb selecting for that argument. So, typically, linguistic theories have come up with new sets of principles, interacting with but different from the ones governing local dependencies, to capture long-distance dependencies such as illustrated in (2): movement and empty category principles, slash feature percolation principles, etc.

(2) a. the tarts which the Hatter offered the March Hare
　　 b.*the tarts which the Hatter offered the March Hare a present
　　 c. the tarts which Alice thought the Hatter offered the March Hare
　　 d. the tarts which the Dormouse said Alice thought ...

Such principles, in the overall design of linguistic theory, are irreducible primitives. As the above discussion shows, there is no unified 'principle-based' account of local and non-local dependencies. Our objective, in searching for the 'logic of grammar', is to present just such a unified account. We approach the problem in two stages: in a first approximation, we restrict our attention to 'multiplicity' issues (i.e. the 'occurrence' aspect of the grammatical resources); then we refine the picture by taking into account also the structural aspects of grammatical composition.

COMPOSITION: THE FORM DIMENSION. A resource-sensitive style of inference would seem to be a good starting point to come to grips with

---

[3]See Pollard & Sag (1994); Chomsky (1981); Kaplan & Bresnan (1982).

issues of grammatical multiplicity.[4] Consider the 'multiplicative' conjunction of linear logic, interpreted as the material composition of parts. The composition operation ($\circ$ in our notation) comes with an implication, which we write as $\multimap$, expressing incompleteness with respect to multiplicative composition. Using a linear implication $A\multimap B$ one actually 'consumes' a datum of type A in order to produce a B. The rules of inference in (3) state how one can *use* a resource implication and how one can *prove* an implicational goal, that is a claim of the form $A\multimap B$. We write $\Gamma \vdash A$ for the judgement that a structure Γ is a well-formed expression of type A. Notice that in the modus ponens rule ($\multimap E$), the use of the implication $\multimap$ goes hand in hand with the introduction of the structure building operation $\circ$ composing the structures Γ and Δ which the premises show to be of type A and $A\multimap B$ respectively. The rule of hypothetical reasoning ($\multimap I$) *withdraws* a component A from the composition structure $A \circ \Gamma$ which the premise shows to be of type B, in order to prove that Γ is of type $A\multimap B$.

(3) ($\multimap E$) from $\Gamma \vdash A$ and $\Delta \vdash A\multimap B$, conclude $\Gamma \circ \Delta \vdash B$
   ($\multimap I$) from $A \circ \Gamma \vdash B$, conclude $\Gamma \vdash A\multimap B$

Using the linear implication to express grammatical incompleteness, we capture the resource-sensitive aspects of grammatical composition in deductive terms. Let us look first at local dependencies. In (4) we represent the type assignment to the lexical resources that would go into the composition of the sentence 'Alice talks to the Footman'. We number the lexical assumptions for future reference.

(4) 1. Alice $\vdash np$ *Lex*
    2. talks $\vdash pp\multimap(np\multimap s)$ *Lex*
    3. to $\vdash np\multimap pp$ *Lex*
    4. the $\vdash n\multimap np$ *Lex*
    5. footman $\vdash n$ *Lex*

The reasoning steps that lead from the lexical assumptions to the conclusion that 'Alice talks to the Footman' is indeed a datum of type s are given below. Each step of modus ponens is justified with a reference to the line which has the supporting judgements. Using Minimalist terminology, at each step of $\multimap$ elimination, the parts are 'merged' by means of the structure building operation $\circ$.

---

[4]See Morrill & Carpenter (1990) for an early assessment of the connection.

(5) 6. the ∘ footman ⊢ np   ─∘E (4, 5)
     7. to ∘ the ∘ footman ⊢ pp   ─∘E (3, 6)
     8. talks ∘ to ∘ the ∘ footman ⊢ np─∘s   ─∘E (2, 7)
     9. Alice ∘ talks ∘ to ∘ the ∘ footman ⊢ s   ─∘E (1, 8)

As desired, subcategorizational principles such as the ones mentioned above are 'encapsulated' into the deductive behaviour of a logical constant: the resource implication ─∘ expressing grammatical incompleteness. In the case of the local dependencies of (1), reasoning proceeds by modus ponens inferences. Moving on to unbounded dependencies such as (2), it turns out that the same constant ─∘ is expressive enough to establish the correlation between a relative pronoun and the absence of certain grammatical material in the relative clause body. This time, *hypothetical reasoning* for the resource implication provides the crucial inference steps.

(6) 0. whom ⊢ (np─∘s)─∘(n─∘n)   *Lex*

Lexical type assignment to the relative pronoun is given in (6). The formula expresses the fact that 'whom' will produce a relative clause (n─∘n) when combined with the relative clause body of type np─∘s. This nested implication launches a process of hypothetical reasoning: in order to establish the claim that the relative clause body is of type np─∘s, we prove that with an extra np resource (line 6′) the body would be of type s (line 9′). At the point where this subproof is completed successfully, the ─∘I inference withdraws the np hypothesis (line 10′).

(7) 6′. │ x ⊢ np   *Hyp*
     7′. │ to ∘ x ⊢ pp   ─∘E (3, 6′)
     8′. │ talks ∘ to ∘ x ⊢ np─∘s   ─∘E (2, 7′)
     9′. │ Alice ∘ talks ∘ to ∘ x ⊢ s   ─∘E (1, 8′)
    10′. Alice ∘ talks ∘ to ⊢ np─∘s   ─∘I (6′, 9′)
    11′. whom ∘ Alice ∘ talks ∘ to ⊢ n─∘n   ─∘E (0, 10′)
    12′. footman ∘ whom ∘ Alice ∘ talks ∘ to ⊢ n   ─∘E (5, 11′)
    13′. the ∘ footman ∘ whom ∘ Alice ∘ talks ∘ to ⊢ np   ─∘E (4, 12′)

COMPOSITION: THE MEANING DIMENSION. So far, we have limited our attention to the 'form' aspect of grammatical composition — to the way in which Introduction and Elimination of the ─∘ connective interacts with the structure-building operation ∘. But as announced at the beginning of this paper, the deductive perspective extends to the composition of grammatical 'meaning'.[5] In (8) we present the inference rules for $\multimap$ with a semantic annotation. The basic declarative units now are pairs $x : A$, where A is a formula and x a term of the simply typed lambda calculus — the representation language we use for grammatical meanings. Each inference rule is associated with an operation providing term decoration for the conclusion, given term decorations to the premises: function application, in the case of $\multimap E$, and function abstraction for $\multimap I$. Given a configuration Γ of assumptions $x_i : A_i$, the *process* of proving $\Gamma \vdash t : B$ produces a program t that specifies how to compute the meaning of the result B out of the input parameters x_i. This essentially *dynamic* (or: 'derivational', 'proof-theoretic') perspective on meaning composition is known as the Curry-Howard interpretation of proofs.

$$(8) \quad \frac{\Gamma \vdash u : A \quad \Delta \vdash t : A \multimap B}{\Gamma \circ \Delta \vdash tu : B} \ (\multimap E) \qquad \frac{x : A \circ \Gamma \vdash t : B}{\Gamma \vdash \lambda x.t : A \multimap B} \ (\multimap I)$$

As an illustration, (9) gives the proofterms for some crucial stages in our earlier derivations. (We use boldface word forms as stand-ins for the unanalysed meanings of the lexical resources.) Line 9 is a pure application term, built up in the four $\multimap E$ steps of (5). Line 10' gives the proofterm for the relative clause body of (7), with abstraction over a variable x of type np as the correlate of the withdrawal of a hypothetical assumption in the $\multimap I$ step. Line 13', then, is the derivational meaning for the full noun phrase 'the footman whom Alice talks to'.

(9) 9. ((**talk** (**to** (**the footman**))) **Alice**)

     10'. $\lambda x.$((**talk** (**to** x)) **Alice**)

     13'. (**the** ((**whom** $\lambda x.$((**talk** (**to** x)) **Alice**)) **footman**))

With respect to the 'syntax-semantics' interface, the grammatical organization proposed here can be situated within the general setting of Montague's Universal Grammar programme. But it improves on Montague's own ('rule-to-rule') execution of this programme, in that we can directly exploit the built-in economy constraints of the grammatical resource logic. We sum up some salient consequences.

- PROOFS AS MEANING PROGRAMS. The composition of form and meaning proceeds in parallel in an 'inference-driven' (rather than

---

[5]The proof-theoretical view on semantics was put on the categorial agenda by Van Benthem in the early Eighties — see his van Benthem (1991,1995) for discussion. The use of resource-sensitive notions of meaning composition has become an important theme within the framework of LFG recently. See Dalrymple (1999) for a representative collection. But LFG 'syntax' is still put together by extra-logical means. We reject this dualism and advocate the stronger position that both grammatical form *and* meaning are put together in a process of resource-sensitive deduction.

'rule-driven') fashion. There is no *structural* representation level of the grammatical resources (such as 'Logical Form') where meaning is read off. Instead, meaning is computed from the derivational process that puts the resources together.

- MEANING PARAMETRICITY.[6] The actual meanings of the resources that enter into the composition process are 'black boxes' for the Curry-Howard computation. No assumptions about the content of the actual meanings can be built into the meaning assembly process.

- RESOURCE SENSITIVITY. Because the grammar logic has a resource-sensitive notion of inference (each assumption is used exactly once), there is no need for 'syntactic' book-keeping stipulations restricting variable occurrences: vacuous abstractions, closed subterms, multiple binding of variables, or unbound variables (other than the proof parameters) simply do not arise.

LEXICAL VERSUS DERIVATIONAL MEANING. The resource constraints impose severe limits on 'derivational' expressivity. The only way a grammar can overcome these limitations is by means of *lexical* instructions for meaning assembly — the lexicon being the 'non-logical' part of the architecture. Consider the single-bind property of the λ abstractor — a consequence of resource-sensitivity. For the relative clause example of (7), we would like to associate the relative pronoun with an instruction to compute a property intersection semantics: intersection of the property obtained by abstracting over a np variable in the relative clause body, and the n property of the common noun which the relative clause combines with. Expressed as a lambda term, this means double binding of an entity type variable: $\lambda x.(\text{RELBODY } x) \wedge (\text{COMMONNOUN } x)$, a term which the derivational system cannot compute. However, we can 'push' the double bind term into the lexical semantics associated with 'whom', as shown in (10a).[7] Substituting the lexical program into the derivational proofterm for (9, line 13'), one obtains (10b) after simplification.

(10) a. whom : $(np{-}\!\circ s){-}\!\circ(n{-}\!\circ n) - \lambda x_1 \lambda x_2 \lambda x_3.(x_1 x_3) \wedge (x_2 x_3)$
      b. **the** $(\lambda x.((\textbf{talk } (\textbf{to } x)) \textbf{ Alice}) \wedge (\textbf{footman } x))$

11.1.2 Grammatical reasoning: logic, structure and control

In the preceding section we have ignored all structural aspects of grammatical composition. This was a deliberate move: we wanted to isolate

---

[6]The term is from Dalrymple e.a. (1999).

[7]The format for lexical entries is WORD FORM: TYPE FORMULA - LEXICAL RECIPE.

the 'resource multiplicity' factor underlying both local and non-local dependencies in pure laboratory conditions, so to speak. As things stand, the $\circ$ operation of linear logic is insensitive to linear order (it does not discriminate between $\Delta_1 \circ \Delta_2$ and $\Delta_2 \circ \Delta_1$), and to hierarchical grouping (the structures $\Delta_1 \circ (\Delta_2 \circ \Delta_3)$ and $(\Delta_1 \circ \Delta_2) \circ \Delta_3$ count as the same). Technically, the structural rules of Commutativity and Associativity are still built-in components of the multiplicative operators of linear logic. Obviously, such a notion of composition is too crude, if we want to take grammatically relevant aspects of linguistic *form* into account.

We refine the tools for grammatical analysis by pushing the strategy of separating 'logic' and 'structure' to its natural conclusion: we drop Associativity and Commutativity as hard-wired components of the grammatical constants, obtaining the truly 'minimal' logic of composition; then we bring these structural options back under explicit logical control. Dropping Associativity, the 'constituent structure' configuration of the resources becomes relevant for grammaticality judgements. Let f and g be resources with types $A{\multimap}B$ and $B{\multimap}C$ respectively. In an associative regime, f and g can be put together, and $f \circ g$ yields a conclusion of type $A{\multimap}C$, with the derivational meaning of function composition $\lambda x.g(fx)$. In a non-associative setting, this inference no longer goes through: the hypothetical A assumption and the implication $A{\multimap}B$ that would have to consume it, are not within the same constituency domain. Dropping also Commutativity, the resource implication $A{\multimap}B$ splits up into a left-handed $A\backslash B$ and a right-handed B/A, implications that insist on following or preceding the A resource they are consuming.

THE BASE LOGIC: RESIDUATION. We are in a position now to introduce the minimal logic of grammatical composition. For an easy presentation format, it is handy to introduce in the formula language a connective $\bullet$, corresponding to the structure building operation $\circ$: whereas $\circ$ puts together *structures* Γ and Δ into the composition structure $\Gamma \circ \Delta$, the $\bullet$ connective puts together *formulas* A and B into the product formula $A \bullet B$. With the explicit product connective, we can express deducibility judgements as statement of the form $A \vdash B$, where A is the $\bullet$ formula-equivalent of the $\circ$ structure Γ in our earlier formulation $\Gamma \vdash B$. The essential deductive principles of the base logic, then, are given by the so-called RESIDUATION laws of Fig 1, which establish the correlation between grammatical incompleteness (as expressed by / and \) and composition ($\bullet$). Together with reflexivity ($A \vdash A$) and transitivity of the derivability relation (from $A \vdash B$ and $B \vdash C$, conclude $A \vdash C$) the residuation laws fully characterize the valid inferences of the base logic.[8]

$$A \vdash C/B \quad \Leftrightarrow \quad A \bullet B \vdash C \quad \Leftrightarrow \quad B \vdash A\backslash C$$

FIGURE 1 The base logic: residuation

Some familiar theorems and derived inference rules of the base logic are given below. It is important to keep in mind that these are 'universal' principles of grammatical composition, in the sense that they hold no matter what the structural properties of the composition relation may be. There is no option for cross-linguistic variation with respect to the principles in (11), in other words. But languages can vary with respect to a principle such as $(A\backslash B) \bullet (B\backslash C) \vdash A\backslash C$, which is not available in the base logic, but dependent on associativity assumptions, as we saw above.

(11) a. Application: $(A/B) \bullet B \vdash A$, $B \bullet (B\backslash A) \vdash A$

    b. Lifting: $A \vdash B/(A\backslash B)$, $A \vdash (B/A)\backslash B$

    c. Monotonicity: $A \vdash B$ and $C \vdash D$ implies $\begin{cases} A/D \vdash B/C \\ A \bullet C \vdash B \bullet D \\ D\backslash A \vdash C\backslash B \end{cases}$

STRUCTURE AND CONTROL. Suppose now that from this base logic, we want to recover the expressivity of the linear logic multiplicatives. A straightforward, but crude way of achieving this would be to simply add the postulates of Commutativity and Associativity.

(12) $A \bullet B \vdash B \bullet A$

    $(A \bullet B) \bullet C \dashv\vdash A \bullet (B \bullet C)$

But what we said above about unrestricted use of waste and duplication of assumptions (Weakening, Contraction) applies to structural resource management as well: instead of global hard-wired settings, we

---

[8]There is a precise technical sense in which we are dealing with the truly 'minimal' logic here. The models for the base logic are specified with respect to *frames* $\langle W, R \rangle$ (as for modal logic), where W is a set of grammatical resources, structured by the composition relation R ('Merge'). Formulas are interpreted as subsets of W. The constant $\bullet$ has the following interpretation: $x \in \|A \bullet B\|$ iff there exist grammatical parts y, z such that $y \in \|A\|, z \in \|B\|$ and $Rxyz$. (The implications $/$ and $\backslash$ are interpreted as the residuation duals.) The basic completeness result then says that $A \vdash B$ is provable iff, for every valuation on every frame, we have $\|A\| \subseteq \|B\|$. The laws of the base logic, in other words, do not impose any restrictions on the interpretation of the composition relation. But the addition of *structural postulates* does indeed restrict the interpretation of R to meet certain structural conditions. The 'modal' perspective on grammatical logics is worked out in depth in Kurtonina (1995).

need lexical *control* over resource management. Consider the Commutativity option. Example (13) gives some alternative ways of rendering a well-known Latin phrase. Although Latin has much greater flexibility with respect to linear order than, say, Dutch or English, it would be wrong to assume that Latin composition obeys a globally commutative regime: as the (c) example shows, a preposition like 'cum' has to precede its nominal complement. The challenge here is to reconcile the structural freedom of, for example, adjectival modifiers, with the rigid order requirements of prepositions.

(13) a. cum magna laude

    b. cum laude magna

    c. magna cum laude

    d.*magna laude cum

Associativity, i.e. flexibility of constituency, has often been called upon to derive instances of 'non-constituent' coordination, such as the Right Node Raising case below. Yet, as the contrast between (14b) and (14c) shows, a global regime allowing restructuring, such as implemented by a structural postulate of Associativity, overgenerates: an associative regime would judge both the transitive verb 'love' and the non-constituent cluster 'thinks Mary loves' to be resources of type $(np\backslash s)/np$, and hence indistinguishable as arguments of 'himself', which as a relation reducer could be typed as $((np\backslash s)/np)\backslash(np\backslash s)$. In this case, one would like to lexically control structural relaxation in such a way that it is only licensed in the presence of the coordination particles.

(14) a. the Lobster loves but the Gryphon hates Turtle Soup
             s/np s/np

    b. the Mad Hatter   loves   himself
                   $(np\backslash s)/np$

    c.*the Mad Hatter thinks Alice loves himself
                   $(np\backslash s)/np$

In order to gain logical control over the structural aspects of grammatical resource management, we now extend the formula language of the grammar logic with a pair of constants, $\Diamond$ and $\Box$ — we refer to them as 'control features'. These constants will play a role analogous to the linear logic modalities governing resource multiplicity. We dissect $\Diamond$ and $\Box$ in their 'logical' and their 'structural' parts, as we did with the binary connectives. As for the logical part, the relation between $\Diamond$ and $\Box$ is the same as that between product and slash: they are residuation duals. In algebraic terms, we have the biconditional law of Fig 2.

$$\Diamond A \vdash B \quad \Leftrightarrow \quad A \vdash \Box B$$

FIGURE 2 Residuation: unary connectives

Section 11.2 below is devoted to an illustration of the linguistic use of the control features. It will be useful here to prepare the ground and present some crucial inferential patterns. Notice that the base logic allows neither $\Box A \vdash A$ nor $A \vdash \Diamond A$. Instead, the basic cancellation law is $\Diamond \Box A \vdash A$, with the dual pattern $A \vdash \Box \Diamond A$, as the reader can check in (15).[9]

(15)   from $\Box A \vdash \Box A$ (Axiom), conclude $\Diamond \Box A \vdash A$ (Res $\Leftarrow$)

from $\Diamond A \vdash \Diamond A$ (Axiom), conclude $A \vdash \Box \Diamond A$ (Res $\Rightarrow$)

As with the binary composition operations, the fixed logical core of $\Diamond, \Box$ can be complemented by variable *structural* extensions. As an illustration, (16) presents modally restricted versions of structural postulates that, in the global form of (12), would destroy structural discrimination with respect to linear order or constituency, as we have seen above. Reordering or restructuring, in (16), has to be explicitly *licensed* by the presence of a $\Diamond$ decorated formula. In §11.2 we will see that this modal marking can be 'projected' from lexical type assignment, the way the structure building operation $\circ$ is driven by the $/, \backslash$ implications in the typing of lexical resources.[10]

(16) $A \bullet \Diamond B \vdash \Diamond B \bullet A$

$(A \bullet B) \bullet \Diamond C \dashv\vdash A \bullet (B \bullet \Diamond C)$

To close this section we present the Natural Deduction format for the grammar logic — our display format for grammatical analysis in §11.2. A proof proceeds from axioms $x : A \vdash x : A$, where A is a formula, and

---

[9]The logic of grammar, in other words, is not a modal logic with principle **T**. Rather, the $\Diamond, \Box$ modalities are related like the inverse duals of *temporal* logic ('will be the case', 'has always been the case'): $x \in \|\Diamond A\|$ iff there exists y such that Rxy and $y \in \|A\|$ versus $x \in \|\Box A\|$ iff for all y, Ryx implies $y \in \|A\|$. Here R is a binary relation interpreting the unary $\Diamond, \Box$, cf. the ternary composition relation interpreting $\bullet$ and its residuals. The initial exploration of modalities in categorial grammar (see Barry & Morrill (1990)) was modeled after the Linear Logic exponential '!', for which the dereliction law $!A \vdash A$ holds. Kurtonina & Moortgat (1997) argues that the dereliction principle is undesirable in the linguistic setting.

[10]The control features, as they are used here, have the status of 'resources' that have to be explicitly checked in the course of a derivation via the cancellation laws of (15, and that can explicitly license structural reasoning via modalized postulates. In this respect, $\Diamond, \Box$ resemble the 'formal features' of minimalist grammars more than the features in unification-based grammar formalisms. Deductive modeling of 'minimalist' views on structural reasoning in terms of $\Diamond, \Box$ is worked out in Vermaat (1999).

x a variable of that type for the construction of the Curry-Howard proof term. Rules of inference for the binary vocabulary are given in Fig 3. We distinguish the two resource implications, and add the inference rules for the • connective. In the absence of Commutativity/Associativity, the structure building operation ∘ now configures the resources as a *tree* (bracketed string). Notice that / and \ introduce refinement in the *form* dimension: with respect to the Curry-Howard derivational meaning, they are both interpreted in terms of function application and abstraction. Term decoration for the • connective associates introduction of this connective with pairing $\langle \cdot, \cdot \rangle$, and elimination with (left $(\cdot)_0$ and right $(\cdot)_1$) projection.

$$[/I]\frac{\Gamma \circ x : B \vdash t : A}{\Gamma \vdash \lambda x.t : A/B} \qquad \frac{\Gamma \vdash t : A/B \quad \Delta \vdash u : B}{\Gamma \circ \Delta \vdash (t\ u) : A}[/E]$$

$$[\backslash I]\frac{x : B \circ \Gamma \vdash t : A}{\Gamma \vdash \lambda x.t : B \backslash A} \qquad \frac{\Gamma \vdash u : B \quad \Delta \vdash t : B \backslash A}{\Gamma \circ \Delta \vdash (t\ u) : A}[\backslash E]$$

$$[\bullet I]\frac{\Gamma \vdash t : A \quad \Delta \vdash u : B}{\Gamma \circ \Delta \vdash \langle t, u \rangle : A \bullet B} \quad \frac{\Delta \vdash u : A \bullet B \quad \Gamma[x : A \circ y : B] \vdash t : C}{\Gamma[\Delta] \vdash t[(u)_0/x, (u)_1/y] : C}[\bullet E]$$

FIGURE 3 Grammatical composition: $/, \bullet, \backslash$

In the natural deduction format, the residuation laws for ◇ and □ turn up as the Introduction and Elimination rules of Fig 4. We use $\langle \cdot \rangle$ as the structure building operation corresponding to the logical constant ◇. In the term language for derivational semantics, we have constructors (the 'cap' operators $\cap, \wedge$) and destructors (the 'cup' operators $\cup, \vee$) for the Introduction and Elimination inferences of ◇ and □ respectively.

$$\frac{\Gamma \vdash t : \Box A}{\langle \Gamma \rangle \vdash {}^\vee t : A} \ (\Box E) \qquad \frac{\langle \Gamma \rangle \vdash t : A}{\Gamma \vdash {}^\wedge t : \Box A} \ (\Box I)$$

$$\frac{\Gamma \vdash t : A}{\langle \Gamma \rangle \vdash {}^\cap t : \Diamond A} \ (\Diamond I) \qquad \frac{\Delta \vdash u : \Diamond A \quad \Gamma[\langle x : A \rangle] \vdash t : B}{\Gamma[\Delta] \vdash t[{}^\cup u/x] : B} \ (\Diamond E)$$

FIGURE 4 Control features

Figures 3 and 4 cover the grammatical base logic. The translation between structural postulates, in the algebraic presentation, and structural rules for the N.D. format is straightforward. A postulate $A \vdash B$ corresponds to a rule of inference licensing replacement of a substructure Δ' in the premise by Δ in the conclusion, where Δ and Δ' are the structure equivalents of the (product) formulas A and B respectively.[11]

(17) $A \vdash B$ (postulate) $\rightsquigarrow$ $\dfrac{\Gamma[\Delta'] \vdash C}{\Gamma[\Delta] \vdash C}$ (N.D. rule)

11.2   Patterns for structural variation

The components of the grammatical architecture proposed in the previous section are summarized below.

Logic. The core logical notions of grammatical composition ('Merge') are characterized in terms of universal laws, independent of the structural properties of the composition relation. The operations of the base logic (introduction/elimination of the grammatical constants) provide the interface to a derivational theory of meaning via the Curry-Howard interpretation of proofs.

Structure. Packages of resource-management postulates function as 'plug-in' modules with respect to the base logic. They offer a logical perspective on structural variation, within languages and cross-linguistically.

Control. A vocabulary of control operators provides explicit means to fine-tune grammatical resource management, by imposing structural constraints or by licensing structural relaxation.

To illustrate the interplay of these three components we return to *wh* dependencies in relativization. In §11.1.1, we concentrated on the 'multiplicity' aspect of these dependencies, and abstracted from structural factors. In the following sections, we look for significant patterns for structural variation. As a case study, we contrast relativization in English and Dutch. The interplay of precedence (linear order) and dominance (constituency) constraints in these two languages is the focus of §11.2.1 and §11.2.2. In §11.2.3, we make a brief remark on the role of dependency asymmetries (head-complement versus specifier-head) in the grammar of *wh* extraction. With respect to these different dimensions, the strategy for uncovering the fine-structure of grammatical resource management will be to make a *minimal* use of structural postulates, thus exploiting the inferential capacity of the base logic to the full.

---

[11] This back-and-forth translation between structures and formulas works on the assumption that we write postulates purely in terms of the connectives $\diamondsuit$ and $\bullet$ (and formula variables), as indeed we will.

11.2.1 English relativization: right branch extraction

Consider the English case first. As remarked above, binding of the subject of the relative clause body is structurally free: the examples in (19) are derivable in the base logic from the lexical assignments shown in (18) for relative pronouns 'who', 'that'. (As (19c) indicates, this type assignment is not appropriate for 'whom'.) A derivation for (19a) is shown in (5).[12]

(18)   who, that : $(n\backslash n)/(np\backslash s) - \lambda x\lambda y\lambda z.(x\ z) \wedge (y\ z)$

(19) a. (the song) that irritated the Gryphon

  b. (the girl) who irritated the Duchess

  c. (the girl) *whom irritated the Duchess

$$
\cfrac{
\begin{array}{c}
\text{that} \vdash (n\backslash n)/(np\backslash s)
\end{array}
\quad
\cfrac{
[x_1 \vdash np]^1
\quad
\cfrac{
\cfrac{
\text{irritated} \vdash (np\backslash s)/np
\quad
\cfrac{
\text{the} \vdash np/n \quad \text{gryphon} \vdash n
}{\text{the gryphon} \vdash np} {\scriptstyle [/E]}
}{\text{irritated (the gryphon)} \vdash np\backslash s} {\scriptstyle [/E]}
}{
\cfrac{
\cfrac{x_1 \text{ (irritated (the gryphon))} \vdash s}{\text{irritated (the gryphon)} \vdash np\backslash s} {\scriptstyle [\backslash I]^1}
}{}
} {\scriptstyle [\backslash E]}
}{\text{irritated (the gryphon)} \vdash np\backslash s} {\scriptstyle [\backslash I]^1}
}{\text{that (irritated (the gryphon))} \vdash n\backslash n} {\scriptstyle [/E]}
$$

FIGURE 5 'that irritated the Gryphon'

Consider now non-subject cases of relativization, such as the binding of the direct object role in 'the book that Dodgson wrote'. We have seen above that implication introduction in the base logic is restricted to the immediate (left or right) daughter of the structural configuration from which the hypothetical resource is withdrawn: the subject is thus accessible in Fig 5,[13] but the direct object, as a daughter of the verb phrase, cannot be reached with a non-subject extraction assignment as given in (20). Under what *structural* assumptions can we make the appropriate set of non-subject positions accessible for relativization?

(20)   that, whom : $(n\backslash n)/(s/np) - \lambda x\lambda y\lambda z.x(z) \wedge y(z)$

(21) $(A \bullet B) \bullet C \vdash A \bullet (B \bullet C)$ $A1$

---

[12] In the derivations, we drop ∘ from the antecedent structure terms, writing $A \circ B$ as $A\ B$. Grouping is indicated by minimal bracketing, dropping outermost brackets.

[13] In using the N.D. format of Figures 3 and 4, we stick to the handy 'sugared' presentation of §11.1.1: we omit the formula part on the left of ⊢, and use the word forms of the lexical assumptions as the term 'variables'.

$$
\cfrac{
\cfrac{
\cfrac{
\cfrac{
\cfrac{
D \vdash np \qquad \cfrac{wrote \vdash (np \backslash s)/np \quad [x_1 \vdash np]^1}{wrote\ x_1 \vdash np \backslash s}\ [/E]
}{D\ (wrote\ x_1) \vdash s}\ [\backslash E]
}{(D\ wrote)\ x_1 \vdash s}\ [A1]
}{D\ wrote \vdash s/np}\ [/I]^1
}{
that \vdash (n \backslash n)/(s/np) \qquad D\ wrote \vdash s/np
}\ [/E]
$$

$$
\cfrac{
\cfrac{
the \vdash np/n \qquad
\cfrac{
book \vdash n \qquad that\ (D\ wrote) \vdash n \backslash n
}{book\ (that\ (D\ wrote)) \vdash n}\ [\backslash E]
}{that\ (D\ wrote) \vdash n \backslash n}
}{the\ (book\ (that\ (D\ wrote))) \vdash np}\ [/E]
$$

FIGURE 6 'the book that Dodgson wrote'

Fig 6 shows that the associativity postulate $A1$ realizes a restructuring that does make the direct object accessible. But does this postulate express the proper structural generalization? The answer must be negative — both on grounds of overgeneration and of undergeneration. As to the latter: $A1$ (in combination with the type assignment in (20)) makes accessible only *right-peripheral* positions in the relative clause body. A relative clause such as 'the book that Dodgson dedicated to Alice Liddell', for example, would still be underivable. As to overgeneration, we have seen in our discussion of (14) that global availability of restructuring destroys constituent information that may be grammatically relevant.

The control operators provide the logical vocabulary to implement a more delicate resource management regime. In (22), the type assignment to non-subject relative pronouns is refined by adding a modal decoration $\Diamond \Box$ to the hypothetical np subtype. The postulate package of Fig 7, keyed to the $\Diamond$ modality, then licenses structural access to non-subject positions. As this section proceeds, we will gradually accumulate motivation for the specific formulation of $P1$ and $P2$. Let it suffice for now to remark that we have not introduced any *global* loss of structure-sensitivity (as an Associativity postulate for • would do); instead, we have narrowed down the structurally 'special' behavior to the 'gap' resource. Moreover, the postulates of Fig 7 do not license access to *arbitrary* positions within the relative clause body: they only allow $\Diamond$ marked resources to communicate recursively with *right* branches of • structures.[14]

---

[14]With the postulates of (16), arbitrary positions would indeed be accessible, making $rel/(s/\Diamond \Box np)$ and $rel/(\Diamond \Box np \backslash s)$ indistinguishable. This indeed was the effect of a permutation modality grafted on the linear logic '!' exponential, as explored in Morrill e.a. (1990) and others. In the text we pursue a more discriminating alternative, exploiting the left/right asymmetry.

(22)   that, whom : $(n\backslash n)/(s/\Diamond\Box np)$ – for semantics, cf. (24b)

$$(A \bullet B) \bullet \Diamond C \vdash (A \bullet \Diamond C) \bullet B \quad P1$$
$$(A \bullet B) \bullet \Diamond C \vdash A \bullet (B \bullet \Diamond C) \quad P2$$

FIGURE 7 Right branch extraction

A derivation for the relative clause '(the book) that Dodgson dedicated to Liddell' is presented in Fig 8. Notice carefully how the structural control inferences interact with the purely logical steps.

- At a certain point in the derivation, the hypothetical $\Diamond\Box np$ resource will have to play the structural role of a simple (non-modalized) np, as a result of the reduction law $\Diamond\Box np \vdash np$. In the example of Fig 8, the np is consumed in the direct object position.
- As long as this reduction has not applied, i.e. as long as the modal prefix $\Diamond\Box$ is intact, the leading $\Diamond$ licenses structural inferences $P1$ and $P2$. These inferences establish the communication between the clause peripheral position, where $\Diamond\Box np$ can be withdrawn in the / Introduction step, and the structural position where np is actually consumed.

$$\dfrac{\begin{array}{c} \dfrac{[x_2 \vdash \Box np]^2}{\langle x_2\rangle \vdash np}\,[\Box E] \end{array}}{}$$

dedicated $\vdash ((np\backslash s)/pp)/np \qquad \langle x_2\rangle \vdash np$

$\dfrac{\text{dedicated } \langle x_2\rangle \vdash (np\backslash s)/pp}{}\,[/E] \qquad \dfrac{\text{to} \vdash pp/np \quad L \vdash np}{\text{to L} \vdash pp}\,[/E]$

$D \vdash np \qquad \dfrac{\text{(dedicated } \langle x_2\rangle)\text{ (to L)} \vdash np\backslash s}{}\,[\backslash E]$

$\dfrac{D \,((\text{dedicated } \langle x_2\rangle)\text{ (to L)}) \vdash s}{}$

$\dfrac{D \,((\text{dedicated (to L)}))\,\langle x_2\rangle) \vdash s}{}\,[P1]$

$$\vdots$$

$$\vdots$$

$\dfrac{}{}\,[P2]$

$[x_1 \vdash \Diamond\Box np]^1 \quad \text{(D (dedicated (to L)))} \langle x_2\rangle \vdash s$

$\dfrac{\text{(D (dedicated (to L)))} x_1 \vdash s}{}\,[\Diamond E]^2$

that $\vdash (n\backslash n)/(s/\Diamond\Box np) \qquad \dfrac{\text{D (dedicated (to L))} \vdash s/\Diamond\Box np}{}\,[/I]^1$

$\dfrac{\text{that (D (dedicated (to L)))} \vdash n\backslash n}{}\,[/E]$

FIGURE 8 'that Dodgson dedicated to Liddell'

The lexical semantics presented above for the non-modalized relative pronouns has to be refined to take the added structure-sensitivity into account. Consider what happens at the end of the conditional subproof for the relative clause body: the $/I$ rule withdraws a $\Diamond\Box np$ hypothetical resource, semantically binding a variable of that type (x_1). But in order to supply the appropriate type for the direct object np argument of 'dedicated' in the body of the relative clause, the $\Diamond$ and $\Box$ Elimination inferences have to 'lower' x_1 to $^{\vee\cup}x_1$.

(23) $[/I]$ $\lambda x_1.(((\textbf{dedicated }^{\vee\cup}x_1)\ (\textbf{to Liddell}))\ \textbf{Dodgson})$

Now compare the 'property intersection' lexical semantics for the non-modalized relative pronouns in (24a) with the refined meaning recipe for the modalized assignment in (24b). In the modal case, the operations $^{\cap\wedge}$ lift the entity-type variable z to the appropriate level to serve as an argument to the x variable, for the relative clause body which is now of type $s/\Diamond\Box np$.

(24)   a. $(n\backslash n)/(np\backslash s) - \lambda x\lambda y\lambda z.(x\ z)\wedge(y\ z)$
       b. $(n\backslash n)/(s/\Diamond\Box np) - \lambda x\lambda y\lambda z.(x\ ^{\cap\wedge}z)\wedge(y\ z)$

The derivational meaning for the complete relative clause 'that Dodgson dedicated to Liddell' is given in (25). Substitution of the lexical semantics (24b) for 'that' leads to a term that can be simplified ('cup-cap' cancellation, twice: $^{\vee\cup\cap\wedge}x_1 = x_1$), which ultimately produces the desired property intersection semantics, when combined with a common noun meaning for the abstraction over y.

(25) $\textbf{that }(\lambda x_1.(((\textbf{dedicated }^{\vee\cup}x_1)\ (\textbf{to L}))\ \textbf{D}))$
         $[\lambda x\lambda y\lambda z.(x\ ^{\cap\wedge}z)\wedge(y\ z)]\ (\lambda x_1.(((\textbf{dedicated }^{\vee\cup}x_1)\ (\textbf{to L}))\ \textbf{D}))\rightsquigarrow$
         $\lambda y.(\lambda z.((((\textbf{dedicated }z)\ (\textbf{to L}))\ \textbf{D})\wedge(y\ z)))$

11.2.2   Dutch relativization: left branch extraction

The observant reader will have noticed that the postulate package of Fig 7 is sensitive to the branching configuration of the structure it interacts with: $\Diamond$ marked material is accessible on right branches, but not on left branches. This choice limits the structural positions which the modalized relative pronoun type $(n\backslash n)/(s/\Diamond\Box np)$ can establish communication with. Some empirical consequences are illustrated below. Prepositions (pp/np) in English can be stranded as in (26a); (embedded[15]) subjects are inaccessible, leading to the so-called 'that-trace' effect of (26b); but the 'that-trace' violation can be avoided as in (26d) via a (complementizer-less) type assignment to 'think' which makes the 'embedded' subject a direct argument of the higher predicate, and realizes

---

[15]Remember we have the type assignment $(n\backslash n)/(np\backslash s)$ for relativization of the main subject of the relative clause body.

the required semantic composition via the associated lexical meaning recipe of (26e).[16]

(26) a. the girl whom Carroll dedicated his book to
      b.*the footman whom Alice thinks that stole the tarts
      c. thinks: $(np\backslash s)/cs$, that: cs/s
      d. the footman whom Alice thinks stole the tarts
      e. thinks: $((np\backslash s)/(np\backslash s))/np - \lambda x\lambda y\lambda z.((\mathbf{think}\ (y\ x))\ z)$

For an SVO language like English, where heads select their complements to the right, the right-branch extraction package of Fig 7 has pleasant consequences. The distinct type-assignment to subject and non-subject cases of relativization correlates with the morphological *who/whom* alternatives. But what about an SOV language, where complement selection is (predominantly) to the left? Considerations of symmetry would suggest the mirror-image left-branch extraction package of Fig 9 here, together with type assignment to the relative pronouns launching the hypothetical 'gap' resource at the *left* periphery of the relative clause body.

(27)   die, dat : $(n\backslash n)/(\Diamond\Box np\backslash s)$

$$\Diamond A \bullet (B \bullet C) \vdash B \bullet (\Diamond A \bullet C)\quad P1'$$
$$\Diamond A \bullet (B \bullet C) \vdash (\Diamond A \bullet B) \bullet C\quad P2'$$

FIGURE 9 Left branch extraction

Let us contrast the empirical consequences of the type assignment (22) and the structural package in Fig 9 with what we found above for Fig 7 and the relative pronoun type-assignments for English. First of all, the asymmetry between subject and non-subject relativization (which in English gives rise to the 'that-trace' effect) disappears with the left-branch extraction package. As the reader can check, the subject-extraction case of (18) which was posited as a separate type-assignment in English, is *derivable* from (22). As a matter of fact, the type transition of (28) is valid already in the base logic — it does not depend on structural assumptions.

(28) $(n\backslash n)/(\Diamond\Box np\backslash s) \vdash (n\backslash n)/(np\backslash s)$

As a result of (28), a Dutch relative clause like (29a) has two possible derivations, paraphrased in (29b) and (29d). The derivation of Fig 10 is obtained by simply reducing the $\Diamond\Box$ prefix, without accessing the structural package. It produces the proofterm (29c) where the relative

---

[16]This is essentially the analysis of Gazdar (1981).

pronoun binds the subject argument of 'vindt'. Communication between the relative pronoun and the direct object position is obtained by means of a $\Diamond$ licensed structural inference $P1'$. See Fig 11 with proofterm (29e).

(29) a. (de lakei) die Alice gek vindt

   b. (the footman) who considers Alice mad

   c. (**who** $\lambda x_0.(((\textbf{considers mad}) \textbf{ Alice}) x_0))$

   d. (the footman) who(m) Alice considers mad

   e. (**who** $\lambda x_0.(((\textbf{considers mad}) x_0) \textbf{ Alice}))$

$$
\cfrac{[x_0 \vdash \Diamond\Box np]^1 \quad \cfrac{\cfrac{[x_1 \vdash \Box np]^2}{\langle x_1 \rangle \vdash np}[\Box E] \quad \cfrac{A \vdash np \quad \cfrac{gek \vdash ap \quad vindt \vdash ap\backslash(np\backslash(np\backslash s))}{gek\ vindt \vdash np\backslash(np\backslash s)}[\backslash E]}{A\ (gek\ vindt) \vdash np\backslash s}[\backslash E]}{\langle x_1 \rangle\ (A\ (gek\ vindt)) \vdash s}[\backslash E]}{x_0\ (A\ (gek\ vindt)) \vdash s}[\Diamond E]^2
$$

$$
\vdots
$$

$$
\cfrac{die \vdash (n\backslash n)/(\Diamond\Box np\backslash s) \quad \cfrac{}{A\ (gek\ vindt) \vdash \Diamond\Box np\backslash s}[\backslash I]^1}{die\ (A\ (gek\ vindt)) \vdash n\backslash n}[/E]
$$

FIGURE 10 'die Alice gek vindt': subject reading

$$
\cfrac{[x_0 \vdash \Diamond\Box np]^1 \quad \cfrac{\cfrac{A \vdash np \quad \cfrac{\cfrac{[x_1 \vdash \Box np]^2}{\langle x_1 \rangle \vdash np}[\Box E] \quad \cfrac{gek \vdash ap \quad vindt \vdash ap\backslash(np\backslash(np\backslash s))}{gek\ vindt \vdash np\backslash(np\backslash s)}[\backslash E]}{\langle x_1 \rangle\ (gek\ vindt) \vdash np\backslash s}[\backslash E]}{A\ (\langle x_1 \rangle\ (gek\ vindt)) \vdash s}[\backslash E]}{\langle x_1 \rangle (A\ (gek\ vindt)) \vdash s}[P1']}{x_0\ (A\ (gek\ vindt)) \vdash s}[\Diamond E]^2
$$

$$
\vdots
$$

$$
\cfrac{die \vdash (n\backslash n)/(\Diamond\Box np\backslash s) \quad \cfrac{}{A\ (gek\ vindt) \vdash \Diamond\Box np\backslash s}[\backslash I]^1}{die\ (A\ (gek\ vindt)) \vdash n\backslash n}[/E]
$$

FIGURE 11 'die Alice gek vindt': direct object reading

Secondly, whereas Dutch verbal heads select to the left, prepositional phrases are head-initial. Prepositional complements, in other words, are inaccessible for the left-branch extraction structural package of Fig 9. And indeed, we do not find stranded prepositions with the regular relative pronouns, witness the ungrammaticality of (30a) as compared to the English counterpart (30b).

(30) a.*(de uitkomst) die de Koningin op rekent

b. (the outcome) which the Queen counts on

c.*op het *versus* er op

d. er : $pp/(pp/np) - \lambda z.(z$ **it**$)$

As we have seen before, given the grammatical architecture proposed here, the only way to overcome the expressive limitations of the derivational system for a language is to use *lexical* resources. For the relativization of prepositional complements, the Dutch relative pronoun 'waar' provides such a lexical device. Dutch has a class of (neuter) personal pronouns, the so-called R-pronouns 'er', 'daar', for which the canonical structural position is to the *left* of the preposition they depend on semantically: see the contrast in (30c). The reader will have understood by now that the grammar doesn't have to rely on structural inferences to realize the required form/meaning composition: the lexical type assignment and meaning recipe of (30d) will do the job in the base logic.

Suppose now we treat 'waar' as a relativizer with respect to an R personal pronoun. Given the type assignment of (31a) (where we use *rpro* as an abbreviation for $pp/(pp/np)$), the relative pronoun 'waar' can establish communication with the left branch home position of an R pronoun by means of the structural inferences of the Dutch extraction package in Fig 9, as the derivation in Fig 12 shows. The derivational meaning for the relative clause body is given in (31b), with an abstraction over a variable x_0 of type $\Diamond\Box rpro$. After the application of the lexical program for 'waar' to (31b), we obtain the property intersection semantics of (31c) for the complete relative clause, with the required binding of the prepositional object.

(31) a. waar : $(n\backslash n)/(\Diamond\Box rpro\backslash s) -$
$\lambda x.(\lambda y.(\lambda z.((x \ ^{\cap\wedge}(\lambda w.(w \ z))) \wedge (y \ z))))$

b. $\Diamond\Box rpro\backslash s - \lambda x_0.((\textbf{counts} \ (^{\vee\cup}x_0 \ \textbf{on})) \ (\textbf{the Queen}))$

c. $n\backslash n - \lambda y.(\lambda z.(((\textbf{counts} \ (\textbf{on} \ z)) \ (\textbf{the Queen})) \wedge (y \ z)))$

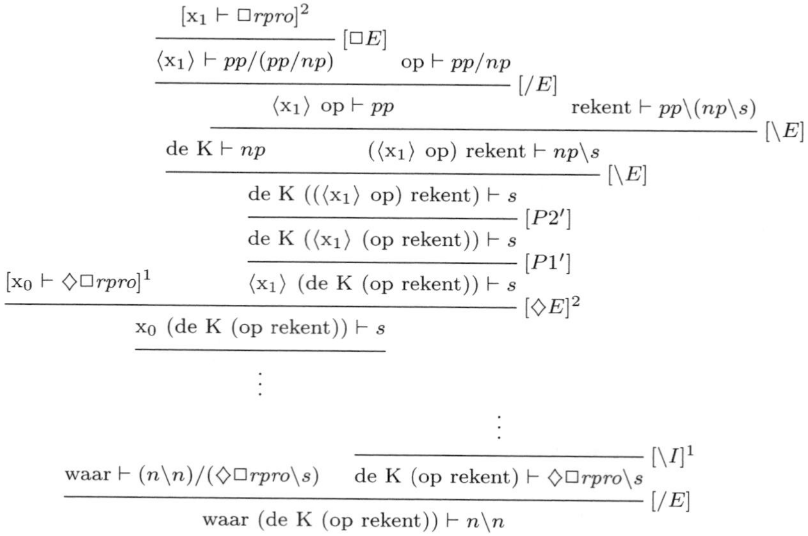

$$\cfrac{\cfrac{[x_0 \vdash \Diamond\Box rpro]^1 \quad \cfrac{\cfrac{\cfrac{\cfrac{de\ K \vdash np \quad \cfrac{\cfrac{\cfrac{[x_1 \vdash \Box rpro]^2}{\langle x_1 \rangle \vdash pp/(pp/np)}[\Box E] \quad op \vdash pp/np}{\langle x_1 \rangle\ op \vdash pp}[/E] \quad rekent \vdash pp\backslash(np\backslash s)}{(\langle x_1 \rangle\ op)\ rekent \vdash np\backslash s}[\backslash E]}{de\ K\ (((\langle x_1 \rangle)\ op)\ rekent) \vdash s}[\backslash E]}{de\ K\ ((\langle x_1 \rangle)\ (op\ rekent)) \vdash s}[P2']}{\langle x_1 \rangle\ (de\ K\ (op\ rekent)) \vdash s}[P1']}{x_0\ (de\ K\ (op\ rekent)) \vdash s}[\Diamond E]^2}{\vdots}$$

waar $\vdash (n\backslash n)/(\Diamond\Box rpro\backslash s)$ $\quad$ $\cfrac{\cfrac{\vdots}{de\ K\ (op\ rekent) \vdash \Diamond\Box rpro\backslash s}[\backslash I]^1}{waar\ (de\ K\ (op\ rekent)) \vdash n\backslash n}[/E]$

FIGURE 12 'waar de Koningin op rekent'

11.2.3 Dependency: blocking extraction from subjects

In the previous sections, we have investigated the structural dimensions of precedence and dominance. The grammars of Dutch and English exploit these dimensions in different ways to pick out 'accessible positions' for extraction. It is not difficult to see that a full account of extraction should include other grammatical dimensions. In this section, we make some brief remarks about the role of dependency relations in grammatical organization, to illustrate the 'multimodal' generalization of the Lambek architecture.

Consider the examples in (32). In these examples, the relative pronoun reasons hypothetically about a position *within* the subject (main or embedded), rather than about the subject as a whole. These examples are derivable with the right branch extraction package $P1/P2$, but they are ill-formed.

(32) a.*a book which the author of admires Alice

b.*a book which Alice thought that the author of was a little crazy

To rule out (32), we need a distinction of a more qualitative character, in addition to the precedence/dominance constraints on tree geometry expressed by $P1/P2$ and $P1'/P2'$. Suppose we take *dependency* information seriously by splitting up the composition relation • into a *head-complement* relation and a *specifier-head* relation. Let us write these as $\bullet_1$ and $\bullet_2$ respectively. Technically, this means moving from a one-dimensional to a multimodal architecture where different composition operations (identified by a *mode* index) live together and interact.[17] The different compositions operations share the same base logic, but structural rules are relativized to the specific composition modes.

For the subject/complement asymmetries with respect to extraction, we can now calibrate $P1/P2$ in the way indicated below. The controlled associativity postulate $P1''$ generalizes over specified-head and head-complement relations. But the controlled reordering postulate $P2''$ operates only in head-complement configurations.

$$P1'' \quad (A \bullet_i B) \bullet_1 \Diamond C \vdash A \bullet_i (B \bullet_1 \Diamond C) \quad \text{(where } i \in \{1,2\})$$
$$P2'' \quad (A \bullet_1 B) \bullet_1 \Diamond C \vdash (A \bullet_1 \Diamond C) \bullet_1 B$$

FIGURE 13 Right branch extraction, dependency sensitive

We leave it to the reader to check that the ungrammatical examples of (32) are indeed underivable with the postulate package of Figure 13 and lexical type assignments where verb phrases are of type $np\backslash_2 s$, designating the subject as a specifier.

11.3 Conclusion

Assessments of the categorial contribution to linguistics tend to be strongly polarized. On the one hand, the categorial approach has been praised for its mathematical elegance and for the transparent design of the syntax-semantics interface. On the other hand, classical categorial systems have been judged to be of limited use for realistic grammar development because of the coarse granularity of the notion of grammatical inference they offer. The criticism is justified, we think, for systems with a fixed resource management regime. However, the enrichment of the type-logical language with an explicit *control* vocabulary changes the black-and-white picture: we hope to have shown that linguistic discrimination is indeed compatible with mathematical sophistication.

This paper adheres to the standard categorial view that macro-grammatical organization, both at the form level and at the meaning level, is fully determined by a deductive process of type inference over lexical assignments. But this standard view has been further articulated in a novel way: by factoring out the structural aspects of grammatical composition from the logical core, we have been able to reconcile the

---

[17]The multimodal formula language is built up from atoms $p, p', p'', \ldots$ by means of binary operations $/_i, \bullet_i, \backslash_i$ and unary $\Diamond_j, \Box_j$, where the indices i and j are taken from given finite sets of composition modes I and J.

cross-linguistic uniformity in the build-up of the form-meaning correspondence with structural variation in the realization of this correspondence. The basic deductive operations of elimination and introduction
of the grammatical constants are semantically interpreted in a uniform
way; packages of structural inferences, triggered by lexically-anchored
control features, determine how the form-meaning correspondence finds
actual expression.

References

Barry, G. and G. Morrill (eds.) (1990), *Studies in Categorial Grammar*.
Edinburgh Working Papers in Cognitive Science, Vol 5. Centre for
Cognitive Science, Edinburgh University.

Benthem, J. van (1991,1995), *Language in Action. Categories, Lambdas,
and Dynamic Logic*. Studies in Logic, North-Holland, Amsterdam.
(Student edition: MIT Press (1995), Cambridge, MA.)

Chomsky, N. (1981), *Lectures on Government and Binding*. Dordrecht.

Chomsky, N. (1995), *The Minimalist Program*. MIT Press, Cambridge,
MA.

Cornell, T.L. (1997), 'A type-logical perspective on minimalist derivations'. In G. Morrill and R.T. Oehrle (eds.) *Formal Grammar 1997*.
Aix-en-Provence.

Dalrymple, M. (ed) (1999), *Semantics and Syntax in Lexical Functional
Grammar. The Resource Logic Approach*. MIT Press, Cambridge,
MA.

Dalrymple, M. e.a. (1999), 'Relating resource-based semantics to categorial semantics'. In Dalrymple (1999).

Gazdar, G. (1981), 'Unbounded dependencies and coordinate structure'.
Linguistic Inquiry **12**: 155–184.

Girard, J.-Y. (1987), 'Linear logic'. *Theoretical Computer Science* **50**,
1–102.

Kaplan, R.M. and J. Bresnan (1982), 'Lexical-Functional Grammar: a
formal system for grammatical representation'. Chapter 4 in J. Bresnan (ed.) *The Mental Representation of Grammatical Relations*, 173–
281. Cambridge, MA.

Kurtonina, N. (1995), *Frames and Labels. A Modal Analysis of Categorial Inference*. Ph.D. Dissertation, OTS Utrecht, ILLC Amsterdam.

Kurtonina, N. and M. Moortgat (1997), 'Structural Control'. In P. Blackburn and M. de Rijke (eds.) *Specifying Syntactic Structures*. CSLI,
Stanford, 1997, 75–113.

Lambek, J. (1958), 'The Mathematics of Sentence Structure', *American
Mathematical Monthly* **65**, 154–170.

Lambek, J. (1961), 'On the calculus of syntactic types'. In Jakobson, R. (ed.) (1961), *Structure of Language and Its Mathematical Aspects*. Proceedings of the Twelfth Symposium in Applied Mathematics. Providence, Rhode Island.

Moortgat, M. (1996), 'Multimodal linguistic inference'. *Journal of Logic, Language and Information,* **5**(3,4), 349–385. Special issue on proof theory and natural language. Guest editors: D. Gabbay and R. Kempson.

Moortgat, M. (1997), 'Categorial Type Logics'. Chapter 2 in J. van Benthem and A. ter Meulen (eds.) *Handbook of Logic and Language.* Elsevier, Amsterdam and MIT Press, Cambridge MA, 1997, 93–177.

Morrill, G. and B. Carpenter (1990), 'Compositionality, implicational logics, and theories of grammar'. *Linguistics & Philosophy,* **13**, 383–392.

Morril, G., N. Leslie, M. Hepple and G. Barry (1990), 'Categorial deductions and structural operations'. In Barry & Morrill (1990), 1–21.

Pollard, C. & I. Sag (1994), *Head-Driven Phrase Structure Grammar.* Chicago.

Stabler, E. (1997), 'Derivational minimalism'. In Ch. Retoré (ed.) *Logical Aspects of Computational Linguistics.* LNAI Lecture Notes, Springer, pp 68–95.

Vermaat, W. (1999) *Controlling Movement. Minimalism in a deductive perspective.* MA Thesis, Utrecht University.

12

Binding as Term Rewriting

RICHARD T. OEHRLE

12.1 Motivation

The goal of the research reported here[1] is to bring binding phenomena into the framework of multimodal type inference Moortgat (1997) in a way that extends the insights of the dynamic semantics tradition to the analysis of intrasentential referential relations. Apart from illustrating one way in which binding phenomena can be accommodated into the perspective of grammatical deduction, the general framework for the analysis of binding developed below allows for the modeling of a wide variety of approaches to binding phenomena. And, as I hope to show, it also yields insights into puzzles connected with such phenomena as crossover restrictions. Before proceeding, I would like to place what follows in perspective by situating it with respect to some alternative approaches.

12.1.1 The categorial grammar binding tradition

There is already a well-developed approach to binding within categorial grammar, building on the work of Bach and Partee (1980) and Chierchia (1988), and developed in differing ways by Szabolcsi (1989), Morrill (1990), Hepple (1990), Dowty (1992, 1999), and, most thoroughly, Jacobson (1999, and the works cited there). Although there are significant distinctions among the proposals within this tradition, a common thread is to assign simple pronouns a functional type with a simple corresponding semantic interpretation, such as the labeled type $\lambda x.x : np^{np}$, where the binary exponential type constructor is distinct from the familiar directionally-sensitive type constructors $/$ and $\backslash$. In

[1]This material is based upon work supported by the National Science Foundation under Grant No. SBR-9510706.

Constraints and Resources in Natural Language Syntax and Semantics.
Gosse Bouma, Erhard W. Hinrichs, Geert-Jan M. Kruijff, and Richard T. Oehrle.

Jacobson's formulation, for example, this type can compose with functor types of the form A/B or $B\backslash A$, with the result that an expression such as *thinks Mary loves him* can be assigned the term-labeled type $\lambda x.(think(love(x)(m))) : (np\backslash s)^{np}$. Expressions of this exponential type can continue to combine with other types by functional composition; alternatively, a combinator (related to Curry's W) can map this term-labeled type to $\lambda x.(think(love(x)(m))(x)) : np\backslash s$, eliminating the exponential type and creating a function which places an additional argument within the scope of the same λ operator that binds the pronoun. (This account of pronouns has interesting affinities with the account of 'variables' in the 'Mitchell-Bénabou language' of a topos: see (MacLane and Moerdijk, 1992, pp. 298ff.).) Similarly, reflexives can be assigned the basic type $\lambda T \lambda x.T(x)(x) : ((np\backslash s)/np)\backslash (np\backslash s)$, which maps a transitive verb to an intransitive verb in a way related syntactically and semantically to Curry's W. The accounts of binding based on this common thread are conceptually elegant and appealing, with insightful empirical applications—particularly when compared to accounts based on the Montagovian tradition in which each pronoun is construed lexically as any one of denumerably many variables.

While acknowledging the fundamental value of this line of research, one may still wonder whether it provides a definitive theoretical framework for research into natural language binding phenomena. For example, by treating anaphoric dependencies in terms of such familiar logical operations as the identity function and the structural operation of contraction (a.k.a. Curry's duplicator W), this work squarely situates binding phenomena within the domain of resource sensitive logical operations; yet it fails to explore (and perhaps exploit) the alternative formulations that this connection opens up.[2]

Moreover, accepting the general lines of these accounts leads one to accept consequences—such as the use of wrapping operations, or the class of parsing theories compatible with passing up dependencies from anaphoric dependent to anaphoric anchor—whose *necessity* one might be skeptical about.

And there are empirical questions. Does this family of theories of quantificational binding extend naturally to cover cases of split quantificational antecedents, as in the case of the sentence *Every teacher reminded every student that they were required to meet twice a semester*, construed schematically as

$$\forall x : teacher(\forall y : student(x \; remind \; y \; ((x \sqcup y) \; meet)))$$

---

[2]Recent papers by Jäger address some of these questions: see Jäger (1997, 1998).

With regard to reflexivization, does this general approach allow for both sloppy and non-sloppy readings in sentences like *Bush voted for himself; Clinton did, too* (where it is likely that each candidate did what was required to forward his candidacy) and *Clinton voted for himself; and a majority of other voters did, too* (where the other voters are taken to endorse Clinton's candidacy)? Does this general approach provide the basis for an adequate account of locality conditions in various languages? And how does this general approach reconcile intra-sentential anaphoric binding with discoure binding (as found, for example, in such cases as *No soldier talked: not about the war; not about himself*).

One may of course try to reconcile these issues with the particular assumptions that have been characteristic of this tradition of categorial binding. But here we shall pursue a different course: by considering alternative approaches to the integration of binding phenomena with type deduction, we hope to focus scrutiny on the possible modes of communication between a pronoun and its anchor, in a way that will strengthen connections between the study of natural language binding phenomena and standard logical methods.

12.1.2   The GB tradition

The Binding Theory of the GB tradition Chomsky (1982) offers a classification of certain anaphoric elements, according to their behavior in simple structures. For example, consider a sentential form such as the following (where indices represent indeterminates associated with arguments):

$$np_i \ told \ np_j \ that \ np_k \ called \ np_l$$

This sentential form offers a small laboratory in which we may investigate how to characterize referential relations in English.

As a first step, we indicate the way the GB Binding categories bear on the interpretation of the referential positions in this sentential form, using a notation in which each referential expression is assigned a fresh indeterminate and binding is indicated by anchoring one indeterminate to another; alternative anchorings are given on separate lines:[3]

---

[3] We depart from the standard GB Binding Theory in allowing anaphors in the subject position of the embedded clause—indicated in the fifth column of the anaphor row—because reciprocals seem to occur in this position (bound by elements in the matrix clause) although reflexive forms do not. Following Brame (1977), we regard this difference as arising from the fact that reflexives have a fixed case incompatible with the contexts that accommodate nominative or possessive pronouns.

	np_i	told	np_j	that	np_k	called	np_l
anaphor:	*	—	$j \mapsto i$	—	$k \mapsto i$	—	$l \mapsto k$
					$k \mapsto j$		
pronominal:	[free]	—	$j \not\mapsto i$	—	[free]	—	$l \not\mapsto k$
R-expr.:	[free]	—	$j \not\mapsto i$	—	$k \not\mapsto i$	—	$l \not\mapsto i$
					$k \not\mapsto j$		$l \not\mapsto j$
							$l \not\mapsto k$

In the GB Binding Theory Chomsky (1982), the properties displayed in this table are characterized by associating each of the descriptive categories in the left-hand column of the table with binding principles formulated in terms of co-indexation, c-command, and governing category. The result is a configurationally based theory of binding, in which referential relations depend on static structures. The GB Binding Theory rests on a slender initial foundation: the essential concepts can be motivated on the basis of a single level of embedding. While this is a theoretical strength in some respects, there are many apparent counterexamples to the basic claims of this theory. Attempts to extend the theory to cover these cases have been ingenious and amplified our descriptive understanding. But one may wonder whether any purely configurational theory can be the basis for an adequate account of natural language referential relations. For example, the import of a sentence like *Dan blamed one person: himself* can be explained dynamically by assigning the subexpression *one person* an indeterminate distinct from semantic value of *Dan* and subsequently anchoring this indeterminate to this value. But this cannot be expressed by any static indexation of expressions using the vocabulary of the GB Binding Theory.

Such examples suggest that we investigate accounts of binding phenomena that are not configurationally based. In the treatment developed below, the configurational concepts of the GB account play no role. Instead, we emphasize communication between structured resources, intrinsically regulated by self-contained logical constants.

12.1.3 Dynamic interpretation

We take the core ideas of dynamic interpretation (Stalnaker (1978), Heim (1982), Kamp (1984), Groenendijk and Stokhof (1991)) to involve two related, fundamental theses:

- interpretation is context-dependent;
- interpretation is context-affecting.

Schematically, then, we can represent the interpretation of an expression α as involving an input context C and an output context C', as pictured below.

$$^C[\alpha]^{C'}$$

This schema raises a number of obvious but important questions:

1. what are the relevant aspects of context?
2. in what ways can the interpretation of α depend on C?
3. what transitions between C and C' are possible?
4. how do these transitions depend on α?
5. given a particular occurrence of α, how is the context C on which it depends determined?

The literature on dynamic semantics already contains an interesting range of answers to these questions. For example, in DRT, one might take a context to be a set of (sorted) constants and indeterminates. In DMG, a context might be regarded as an assignment function. Similarly, the 'boxes' of DRT provide an example of how contexts can be structured. In the developments to follow, we will follow the lead of DRT and regard contexts as structured sets of constants and indeterminates. Later, we will briefly consider some other possible ways of setting these parameters as well.

Regardless of how exactly we think of contexts in the schema above, its form suggests that we regard the meaning of α as a binary relation among input contexts C and output contexts C'. Concretely, we may regard this meaning as a *non-deterministic program*. The *internal* dynamics of this program involve its sensitivity to context and its potential contribution to context. The *external* dynamics of the program involve what context serves as the input to the program and how the output of the program affects the context of its occurrence.

For example, compare:

> *The person who gave Jones a present wrapped it carefully.*
> *The person who gave noone a present wrapped it carefully.*

The first example suggests that *a present* can affect the context by introducing a fresh discourse referent accessible to the subsequent occurrence of the pronoun *it*. If the second example is interpreted in the natural way with *noone* having scope over *a present*, the lack of a referent for *it* suggests that the discourse referent introduced internally by *a present* can be subject to the external requirements of the quantifier *noone*.

These three aspects of dynamic interpretation—the internal dynamics of an expression, the input contribution of the context in which it finds itself, and the output contribution it makes to the context—provide a natural division of labor which can be exploited in the setting of multi-modal grammatical inference. To see how this can be achieved, we start with a brief review of the multimodal setting.

12.2 The multimodal setting

12.2.1 Multimodal type inference

Unimodal categorial type logics—non-associative, non-commutative **NL**, associative, non-commutative **L**, and associative, commutative **LP**—contain a single product type-constructor, and its left and right residuals, and the set of valid sequents are closed under identity, cut, residuation, and, where appropriate, the structural rules of associativity (**L**, **LP**) and commutativity (**LP**). These systems represent absolute choices among the options of resource-sensitivity offered by different packages of structural rules. Natural languages fail to conform to such absolute standards. For example, sensitivity to order may be enforced with respect to some structures but not with respect to others. (Thus, Japanese is rigidly verb final, but subject and object are not rigidly ordered with respect to each other.) The multimodal setting is compatible with this more refined resource-sensitivity. We start with a set of modes (here: unary and binary). Each mode yields a product type-constructor and associated residuals. Just as in the unimodal setting, valid sequents are closed under identity, cut, and residuation. Individual modes behave in a way dictated by a package of structural rules (possibly empty). Communication between modes is governed by interaction postulates. Just as in the unimodal case, there are a variety of presentations of multimodal type inference. Here is one, starting with a set $\mathcal{A}$ of atomic types, a set $\mathcal{U}$ of unary modes, and a set $\mathcal{B}$ of binary modes, with u and b variable indices ranging over $\mathcal{U}$ and $\mathcal{B}$, respectively:

$$
\begin{aligned}
\text{formulae } \mathcal{F} \quad &:= \mathcal{A} \mid \Diamond_u \mathcal{F} \mid \Box_u^\downarrow \mathcal{F} \mid \mathcal{F} \bullet_b \mathcal{F} \mid \mathcal{F}/_b\mathcal{F} \mid \mathcal{F}\backslash_b\mathcal{F} \\
\text{structures } \mathcal{S} \quad &:= \mathcal{F} \mid (\mathcal{S})^u \mid (\mathcal{S},\mathcal{S})^b \\
\text{sequents} \quad &:= \mathcal{S} \Rightarrow \mathcal{F} \\
\text{identity:} \quad & A \to A \\
\text{cut:} \quad & \frac{\Gamma \to A \quad \Delta[A] \to B}{\Delta[\Gamma] \to B} \\
\text{residuation / adjointness:} \quad & A \to C/_bB \Leftrightarrow A \bullet_b B \to C \Leftrightarrow B \to A\backslash_bC \\
& \Diamond_u A \to B \Leftrightarrow A \to \Box_u^\downarrow B \\
\text{structural rules:} \quad & \ldots \\
\text{interaction postulates:} \quad & \ldots
\end{aligned}
$$

Since residuation holds for all modes, the following direct consequences of it are valid for any binary mode. (Note that all the proofs below start from valid instances of the identity axiom.)

$$\frac{A/_bB \to A/_bB}{A/_bB \bullet_b B \to A} \; residuation \qquad \frac{A\backslash_bB \to A\backslash_bB}{A \bullet_b A\backslash_bB \to B} \; residuation$$

$$\frac{A \bullet_b B \to A \bullet_b B}{A \to (A \bullet_b B)/_bB} \; residuation \qquad \frac{A \bullet_b B \to A \bullet_b B}{B \to A\backslash_b(A \bullet_b B)} \; residuation$$

Moreover, since residuation holds for all unary modes, the same reasoning shows the validity of unary analogs of the above binary cases:

$$\frac{\Box_u^{\downarrow}A \to \Box_u^{\downarrow}A}{\Diamond_u\Box_u^{\downarrow}A \to A} \; residuation \qquad \frac{\Diamond_uA \to \Diamond_uA}{A \to \Box_u^{\downarrow}\Diamond_uA} \; residuation$$

These direct consequences of residuation will play a pivotal role in what follows.

For much more extensive discussion of the properties of multimodal grammatical inference, see Moortgat (1997).

12.2.2 Proofs and terms

We now label types with λ-terms and use the Curry-Howard correspondence to label proofs. This is particularly transparent in the Natural Deduction presentation, where the product introduction rule corresponds to pairing, product elimination to projection, residual introduction to abstraction, and residual elimination to application, as shown below (where undischarged, term-labeled assumptions appear on the left of the sequent sign and a single term-labeled type of the form *term: type* appears on the right):

$$x : A \vdash x : A$$

$$[/I]\frac{(\Gamma, x : B) \vdash t : A}{\Gamma \vdash \lambda x.t : A/B} \qquad \frac{\Gamma \vdash t : A/B \quad \Delta \vdash u : B}{(\Gamma, \Delta) \vdash t(u) : A}[/E]$$

$$[\backslash I]\frac{(x : B, \Gamma) \vdash t : A}{\Gamma \vdash \lambda x.t : B\backslash A} \qquad \frac{\Gamma \vdash u : B \quad \Delta \vdash t : B\backslash A}{(\Gamma, \Delta) \vdash t(u) : A}[\backslash E]$$

$$[\bullet I]\frac{\Gamma \vdash t : A \quad \Delta \vdash u : B}{(\Gamma, \Delta) \vdash \langle t, u \rangle : A \bullet B}$$

$$\frac{\Delta \vdash u : A \bullet B \quad \Gamma[(x : A, y : B)] \vdash t : C}{\Gamma[\Delta] \vdash t[(u)_0/x, (u)_1/y] : C}[\bullet E]$$

The same method carries over to the unary operators: the 'product' $\Diamond_u$ corresponds to a term constructor $^\wedge$; its residual $\Box_u^\downarrow$ corresponds to a term destructor $^\vee$:

$$\frac{\Gamma \vdash t : \Box^\downarrow A}{\langle \Gamma \rangle \vdash {}^\vee t : A} \ (\Box^\downarrow E) \qquad \frac{\langle \Gamma \rangle \vdash t : A}{\Gamma \vdash {}^\wedge t : \Box^\downarrow A} \ (\Box^\downarrow I)$$

$$\frac{\Gamma \vdash t : A}{\langle \Gamma \rangle \vdash {}^\cap t : \Diamond A} \ (\Diamond I) \qquad \frac{\Delta \vdash u : \Diamond A \quad \Gamma[\langle x : A \rangle] \vdash t : B}{\Gamma[\Delta] \vdash t[{}^\cup u/x] : B} \ (\Diamond E)$$

In this way, then, each valid proof determines a λ-term that can be associated with its succedent.

In the next section, we illustrate how this correspondence can accommodate the basic properties of dynamic semantics. Essentially, the picture that will emerge is this:

- *external dynamics* will be controlled by product modes;
- *internal dynamics* will be controlled by unary modalities;
- *nondeterminism* will be introduced by term re-writing rules.

Before turning to details, it might be useful to sketch the broad lines of the architecture that these details express. Communication between an anaphoric element and its anchor is treated here through the dynamic allocation of structured contexts. Particular expressions can both depend and affect the contexts in which they can occur. In contrast to the traditional categorial binding account, where access to the term associated with a pronoun is carried up through the larger term structure containing it by functional composition, the account here carries information from the anchor to the anaphoric element. Instead of taking the term associated with non-reflexive pronouns, say, to be the identity function $\lambda x.x$, and selecting an argument to pass to this function, we associate each pronoun with a designated non-determinate x and directly bind this indeterminate to the term selected as the anchor. It would be equally possible in the present setting to associate pronouns with the identity function, which would bring the account closer to the categorial binding tradition discussed above. Rather than doing so, however, we note the treatment proposed here may be regarded as compiling the steps of application and subsequent β-reduction into a single step corresponding to the substitution phase of β-reduction. Finally, although the exposition to follow fleshes out this general architecture in the guise of term-rewriting, the same general architecture can be instantiated in other ways, for example, in the form of a multi-modal logical calculus in the style developed by Jäger (1997, 1998).

12.3 Initial development: names, reflexive and nonreflexive pronouns

12.3.1 Lexicon

We start with a lexicon in which each element is 'locked' with a lexical box.

expression	term	type
mary :=	$\overset{\vee}{pn}m$:	$\Box^{\downarrow}np$
john :=	$\overset{\vee}{pn}j$:	$\Box^{\downarrow}np$
him :=	$\overset{\vee}{f}x$:	$\Box^{\downarrow}_c np$
he :=	$\overset{\vee}{n}x$:	$\Box^{\downarrow}_s np$
himself :=	$\overset{\vee}{r}x$:	$\Box^{\downarrow}_c np$
admire :=	$admire$:	$\Box^{\downarrow}_c (np\backslash_s(s/_c np))$
tell :=	$tell$:	$\Box^{\downarrow}_c (np\backslash_s((s/_c s)/_c np))$

Expressions which exhibit distinct patterns of sensitivity to referential context are marked with different boxes. Note as well that verbs are taken to combine first with subjects, rather than last. In the present setting, this simplifies the correspondence between syntactic combination and anaphoric dependence. (A referee points out that one could achieve a similar simplification by preserving the traditional structure in which the subject is the final argument and adopting a directionally sensitive term calculus, as found in the work of Buszkowski and Wansing.) The assumption that the subject combines first with the verb, rather than last, need not be taken to be at odds with having a syntactic constituent representing the verb phrase: just take a transitive verb such as *admire* to have the type $np\backslash_s((s/vp) \oplus (vp/_c np))$ (where the binary product $\oplus$ is (at least) right associative with respect to subsequent arguments).

12.3.2 Postulates

Each lexical box must be 'unlocked' by the presence of a corresponding diamond (using a variant of the basic residuation inference $\Diamond \Box A \rightarrow A$). This diamond will have its source as a box on the goal type and communicate (as a diamond) with resource assumptions according to the postulates below:

$$P1 \quad \Diamond_c(A \bullet_c B) \longrightarrow \Diamond_c A \bullet_c \Diamond_c B$$
$$P2 \quad \Diamond_c(A \bullet_s B) \longrightarrow \Diamond_s A \bullet_s \Diamond_c B$$
$$P3 \quad \Diamond_c A \longrightarrow \Diamond A$$
$$P4 \quad \Diamond_s A \longrightarrow \Diamond A$$

The following proof illustrates the interplay of lexical information and type inference in a simple transitive sentence.

$$
\cfrac{
  \cfrac{
    \cfrac{
      \cfrac{\alpha \vdash \alpha' : \Box^{\downarrow} np}{\alpha \vdash \alpha' : \Box^{\downarrow}_s np} \, P4
    }{\langle \alpha \rangle_s \vdash {}^{\vee}_s \alpha' : np} \, \Box^{\downarrow}_s E
    \qquad
    \cfrac{a \vdash a : \Box^{\downarrow}_c(np \backslash_s (s/_c np))}{\langle a \rangle_c \vdash {}^{\vee}_c a : np \backslash_s (s/_c np)} \, \Box^{\downarrow}_c E
  }{
    \cfrac{
      \cfrac{\langle \alpha \rangle_s \circ_s \langle a \rangle_c \vdash ({}^{\vee}_c a)({}^{\vee}_s \alpha') : s/_c np}{\langle \alpha \circ_s a \rangle_c \vdash ({}^{\vee}_c a)({}^{\vee}_s \alpha') : s/_c np} \, P2
      \qquad
      \cfrac{
        \cfrac{\cfrac{\beta \vdash \beta' : \Box^{\downarrow} np}{\beta \vdash \beta' : \Box^{\downarrow}_c np} \, P3}{\langle \beta \rangle_c \vdash {}^{\vee}_c \beta' : np} \, \Box^{\downarrow}_c E
      }{}
    }{
      \cfrac{\langle \alpha \circ_s a \rangle_c \circ_c \langle \beta \rangle_c \vdash ({}^{\vee}_c a)({}^{\vee}_s \alpha')({}^{\vee}_c \beta') : s}{\langle (\alpha \circ_s a) \circ_c \beta \rangle_c \vdash ({}^{\vee}_c a)({}^{\vee}_s \alpha')({}^{\vee}_c \beta') : s} \, P1
    } \, /_c E
  }{((\alpha \circ_s admire) \circ_c \beta) \vdash {}^{\wedge}_c (({}^{\vee}_c admire)({}^{\vee}_s \alpha')({}^{\vee}_c \beta')) : \Box^{\downarrow}_c s} \, \Box^{\downarrow}_c I
}{} \, \backslash_s E
$$

Special cases of this proof arise by making specific lexical choices for the arguments:

$$((\text{john} \circ_s \text{admire}) \circ_c \text{mary}) \vdash {}^{\wedge}_c (({}^{\vee}_c admire)({}^{\vee}_{s\ pn}{}^{\vee} j)({}^{\vee}_{c\ pn}{}^{\vee} m)) : \Box^{\downarrow}_c s$$
$$((\text{john} \circ_s \text{admire}) \circ_c \text{himself}) \vdash {}^{\wedge}_c (({}^{\vee}_c admire)({}^{\vee}_{s\ pn}{}^{\vee} j)({}^{\vee}_{c\ r}{}^{\vee} x)) : \Box^{\downarrow}_c s$$
$$((\text{john} \circ_s \text{admire}) \circ_c \text{him}) \vdash {}^{\wedge}_c (({}^{\vee}_c admire)({}^{\vee}_{s\ pn}{}^{\vee} j)({}^{\vee}_{c\ f}{}^{\vee} x)) : \Box^{\downarrow}_c s$$
$$((\text{john} \circ_s \text{admire}) \circ_c \text{john}) \vdash {}^{\wedge}_c (({}^{\vee}_c admire)({}^{\vee}_{s\ pn}{}^{\vee} j)({}^{\vee}_{c\ pn}{}^{\vee} j)) : \Box^{\downarrow}_c s$$

These examples all represent valid sequents: instances of a relation between a structured set of resource assumptions and a term-labeled type. In each case, the proof takes the form exhibited above.

12.3.3   Term rewriting

We wish to regard the term associated with a proof as a program that takes a representation of the context of utterance as input and nondeterministically computes both a specific value and an output context from this input. This can be done by term rewriting rules such as the following:

In the rewriting rules below, we take contexts to consist of two domains of symbols of the term language: a domain of local binders (denoted L) and a domain of discourse binders (denoted D). The customary braces of standard set theory are suppressed, so that we write 'j' to represent the singleton set $\{j\}$. And we write $L \setminus t$ to indicate that $t \notin L$ and $L[t]$ $(D[t])$ to indicate that $t \in L$ $(t \in D)$.

Internal dynamics of terms

Proper Names—locally free and possibly new:

$$\underset{L \setminus \alpha}{\overset{D}{}} pn \overset{\vee}{} \alpha \quad \rightarrow \quad \alpha^{D \cup \alpha}_{(L \setminus \alpha) \cup \alpha}$$

Accusative pronouns—bound to t in D but not in L:

$$\underset{L \setminus t}{\overset{D[t]}{}} f \overset{\vee}{} x \quad \rightarrow \quad t^{D[t]}_{(L \setminus t) \cup t}$$

Nominative pronouns—bound to t in D:

$$\underset{L}{\overset{D[t]}{}} n \overset{\vee}{} x \quad \rightarrow \quad t^{D[t]}_{L \cup t}$$

Reflexives—bound to t in L:

$$\underset{L[t]}{\overset{D}{}} r \overset{\vee}{} x \quad \rightarrow \quad t^{D}_{L[t]}$$

Other constants—neutral:

$$\underset{L}{\overset{D}{}} \text{constant} \quad \rightarrow \quad \text{constant}^{D}_{L}$$

External dynamics of terms

Each term operator must pass its input context to its argument and then regulate how the output of the internal dynamics of the argument is passed on to its own output. Thus, there are two rules for each of the term operators below:

$\hat{c}$ copies input and promotes output:

$$\underset{L\,c}{\overset{D \wedge}{}} \phi \quad \rightarrow \quad \underset{L\,c}{\overset{D \wedge}{}} (\underset{L}{\overset{D}{}} \phi) \qquad\qquad \hat{c}(\phi^{D'}_{L'}) \quad \rightarrow \quad (\phi)^{D'}_{L'}$$

$\overset{\vee}{c}$ commutes with input context and promotes output:

$$\underset{L}{\overset{D}{}} (\overset{\vee}{c} \phi) \quad \rightarrow \quad \underset{c\,L}{\overset{\vee D}{}} \phi \qquad\qquad \overset{\vee}{c}(\phi^{D'}_{L'}) \quad \rightarrow \quad (\phi)^{D'}_{L'}$$

$\overset{\vee}{s}$ commutes with input context and resets output L':

$$\underset{L}{\overset{D}{}} (\overset{\vee}{s} \phi) \quad \rightarrow \quad \overset{\vee}{s} (\underset{L}{\overset{D}{}} \phi) \qquad\qquad \overset{\vee}{s}(t^{D'}_{L'}) \quad \rightarrow \quad (t)^{D'}_{t}$$

Examples: names and pronouns

The action of term rewriting rules is illustrated in the following examples. The context variables D and L may be taken arbitrarily, for the most part. In particular, they may be empty. In some examples, however, we have indicated that the local context does not contain j, because if it did, term rewriting would fail due to the requirements of the subterm $\overset{\vee}{pn}j$ corresponding to the subject *John*.

EXAMPLE: *John admires Mary*

$$
\begin{aligned}
((\text{john} \circ_s \text{admire}) \circ_c \text{mary}) \;\vdash\;\; & {}^{D}_{L\backslash j}(\hat{c}((\overset{\vee}{c}\,admire)(\overset{\vee}{s}\overset{\vee}{pn}j)(\overset{\vee}{c}\overset{\vee}{pn}m))) : \square^{\downarrow}_{c}s \\
\rightarrow\;\; & {}^{D}_{L\backslash j}{}_{c}(\overset{D}{L\backslash j}(\overset{\vee}{c}\,admire)(\overset{\vee}{s}\overset{\vee}{pn}j)(\overset{\vee}{c}\overset{\vee}{pn}m)) : \square^{\downarrow}_{c}s \\
\rightarrow\;\; & {}^{D}_{L\backslash j}{}_{c}(\overset{\vee}{c}(\overset{D}{L\backslash j}admire)(\overset{\vee}{s}\overset{\vee}{pn}j)(\overset{\vee}{c}\overset{\vee}{pn}m)) : \square^{\downarrow}_{c}s \\
\rightarrow\;\; & {}^{D}_{L\backslash j}{}_{c}(\overset{\vee}{c}(admire^{D}_{L\backslash j})(\overset{\vee}{s}\overset{\vee}{pn}j)(\overset{\vee}{c}\overset{\vee}{pn}m)) : \square^{\downarrow}_{c}s \\
\rightarrow\;\; & {}^{D}_{L\backslash j}{}_{c}((admire)^{D}_{L\backslash j}(\overset{\vee}{s}\overset{\vee}{pn}j)(\overset{\vee}{c}\overset{\vee}{pn}m)) : \square^{\downarrow}_{c}s \\
\rightarrow\;\; & {}^{D}_{L\backslash j}{}_{c}((admire)_{s}(\overset{D}{L\backslash j}\overset{\vee}{pn}j)(\overset{\vee}{c}\overset{\vee}{pn}m)) : \square^{\downarrow}_{c}s \\
\rightarrow\;\; & {}^{D}_{L\backslash j}{}_{c}((admire)_{s}(j^{D\cup j}_{L\backslash j\cup j})(\overset{\vee}{c}\overset{\vee}{pn}m)) : \square^{\downarrow}_{c}s \\
\rightarrow\;\; & {}^{D}_{L\backslash j}{}_{c}((admire)(j)^{D\cup j}_{j}(\overset{\vee}{c}\overset{\vee}{pn}m)) : \square^{\downarrow}_{c}s \\
\rightarrow\;\; & {}^{D}_{L\backslash j}{}_{c}((admire)(j)^{\vee}_{c}(j^{D\cup j}\overset{\vee}{pn}m)) : \square^{\downarrow}_{c}s \\
\rightarrow\;\; & {}^{D}_{L\backslash j}{}_{c}((admire)(j)^{\vee}_{c}(m^{D\cup j\cup m}_{j\cup m})) : \square^{\downarrow}_{c}s \\
\rightarrow\;\; & {}^{D}_{L\backslash j}{}_{c}((admire)(j)(m)^{D\cup j\cup m}_{j\cup m}) : \square^{\downarrow}_{c}s \\
\rightarrow\;\; & {}^{D}_{L\backslash j}((admire)(j)(m))^{D\cup j\cup m}_{j\cup m} : \square^{\downarrow}_{c}s
\end{aligned}
$$

EXAMPLE: *John admires himself*

$$
\begin{aligned}
((\text{john} \circ_s \text{admire}) \circ_c \text{himself}) \;\vdash\;\; & {}^{D}_{L\backslash j}(\hat{c}((\overset{\vee}{c}\,admire)(\overset{\vee}{s}\overset{\vee}{pn}j)(\overset{\vee}{c}\overset{\vee}{r}x))) : \square^{\downarrow}_{c}s \\
\dots \rightarrow\;\; & {}^{D}_{L\backslash j}{}_{c}((admire)(j)^{D\cup j}_{j}(\overset{\vee}{c}\overset{\vee}{r}x)) : \square^{\downarrow}_{c}s \\
\rightarrow\;\; & {}^{D}_{L\backslash j}{}_{c}((admire)(j)^{\vee}_{c}(j^{D\cup j}\overset{\vee}{r}x)) : \square^{\downarrow}_{c}s \\
\rightarrow\;\; & {}^{D}_{L\backslash j}{}_{c}((admire)(j)^{\vee}_{c}(j^{D\cup j})) : \square^{\downarrow}_{c}s \\
\rightarrow\;\; & {}^{D}_{L\backslash j}{}_{c}((admire)(j)(j)^{D\cup j}_{j}) : \square^{\downarrow}_{c}s \\
\rightarrow\;\; & {}^{D}_{L\backslash j}((admire)(j)(j))^{D\cup j}_{j} : \square^{\downarrow}_{c}s
\end{aligned}
$$

EXAMPLE: *John admires him*

$$
\begin{aligned}
((\text{john} \circ_s \text{admire}) \circ_c \text{him}) \;\vdash\;\; & {}^{D[k]}_{L\backslash j}(\hat{c}((\overset{\vee}{c}\,admire)(\overset{\vee}{s}\overset{\vee}{pn}j)(\overset{\vee}{c}\overset{\vee}{f}x))) : \square^{\downarrow}_{c}s \\
\dots \rightarrow\;\; & {}^{D[k]}_{L\backslash j}{}_{c}((admire)(j)^{D[k]\cup j}_{j}(\overset{\vee}{c}\overset{\vee}{f}x)) : \square^{\downarrow}_{c}s \\
\rightarrow\;\; & {}^{D[k]}_{L\backslash j}{}_{c}((admire)(j)^{\vee}_{c}(j^{D[k]\cup j}\overset{\vee}{f}x)) : \square^{\downarrow}_{c}s \\
\rightarrow\;\; & {}^{D[k]}_{L\backslash j}{}_{c}((admire)(j)^{\vee}_{c}(k^{D[k]\cup j}_{j\cup k})) : \square^{\downarrow}_{c}s \\
\rightarrow\;\; & {}^{D[k]}_{L\backslash j}{}_{c}((admire)(j)(k)^{D[k]\cup j}_{j\cup k}) : \square^{\downarrow}_{c}s \\
\rightarrow\;\; & {}^{D[k]}_{L\backslash j}((admire)(j)(k))^{D[k]\cup j}_{j\cup k} : \square^{\downarrow}_{c}s
\end{aligned}
$$

N.B. the transition from $_j^{D[k]\cup j}\overset{\vee}{_f}x$ to $k_{j\cup k}^{D[k]\cup j}$ requires that $k \neq j$, by the term rewriting rule

$$_{L\setminus t}^{D[t]\vee}{}_f x \quad \rightarrow \quad t_{(L\setminus t)\cup t}^{D[t]}$$

EXAMPLE: *John admires John*

$$
\begin{aligned}
((\text{john} \circ_s \text{admire}) \circ_c \text{john}) \vdash \; & \overset{\wedge}{_c}((\overset{\vee}{_c}\,admire)(\overset{\vee\vee}{_{s\,pn}}j)(\overset{\vee\vee}{_{c}\,pn}j)) : \square^{\downarrow}_c s \\
\cdots \rightarrow \; & \overset{D}{_{L\setminus j}}\overset{\wedge}{_c}((admire)(j)_j^{D\cup j}(\overset{\vee\vee}{_c\,pn}j)) : \square^{\downarrow}_c s \\
\rightarrow \; & \overset{D}{_{L\setminus j}}\overset{\wedge}{_c}((admire)(j)\overset{\vee}{_c}(\overset{D\cup j\vee}{_j\;pn}j)) : \square^{\downarrow}_c s \\
\rightarrow \; & ?
\end{aligned}
$$

At this point, term rewriting halts, since the action of a term of the form $\overset{\vee}{_{pn}}j$ is not defined on local contexts that contain j.

Embedding and nondeterminism

The proof below gives rise to a family of slightly more complex examples. (For typographical reasons, the proof is stretched into two parts, connected at the vertical ellipsis signs.)

$$
\cfrac{
\cfrac{
\cfrac{\cfrac{\alpha \vdash \alpha' : \square^{\downarrow}np}{\alpha \vdash \alpha' : \square^{\downarrow}_s np}P4}{\langle\alpha\rangle_s \vdash \overset{\vee}{_s}\alpha' : np}\square^{\downarrow}_s E \quad \cfrac{t \vdash t : \square^{\downarrow}_c np\backslash_s((s/_c s)/_c np)}{\langle t\rangle_c \vdash \overset{\vee}{_c}t : np\backslash_s((s/_c s)/_c np)}
}{
\cfrac{((\langle\alpha\rangle_s \circ_s \langle t\rangle_c) \vdash (\overset{\vee}{_c}t)(\overset{\vee}{_s}\alpha') : (s/_c s)/_c np}{((\alpha \circ_s t)_c) \vdash (\overset{\vee}{_c}t)(\overset{\vee}{_s}\alpha') : (s/_c s)/_c np}P2}\backslash_s E \quad
\cfrac{\cfrac{\beta \vdash \beta' : \square^{\downarrow}np}{\beta \vdash \beta' : \square^{\downarrow}_c np}P3}{\langle\beta\rangle_c \vdash \overset{\vee}{_c}\beta' : np}\square^{\downarrow}_c E
}{
\cfrac{(\langle\alpha \circ_s t\rangle_c \circ_c \langle\beta\rangle_c) \vdash (\overset{\vee}{_c}t)(\overset{\vee}{_s}\alpha')(\overset{\vee}{_c}\beta') : s/_c s}{\langle(\alpha \circ_s t) \circ_c \beta\rangle_c \vdash (\overset{\vee}{_c}t)(\overset{\vee}{_s}\alpha')(\overset{\vee}{_c}\beta') : s/_c s}P1}/_c E
$$

$$\vdots$$

$$
\cfrac{
\cfrac{
\vdots \quad \cfrac{\cfrac{\sigma \vdash \sigma' : \square^{\downarrow}_c s}{\langle\sigma\rangle_c \vdash \overset{\vee}{_c}\sigma' : s}\square^{\downarrow}_c E}{}
}{
\cfrac{\langle(\alpha \circ_s t) \circ_c \beta\rangle_c \circ_c \langle\sigma\rangle_c \vdash (\overset{\vee}{_c}t)(\overset{\vee}{_s}\alpha')(\overset{\vee}{_c}\beta')(\overset{\vee}{_c}\sigma') : s}{\langle((\alpha \circ_s t) \circ_c \beta) \circ_c \sigma\rangle_c \vdash (\overset{\vee}{_c}t)(\overset{\vee}{_s}\alpha')(\overset{\vee}{_c}\beta')(\overset{\vee}{_c}\sigma') : s}P1}/_c E
}{
(((\alpha \circ_s \text{told}) \circ_c \beta) \circ_c \sigma) \vdash \overset{\wedge}{_c}(\overset{\vee}{_c}told)(\overset{\vee}{_s}\alpha')(\overset{\vee}{_c}\beta')(\overset{\vee}{_c}\sigma') : \square^{\downarrow}_c s}\square^{\downarrow}_c I
$$

EXAMPLE: *John told Bill he admired him.*

$$(((\text{john} \circ_s \text{told}) \circ_c \text{Bill}) \circ_c ((\text{he} \circ_s \text{admired}) \circ_c \text{him})) \vdash$$
$$\hat{c}((\overset{\vee}{c}\,told)(\overset{\vee\,\vee}{s\,pn}j)(\overset{\vee\,\vee}{c\,pn}b)(\overset{\vee}{c}(\overset{\vee}{c}\,admire)(\overset{\vee\,\vee}{s\,n}x)(\overset{\vee\,\vee}{c\,f}x))) : \square_c^{\downarrow}s$$

$$\overset{\emptyset}{L\backslash j}\hat{c}((\overset{\vee}{c}\,told)(\overset{\vee\,\vee}{s\,pn}j)(\overset{\vee\,\vee}{c\,pn}b)(\overset{\vee}{c}(\overset{\vee}{c}\,admired)(\overset{\vee\,\vee}{s\,n}x)(\overset{\vee\,\vee}{c\,f}x)))$$
$$\rightarrow \quad \overset{\emptyset}{L\backslash j}((told)(j)(b)((admired)(j)(b)))^{j,b}_{j,b}$$
$$\text{OR} \quad \overset{\emptyset}{L\backslash j}((told)(j)(b)((admired)(b)(j)))^{j,b}_{j,b}$$

$$\overset{k}{L\backslash j}\hat{c}((\overset{\vee}{c}\,told)(\overset{\vee\,\vee}{s\,pn}j)(\overset{\vee\,\vee}{c\,pn}b)(\overset{\vee}{c}(\overset{\vee}{c}\,admired)(\overset{\vee\,\vee}{s\,n}x)(\overset{\vee\,\vee}{c\,f}x)))$$
$$\rightarrow \quad \overset{k}{L\backslash j}((told)(j)(b)((admired)(j)(b)))^{k,j,b}_{j,b}$$
$$\text{OR} \quad \overset{k}{L\backslash j}((told)(j)(b)((admired)(b)(j)))^{k,j,b}_{j,b}$$
$$\text{OR} \quad \overset{k}{L\backslash j}((told)(j)(b)((admired)(k)(b)))^{k,j,b}_{k,b}$$
$$\text{OR} \quad \overset{k}{L\backslash j}((told)(j)(b)((admired)(k)(j)))^{k,j,b}_{k,j}$$
$$\text{OR} \quad \overset{k}{L\backslash j}((told)(j)(b)((admired)(j)(k)))^{k,j,b}_{j,k}$$
$$\text{OR} \quad \overset{k}{L\backslash j}((told)(j)(b)((admired)(b)(k)))^{k,j,b}_{b,k}$$

EXAMPLE: *John told Bill he admired himself.*

$$(((\text{john} \circ_s \text{told}) \circ_c \text{Bill}) \circ_c ((\text{he} \circ_s \text{admired}) \circ_c \text{himself})) \vdash$$
$$\hat{c}((\overset{\vee}{c}\,told)(\overset{\vee\,\vee}{s\,pn}j)(\overset{\vee\,\vee}{c\,pn}b)(\overset{\vee}{c}(\overset{\vee}{c}\,admired)(\overset{\vee\,\vee}{s\,n}x)(\overset{\vee\,\vee}{c\,r}x))) : \square_c^{\downarrow}s$$

$$\overset{k}{L\backslash j}\hat{c}((\overset{\vee}{c}\,told)(\overset{\vee\,\vee}{s\,pn}j)(\overset{\vee\,\vee}{c\,pn}b)(\overset{\vee}{c}(\overset{\vee}{c}\,admired)(\overset{\vee\,\vee}{s\,n}x)(\overset{\vee\,\vee}{c\,r}x)))$$
$$\rightarrow \quad \overset{k}{L\backslash j}((told)(j)(b)((admired)(j)(j)))^{k,j,b}_{j}$$
$$\text{OR} \quad \overset{k}{L\backslash j}((told)(j)(b)((admired)(b)(b)))^{k,j,b}_{b}$$
$$\text{OR} \quad \overset{k}{L\backslash j}((told)(j)(b)((admired)(k)(k)))^{k,j,b}_{k}$$

12.4 Parametric variation

Obviously, of course, we have not tried to sort pronouns by person, number, and gender. Nothing in the present approach prevents this, though many interesting issues involving the interplay among syntactic, semantic, and pragmatic factors in agreement phenomena. The structural representation of context adopted in the examples above raises other choices, however. In particular, the representation of context in the above examples as consisting of two sets of discourse referents, a set of discourse referents and a set of local binders, is convenient, but by no means necessary.

For example, to model the effects of Condition C of the GB account sketched earlier, according to which names cannot be co-indexed with any c-commanding expression, one can take contexts to have further structure, keeping track of global c-commanders as well as local binders and discourse referents.

Moreover, instead of regarding the discourse referents, say, as an unstructured set, this component of the representation of context may be structurally refined. For example, following work in the DRT literature, it is useful to distinguish constant terms and indeterminates introduced in the scope of certain quantifiers. Constants persist in the collection of discourse referents beyond the scope of these quantifiers; indeterminates do not.

It is also possible to manage the dynamics of the context representation in different ways. As an example, consider a language in which a reflexive must be bound by the subject of its clause. From the perspective adopted here, this can be treated by preventing the referents of non-subjects from being added to the set of reflexive-binders. That is, this typological distinction corresponds to a simple resource-management parameter.

Finally, the literature on dynamic semantics offers other possibilities. In DMG, for example, contexts are represented by assignment functions. It would be possible to develop an account along present lines in which representations of contexts are taken to be not structured sets of terms, but rather a structured set of assignment functions, one function for each class of context-dependent referring expressions. Thus, the domain of one such function might consist of just the reflexive pronouns; its co-domain would consist of just the set of acessible referents.

Although such possibilities cannot be pursued in detail here, it is worth noting a basic distinction between the present point of view and the GB tradition: instead of characterizing referential relations in terms of configurations defined on rigid syntactic structures (such as c-command), we emphasize here communication among linguistic resources. This point of view has affinities with work in the Eighties, especially that of Bach and Partee (1980) and Johnson and Klein (1986).

12.5 Extension to quantifiers

Consider now how an account along these lines can be extended to quantifiers. We begin with the treatment of quantifiers proposed by Moortgat (1996). Quantifiers are assigned the type

$$\diamond_q(s/_q(\square_q^\downarrow np\backslash_q s))$$

The type constructors involved are governed by the postulates below, where **t** is a designated type constant which serves as a place-holder:

$$(P0) \qquad \qquad \Diamond_q A \longleftrightarrow A \circ_q \mathbf{t} \qquad \qquad (P0')$$
$$(P1) \quad (A \circ_q B) \bullet C \longleftrightarrow A \circ_q \langle 0 \rangle (B \bullet C) \quad (P1')$$
$$(P2) \quad A \bullet (B \circ_q C) \longleftrightarrow B \circ_q \langle 1 \rangle (A \bullet C) \quad (P2')$$

The proof below shows how a quantifier non-deterministically finds its scope.

$$
\cfrac{
\cfrac{
\cfrac{
\cfrac{
\cfrac{
\cfrac{\Delta[A] \Rightarrow B}{\Delta[\Diamond_q \Box_q^\downarrow A] \Rightarrow B} \Box_q^\downarrow L
}{\Delta[\Box_q^\downarrow A \circ_q \mathbf{t}] \Rightarrow B} P0'
}{\Box_q^\downarrow A \circ_q \Diamond_r^l \Delta[\mathbf{t}] \Rightarrow B} P1'/P2'
}{\Diamond_r^l \Delta[\mathbf{t}] \Rightarrow \Box_q^\downarrow A \backslash_q B} \backslash_q R \qquad \Gamma[C] \Rightarrow D
}{\Gamma[s/_q(\Box^\downarrow np \backslash_q s) \circ_q \Diamond_r^l \Delta[\mathbf{t}]] \Rightarrow D} /_q L
}{\Gamma[\Delta[s/_q(\Box^\downarrow np \backslash_q s) \circ_q \mathbf{t}]] \Rightarrow D} P1/P2
}{\Gamma[\Delta[\Diamond_q(s/_q(\Box^\downarrow np \backslash_q s))]] \Rightarrow D} P0
$$

As the reader is invited to show, the non-determinism involved gives rise to scope ambiguities in the presence of two quantifiers.

Determiners, such as *every* and *no*, look for an n on their right to form a quantifier:

$$(\Diamond_q s/_q(\Box^\downarrow np \backslash_q s))/n$$

We call the n argument of the determiner its *restriction* and the $\Box_q^\downarrow np \backslash_q s$ argument of the quantifier its *scope*. Suppressing the effect of the modalities here, the Curry-Howard term assigned to a proof of a sentence in which such a static determiner takes wide scope will have the form

$$\mathcal{D}(R)(\lambda x.S),$$

with $\mathcal{D}$ a variable associated with the determiner, R a variable associated with n, and $\lambda x.S$ the term associated with the scope.

Now, a dynamic analog of this term compatible with the developments above needs two properties: first, it must contain a bound variable which can serve as anchor for pronouns in an appropriate domain; second, it will contain term-constructors that control the dynamic flow of contextual information.

Below, we show how the dynamics of various cases can be treated as a first approximation. The set of discourse binders, represented in examples above as D is split up here into two disjoint sets consisting of constants C and indeterminates I.

$$\overset{C;I\backslash z}{L}(\forall z^{C;I\cup z}_{L\cup z}(R)^{C';I'\cup z}_{L'}(\lambda x.S)^{C'';I''\cup z}_{L''})^{C'';I\backslash z}_{\emptyset}$$

$$\overset{C;I\backslash z}{L}(\exists z^{C;I\cup z}_{L\cup z}(R)^{C';I'\cup z}_{L'}(\lambda x.S)^{C'';I''\cup z}_{L''})^{C'';I}_{\emptyset}$$

These representations are inspired by the treatment of universals and indefinites in DRT and DMG and by the behavior of particular cases. They have a number of properties familiar in the dynamics literature.

First, the bound variable involved is sensitive to the properties of the context in which it occurs: it must be *fresh*.

Second, this variable must be passed as input to the term representing the restriction, in view of the well-formedness of sentences such as *every farmer with his own donkey protects it.*

Third, the output of the restrictor, including the distinguished bound variable associated with the quantifier is passed as input to the scope. And in particular, the local context which serves as input to the scope contains the distinguished bound variable. Note that the sentence *A picture of himself was the favorite of each of the judges* is grammatical when the universal has wide scope but not otherwise, for in the latter case, there is no available referent anchor for the reflexive. This shows that the the universal quantifier passes its bound variable to the local context which serves as input for the scope of the quantifier.

Fourth, for determiners like *every* and *no*, constants introduced by proper names within the restriction or the scope are passed to the output; indeterminates introduced by indefinites are not.

Just as earlier, we can enforce this referential behavior by a suitable choice of lexical term decorations (for lexical determiners), modes governing the external dynamics involved, and term re-writing rules. Instead of carrying out this program here, however, we comment on the bearing of the schema above on a small but still interesting puzzle involving crossover phenomena.

The puzzle can be illustrated as follows:

(1) A detective followed each schurk.
  $\approx$ $\forall x(schurk(x) \to \exists y(detective(y) \land followed(y,x)))$

(2) Every striker blamed himself.
  $\approx$ $\forall x(striker(x) \to blamed(x,x))$

(3) He blamed every striker.
  $\not\approx$ $\forall x(striker(x) \to blamed(x,x))$

(4) A picture of its author graces each book.
  $\forall x(book(x) \to \exists y(pic(y,\iota z(author(z,x)) \land graces(y,x))))$

(1) allows the wide-scope univeral interpretation. (2) shows that a quantifier can provide the anchor for a reflexive. But (3) doesn't allow the wide-scope universal reading which might be expected to permit the quantifier to bind the subject. On the other hand, (4) shows that a wide-scope universal reading allows the quantifier to bind a pronoun which precedes it.

To see how this behavior can be modeled, note first that the scope of the quantifier in the Curry-Howard term associated with a proof containing it will take the form of a λ-abstraction (apart from any additional modal decoration it may bear). As a consequence, the *np* assumption introduced by hypothetical reasoning can be chosen so that it has the following properties: it is fresh both with respect to discourse binders and with respect to local binders. Now, in any simple transitive sentence, the interpretation of the term associated with the object *np* is always carried out relative to a context which includes a representation of the value of the subject and the value of the possessor(s) within the subject (if any). (This latter claim can be supported by the fact that negative determiners in subject *np*'s always induce positive tags: *No student's exam was mediocre, was it / *wasn't it.*) Putting these two properties together, we see that the term associated with the hypothetical assumption must always be taken to be distinct from the individual term associated with the subject and from the individual terms (if any) of possessive determiners. On the other hand, given this interpretation of 'fresh', if the term associated with an *np* preceding the gap associated with the hypothetical assumption is *not* contained in the discourse context or local context relative to which the term associated with the hypothetical assumption is interpreted, then the distinctness of these two terms need not be enforced. This is one half of the solution: the term associated with the hypothetical assumption must be distinct from both a (c-commanding) subject and any (non-c-commanding) possessor within the subject; but distinctness with terms not represented in the discourse context it is interpreted relative to is not enforced. The other half of the solution deals with how such pronouns are anchored. The solution proposed here is simply that they can be anchored to the bound variable introduced by the quantifier within whose scope they fall.

There is a way to test this hypothesis. The hypothesis depends on the assumption that in a case such as *A picture of its author graces each book*, *each book* has wide scope, and the term associated *its* does not occur in the discourse context relative to which the distinguished variable in the scope of the quantifier is interpreted. Accordingly, then, if we replace the pronoun with an indefinite and the quantifier with a pronoun, the pronoun should *not* be anchorable to the indefinite. In the case at hand, the hypothesis gains support: sentences like *A picture of an employee appeared on his lapel pocket* cannot be interpreted in a way that anchors *his* to the term associated with *an employee* (unless the latter is interpreted with wide scope relative to the subject).

Finally, note that this argument can be run the other way as well. A referee points out that a sentence like *A cousin of his invited no man to the party* fails to have the interpretation

$$\neg\exists x(\exists y(man(x) \wedge cousin(y,x) \wedge invite\_to\_the\_party(y,x)))$$

But compare the possibility of binding a definite pronominal object to an indefinite in the position of *his* in this case: *A cousin of a mafioso just shot him in the middle of the street.* If we can construe this in a way that anchors *him* to the value of *a mafioso*—and I think we can—then this fact is consistent with the requirement that when a fresh value for the hypothetical *np* introduced by the quantifier *no man* in the example under consideration is chosen, the choice is made in a context which contains a value for *a mafioso*.

12.6 Acknowledgments

A written version of an earlier conception of the approach developed here was circulated in the summer of 1995 and presented at Utrecht and Groningen in June 1995 and at the Symposium on Language and Proof Theory at the ESSLLI Summer School in Barcelona in August 1995. More recent versions were presented in Fall 1996 and Spring 1997 to audiences in Columbus, Amsterdam, and Utrecht. The present conception was first presented at UCLA in April 1997. The comments of these audiences have been very helpful. In addition, any work of this kind rests on the insights of many others, especially in the empirical work of Generative Grammar and the theoretical ideas that form the basis of dynamic semantics. Although I shall not try to trace particular ideas to their historical sources in the literature here, I hope to be able to do so elsewhere in a larger work. Finally, I would like to thank Jean Braithwaite, Jaap van der Does and Michael Moortgat for comments and very constructive criticism, and two anonymous referees for their helpful comments. Errors are mine.

References

Bach, E. and B. H. Partee. 1980. Anaphora and semantic structure. In C. M. et al., ed., *Papers from the Parasession on Anaphora and Pronouns at the Sixteenth Regional Meeting of the Chicago Linguistic Society*, pages 1–28. Chicago: Chicago Linguistic Society.

Brame, M. 1977. Alternatives to the tensed-s and specified subject conditions. *Linguistics and Philosophy* 1:381–411.

Chierchia, G. 1988. Aspects of a categorial theory of binding. In R. T. Oehrle, E. Bach, and D. W. Wheeler, eds., *Categorial Grammar and Natural Languages Structures*, pages 125–151. Dordrecht: D. Reidel.

Chomsky, N. 1982. *Some concepts and consequences of the theory of Government and Binding*, vol. 6 of *Linguistic Inquiry Monographs*. Cambridge, Massachusetts: MIT Press.

Dowty, D. 1992. 'Variable-free' syntax, variable-binding syntax, the natural deduction lambek calculus, and the crossover constraint. In *Proceedings of the 11th Meeting of the West Coast Conference on Formal Linguistics*. Stanford: CSLI Publications.

Dowty, D. 1999. Abstract: Bound anaphora and type logical grammar. http://www.ling.ohio-state.edu/ dowty.

Groenendijk, J. and M. Stokhof. 1991. Dynamic predicate logic. *Linguistics and Philosophy* 14:39–100.

Heim, I. 1982. *The semantics of definite and indefinite noun phrases*. Ph.D. thesis, University of Massachusetts at Amherst.

Hepple, M. 1990. *The Grammar and Processing of Order and Dependency: A Categorial Approach*. Ph.D. thesis, University of Edinburgh.

Jacobson, P. 1999. Towards a variable-free semantics. *Linguistics and Philosophy* .

Jäger, G. 1997. A multi-modal analysis of anaphora and ellipsis. Manuscript. IRCS, University of Pennsylvania.

Jäger, G. 1998. Anaphora and ellipsis in type-logical grammar. In *Proceedings of the 11th Amsterdam Colloquium*. ILLC, Universiteit van Amsterdam, Amsterdam.

Johnson, M. and E. Klein. 1986. Discourse, anaphora and parsing. Tech. Rep. CSLI-86-63, CSLI, Stanford.

Kamp, H. 1984. A theory of truth and semantic representation. In J. Groenendijk, T. Janssen, and M. Stokhof, eds., *Truth, interpretation, and information*. Dordrecht: Foris Publications.

MacLane, S. and I. Moerdijk. 1992. *Sheaves in Geometry and Logic: A First Introduction to Topos Theory*. Berlin: Springer.

Moortgat, M. 1996. In situ binding. In *Proceedings of the 10th Amsterdam Colloquium*. ILLC, Universiteit van Amsterdam, Amsterdam.

Moortgat, M. 1997. Categorial type logics. In J. van Benthem and A. ter Meulen, eds., *Handbook of Logic and Language*. Amsterdam: Elsevier.

Morrill, G. 1990. Intensionality and boundedness. *Linguistics and Philosophy* 13:699–726.

Stalnaker, R. 1978. Assertion. In P. Cole, ed., *Syntax and Semantics 9: Pragmatics*, pages 315–332. New York: Academic Press.

Szabolcsi, A. 1989. Bound variables in syntax: Are there any? In R. Bartsch, J. van Benthem, and P. van Emde Boas, eds., *Semantics and Contextual Expressions*, pages 295–318. Dordrecht: Foris Publications.

Part III

Formal and Computational Issues

13

Synchronous Local TDGs and Scope Ambiguities

Laura Kallmeyer

This paper proposes to describe the relation between syntax and semantics of natural languages using two local Tree Description Grammars (TDG) connected by a synchronization relation. The use of tree descriptions (instead of structures, e.g., trees in Tree Adjoining Grammars) allows an underspecification of the dominance relation between nodes in a tree and consequently underspecified representations for scope ambiguities can be generated in an elegant way. Furthermore, local TDGs offer an extended domain of locality such that local dependencies can be expressed in single elements of the grammar and island constraints are respected because of the locality of the derivations.

13.1 Introduction

Local TDGs (Kallmeyer 1997, 1999) were developed as an extension of Tree Adjoining Grammars (TAG) generating tree descriptions.

To incorporate semantics into TAGs, Shieber and Schabes 1990 propose to use synchronous TAGs. Following their ideas, I will present a syntax-semantics interface using synchronous local TDGs. For semantic representations a TDG G_{sem} will be developed. G_{sem} depends on the syntax in some compositional way which is realized by synchronizing the syntax TDG G_{syn} with G_{sem}.

Most theories in the Montagovian tradition assume syntax and semantics to be closely related. Usually, trees of height 1 (which corresponds to phrase structure rules) are related to semantic rules describing how to obtain the semantic interpretation of the mother node from the interpretations of the daughters. These systems need higher order logics

Constraints and Resources in Natural Language Syntax and Semantics.
Gosse Bouma, Erhard W. Hinrichs, Geert-Jan M. Kruijff, and Richard T. Oehrle.
Copyright © 1999, Stanford University.

for truth conditions and rules like *Quantifying In*. With synchronous local TDGs, the semantics also depends on the syntax in a compositional way, but the relation is less close. In this framework a syntactic tree description is related to a second tree description that characterizes the contribution of the first one to the semantic interpretation. These tree descriptions can be larger than a tree of height 1 and there need not be a direct correspondence between the node names in these two descriptions. Consequently, no additional mechanisms are required to account for differences between (surface) word order and semantic interpretation, and the truth-conditional logic can be relatively simple.

The structure of the paper is as follows: in Section 13.2 I briefly present two prominent approaches to deal with quantifier scope and I motivate the need for underspecified representations. Then, in 13.3 I give an informal introduction to synchronous local TDGs. In the following section a fragment of a syntax-semantics interface is proposed. After that I show in 13.5 that this grammar allows the derivation of underspecified representations for scope ambiguities in such a way that island constraints are respected.

13.2 Quantifier scope

In this section two important approaches proposed for quantifying noun phrases are sketched, namely Montague 1974 and Cooper 1983, and underspecified representations are motivated.

13.2.1 Quantifying in and quantifier storage

Montague (1974) analyzes noun phrases as sets of properties: *every man* denotes the set of properties that are true for all men, and *a man* the set of properties that are true for at least one man.

(1) a. A man sings.

    b. A man loves every woman.

(1)a. can be interpreted in the following way: there is some individual x such that: x is a man and x is singing. The part "there is some individual x such that: x is P_1 and x is P_2" can be regarded as the denotation of the determiner a. This must be applied to two predicates (P_1 and P_2), in this case the denotations of *man* and *sings*. Following Barwise and Cooper 1981, I will call the interpretation of an NP a *quantifier*, and the interpretation of a determiner a *quantifying phrase*. A quantifying phrase has two arguments both denoting properties. The first argument of a quantifying phrase is called its *restriction* and the second its *body*.

Montague uses one rule that combines a subject NP with an intransitive verb as described above. Another rule combines a transitive verb as in (1)b. with an object NP in such a way that the transitive verb is applied to the quantifier corresponding to the NP. The result is a predicate. With these rules, in (1)b. *loves* is applied to *every woman*, and the result becomes the argument of *a man*. However, with this analysis only the reading with narrow scope of *every woman* is obtained. To account for wide scope of quantifiers, Montague proposes a *quantifying-in* mechanism. The idea is that a sentence can be formed by lowering an NP with denotation α into a position marked by a variable x, and then the sentence is true iff $\alpha(\lambda x \phi)$ is true, where ϕ is the denotation of the sentence with the variable x. This analysis accounts for wide scope of *every woman* by a specific derivation of the syntactic structure.

As Cooper (1983) points out, quantifying-in creates unnecessary syntactic ambiguity. Even (1)a. can be derived either by quantifying-in or by the rule combining subject-NP and intransitive verb. In the case of (1)b., there is also more than one syntactic derivation for each of the two scope orders. Furthermore, the syntactic structures derived for different scope orders are the same, they differ only in the way they are derived, and they can also be derived without quantifying-in. For these reasons, Cooper argues that there is no syntactic motivation for quantifying-in.

Cooper proposes a storage mechanism, *Cooper Storage*, in order to eliminate the operation of quantifying-in from the syntactic domain: if a quantifier is supposed to have wide scope, it is put into a store, and later, at an appropriate moment, it is quantified in. This mechanism also gives a way to defer the disambiguation process: quantifiers with underspecified scope can be put in a store and thereby an underspecified representation is obtained. In the course of a disambiguation, the order of the quantifiers is specified.

This approach however does not exclude any readings. Quantifiers can stay arbitrarily long in the store and there is no restriction with respect to the order of retrieval. Therefore all combinatorially possible combinations of quantifier scope might be created. Afterwards ungrammatical readings must be explicitly excluded by extra rules.

Clearly, it would be preferable if the ungrammaticality of certain scope orders was already predicted by the form of the underspecified representation without the necessity of any extra rules. We will see that this is the case with local TDGs.

13.2.2 Scope ambiguities and underspecification

A lot of attention has been paid to underspecification recently, mainly to underspecified semantic representations. There are two reasons for replacing several analyses of a single expression by one underspecified analysis. The more practical reason is the desire to avoid combinatorial explosion. Examples like (2), taken from Poesio 1996, with 14400 readings show that it is desirable to allow scope ambiguities to exist for some time instead of resolving them immediately. For this purpose a level of underspecified representations is necessary.

(2) A politician can fool most voters on most issues most of the time, but no politician can fool all voters on every single issue all of the time.

The second reason for exploring underspecification concerns considerations of psychological plausibility. From a cognitive point of view it does not seem plausible that we process sentences such as (2) by first generating all readings and then testing them. It appears more cognitively adequate to generate underspecified representations and to postpone the resolution of ambiguities.

Most theories of underspecified semantics (e.g., Reyle 1993, Bos 1995, Muskens 1995, and Niehren et al. 1997) propose to represent scope by a partial order and to obtain underspecified representations by a relaxation of this ordering relation.

As we will see, local TDGs allow a relaxation of the dominance relation between nodes in a tree (reflexive transitive closure of the parent relation), a partial order that can be used to represent scope.

13.3 Synchronous local TDGs

In this section, I will informally introduce synchronous local TDGs as defined in Chapter 4 of Kallmeyer 1999.

13.3.1 Local TDGs

Local TDGs consist of tree descriptions, so-called *elementary descriptions*, and a specific *start description*. These descriptions are negation- and disjunction-free formulas in a quantifier-free first order logic. The tree logic allows the description of relations between node names k_1, k_2 such as parent relation (immediate dominance) $k_1 \lhd k_2$, dominance (reflexive transitive closure of the parent relation) $k_1 \lhd^* k_2$, linear precedence $k_1 \prec k_2$ and equality $k_1 \approx k_2$. Furthermore, nodes are supposed to be labelled by terminals or by atomic feature structures. The labeling function is denoted by δ, and for a node name k, $\delta(k) \approx t$ signifies that k has a terminal label t, and $a(\delta(k)) \approx v$ signifies that k is labelled by a feature structure containing the attribute value pair $\langle a, v \rangle$. In an elementary ψ, some of the node names are marked, namely those in the set K_ψ. Marked names influence the derivation in local TDGs. Fig. 1 shows a sample local TDG. In the graphical representations, marked names are equipped with an asterisk. A subscript i stands for the node name k_i.

Local TDG with start description ϕ_S and elementary descriptions ψ_1, ψ_2:

$$\phi_S \;=\; k_1 \lhd^* k_2 \wedge k_2 \lhd k_3 \wedge cat(\delta(k_1)) \approx N \wedge cat(\delta(k_2)) \approx N \wedge$$
$$\delta(k_3) \approx professor$$

$$\psi_1 \;=\; k_4 \lhd^* k_5 \wedge k_5 \lhd k_6 \wedge k_6 \lhd k_7 \wedge k_5 \lhd k_8 \wedge k_8 \lhd^* k_9 \wedge k_6 \prec k_8$$
$$\wedge\; cat(\delta(k_4)) \approx N \wedge cat(\delta(k_5)) \approx N \wedge cat(\delta(k_6)) \approx AP$$
$$\wedge\; \delta(k_7) \approx former \wedge cat(\delta(k_8)) \approx N \wedge cat(\delta(k_9)) \approx N$$

$$\psi_2 \;=\; k_{10} \lhd^* k_{11} \wedge k_{11} \lhd k_{12} \wedge k_{12} \lhd^* k_{13} \wedge k_{11} \lhd k_{14} \wedge k_{14} \lhd k_{15}$$
$$\wedge\; k_{12} \prec k_{14} \wedge cat(\delta(k_{10})) \approx N \wedge cat(\delta(k_{11})) \approx N$$
$$\wedge \ldots$$

$K_{\psi_1} = \{k_9\}$, $K_{\psi_2} = \{k_{13}\}$.

Graphical representations:

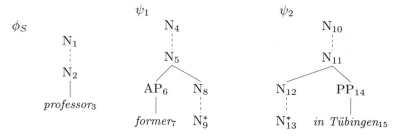

FIGURE 1 Sample local TDG

13.3.2 Derivation in local TDGs

Local TDGs generate tree descriptions. A derivation starts with the start description. In each derivation step, a derived description ϕ_1 and an elementary ψ are used to obtain a new description ϕ_2. Roughly said, ϕ_2 can be viewed as a conjunction $\phi_2 = \phi_1 \wedge \psi \wedge k_1 \approx k'_1 \wedge \cdots \wedge k_n \approx k'_n$ where k_i are names from ϕ_1 and k'_i are names from ψ for $1 \le i \le n$. This derivation step must be such that

1. for a k_ψ in ψ, there is a new equivalence iff k_ψ is either marked or minimal (dominated by no other name, e.g., k_4 in ψ_1 in Fig. 1),
2. the names $k_1, \ldots, k_n$ from ϕ_1 that are used for new equivalences are part of one single elementary or start description, the so-called *derivation description* of this derivation step (locality condition),
3. and the result ϕ_2 is as underspecified as possible, i.e. up to some renaming of node names, ϕ_2 does not entail any other possible result of the derivation step.

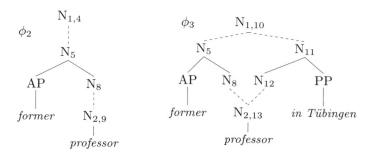

FIGURE 2 Sample derived descriptions

With the first condition, one can say that the marking of names some-how specifies how to put the two descriptions (the old ϕ_1 and the new elementary ψ) together. Marked names indicate those parts of ψ that must be connected (by new equivalences) to ϕ_1. In this sense, marked names resemble foot nodes in TAGs. Only elementary descriptions have marked names, i.e., after adding an elementary ψ in a derivation step to a description ϕ_1, the marked names in ψ are no longer distinguished from other names in ψ.

The idea of the locality condition is that the modifications of ϕ_1 caused by a single derivation step should be local in the sense that only parts of ϕ_1 belonging to the same elementary or start description are modified. As a consequence of this condition, semilinearity of local TDGs can be shown (see Kallmeyer 1997) since the derivation process becomes context-free.

The description of derivation in local TDGs given here is only an informal presentation that is sufficient to follow the proposals of this paper. For a formal definition of local TDGs and of derivations in local TDGs (see Kallmeyer 1999, Chapter 4).

As an example, consider again the grammar in Fig. 1. Derivation steps in this local TDG are for example $\phi_S \overset{\psi_1}{\Rightarrow} \phi_2$ with $\phi_2 = \phi_S \wedge \psi_1 \wedge k_1 \approx k_4 \wedge k_2 \approx k_9$ and also $\phi_2 \overset{\psi_2}{\Rightarrow} \phi_3$ with $\phi_3 = \phi_2 \wedge \psi_2 \wedge k_1 \approx k_{10} \wedge k_2 \approx k_{13}$. ϕ_2 and ϕ_3 are shown in Fig. 2. In the second derivation step, ϕ_3 is the only description that can be derived combining ϕ_2 and ψ_2 with derivation description ϕ_S because the result must be maximally underspecified.

13.3.3 Minimal trees

A local TDG G generates a set of descriptions, namely all descriptions that are derived from the start description of G. From these descriptions, corresponding so-called *minimal trees* can be obtained. A description such as ϕ_3 in Fig. 2 is satisfied by an infinite number of trees. However, as "smallest" models this description is intended to describe the two syntactic structures of *former professor in Tübingen*. Therefore, a tree γ is a minimal tree of a description ϕ, iff γ satisfies ϕ in such a way that

1. all parent relations in γ are described in ϕ, and
2. if two node names that are not equivalent in ϕ denote the same node in γ, then one node name lacks a parent in ϕ and one node name lacks a daughter in ϕ.

The minimal trees of a given description can be obtained by adding equivalences between node names and equivalences between labels.

13.3.4 Synchronization

Synchronous local TDGs consist of two local TDGs G_1, G_2 and a synchronization relation Σ between the elementary descriptions of G_1 and G_2. For each pair in Σ, there is an additional relation σ between the node names of the two descriptions, i.e. the elements of Σ are triples $\langle \psi_1, \psi_2, \sigma \rangle$, so-called *elementary configurations*. Besides Σ, there is a *start configuration* κ_s consisting of the two start descriptions of G_1 and G_2 and a relation between the sets of node names of these descriptions.

Derivation in the two TDGs is done in parallel. Starting from κ_s, further configurations (triples of two descriptions and a relation between node names) are derived by adding an elementary configuration in each derivation step. A derivation step $\langle \phi_1, \phi_2, \sigma \rangle \Rightarrow \langle \phi_1', \phi_2', \sigma' \rangle$ with an elementary $\langle \psi_1, \psi_2, \sigma_\psi \rangle$ is such that

1. $\phi_i \overset{\psi_i}{\Rightarrow} \phi_i'$ is a local derivation step in G_i for $i \in \{1, 2\}$,
2. the derivation descriptions used in these two steps are related by Σ,
3. and if equivalences $k_1 \approx k_2$ and $k_3 \approx k_4$ are added to derive ϕ_1' and ϕ_2' respectively, such that k_1 is related to k_3 and there is a node name related to k_2 or k_4, then k_2 and k_4 must be also related to each other.
4. σ' is the union of σ and σ_ψ.

The third condition makes sure that for example in derivations such as the derivation of the configuration in Fig. 5 from the descriptions in Fig. 3 and 4, when adding ψ_2 as subject NP to ψ_1, χ_2 must be inserted at the corresponding argument slot in χ_1.

A pair G_s of synchronous local TDGs generates the set of pairs $\langle \phi_1, \phi_2 \rangle$ where there is a σ such that $\kappa_s \overset{*}{\Rightarrow} \langle \phi_1, \phi_2, \sigma \rangle$. The tree language of G_s is then the set of pairs $\langle B_1, B_2 \rangle$ where there is a pair $\langle \phi_1, \phi_2 \rangle$ generated by G_s such that B_1 is a minimal tree of ϕ_1 and B_2 a minimal tree of ϕ_2.

13.4 The syntax-semantics interface

In this section I propose (a fragment of) a syntax-semantics interface where one local TDG G_{syn} describes the syntactic structures, and a second local TDG G_{sem} gives a truth-conditional semantics. G_{syn} and G_{sem} are related by a synchronization relation Σ.

As string language of G_{sem}, a traditional truth-conditional logic with model-theoretic semantics is chosen, and semantic interpretations are defined only for this logic. Minimal trees in G_{sem} are syntax trees for logical expressions, they do not have a meaning themselves. The logic is a typed first order logic allowing λ-abstraction with individuals e, truth values t and situations s as basic types. Terms are built in the usual way with sets K_T of constants of all types T, a set V of individual variables, the λ-abstractor and brackets.

Since trees in G_{sem} are supposed to describe the syntax of logical expressions, nonterminals should be names of some kind of syntactic (semantic) categories. Several types are summarized under one semantic category, and there is an attribute CAT with these semantic categories as possible values. Semantic categories are

- *prop* for propositions (type $\langle s, t \rangle$),
- *ind* for individuals (type e),
- *pred* for predicates that take individuals as arguments and that give a proposition (types $\langle e, \langle s, t \rangle \rangle$ or $\langle e, \langle e, \langle s, t \rangle \rangle \rangle$ or $\langle e, \langle e, \langle e, \langle s, t \rangle \rangle \rangle \rangle$ etc.),
- *mod* for objects of a type $\langle T, T \rangle$, where T is a type,
- *qp* for quantifying phrases (type $\langle \langle e, \langle s, t \rangle \rangle, \langle \langle e, \langle s, t \rangle \rangle, \langle s, t \rangle \rangle \rangle$),
- *quant* for quantifiers (type $\langle \langle e, \langle s, t \rangle \rangle, \langle s, t \rangle \rangle$)
- *con* for objects that take an argument of some type T and then give a modifier of type $\langle T, T \rangle$

13.4.1 Verbs and proper names

First, I will introduce the elementary configurations needed to analyze simple sentences such as

(3) John loves Mary.

The derivation for (3) starts with the elementary descriptions for *loves*, since this is the anchor of the whole sentence. The minimal names of these elementary descriptions have the categories S and *prop* respectively, and love is of type $\langle e, \langle e, \langle s, t \rangle \rangle \rangle$. The elementary configuration for *loves* is shown in Fig. 3. (In the graphical representations, syntactic descriptions are depicted on the left and semantic descriptions on the right.) The predicate love is first applied to an individual which corresponds to the object-NP and then to an argument corresponding

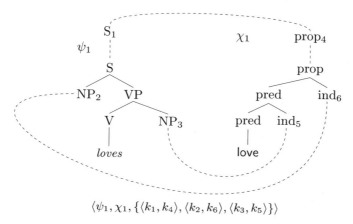

$$\langle \psi_1, \chi_1, \{\langle k_1, k_4 \rangle, \langle k_2, k_6 \rangle, \langle k_3, k_5 \rangle\}\rangle$$

FIGURE 3 Elementary configurations for *loves*

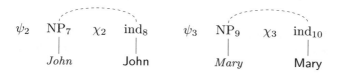

FIGURE 4 Elementary configurations for *John* and *Mary*

to the subject-NP. These correspondences are expressed by $\langle k_2, k_6 \rangle$ and $\langle k_3, k_5 \rangle$ in the synchronization relation. Elementary configurations for intransitive verbs are similar, only the object slot is omitted.

Proper names are treated as constants of type e, and I adopt elementary configurations as in Fig. 4.

For (3), starting with the elementary configuration for *loves*, the configurations for *John* and for *Mary* are added. The result is the configuration shown in Fig. 5.

13.4.2 Quantifiers

Following Montague, I will analyze quantifiers as sets of predicates (type $\langle\langle e, \langle s, t \rangle\rangle, \langle s, t \rangle\rangle$) and quantifying phrases as objects that take a predicate and give a quantifier (type $\langle\langle e, \langle s, t \rangle\rangle, \langle\langle e, \langle s, t \rangle\rangle, \langle s, t \rangle\rangle\rangle$).

(4) Every man sings.

Quantifying phrases are first applied to their restriction, and then to their body. The body can be obtained by λ-abstraction of the whole proposition with respect to the argument corresponding to the quantified NP. Therefore I propose elementary configurations like the one for *every*

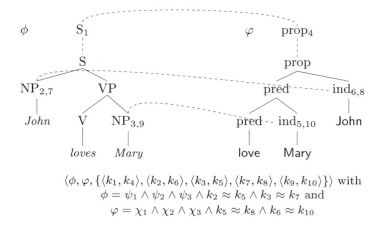

$$\langle \phi, \varphi, \{\langle k_1, k_4\rangle, \langle k_2, k_6\rangle, \langle k_3, k_5\rangle, \langle k_7, k_8\rangle, \langle k_9, k_{10}\rangle\}\rangle \text{ with}$$
$$\phi = \psi_1 \wedge \psi_2 \wedge \psi_3 \wedge k_2 \approx k_5 \wedge k_3 \approx k_7 \text{ and}$$
$$\varphi = \chi_1 \wedge \chi_2 \wedge \chi_3 \wedge k_5 \approx k_8 \wedge k_6 \approx k_{10}$$

FIGURE 5 Configuration derived for *John loves Mary*.

shown in Fig. 6 for quantifying phrases. The relation between k_7 and k_9 guarantees that the noun added in G_{syn} under k_7 denotes the restriction of the quantifying phrase. With $\langle k_6, k_{11}\rangle$, the body of the quantifying phrase must be a predicate that is applied to the individual corresponding to the quantified NP. Each time such an elementary configuration is used, x must be instantiated with a new individual variable.

Common nouns like *man* in (4) are of type $\langle e, \langle s, t\rangle\rangle$. Their elementary configurations are as shown in Fig. 6. The dominances between k_{12} and k_{13} and between k_{14} and k_{15} account for the fact that the predicate might be modified in further derivation steps.

The analysis of (4) (see Fig. 6) starts with the configuration for *sings*. First the configuration for *every* is added and then the configuration for *man*. The result in G_{sem} has exactly one minimal tree yielding the term every(man)(λx(sing(x))).

13.4.3 Relative clauses

Relative clauses are considered here because they provide an example for island constraints for quantifier scope in Section 13.5. I treat only so-called *restrictive* relative clauses as in (5):

(5) a girl who adores John

Roughly, this NP denotes the set of all properties that are true for at least one x such that x is a girl and x adores John. More generally, a restrictive relative clause modifies (restricts) a predicate P_1 by adding a new predicate P_2. The resulting predicate is true for an individual a in

Synchronization:
ψ_1 and χ_1: $\langle k_1, k_3 \rangle, \langle k_2, k_5 \rangle$
ψ_2 and χ_2: $\langle k_6, k_{11} \rangle, \langle k_7, k_9 \rangle$
ψ_3 and χ_3: $\langle k_{12}, k_{14} \rangle, \langle k_{13}, k_{15} \rangle$

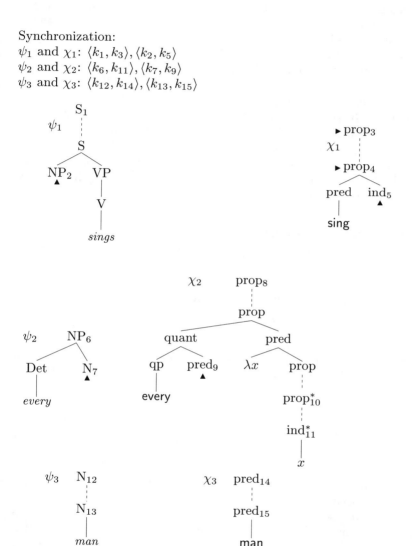

FIGURE 6 Derivation steps for *Every man sings*.

a situation s iff both P_1 and P_2 are true for a in s. In order to account for this interpretation, I propose elementary configurations as in Fig. 7 for verbs that are anchors of relative clauses. The combination and of two propositions is the usual conjunction with type $\langle\langle s, t\rangle, \langle\langle s, t\rangle, \langle s, t\rangle\rangle\rangle$. Fig. 7 captures the case that the subject-NP is relativized. The slot k_1 for the relative pronoun in ψ_1 is related to k_4 and k_6, the argument slots of P_1 and P_2.

The relative pronoun is a λ-abstractor, i.e. introduces λx for a new variable x. In the scope of λx, x occurs once as argument of P_1 and once as argument of P_2. Therefore I propose elementary configurations for relative pronouns as shown in Fig. 7 for *who*. If such a configuration is added to the configuration for *adores*, the synchronization makes sure that the NP with the empty word is inserted under k_2 and that the two variables x are inserted under k_4 and k_6.

13.5 Underspecified representations

In this section I will show how to deal with scope ambiguities in the framework presented above.

13.5.1 Quantifier scope ambiguities

(6) A man loves every woman.

For (6), the description in Fig. 8 is derived in G_{sem}. It has two minimal trees: since all parent relations in minimal trees must occur in the description, either k_1 and k_2 denote the same node or k_1 and k_4. In the first case, k_3 and k_4 and also k_5 and k_6 denote the same nodes as well and a minimal tree for the stronger reading (wide scope of *a man*) is obtained. In the second case, k_5 and k_2 also denote the same node and k_3 and k_6 as well. The interpretations of the terms yielded as strings by the corresponding two minimal trees are the two possible scope orders.

As this example shows, synchronous local TDGs allow the derivation of underspecified representations for quantifier scope ambiguities. The underspecification in this case arises from not fully specifying the dominance relation. This distinguishes (synchronous) local TDGs from more traditional approaches dealing with structures (i.e., fully specified objects) such as synchronous TAGs where instead of one underspecified representations two different analyses are generated for the two readings of a scope ambiguitiy as (6).

The description generated for (6) in G_{syn} is not ambiguous; in this system quantifier scope ambiguities are analyzed as semantic ambiguities and unnecessary syntactic ambiguities do not arise.

Synchronization:

ψ_1 and χ_1: $\{\langle k_1, k_4 \rangle, \langle k_1, k_6 \rangle, \langle k_2, k_6 \rangle, \langle k_3, k_5 \rangle\}$

ψ_2 and χ_2: $\{\langle k_7, k_9 \rangle, \langle k_7, k_{10} \rangle, \langle k_8, k_{10} \rangle\}$

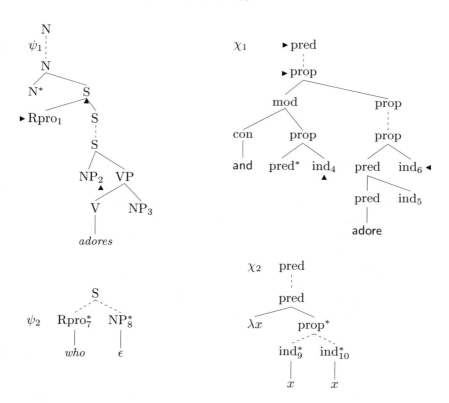

FIGURE 7 Elementary descriptions for restrictive relative clauses

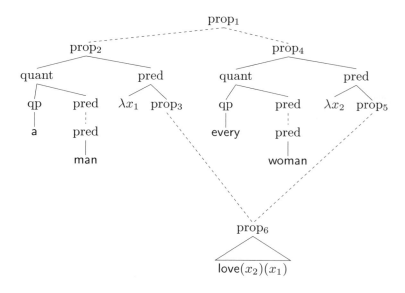

FIGURE 8 Description derived in G_{sem} for (6)

Since the description of the dominance relation is part of the grammar in this tree description based formalism, underspecified representations for scope ambiguities can be obtained in a natural and elegant way without adding any extra mechanisms (as in Reyle 1993 and Bos 1995 for example).

This analysis is not restricted to quantifiers. In Kallmeyer 1999, similar descriptions are generated for de re – de dicto ambiguities and for ambiguities with nominal modifiers.

13.5.2 Island constraints

Similar to wh-movement, quantifier raising is subject to island constraints. For this paper I will consider only the

Relative clause constraint: A quantifier occuring in a relative clause cannot have scope over the element modified by this relative clause.

(7) John loves a princess who adores every frog.

In (7) for the quantifier *every frog* it is not possible to outscope *a princess*. This constraint is respected within the analysis proposed above: in G_{sem} first the description for *John loves a princess* is derived, and the description for *adores* anchoring a relative clause is added as modifier of *princess* (see Fig. 9). Since the minimal name in χ must

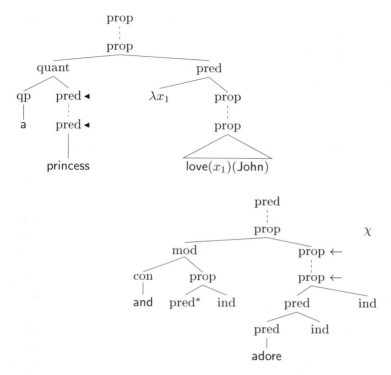

FIGURE 9 Derivation step adding the relative clause in (7)

be identified with a name belonging to the elementary description of *princess*, i.e., belonging to the restriction of the quantifying phrase *a*, the whole relative clause becomes part of the restriction of *a*.

In the next derivation steps the configurations for *who* and for *every* must be added in such a way that in both cases the elementary description for *adores* is the derivation description. Therefore the quantifying phrase *every* must be "inserted" between the two node names marked by an arrow in Fig. 9. This excludes wide scope of *every frog*, since *every frog* is part of the restriction of *a* and therefore cannot outscope *a princess*. Without the locality condition for the derivations, wide scope of *every frog* would have been possible since the minimal name of the elementary description of *every* would have become equivalent to the minimal name of the whole description.

As this example shows, within the syntax-semantics interface presented above, the Relative clause constraint is respected. It follows from the fact that the elementary configuration for the anchor of the relative clause is added to the elementary descriptions of the modified noun. The locality restriction for the derivation in synchronous local TDGs then signifies that a quantifier occurring in the relative clause cannot raise out of the predicate denoted by the modified noun.

In frameworks such as synchronous local TDGs (also TAGs and tree- and set-local MC-TAGs) that combine an extended domain of locality with a locality restriction on the derivations, island constraints need not be explicitly stated. They hold as a consequence of the choice of elementary descriptions (which is motivated by independent linguistic principles such as the predicate-argument cooccurrence principle) and of the locality of derivations. A recent approach that also shows these properties, is Joshi and Vijay-Shanker 1999. However, the semantic representations used in this proposal are only sketched, and therefore it is difficult to compare it to the approach presented here. In frameworks that do not offer this extended domain of locality, island constraints must be explictely stated: they are not given by the lexical entries themselves. This distinguishes local TDGs from approaches such as Muskens 1995 and Niehren et al. 1997 that also use tree descriptions as underspecified representations for scope ambiguities. Even Muskens and Krahmer (1998), who make use of the extended domain of locality provided by TAG-like grammar, still suppose each node in the syntactic tree to be related to some semantic expression. Therefore they also have to impose island constraints explicitly.

It is important to mention that the locality condition for the derivation in local TDGs was not proposed in order to produce island effects but (see Kallmeyer 1997,1999) in order to restrict the generative capacity of the grammar formalism to semilinear languages. In other words, the locality condition arises from more general considerations concerning the generative power of the grammar.

13.6 Conclusion

In this paper, I have presented a fragment of a syntax-semantics interface based on synchronous local TDGs. One TDG G_{syn} describes the syntactic structure of a natural language, and a second TDG G_{sem} describes the syntactic structure of a truth conditional logic. G_{syn} and G_{sem} are related to each other by a synchronization relation.

The use of synchronous local TDGs has several advantages:

Local TDGs generate underspecified representations for scope ambiguities in a very elegant and natural way since they deal with tree descriptions that allow an underspecification of the dominance relation.

Furthermore, since the same formalism is used for syntax and semantics, syntactic scope ambiguities are accounted for in the same way as semantic scope ambiguities (cf. the examples of nominal modifier scope ambiguities in Kallmeyer 1999).

Syntax and semantics depend on each other in a compositional way but this dependence is less close than in more traditional Montagovian approaches. As a consequence of this, a quantifying-in mechanism is not needed. Furthermore, a simple first-order logic is sufficient as truth-conditional semantics and trees in G_{sem} can be simply seen as syntactic trees of logical expressions. There is no need to define specific semantic operations for internal nodes.

Because of the combination of an extended domain of locality with a locality condition on derivations, island constraints for quantifier scope are respected. More precisely, these constraints are a consequence of the locality condition and the linguistic principles underlying the choice of elementary descriptions.

Acknowledgments

For many helpful comments and useful discussions I would like to thank Erhard W. Hinrichs and Graham Katz. Furthermore, I am very grateful to two anonymous reviewers who made very detailed comments and suggestions and thereby helped me to make some points more clear and explicit.

References

Barwise, J. and R. Cooper. 1981. Generalized quantifiers and natural language. *Linguistics and Philosophy* 4:159–219.

Bos, J. 1995. Predicate logic unplugged. In P. Dekker and M. Stokhof, eds., *Proceedings of the 10th Amsterdam Colloquium*, pages 133–142.

Cooper, R. 1983. *Quantification and Syntactic Theory*. Synthese Language Library. Dordrecht: Reidel.

Joshi, A. K. and K. Vijay-Shanker. 1999. Compositional Semantics with Lexicalized Tree-Adjoining Grammar (LTAG): How Much Underspecification is Necessary? In H. C. Blunt and E. G. C. Thijsse, eds., *Proceedings ot the Third International Workshop on Computational Semantics (IWCS-3)*, pages 131–145. Tilburg.

Kallmeyer, L. 1997. Local Tree Description Grammars. In *Proceedings of the Fifth Meeting on Mathematics of Language, DFKI Research Report*, pages 77–84.

Kallmeyer, L. 1999. *Tree Description Grammars and Underspecified Representations*. Ph.D. thesis, Universität Tübingen. To appear as

Technical Report at the Institute for Research in Cognitive Science, University of Pennsylvania, Philadelphia.

Montague, R. 1974. The Proper Treatment of Quantification in Ordinary English. In R. H. Thomason, ed., *Formal Philosophy: Selected Papers of Richard Montague*, pages 247–270. New Haven: Yale University Press.

Muskens, R. 1995. Order-independence and underspecification. In J. Groenendijk, ed., *Ellipsis, Underspecification, Events and More in Dynamic Semantics*. DYANA Report R2.2.C.

Muskens, R. and E. Krahmer. 1998. Description Theory, LTAGs and Underspecified Semantics. In *Fourth International Workshop on Tree Adjoining Grammars and Related Frameworks, IRCS Report 98–12*. University of Pennsylvania, Philadelphia.

Niehren, J., M. Pinkal, and P. Ruhrberg. 1997. A Uniform Approach to Underspecification and Parallelism. In *Proceedings of ACL*. Madrid.

Poesio, M. 1996. Semantic ambiguity and perceived ambiguity. In K. van Deemter and S. Peters, eds., *Semantic Ambiguity and Underspecification*, pages 159–201. CLSI Publications Stanford.

Reyle, U. 1993. Dealing with ambiguities by underspecification: Construction, representation and deduction. *Journal of Semantics* 10:123–179.

Shieber, S. M. and Y. Schabes. 1990. Synchronous Tree-Adjoining Grammars. In *Proceedings of COLING*, pages 253–258.

14

LIGs with Reduced Derivation Sets

JENS MICHAELIS AND CHRISTIAN WARTENA

14.1 Introduction

The potential of indexed grammars (Aho 1968) to account for non–local dependencies in natural languages was first exploited in Gazdar 1988, which introduced the formalism of linear indexed grammar (LIG). In an LIG–derivation each nonterminal has an associated stack of indices. If a nonterminal is rewritten, the indices are passed on to exactly one daughter, the *distinguished child*, specified in the applied production. As for grammars of natural languages it seems to be possible to place general constraints on the position of the distinguished child among its sisters. In this paper we investigate the consequences of restricting the set of possible candidates for inheritance of the index stack. First we consider LIGs in which the distinguished child always has to be the rightmost symbol in the righthand side of a production. We call an LIG in this format a right LIG (RLIG). Left LIGs (LLIGs) are defined analogously. Both RLIGs and LLIGs are special cases of a type of LIG we introduce below, unidirectional indexed grammars (UIGs). In a UIG a stack of indices can be passed on either to a leftmost or to a rightmost daughter. But once the stack is inherited to the right (left) it cannot "change direction" until it is empty again. For many languages this restriction seems to be too strong, though index inheritance is in some sense still rightmost as we argue in Section 14.2. We therefore define a slightly relaxed, but still restricted form of LIGs, extended UIGs (EUIGs), in Section 14.4. Though UIGs define non–recognizable (tree–)sets, the class of generated (string–)languages is that of context–free languages (Section 14.5). The weak generative capacity of EUIGs is located properly between that of CFGs and LIGs (Section 14.7). In Section 14.6 we argue that there are strong connections between the UIG–formalism and tree insertion gram-

Constraints and Resources in Natural Language Syntax and Semantics.
Gosse Bouma, Erhard W. Hinrichs, Geert-Jan M. Kruijff, and Richard T. Oehrle.
Copyright © 1999, Stanford University.

mars (TIGs) (Schabes and Waters 1995) and we sketch how extended
TIGs (ETIGs) corresponding to EUIGs can be defined.

14.2   A note on extraction paths

Without tying us down to a derivational or representational approach,
we use the movement metaphor and exploit traces in structural analyses
for the sake of clarity. Also, we sometimes refer to the sequence of nodes
between two dependent positions as an extraction path.

An extraction path tends to coincide with a rightmost path. This
is due to the interplay of the principles regarding the linearization of
clauses on the one hand and those determining the opacity of constituents on the other. Subjects, indirect objects and adjuncts behave
in many languages like islands for extraction in contrast to the transparency of objects as is illustrated in (1) and (2), respectively.

(1) a. Who_i did Mary think [that John loves t_i]?
   b. Who_i does Mary know [a friend of t_i]?
   c. [Of which month]$_i$ does John hate [every day t_i]?

(2) a. $*Who_i$ did [that John loves t_i] annoy Mary?
   b. $*Who_i$ did John give [a friend of t_i] a book?
   c. $*$[Of which month]$_i$ does John strike his donkey [every day t_i]?

Further, objects are mostly positioned near the right edge of each clause.
In English and other languages in which the object is really clause–final
the directedness of extraction thus becomes most clear. As for verb–
final languages the situation is somewhat more intricate. According to
Haider 1993, specifiers and adjuncts universally appear to the left of
the head whereas the position of complements is lexically determined by
the head, either to the left or to the right. Given the fact that objects
are assumed to be realized as complements, the only kind of movement
allowed in this framework is raising out of a constituent whose root has
either nothing or a (verbal) head to its right. This chimes in as well
with the movement theory in Müller 1995, in which every NP within
a VP constitutes a barrier unless its head can (abstractly) incorporate
into the verb. This in turn is only possible if this NP is a sister of the
verb. Thus we assume that movement in general is always out of the
rightmost nonterminal.

There are a few counterexamples like wh–movement out of infinitival subject sentences (3a) and movement of prepositional adjuncts out
of subject NPs (3b) in German.

(3) a. Was$_i$ hat [$_\text{CP}$PRO t_i zu beanstanden] sich nicht gehört ?
　　　　 what has 　　　　 to complain of REFL not 　 befitted

　 b. [Von wem]$_i$ würde [jeder Roman t_i] den Preis gewinnen?
　　　 Of whom 　 would every novel 　　 the award win

Anyhow, there is no possibility to pursue this kind of extraction recursively, i.e. there are no similar constructions in which a constituent is moved out of the subject of a subject. In the grammar formalisms we introduce below one could therefore, if need be, use another way than the general mechanism handling non–local dependencies to account for this kind of bounded movement. For the moment we simply assume the initial observation to be correct.

14.3　From extraction paths to spines

A linear indexed grammar (LIG) constitutes a simple model for investigations on movement. At the righthand side of each (nonterminal) production in an LIG, one symbol is distinguished, explicitly indicating the next branch of a path along which (a stack of) indices can be passed on. Such a path is called a spine. Spines can serve as a formalization of the more informal notion of extraction paths.

Definition 1 (LIG) A *linear indexed grammar (LIG)* G is a five–tuple (N, Σ, I, P, S), where N, Σ and I are finite sets, pairwise disjoint, which respectively denote the sets of *nonterminal, terminal* and *index symbols*. S denotes a distinguished nonterminal (the *start symbol*). P is a finite set of pairs, called *productions*, of one of the forms:

$$1.\ A[\zeta...] \to \beta_l B[\eta...]\beta_r \qquad\qquad 2.\ A[\zeta] \to w$$

for some $A, B \in N$, $\zeta, \eta \in I^*$, $\beta_l, \beta_r \in (O \cup \Sigma)^*$ and $w \in \Sigma^*$.[1] $[\,,]$ and $...$ are extra symbols not in $N \cup \Sigma \cup I$, O is the set $\{A[\eta] \mid A \in N, \eta \in I^*\}$, the set of *nonterminal objects (in G)*. Productions of the 1$^\text{st}$ form are *nonterminal*, those of the 2$^\text{nd}$ form are *terminal*.

Let $G = (N, \Sigma, I, P, S)$ be an LIG. A string $\sigma \in (O \cup \Sigma)^*$ is said to *directly generate (directly derive)* a string $\tau \in (O \cup \Sigma)^*$, written $\sigma \underset{G}{\Rightarrow} \tau$, if either (1) or (2):

$$(1)\quad \sigma = \gamma_l A[\zeta\theta]\gamma_r \qquad\qquad (2)\ \sigma = \gamma_l A[\zeta]\gamma_r$$
$$A[\zeta...]{\to}\beta_l B[\eta...]\beta_r \in P \qquad\qquad A[\zeta]{\to}w \in P$$
$$\tau = \gamma_l \beta_l B[\eta\theta]\beta_r\gamma_r \qquad\qquad \tau = \gamma_l w \gamma_r$$

for some $A, B \in N$, $\zeta, \eta, \theta \in I^*$, $\beta_l, \beta_r, \gamma_l, \gamma_r \in (O \cup \Sigma)^*$ and $w \in \Sigma^*$.

---

[1]For any set M, M^* is the set of finite strings in M including the empty string ϵ.

If $\sigma \underset{G}{\Rightarrow} \tau$ by applying $p \in P$, we also write $\sigma \overset{p}{\underset{G}{\Rightarrow}} \tau$. When $I \neq \emptyset$, a nonterminal production is applicable to instances of infinitely many different nonterminal objects. A terminal production is applicable to instances of exactly one nonterminal object. It is helpful to think of an element in O as a nonterminal associated with a stack of indices. Thus, we see that in (1) such a stack is passed on from the mother to exactly one daughter, while the upper part ζ is replaced by η. Then, w.r.t. the corresponding occurrences, $B[\eta\theta]$ is the *distinguished child* of $A[\zeta\theta]$.

We will write $A[\,]$ instead of $A[\zeta] \in O$, if $\zeta = \epsilon$, and take $N_{[]}$ to denote $\{A[\,] \mid A \in N\} \subseteq O$, the set of nonterminal objects associated with the empty stack. By $\underset{G}{\overset{*}{\Rightarrow}}$ we denote the reflexive and transitive closure of the relation $\underset{G}{\Rightarrow}$. Let $n \in \mathbb{N}$,[2] and let $d = \sigma_0 \ldots \sigma_n$ be a sequence of strings in $(O \cup \Sigma)^*$ with $\sigma_i \underset{G}{\Rightarrow} \sigma_{i+1}$ for $0 \leq i < n$. d is a *derivation (in G from σ_0 to σ_n)*. When $\sigma_0 = S[\,]$ we also call d a *derivation of σ_n*. If in each string σ_i the leftmost (rightmost) nonterminal object is rewritten to directly derive σ_{i+1}, then d is called a *leftmost (rightmost)* derivation. The set $L(G) = \{w \in \Sigma^* \mid S[\,] \underset{G}{\overset{*}{\Rightarrow}} w\}$, the language generated by G, is called a *linear indexed language (LIL)*.

In order to introduce the notion of a spine, we start by defining a *(finite) ordered tree* $\tau = (N_\tau, \vartriangleleft_\tau^*, \prec_\tau)$ in the usual sense: $\vartriangleleft_\tau^*$ and $\prec_\tau$ denote the binary relations of *dominance* and *precedence*, respectively, defined on the (finite) set of nodes N_τ, the *tree domain*.[3] $\vartriangleleft_\tau^*$ is the reflexive and transitive closure of $\vartriangleleft_\tau \subseteq N_\tau \times N_\tau$, the relation of *immediate dominance*. A *labeled ordered tree* $\tau = (N_\tau, \vartriangleleft_\tau^*, \prec_\tau, \ell_\tau)$ is an ordered tree $(N_\tau, \vartriangleleft_\tau^*, \prec_\tau)$ with a mapping ℓ_τ from N_τ into a set of *labels*.

Let $G = (N, \Sigma, I, P, S)$ be an LIG, and $d = \sigma_0 \ldots \sigma_n$ a derivation in G with $\sigma_0 \in O \cup \Sigma$. The *derivation tree* $\delta = (N_\delta, \vartriangleleft_\delta^*, \prec_\delta, \ell_\delta)$ *(induced by d)* is the labeled ordered tree inductively given in the usual way depending on the derivation steps of d. In particular, $\ell_\delta : N_\delta \to O \cup \Sigma$. A *spine (of δ or of d)* is a sequence $\chi_0 \ldots \chi_k$ of nodes $\chi_i \in N_\delta$ with label $\ell_\delta(\chi_i) \in O$ such that χ_{i+1} is the distinguished child of χ_i w.r.t. d. χ_k is called a *distinguished descendant* of χ_0. Hence, a spine is a path along which a stack is successively passed on.

The observation that an extraction path successively descends along rightmost branches can now be formalized in terms of LIGs by requiring that only productions of the following type are used:

$$1.\ A[\zeta...] \to \beta B[\eta...] \qquad\qquad 2.\ A[\zeta] \to w$$

---

[2] $\mathbb{N}$ denotes the set of all non-negative integers.

[3] Up to an isomorphism, N_τ is a unique subset of $\mathbb{N}^*$ such that N_τ is *prefix closed* and *left closed*: $\phi \in N_\tau$ if $\phi\chi \in N_\tau$, and $\phi i \in N_\tau$ if $\phi j \in N_\tau$, where $\phi, \chi \in \mathbb{N}^*$ and $i, j \in \mathbb{N}$ with $i < j$.

for some $A, B \in N$, $\zeta, \eta \in I^*$, $\beta \in (O \cup \Sigma)^*$ and $w \in \Sigma^*$.

Definition 2 (RLIG) An LIG G is called a *right linear indexed grammar (RLIG)* if each production is of one of the two forms just given.

Following the argumentation of Section 14.2, the expressive power of LIGs useful for the description of many languages is already provided by RLIGs. Therefore RLIGs are of some interest. At a glance it might be surprising that RLIGs turn out to be weakly equivalent to context–free grammars (CFGs): A language derivable by an RLIG $G = (N, \Sigma, I, P, S)$ can be recognized by a pushdown automaton (PDA) and, consequently, is context–free. The idea is that an appropriate PDA simulates a left-most derivation in G. The construction of such a PDA is straightforward, since G can be considered as a highly restricted type of phrase structure grammar in the usual sense with nonterminal set $N \cup I \cup \{[\}$. In terms of strings, applying a production p to a nonterminal object $A[\zeta\theta]$ is simply a replacement of $A[\zeta$ by a string in $(N \cup I \cup \{[\} \cup \Sigma)^*$, namely the righthand side of p up to ...]. That is to say, the PDA does in fact not need to take care of the inheritance of indices. Only for the permitted change of the upper part of a stack a small look-ahead (bounded in size, because P is finite) is required. The construction of a PDA for an RLIG in normalized form is given in Michaelis and Wartena 1997. Here, we will prove the weak equivalence of CFGs and a generalization of RLIGs, unidirectional indexed grammars (UIGs) (Section 14.5).[4]

According to Section 14.2, for verb–final languages the appropriate formalization of the restrictions on index inheritance could be approximated by the exclusive use of productions in which the distinguished symbol is the rightmost nonterminal symbol on the righthand side. Thus we need productions of only the following type:

$$\text{1. } A[\zeta...] \to \beta B[\eta...]w \qquad\qquad \text{2. } A[\zeta] \to w$$

for some $A, B \in N$, $\zeta, \eta \in I^*$, $\beta \in (O \cup \Sigma)^*$ and $w \in \Sigma^*$.

Definition 3 (ERLIG) An LIG G is an *extended right linear indexed grammar (ERLIG)* if each production is of the form 1. or 2. above.

It is easy to see that ERLIGs generate non–context–free languages. The ERLIG–formalism can e.g. cope with the cross–serial dependencies found in Dutch.[5] Nevertheless, the ERLIG–restriction on the production for-

---

[4]Note that RLIGs can in turn be considered as a non–trivial extension of *right linear indexed right linear grammars*. The latter were introduced and shown to be weakly context–free in Aho 1968.

[5]Figure 1 provides an ERLIG–tree for the Dutch verb raising structure. We assume that the "base structure" involves nested dependencies from which the verbs are moved out to the right. This is more or less in line with the traditional analysis

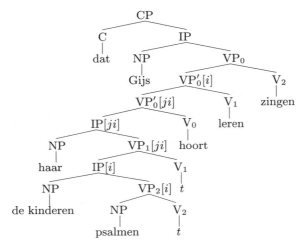

' ...that Gijs hears her teaching the children to sing psalms'

FIGURE 1 Dutch VR-Structure as an ERLIG–tree

mat reduces the weak generative power of LIGs. Again, we will show this for a more general class of grammars, Extended UIGs.[6]

14.4   Unidirectional inheritance of indices

Unidirectional indexed grammars (UIGs) are a generalization of RLIGs as well as of their counterpart, left LIGs (LLIGs).[7] The UIG–formalism allows one to combine an RLIG and an LLIG in a particular way: A spine can successively follow the leftmost or rightmost child. The restriction imposed is that the direction of passing on the stack, leftmost or rightmost, can only be changed if the stack is empty.[8] This concept can be loosened by requiring that the distinguished symbol is the rightmost (leftmost) nonterminal. In the latter case the resulting grammars are called extended UIGs (EUIGs).

(Evers 1975). However we cannot describe the verbal cluster exactly in the way it is usually done, disregarding c–command in its strictest interpretation.

[6] In Wartena 1998 automata are investigated that accept exactly the languages generable by ERLIGs.

[7] Just in order to complete the picture, we formally define an LLIG as an LIG with each production of type $A[\zeta...] \rightarrow B[\eta...]\beta$ or $A[\zeta] \rightarrow w$, and an extended LLIG (ELLIG) as an LIG with each production of the form $A[\zeta...] \rightarrow wB[\eta...]\beta$ or $A[\zeta] \rightarrow w$, where $A, B \in N$, $\zeta, \eta \in I^*$, $\beta \in (O \cup \Sigma)^*$ and $w \in \Sigma^*$.

[8] From a linguistic point of view, this might allow an appropriate formalization for some rare examples of non–local dependencies along left branches (cf. Gazdar 1988, p. 77), which could not be accounted for within the RLIG–formalism.

Definition 4 (UIG) A five–tuple $G = (N, \Sigma, I, P, S)$ with N, Σ, I, P and S defined as in an LIG is called a *unidirectional indexed grammar (UIG)* if each $p \in P$ is of one the types

$$\text{u.1 } A[\zeta..] \to \beta B[\eta...] \qquad \text{u.2 } A[\zeta..] \to B[\eta...]\beta \qquad 2. \ A[\zeta] \to w$$

for some $A, B \in N$, $\zeta, \eta \in I^*$, $\beta \in (O \cup \Sigma)^*$ and $w \in \Sigma^*$, and if G is interpreted by the restricted derives–relation $\underset{G}{\overset{\text{ui}}{\Rightarrow}} \subseteq \underset{G}{\overset{*}{\Rightarrow}}$ depending on these types (see below).

A $p \in P$ of type u.1 is called *rightmost indexed (in G)*, a $p \in P$ of type u.2 is called *leftmost indexed (in G)*. The sets of rightmost indexed and leftmost indexed productions in G are denoted by P_{ri} and P_{li}, respectively.

Definition 5 (EUIG) A five–tuple $G = (N, \Sigma, I, P, S)$ with N, Σ, I, P and S defined as in an LIG is called an *extended unidirectional indexed grammar (EUIG)* if each $p \in P$ is of one of the types

$$\text{e.1 } A[\zeta..] \to \beta B[\eta...]v \qquad \text{e.2 } A[\zeta..] \to vB[\eta...]\beta \qquad 2. \ A[\zeta] \to w$$

for some $A, B \in N$, $\zeta, \eta \in I^*$, $\beta \in (O \cup \Sigma)^*$ and $v, w \in \Sigma^*$, and if G is interpreted by the restricted derives–relation $\underset{G}{\overset{\text{ui}}{\Rightarrow}} \subseteq \underset{G}{\overset{*}{\Rightarrow}}$ depending on these production types (see below).

A $p \in P$ of type e.1 is called *rightmost indexed (in G)*, a $p \in P$ of type e.2 is called *leftmost indexed (in G)*. The sets of rightmost indexed and leftmost indexed productions in G are denoted by P_{ri} and P_{li}, respectively.[9]

Let $G = (N, \Sigma, I, P, S)$ be an (E)UIG. A string $\sigma \in (O \cup \Sigma)^*$ is said to *directly derive rightmost indexed (leftmost indexed)* a string $\tau \in (O \cup \Sigma)^*$, written $\sigma \underset{G}{\overset{\text{ri}}{\Rightarrow}} \tau$ ($\sigma \underset{G}{\overset{\text{li}}{\Rightarrow}} \tau$), if (1) or (2):

$$(1) \quad \sigma = \gamma_l A[\zeta\theta]\gamma_r \qquad\qquad (2) \ \sigma = \gamma_l A[\zeta]\gamma_r$$
$$A[\zeta...] \to \beta_l B[\eta...]\beta_r \in P_{\text{ri}} \ (\in P_{\text{li}}) \qquad A[\zeta] \to w \in P$$
$$\tau = \gamma_l \beta_l B[\eta\theta]\beta_r \gamma_r \qquad\qquad \tau = \gamma_l w \gamma_r$$

for some $A, B \in N$, $\zeta, \eta, \theta \in I^*$, $\beta_l, \beta_r, \gamma_l, \gamma_r \in (O \cup \Sigma)^*$ and $w \in \Sigma^*$. We say a string $\sigma \in (O \cup \Sigma)^*$ *directly derives ((extended) unidirectional indexed in G)* a string $\tau \in (O \cup \Sigma)^*$, written $\sigma \underset{G}{\Rightarrow} \tau$, if $\sigma \underset{G}{\overset{\text{ri}}{\Rightarrow}} \tau$ or $\sigma \underset{G}{\overset{\text{li}}{\Rightarrow}} \tau$. Now, generalizing $\underset{G}{\Rightarrow}$ we will inductively define a binary relation $\underset{G}{\overset{\text{ui}}{\Rightarrow}}$ on the set $\sigma \in (O \cup \Sigma)^*$. But contrasting with the general LIG–case, $\underset{G}{\overset{\text{ui}}{\Rightarrow}}$ will characterize only a subset of $\underset{G}{\overset{*}{\Rightarrow}}$, the reflexive and transitive closure of

---

[9]Note that each production of type e.1 (type e.2) with $\beta \in \Sigma^*$ also is of type e.2 (type e.1), but a production of type u.1 (type u.2) also is of type u.2 (type u.1) only for $\beta = \epsilon$.

$\Rightarrow_{\overrightarrow{G}}$:[10] For each string $\sigma \in (O \cup \Sigma)^*$ set $\sigma \overset{ui}{\underset{\overrightarrow{G}}{\Rightarrow}}{}^0 \sigma$. For $n \in \mathbb{N}$ let $\sigma_0 \ldots \sigma_{n+1}$ be a sequence of strings in $(O \cup \Sigma)^*$ such that $\sigma_i \underset{\overrightarrow{G}}{\Rightarrow} \sigma_{i+1}$ for $0 \le i \le n$ and such that $\sigma_0 \overset{ui}{\underset{\overrightarrow{G}}{\Rightarrow}}{}^n \sigma_n$. Thus, a particular occurrence of some $A_n[\zeta_n] \in O$ is rewritten in $\sigma_n \underset{\overrightarrow{G}}{\Rightarrow} \sigma_{n+1}$ by applying some $p_n \in P$. Consider the case $\zeta_n \ne \epsilon$ such that for some $0 \le i < n$ the instance of $A_n[\zeta_n]$, rewritten in $\sigma_n \overset{p_n}{\underset{\overrightarrow{G}}{\Rightarrow}} \sigma_{n+1}$, has been introduced as a distinguished child in $\sigma_i \underset{\overrightarrow{G}}{\Rightarrow} \sigma_{i+1}$ by applying some $p_i \in P_{\mathrm{ri}}$ ($p_i \in P_{\mathrm{li}}$). Then $\sigma_0 \overset{ui}{\underset{\overrightarrow{G}}{\Rightarrow}}{}^{n+1} \sigma_{n+1}$ only if also $p_n \in P_{\mathrm{ri}}$ ($p_n \in P_{\mathrm{li}}$). In all other cases $\sigma_0 \overset{ui}{\underset{\overrightarrow{G}}{\Rightarrow}}{}^{n+1} \sigma_{n+1}$ holds without restriction. We say a string $\sigma \in (O \cup \Sigma)^*$ derives ((extended) unidirectional indexed in G) a string $\tau \in (O \cup \Sigma)^*$, written $\sigma \overset{ui}{\underset{\overrightarrow{G}}{\Rightarrow}} \tau$, if $\sigma \overset{ui}{\underset{\overrightarrow{G}}{\Rightarrow}}{}^n \tau$ for some $n \in \mathbb{N}$. The set $L(G) = \{w \in \Sigma^* \mid S \overset{ui}{\underset{\overrightarrow{G}}{\Rightarrow}} w\}$ is the language generated by G. $L(G)$ is a unidirectional indexed language (UIL) in case G is a UIG, and an extended UIL (EUIL) in case it is an EUIG.

To make the definition of $\overset{ui}{\Rightarrow}$ somewhat more transparent, recall that a spine is a sequence of distinguished children w.r.t. to some derivation tree in G. In an (E)UIG, as long as the stack which is passed on is not empty, a spine necessarily is a path from some node to its rightmost (leftmost) descendant labeled by a nonterminal object.

Take $\overset{ri}{\underset{\overrightarrow{G}}{\Rightarrow}}{}^*$ and $\overset{li}{\underset{\overrightarrow{G}}{\Rightarrow}}{}^*$ to denote the reflexive and transitive closure of $\overset{ri}{\underset{\overrightarrow{G}}{\Rightarrow}}$ and $\overset{li}{\underset{\overrightarrow{G}}{\Rightarrow}}$, respectively. Note that $\overset{ri}{\underset{\overrightarrow{G}}{\Rightarrow}}{}^* \cup \overset{li}{\underset{\overrightarrow{G}}{\Rightarrow}}{}^* \subseteq \overset{ui}{\underset{\overrightarrow{G}}{\Rightarrow}} \subseteq \overset{}{\underset{\overrightarrow{G}}{\Rightarrow}}{}^*$. Equality for both inclusions holds if $I = \emptyset$, but also if all nonterminal productions belong to P_{ri} (to P_{li}). If the latter then G is an ERLIG (an ELLIG), even an RLIG (an LLIG) in case that G is an UIG, and we have $\overset{ri}{\underset{\overrightarrow{G}}{\Rightarrow}}{}^* = \overset{ui}{\underset{\overrightarrow{G}}{\Rightarrow}}$ ($\overset{li}{\underset{\overrightarrow{G}}{\Rightarrow}}{}^* = \overset{ui}{\underset{\overrightarrow{G}}{\Rightarrow}}$). If $I = \emptyset$, the (E)UIG can simply be taken as a CFG.

Let $G = (N, \Sigma, I, P, S)$ be a UIG, and let $<_{\mathrm{lex}}$ be the lexicographical order on $\mathbb{N}^*$: $\omega <_{\mathrm{lex}} \omega i \varphi$ and $\omega j \chi <_{\mathrm{lex}} \omega k \psi$ for all $\omega, \varphi, \chi, \psi \in \mathbb{N}^*$ and $i, j, k \in \mathbb{N}$, where $j < k$. Then, w.r.t. $<_{\mathrm{lex}}$ a particular (linear) derivation strategy can be defined for $\overset{ui}{\Rightarrow}$.[11] The strategy contrasts with the concept of a rightmost or a leftmost derivation, respectively, since it works "developing spines last." To achieve this, an address $\omega \in \mathbb{N}^*$ will be assigned to each instance of a nonterminal object $A[\zeta]$ within a $\sigma \in (O \cup \Sigma)^*$ in a canonical way. We present this method in some more detail, since it will be of particular interest, when we prove UIGs to be weakly equivalent to CFGs. Within a derivation the corresponding addresses are defined inductively depending on the length of the derivation in the following way: Consider nonterminal production

---

[10] Up to here, each (E)UIG could just be taken as an LIG with a particular type of permissible productions, while the class of grammars defined this way would be weakly equivalent to the proper superclass formed by all LIGs.

[11] As e.g. Boullier (1996) does considering LIGs in normal 2–form.

$p \in P$. Hence, $p \in P_{\mathrm{ri}} \cup P_{\mathrm{li}}$, and therefore $p = A[\zeta...] \to \beta_l B[\eta...]\beta_r$ for some $A, B \in N$, $\zeta, \eta \in I^*$ and $\beta_l, \beta_r \in (O \cup \Sigma)^*$ with $\beta_l = \epsilon$ or $\beta_r = \epsilon$. Set $m(p) = |\beta_l\beta_r|$. Then, there are $X_0, \ldots, X_{m(p)-1} \in O \cup \Sigma$ such that (ri) or (li) holds.

(ri) $\beta_r = \epsilon$, $\beta_l = X_0 \ldots X_{m(p)-1}$ (li) $\beta_l = \epsilon$, $\beta_r = X_{m(p)-1} \ldots X_0$

Suppose that, for some $\theta \in I^*$, p is applied to an instance of $A[\zeta\theta]$ with address $\omega \in \mathbb{N}^*$. In both cases, (ri) and (li), the address of the distinguished child $B[\eta\theta]$ is $\omega\, m(p)$. For $0 \le k < m(p)$, if $X_k \in O$ then the address of the corresponding child is ωk. If $X_k \in \Sigma$ then no address is assigned to the corresponding instance.

Let $\sigma \in (O \cup \Sigma)^*$ be such that for each instance of a nonterminal object in σ a unique address in $\mathbb{N}^*$ is defined. We also refer to such an address simply as an *address of* σ. Now, assume d to be a derivation in G starting with σ.[12] Then, according to the just mentioned method a (unique) address is assigned to each new instance of a nonterminal object introduced in a derivation step. Say, $d = \sigma_0 \ldots \sigma_n$ such that $\sigma_i \overset{p_i}{\underset{G}{\Rightarrow}} \sigma_{i+1}$ for some $p_i \in P$ applied to a particular occurrence of some $A_i[\zeta_i] \in O$ with address $\omega_i \in \mathbb{N}^*$. We call the derivation d *linear (w.r.t.* $<_{\mathrm{lex}}$*)* if in each derivation step p_i rewrites that instance of a nonterminal object with the smallest address (w.r.t. $<_{\mathrm{lex}}$) of σ_i, i.e. if ω_i is the smallest address among all addresses assigned to some instance of a nonterminal object in σ_i. If ω_i is also the highest address of σ_i then we have $\sigma_i = u_i A_i[\zeta_i]v_i$ for some $u_i, v_i \in \Sigma^*$.

Now, suppose that $d = \sigma_0 \ldots \sigma_n$ is a linear derivation and that we have $\sigma_i = \tau_i B_i[\eta_i]$ ($\sigma_i = B_i[\eta_i]\tau_i$) for $0 \le i < n$ with $B_i[\eta_i] \in O$ and $\tau_i \in (O \cup \Sigma)^*$. If, in addition, for $0 \le i < n$ the highest address of σ_i belongs to the rightmost (leftmost) instance of $B_i[\eta_i]$ then d is also called *weakly right linear (weakly left linear)*. In this case the rightmost (leftmost) occurrence of $B_i[\eta_i]$ can be rewritten only if $\tau_i \in \Sigma^*$.

Lemma 1 *Let $G = (N, \Sigma, I, P, S)$ be a UIG. For each derivation in G from some $\sigma \in (O \cup \Sigma)^*$ to some $w \in \Sigma^*$ there is also a linear derivation in G from σ to w.*   □

Definition 6 We say an (E)UIG/LIG $G = (N, \Sigma, I, P, S)$ is in *normalized form* if each $p \in P$ obeys type 1.1, 1.2 or 2.

  1.1 $A[f...] \to \beta B[g...]$ 1.2 $A[f...] \to B[g...]\beta$ 2. $A[] \to w$

for some $A, B \in N$, $f, g \in I \cup \{\epsilon\}$ with $|fg| \le 1$, $\beta \in (N_{[]} \cup \Sigma)^*$ and $w \in \Sigma^*$. If furthermore $|\beta| \le 1$ and $|w| \le 2$ for each $p \in P$ of the

---

[12]If not defined for some other reasons, in any derivation $\tilde{d}$ starting with some $\tilde{\sigma} \in (O \cup \Sigma)^*$, $\tilde{\sigma}$ is tacitly assumed to be addressed in the same manner as σ here.

respective types 1.1, 1.2 and 2 then G is in *normal 2–form.*

Each nonterminal $p \in P$ is either *index introducing* (if $g \in I$), *index absorbing* (if $f \in I$) or *constraint free* (if $fg = \epsilon$). The sets of index introducing, index absorbing and constraint free productions are denoted by P_{in}, P_{ab} and P_{cf}, respectively.

An (E)UIG/LIG $G = (N, \Sigma, I, P, S)$ in normal 2–form is in *strict normal 2–form* in case that (a) if $A[] \to \epsilon \in P$ then $A = S$, and (b) if $S[] \to \epsilon \in P$ then S does not appear on the righthand side of any $p \in P$.

Note that e.g. each CFG in Chomsky normal form can be interpreted as a UIG with $I = \emptyset$. Thus, each CFL turns out as a UIL. In order to show the converse in the next section, we finally fix

Lemma 2 *For every UIG there exists some weakly equivalent UIG in normalized form.* □

14.5 Weak generative capacity of UIGs

Let $G = (N, \Sigma, I, P, S)$ be a UIG in normalized form. We give a method for constructing a CFG $G' = (N', \Sigma, P', S')$ which is weakly equivalent to G: First, the nonterminal set N' is defined as the set of all pairs (A, x) with $A \in N$ and $x \in P_{\text{ab}} \cup \{\epsilon\}$, (S, ϵ) the start symbol S'. Then, for all $A, B, C, D \in N$, $f \in I$, and $\gamma, \beta \in (N_{[]} \cup \Sigma)^*$, $w \in \Sigma^*$ the production set P' is defined as[13]

(R1) $(A, x) \to (\gamma, \epsilon)(C, q)(\beta, \epsilon)(B, x) \in P'$ for all $x \in (P_{\text{ri}} \cap P_{\text{ab}}) \cup \{\epsilon\}$
 if $p = A[...] \to \gamma C[f...] \in P_{\text{ri}}$ and $q = D[f...] \to \beta B[...] \in P_{\text{ri}}$

(L1) $(A, x) \to (B, x)(\beta, \epsilon)(C, q)(\gamma, \epsilon) \in P'$ for all $x \in (P_{\text{li}} \cap P_{\text{ab}}) \cup \{\epsilon\}$
 if $p = A[...] \to C[f...]\gamma \in P_{\text{li}}$ and $q = D[f...] \to B[...]\beta \in P_{\text{li}}$

(R2) $(A, x) \to (\gamma, \epsilon)(C, x) \in P'$ for all $x \in (P_{\text{ri}} \cap P_{\text{cf}}) \cup \{\epsilon\}$
 if $p = A[...] \to \gamma C[...] \in P_{\text{ri}}$

(L2) $(A, x) \to (C, x)(\gamma, \epsilon) \in P'$ for all $x \in (P_{\text{li}} \cap P_{\text{cf}}) \cup \{\epsilon\}$
 if $p = A[...] \to C[...]\gamma \in P_{\text{li}}$

 (3) $(A, \epsilon) \to w \in P'$ if $p = A[] \to w \in P$

(R4) $(D, q) \to \epsilon \in P'$ if $q = D[f...] \to \beta B[...] \in P_{\text{ri}}$

(L4) $(D, q) \to \epsilon \in P'$ if $q = D[f...] \to B[...]\beta \in P_{\text{li}}$

The productions of the form (R1) and (R2) (the form (L1) and (L2)) build the set of *passing on rightmost (passing on leftmost)* productions which is denoted by P'_r (by P'_l).[14]

---

[13]For $\alpha \in (N_{[]} \cup \Sigma)^*$ the string $(\alpha, \epsilon) \in (N' \cup \Sigma)^*$ is inductively defined as follows: First, let $(\epsilon, \epsilon) := \epsilon$. Then, for $\beta \in (N_{[]} \cup \Sigma)^*$, $a \in \Sigma$ and $A \in N$ set $(a\beta, \epsilon) := a(\beta, \epsilon)$

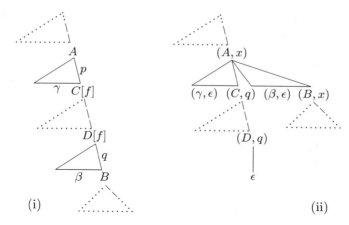

FIGURE 2 (i) A partial weakly right linear tree in G and (ii) the corresponding CFG-tree in G'.

In terms of trees what G' does with a given UIG–tree in G is flatten the structure by recursively splitting up spines in a particular way without changing the yield of the original tree. I.e. productions of the form (R2), (L2) and (3) simply imitate the constraint free and terminal productions from the original UIG G. But, a $p' \in P'$ of the form (R1) or (L1) crucially imitates the introduction of an index and its absorption in one step (the "structure–flattening" step). The second component of the corresponding (C, q) stores the information that the index f introduced with C applying $p \in P_{in}$ has been popped applying $q \in P_{ab}$. Since $q \neq \epsilon$, no $(Z, q) \in N'$ can subsequently be rewritten as a terminal string except by using a production of the form (R4) or (L4) at some derivation step. This kind of constraint ensures the "instant popping" of f to be a legitimate operation (see also Figure 2 indicating the case with regard to (R1) and (R4)).[15]

The linear derivation strategy for UIGs can be transferred to G' by means of the following: For any $p' = A' \to \alpha' \in P'_r \cup P'_l$ we define $m(p') = |\alpha'| - 1$. Then we fix existing $X_0, \dots, X_{m(p')} \in (N' \cup \Sigma)^*$, such that $\alpha' = X_0 \dots X_{m(p')}$ if $p' \in P'_r$, or such that $\alpha' = X_{m(p')} \dots X_0$ if

and $(A[]\beta, \epsilon) := (A, \epsilon)(\beta, \epsilon)$, respectively.

[14]The respective term has been chosen because the second component of the mother can be considered as being passed onto the rightmost (leftmost) child while applying such a production.

[15]Note that a less complex second component would actually be sufficient to prove $L(G) = L(G')$. All that has to be stored is the nonterminal of the left hand side of q and whether $q \in P_{ri}$ or $q \in P_{li}$. Storing the whole production seems useful in order to make somewhat more explicit the leading idea.

$p' \in P_1'$. If $\omega \in \mathbb{N}^*$ is the address of A', for $0 \leq k \leq m(p')$ the address of X_k is ωk in case $X_k \in N'$. No address is assigned if $X_k \in \Sigma$. It should be clear what is meant when a derivation d' or a parse π' in G' is called *linear, weakly right linear* or *weakly left linear (w.r.t. $<_{\text{lex}}$)*.

Lemma 3 *For each derivation in G' from some $\sigma' \in (N' \cup \Sigma)^*$ to some $w \in \Sigma^*$ there is also a linear derivation in G' from σ' to w.* □

To conclude that $L(G) = L(G')$, we prove the somewhat more specific

Proposition 4 *It can be shown that*

a) $A[\,] \Rightarrow_{\overline{G}}^{\text{ui}} wX[\,]$ *weakly right linear iff* $(A,x) \Rightarrow_{G'}^* w(X,x)$ *weakly right linear,*

b) $A[\,] \Rightarrow_{\overline{G}}^{\text{ui}} Y[\,]w$ *weakly left linear iff* $(A,y) \Rightarrow_{G'}^* (Y,y)w$ *weakly left linear,*

c) $\sigma \Rightarrow_{\overline{G}}^{\text{ui}} w$ *linear iff* $(\sigma,\epsilon) \Rightarrow_{G'}^* w$ *linear,*

for all $A, X, Y \in N$, $\sigma \in (N_{[\,]} \cup \Sigma)^*$, $w \in \Sigma^*$, $x \in P_{\text{ri}} \cap P_{\text{ab}}$, $y \in P_{\text{li}} \cap P_{\text{ab}}$.

Proposition 4 c) especially holds for $\sigma = S[\,]$. Lemmata 1, 3 and 2 yield

Corollary 5 *For each UIG there is a weakly equivalent CFG.*

Note that a proof of Proposition 4 can be done simultaneously for a), b), and c) by an induction on the length of a derivation in G and G' to see the "only if" and the "if", respectively. Roughly speaking, the crucial fact consists in the connection between partial weakly right (left) linear derivations in G and G' as indicated in Figure 2 displaying the weakly right linear case: applying $q \in P_{\text{ri}}$ to $D[f] \in O$ absorbs the instance of $f \in I$ introduced by applying $p \in P_{\text{ri}}$ to $A[\,] \in O$.

14.6 TIGs: Another way to constrain spines

UIGs still permit one to characterize tree–sets that cannot be generated by any CFG, and moreover UIGs can be shown to be parsable in cubic–time (Michaelis and Wartena 1998). Because the class of LIGs is weakly equivalent to the class of *tree adjoining grammars (TAGs)*,[16] our work on UIGs is directly comparable to work of Rogers (1994) and of Schabes and Waters (1995). Both approaches constrain the TAG–formalism yielding a cubic time parsable formalism which is weakly equivalent to CFGs.

In general contrast to our work Rogers in particular defines a sub-class of TAGs such that each member (in terms of trees) generates a *recognizable set*, and thus is strongly equivalent *(modulo projection)* to some CFG (Thatcher 1967). *Tree insertion grammars (TIGs)* as defined in Schabes and Waters 1995 have deeper parallels to UIGs. Though their

---

[16]TAGs as defined e.g. in Vijay-Shanker and Weir 1994, where also a proof of the mentioned weak equivalence can be found.

motivation is different, the underlying idea of TIGs resembles the restrictions used in UIGs. TIGs can be viewed as a form of restricted TAGs. Recall that a TAG has a set of initial and a set of elementary auxiliary trees. Each auxiliary tree (elementary or derived) has a node on the frontier marked as the *foot* with the same nonterminal label as the root. The path from the root to the foot is called the *spine*. An auxiliary tree is called *left (right) auxiliary* if the foot is the rightmost (leftmost) node on the frontier not labeled with the empty string, otherwise it is called *wrapping auxiliary*. A subtree can be replaced by an auxiliary tree if their roots have the same label. The replaced subtree is inserted (up to its root) below the foot of the auxiliary tree. A TIG is defined as a TAG without elementary wrapping auxiliary trees and with the constraints that no node on the spine of a right (left) auxiliary tree can be replaced by a left (right) auxiliary tree and that no adjunction at all is allowed to the right (left) of the spine of an elementary left (right) auxiliary tree. A "change of direction" of a spine can be achieved only by simultaneous left and right adjunction. Up to the fact that to the left (right) of the spine of an elementary right (left) auxiliary tree, "non–productive" nodes can appear, the restriction on spines is comparable to the one we have defined for UIGs. Indeed, Schabes and Waters (1995) show that TIGs are weakly equivalent to CFGs.

As argued, the potential of LIGs to describe SVO languages like English is already provided by UIGs. The argumentation should be accurate as well for the relation between TIGs and TAGs. This is actually confirmed empirically by the fact that a large scale TAG developed by the XTAG Research Group is almost compatible with the TIG restrictions (Schabes and Waters 1995). Likewise we expect an extension along the lines of EUIGs to be necessary for head–final languages. Then *extended TIGs (ETIGs)* could be defined by relaxing the conditions on left (right) auxiliary trees, allowing terminal symbols to the right (left) of the foot on the frontier. If in addition selective adjunction is incorporated as for TAGs (cf. Vijay-Shanker and Weir 1994), the result on the weak generative capacity of EUIGs could be transferred to ETIGs.

14.7   Weak generative capacity of EUIGs

The class of EUILs is a proper subclass of LILs: As an immediate consequence of Proposition 7, Corollary 8 provides an example of a language that is an LIL, but not an EUIL. To finally prove the corollary, assume that $G = (N, \Sigma, I, P, S)$ is an LIG in strict normal 2–form for which $\Sigma = \Sigma_1 \cup \Sigma_2 \cup \Sigma_3$, where $\Sigma_3 = \{a, b, c, d\}$ and the Σ_i's are pairwise disjoint. Further, suppose that $L_1 \subseteq \Sigma_1^*$ and $L_2 \subseteq \Sigma_2^*$ are such that

$L(G) = \{a^n u b^n c^n v d^n \mid n \in \mathbb{N}, u \in L_1, v \in L_2\}$. We proceed to establish some claims concerning G illustrated by Figure 3.

For some $n \in \mathbb{N}$, $u \in L_1$ and $v \in L_2$ consider $\delta(n, u, v)$, the derivation tree $\delta = (N_\delta, \lhd_\delta^*, \prec_\delta, \ell_\delta)$ induced by some derivation of $a^n u b^n c^n v d^n$ in G.[17] For $1 \leq i \leq n$ there are leaves $\lambda_i^{(n)} \in N_\delta$ labeled a, $\lambda_{n+i}^{(n)} \in N_\delta$ labeled b, $\mu_{n+i}^{(n)} \in N_\delta$ labeled c, and $\mu_i^{(n)} \in N_\delta$ labeled d such that $\lambda_i^{(n)} \prec \lambda_{i+1}^{(n)}$ and $\mu_{i+1}^{(n)} \prec \mu_i^{(n)}$. Thus, $\lambda_{2n}^{(n)} \prec \mu_{2n}^{(n)}$. Furthermore, for $1 \leq i \leq 2n$ we fix existing $\nu_i^{(n)} \in N_\delta$ with $\nu_i^{(n)} \lhd^* \lambda_i^{(n)}$ and $\nu_i^{(n)} \lhd^* \mu_i^{(n)}$ such that for each $\nu \in N_\delta$ with $\nu \lhd^* \lambda_i^{(n)}$ and $\nu \lhd^* \mu_i^{(n)}$ we have $\nu \lhd^* \nu_i^{(n)}$.

Claim 1 $\nu_i^{(n)} \lhd^* \nu_{i+1}^{(n)}$ for all $n \in \mathbb{N}$ and $1 \leq i \leq 2n$. $\qquad\square$

Claim 2 There is a $k(G) \in \mathbb{N}$ such that for any $n \in \mathbb{N}$ and $1 \leq i \leq 2n$, if $\nu_i^{(n)} = \nu_{i+1}^{(n)} = \ldots = \nu_{i+k}^{(n)}$ for some $k \in \mathbb{N}$ then $k < k(G)$. $\qquad\square$

Let $n > k(G)$. For some $k(n) \in \mathbb{N}$ there are $\xi_0^{(n)}, \ldots, \xi_{k(n)}^{(n)} \in N_\delta$ with $\xi_i^{(n)} \lhd \xi_{i+1}^{(n)}$, where $\xi_0^{(n)} = \nu_n^{(n)}$ and $\xi_{k(n)}^{(n)} = \nu_{n+1+k(G)}^{(n)}$. Then we have $\lambda_{n-k(G)}^{(n)} \prec \nu_n^{(n)} \prec \mu_{n-k(G)}^{(n)}$ and $\lambda_{n+1}^{(n)} \prec \nu_{n+1+k(G)}^{(n)} \prec \mu_{n+1}^{(n)}$ by Claim 2. Let $A_i^{(n)}[\theta_i^{(n)}] \in O$ be the label of $\xi_i^{(n)}$.

Claim 3 For $k(G) < n$ and for $0 \leq i \leq k(n)$ we have

$$S[] \underset{G}{\Rightarrow}^* a^{n-p(i,n)} w(i,n) A_i^{(n)}[\theta_i^{(n)}] z(i,n) d^{n-s(i,n)} \text{ and}$$

$$A_i^{(n)}[\theta_i^{(n)}] \underset{G}{\Rightarrow}^* x(i,n) b^{n-q(i,n)} c^{n-r(i,n)} y(i,n)$$

with non–negative integers $p(i,n), q(i,n), r(i,n), s(i,n) \leq k(G)$, and with strings $w(i,n), x(i,n), y(i,n), z(i,n) \in (\Sigma_1 \cup \Sigma_2 \cup \Sigma_3)^*$ such that $w(i,n)\,x(i,n) = a^{p(i,n)} u\, b^{q(i,n)}$ and $y(i,n)\,z(i,n) = c^{r(i,n)} v\, d^{s(i,n)}$. $\qquad\square$

Claim 4 An $\widetilde{n} \in \mathbb{N}$ exists such that $\theta_0^{(n)}, \ldots, \theta_{k(n)}^{(n)} \neq \epsilon$ for any $n \geq \widetilde{n}$.

Proof. If not, there is a strictly increasing sequence $(n_j)_{j \in \mathbb{N}}$ of non–negative integers with $A_{i_j}^{(n_j)}[\theta_{i_j}^{(n_j)}] = A_{i_j}^{(n_j)}[]$ for some $0 \leq i_j \leq k(n_j)$. Because the nonterminal set N is finite, we may w.l.o.g. assume that there is some $A \in N$ such that $A_{i_j}^{(n_j)} = A$ for each $j \in \mathbb{N}$. Then, by Claim 3 we are able to choose an $n_j > n_0 + k(G)$ to derive

$$w = a^{n_0 - p(i_0, n_0)} w(i_0, n_0) x(i_j, n_j) b^{n_j - q(i_j, n_j)}$$
$$c^{n_j - r(i_j, n_j)} y(i_j, n_j) z(i_0, n_0) d^{n_0 - s(i_0, n_0)}$$

from $S[]$. But, this is a contradiction, because e.g. the respective numbers of instances of a and b in w are different. $\qquad\square$

Claim 5 For $n \geq \widetilde{n}$ the path $\xi_0^{(n)} \ldots \xi_{k(n)}^{(n)}$ is a spine and part of the spine that starts at the root of the derivation tree $\delta(n, u, v)$.

---

[17] For the sake of clarity we write $\lhd$, $\lhd^*$ and $\prec$ instead of $\lhd_\delta$, $\lhd_\delta^*$ and $\prec_\delta$, respectively.

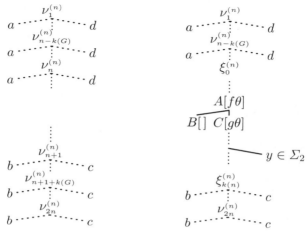

FIGURE 3 Structure of the language $a^n L_1 b^n c^n L_2 d^n$

Proof. By Claim 4, because G is in strict normal 2–form. $\qquad\square$

Claim 6 Let $n \in \mathbb{N}$ with $n \geq \tilde{n}$ be such that for all $u \in L_1$ $(v \in L_2)$ there is an $v \in L_2$ $(u \in L_1)$ and a derivation of $a^n u b^n c^n v d^n$ such that each $p \in P$ with righthand side including an $x \in \Sigma_1$ $(y \in \Sigma_2)$ that applies, applies to some node on the spine $\xi_0^{(n)} \dots \xi_{k(n)}^{(n)}$. Then L_1 (L_2) is a CFL.

Proof (sketch). Consider the case for L_1. Recall, G is in normal 2–form. Define an LIG $G' = (N, \Sigma, I, P', S)$, where $A, B, C \in N$, $f, g \in I \cup \{\epsilon\}$:

- $A[f...] \to B[g...] \in P'$ if $A[f...] \to C[\,]B[g...] \mid B[g...]C[\,] \in P$
- $A[f...] \to B[g...] \in P'$ if $A[f...] \to xB[g...] \mid B[g...]x \in P$ for
  $$x \in \Sigma_2 \cup \{a, b, c, d\} \cup \{\epsilon\}$$
- $A[f...] \to xB[g...] \in P'$ if $A[f...] \to xB[g...] \in P$ for $x \in \Sigma_1$
- $A[f...] \to B[g...] \in P'$ if $A[f...] \to B[g...]x \in P$ for $x \in \Sigma_1$
- $A[f...] \to \epsilon \in P'$ if $A[f...] \to x \in P$ for $x \in \Sigma_2 \cup \{a, b, c, d\} \cup \{\epsilon\}$
- $A[f...] \to x \in P'$ if $A[f...] \to x \in P$ for $x \in \Sigma_1$

$L(G') = L_1$ essentially by assumption and Claim 5. $L(G')$ is a CFL by Corollary 5, since G' is an RLIG and thus a UIG. $\qquad\square$

Lemma 6 For each EUIG G there is a weakly equivalent EUIG G' in strict normal 2–form such that $\underset{G'}{\Rightarrow}^{\mathrm{ui}} = \underset{G'}{\Rightarrow}^*$, i.e. G' is also an LIG. $\qquad\square$

Proposition 7 Let Σ be a finite set with $\Sigma_1, \Sigma_2, \{a, b, c, d\} \subseteq \Sigma$. If the language $L = \{a^n u\, b^n c^n v\, d^n \mid n \in \mathbb{N}, u \in L_1, v \in L_2\}$ is an EUIL for some $L_1 \subseteq \Sigma_1^*$ and $L_2 \subseteq \Sigma_2^*$ then L_1 or L_2 is a CFL.

Proof (sketch). Let G be an EUIG with $L(G) = L$. W.l.o.g. G is also an LIG in strict 2–normal form by Lemma 6, and we may suppose the sets Σ_1, Σ_2 and $\{a, b, c, d\}$ to be pairwise disjoint. Assume that L_1 is a non–CFL (the case that L_2 is a non–CFL is analogous).

In particular, contraposition of Claim 6 implies the existence of an $n \geq \tilde{n}$ and $u \in L_1$ such that $a^n u b^n c^n v d^n$ for any $v \in L_2$ is derivable only by applying some $p \in P_{\mathrm{ri}}$ of the form $A[f...] \to B[\,]C[g...]$ to some node on the spine $\xi_0^{(n)} \ldots \xi_{k(n)}^{(n)}$, where $A, B, C \in N$ and $f, g \in I \cup \{\epsilon\}$. Then in any corresponding derivation, by Claim 4 and the definition of $\underset{G}{\Rightarrow}^{\mathrm{ui}}$, only productions from P_{ri} apply to the spine $\xi_0^{(n)} \ldots \xi_{k(n)}^{(n)}$. Thus, since $n \geq \tilde{n}$ and G is in strict normal 2–form, the assumption of Claim 6 holds in such a way that L_2 must be a CFL. □

Corollary 8 *The language* $\{a_1^n\, b_1^l\, b_2^l\, b_3^l\, a_2^n\, a_3^n\, c_1^m c_2^m c_3^m\, a_4^n \mid l, m, n \in \mathbb{N}\}$ *is an LIL, but not an EUIL.* □

14.8 Conclusion

Starting from some linguistic observations on extraction paths, we have identified a weakly context–free subclass of LIGs, namely UIGs. Slightly loosening the restrictions on index inheritance to cope with head–final languages, as well, we have introduced EUIGs and proved them to give rise to a language–class that falls properly between CFLs and LILs. Exploring the formal potential of LIGs, these results shed some light upon the nature of non–local dependencies in natural languages.

Acknowledgment

This paper has been worked out at the University of Potsdam within the *Innovationskolleg 'Formale Modelle kognitiver Komplexität' (INK 12)* funded by the Deutsche Forschungsgemeinschaft (DFG). Especially, we want to thank Peter Staudacher for constructive discussions and many helpful comments.

References

Aho, A. V. 1968. Indexed grammars — an extension of context–free grammars. *Journal of the Association for Computing Machinery* 15:647–671.

Boullier, P. 1996. Another facet of LIG parsing. In *34st Annual Meeting of the ACL*, pages 87–94. ACL, Santa Cruz, CA.

Evers, A. 1975. *The Transformational Cycle in Dutch and German.* Ph.D. thesis, Rijksuniversiteit Utrecht. Reprinted by Indiana University Linguistics Club, Bloomington.

Gazdar, G. 1988. Applicability of indexed grammars to natural languages. In U. Reyle and C. Rohrer, eds., *Natural Language Parsing and Linguistic Theories*, pages 69–94. Dordrecht: D. Reidel Publishing Company.

Haider, H. 1993. *Deutsche Syntax – generativ. Vorstudien zur Theorie einer Projektiven Grammatik*. Tübingen: Gunter Narr Verlag.

Michaelis, J. and C. Wartena. 1997. How linguistic constraints on movement conspire to yield languages analyzable with a restricted form of LIGs. In *Proceedings of the Conference on Formal Grammar (FG '97)*, pages 158–168. Aix en Provence.

Michaelis, J. and C. Wartena. 1998. Unidirectional inheritance of indices. A weakly context–free facet of LIGs. In *Proceedings of the Joint Conference on Formal Grammar, Head–Driven Phrase Structure Grammar and Categorial Grammar (FHGC '98)*, pages 258–267. Saarbrücken.

Müller, G. 1995. *A–Bar–Syntax. A Study in Movement Types*, vol. 42 of *Studies in Generative Grammar*. Berlin: Mouton de Gruyter.

Rogers, J. 1994. Capturing CFLs with tree adjoining grammars. In *32st Annual Meeting of the ACL*, pages 155–162. ACL, Las Cruces, NM.

Schabes, Y. and R. C. Waters. 1995. Tree insertion grammar: A cubic–time parsable formalism that lexicalizes context–free grammar without changing the trees produced. *Computational Linguistics* 21(4):479–513.

Thatcher, J. W. 1967. Characterizing derivation trees of context–free grammars through a generalization of finite automata theory. *Journal of Computer and System Sciences* 1:317–322.

Vijay-Shanker, K. and D. J. Weir. 1994. The equivalence of four extensions of context–free grammars. *Math. Systems Theory* 27:511–546.

Wartena, C. 1998. Grammars with composite storages. In *Proceedings of the Conference on Logical Aspects of Computational Linguistics (LACL '98)*, pages 11–14. Grenoble.

15

A Formal Interpretation of Relations and Quantification in HPSG

FRANK RICHTER, MANFRED SAILER AND GERALD PENN

15.1 Introduction[1]

This paper formalizes the language used for expressing the principles found in Pollard and Sag (1994). In a sense, this is not a new language, but rather the language that Pollard and Sag (1994) and other HPSG linguists have already been using. There have been many logics proposed for the task of unification-based processing with constraint-based grammars such as HPSG, for instance, Höhfeld and Smolka (1988), and Carpenter (1992); but because of certain practical considerations, they have eschewed some of the formal devices that a declarative, formal specification of the constraints themselves requires. The major properties that distinguish our formal language will be described below.

The language is called RSRL, a relational extension of SRL (Speciate Re-entrant Logic, see King, 1989).

SRL is actually a logic that was proposed as a formalization and refinement of the language used in Pollard and Sag (1987); and Pollard and Sag (1994) incorporated many of those refinements. SRL is nevertheless not an adequate formalism for Pollard and Sag 1994, *pace* King (1999) and Pollard (1999), as it crucially lacks an explicit means of quantification, which is necessary to express the quantification either understood or explicitly stated in many of the principles of Pollard and Sag (1994). In fact, the principal contribution that RSRL makes is not

[1]We are most grateful to Mike Calcagno, Tom Cornell, Thilo Götz, Tilman Höhle, Hans-Peter Kolb, Detmar Meurers, Uwe Mönnich, Frank Morawietz, Carl Pollard, Adam Przepiórkowski, Kiril Simov and Shuly Wintner for discussions, comments and support. Paul King assisted in the final formulation of RSRL.

Constraints and Resources in Natural Language Syntax and Semantics.
Gosse Bouma, Erhard W. Hinrichs, Geert-Jan M. Kruijff, and Richard T. Oehrle.

its addition of relations but its formalization of what the quantification of Pollard and Sag (1994) really means: not quantification over some or all objects in a model, but over the components of a given object, such as a linguistic sign. The components of an object in an interpretation are those objects that are accessible from that object by a (finite) path. This different notion of quantification gives RSRL the ability to formalize linguistic principles from the HPSG literature very naturally; and it provides an important insight into the relation between HPSG and the logics underlying HPSG-based computational systems.

We do not suppose that the reader is familiar with SRL. Since the language of SRL is a proper sublanguage of RSRL, all relevant aspects of SRL will be introduced. In fact, from a more general perspective, our augmentation of SRL by restricted quantification and relations can be viewed as the characterization of an extension that could be applied to other description languages that are more loosely related to HPSG, just as Höhfeld and Smolka (1988) provides a method to augment constraint languages with relations. The reason that we choose SRL as our starting point is that, unlike other logics of descriptions, it was expressly designed for HPSG and, therefore, implicitly incorporates several HPSG-specific mechanisms that others do not. They include HPSG's view of appropriateness specifications for sorts and attributes, and the assumption that the maximally specific sorts partition the universe of linguistic objects. Moreover, SRL is furnished with a theory of what it means for an HPSG grammar to be true of a natural language, which we can easily adapt to RSRL, as will be discussed below.

15.2 Relations

Relations are used prolifically in Pollard and Sag (1994) and elsewhere in the HPSG literature. Some are explicitly referred to as such, e.g., the o-command and local o-command relations of the binding theory, while others are implicitly required by the natural language descriptions of principles. The Subject Condition (p. 400), for example, says:

"If the initial element of the SUBCAT value of a word is slashed, then so is some other element of that list."

The consequent of this implication requires the use of a member relation to pinpoint another slashed element on the SUBCAT list. The recursive nature of lists requires the use of the relation.

RSRL is not the first extension of a constraint language to provide relations. Höhfeld and Smolka (1988), for example, provides a restricted kind of relational extension that can be used for logic programming over a wide range of constraint languages, including several feature logics.

This relational extension, however, does not permit relations to occur in the scope of negation, which includes the antecedents of implicational constraints. The Subject Condition above does not have the member relation in its antecedent; but the Relative Uniqueness Principle (p. 212) does:

"A member of the INHERITED REL *set on a headed constituent may be inherited from . . . at most one daughter."*[2]

Perhaps the most famous instance of a negated HPSG relation can be found in principle B of HPSG's binding theory (p. 401), in which a personal pronoun is required to be locally o-free, i.e., not locally o-bound. The formalization of principle B and its relations can be found in Appendix 1.

True negation, of course, is very difficult to compute with; so it is only natural for definite clause languages such as Höhfeld and Smolka (1988) or systems such as ALE (Carpenter and Penn, 1996) to rely on negation by failure or some other substitute. For a formal language with which we want to precisely specify models of our theories, however, these substitutes will not provide us with the usual set-theoretic interpretation of negation that matches its intended use in linguistic principles. Junk slots, the encoding of relations as components of an object by means of extra attributes and extra sorts (Ait-Kaci, 1984; Carpenter, 1992), cannot also encode relational negation, and require the signature to contain uninteresting and unmotivated sorts.[3]

It has been suggested (Kasper et al., 1995) that one might be able to restrict the use of negated relations to an inventory of decidable ones that can be replaced by new (computable) relations that have the opposite meaning. For example, instead of using $(\neg$ member$(x,y))$ in a description, we might simply define a new relation, non-member, and use non-member(x,y) instead. The problem is that relations are often used with quantification over at least one of their arguments. Consider, as a simple example, the following constraint, taken from Abeillé and Godard (1996), that assists in predicting the distribution of *avoir* and *être* in French:

$$\begin{bmatrix} \text{VFORM } \textit{part-passé} \\ \text{S-ARG } \langle \dots \textit{aff\_r} \dots \rangle \end{bmatrix} \rightarrow \begin{bmatrix} \text{V-AUX } \textit{etre} \end{bmatrix}$$

Formalized in RSRL, this says:

$[: \text{VFORM} \sim \textit{part-passé} \land \exists x[x \sim \textit{aff\_r} \land \text{member}(x,: \text{S-ARG})]]$
$\rightarrow [: \text{V-AUX} \sim \textit{etre}]$

---

[2]RSRL can also be used to encode finite sets and the necessary access relations, such as membership and union, for them.

[3]See below for further problems with a junk slot approach.

If the VFORM value is of sort *part-passé*, and there exists a member of the S-ARG list which is of sort *aff_r*, i.e., which is a reflexive clitic, then the V-AUX value must be *etre*. Because member is in the antecedent of an implication, it occurs in the scope of a negation. It is also in the scope of an implicit existential quantifier, made explicit in our formalization, which is in the scope of the negation as well. If, in the disjunctive form of the original implication, we simply used non-member for member, we would negate the relation but not the quantifier (which must become universal). Computability properties aside, introducing new relations with negation built-in simply will not preserve the intended meaning, even in straightforward principles such as this.

A formal language for HPSG must have true relations with true negation. We extend the usual SRL-style signatures with relational symbols and an arity function to express them:

Definition 1 Σ is a signature iff
Σ is a septuple $\langle \mathcal{G}, \sqsubseteq, \mathcal{S}, \mathcal{A}, \mathcal{F}, \mathcal{R}, \mathcal{AR} \rangle$,
$\langle \mathcal{G}, \sqsubseteq \rangle$ is a finite partial order,
$$\mathcal{S} = \left\{ \sigma \in \mathcal{G} \,\middle|\, \begin{array}{l} \text{for each } \sigma' \in \mathcal{G}, \\ \text{if } \sigma' \sqsubseteq \sigma \text{ then } \sigma = \sigma' \end{array} \right\},$$
$\mathcal{A}$ is a set,
$\mathcal{F}$ is a partial function from the Cartesian product of $\mathcal{G}$ and $\mathcal{A}$ to $\mathcal{G}$,
for each $\sigma_1 \in \mathcal{G}$, for each $\sigma_2 \in \mathcal{G}$ and for each $\alpha \in \mathcal{A}$,

> if $\mathcal{F}\langle \sigma_1, \alpha \rangle$ is defined and $\sigma_2 \sqsubseteq \sigma_1$
> then $\mathcal{F}\langle \sigma_2, \alpha \rangle$ is defined and $\mathcal{F}\langle \sigma_2, \alpha \rangle \sqsubseteq \mathcal{F}\langle \sigma_1, \alpha \rangle$,

$\mathcal{R}$ is a finite set, and
$\mathcal{AR}$ is a total function from $\mathcal{R}$ to $\mathbb{N}^+$.

$\langle \mathcal{G}, \sqsubseteq \rangle$ is a sort hierarchy for a theory, and $\mathcal{S}$ is the set of maximally specific sorts (*species*) that will partition the objects of our interpretations. $\mathcal{A}$ is the set of attributes; and $\mathcal{F}$ encodes the appropriateness conditions on an HPSG signature. $\mathcal{R}$ and $\mathcal{AR}$ are for the relation symbols and their arities, respectively. We interpret RSRL signatures as follows:

Definition 2 For each signature Σ, I is a Σ interpretation iff
I is a quadruple $\langle U, S, A, R \rangle$,
U is a set,
S is a total function from U to $\mathcal{S}$,
A is a total function from $\mathcal{A}$ to the set of partial functions from U to U,
for each $\alpha \in \mathcal{A}$, for each $u \in U$,

> if $A(\alpha)(u)$ is defined
> then $\mathcal{F}\langle S(u), \alpha \rangle$ is defined, and $S(A(\alpha)(u)) \sqsubseteq \mathcal{F}\langle S(u), \alpha \rangle$,

for each $\alpha \in \mathcal{A}$, for each $u \in U$,

if $\mathcal{F}\langle S(u), \alpha \rangle$ is defined then $A(\alpha)(u)$ is defined,

R is a total function from $\mathcal{R}$ to the power set of U^*, and for each $\rho \in \mathcal{R}$, $R(\rho) \subseteq U^{\mathcal{AR}(\rho)}$.

where S^* is the set of finite sequences or tuples over elements of a set S. Similarly, for each natural number n, S^n is the set of n-tuples over elements of a set S. Below, we will also write S^+ for the set of nonempty finite tuples over elements of a set S, and $\overline{S}$ as an abbreviation for $S \cup S^*$.

U is the set of objects in the universe. S partitions the objects of the universe by assigning a maximally specific sort to each object. A provides an interpretation of attributes as functions that map from objects to their object values at that attribute, along with conditions to enforce appropriateness. R interprets a relation as a set of n-tuples of objects, where n is the arity of that relation.

In a definite clause extension of a constraint language, we would define descriptions for that constraint language, and then an additional stratum of descriptions in which relations could be used. Because we want to use relations on a par with other descriptions in our formal language, for example, in the scope of negation and/or quantification, relations in RSRL are part of the core description language itself. $\mathcal{VAR}$ is a countably infinite set of symbols, the variables of our language.

Definition 3 For each signature Σ, $\mathcal{T}^\Sigma$ and $\mathcal{D}^\Sigma$ are the smallest sets such that
: $\in \mathcal{T}^\Sigma$,
for each $v \in \mathcal{VAR}$, $v \in \mathcal{T}^\Sigma$,
for each $\alpha \in \mathcal{A}$ and each $\tau \in \mathcal{T}^\Sigma$, $\tau\alpha \in \mathcal{T}^\Sigma$,
for each $\sigma \in \mathcal{G}$, for each $\tau \in \mathcal{T}^\Sigma$, $\tau{\sim}\sigma \in \mathcal{D}^\Sigma$,
for each $\tau_1 \in \mathcal{T}^\Sigma$, for each $\tau_2 \in \mathcal{T}^\Sigma$, $\tau_1 \approx \tau_2 \in \mathcal{D}^\Sigma$,
for each $\rho \in \mathcal{R}$, for each $x_1 \in \mathcal{VAR}$, ... , for each $x_{\mathcal{AR}(\rho)} \in \mathcal{VAR}$,
$\quad \rho(x_1, \dots, x_{\mathcal{AR}(\rho)}) \in \mathcal{D}^\Sigma$,
for each $x \in \mathcal{VAR}$, for each $\delta \in \mathcal{D}^\Sigma$, $\exists x\, \delta \in \mathcal{D}^\Sigma$,
for each $x \in \mathcal{VAR}$, for each $\delta \in \mathcal{D}^\Sigma$, $\forall x\, \delta \in \mathcal{D}^\Sigma$,
for each $\delta \in \mathcal{D}^\Sigma$, $\neg\delta \in \mathcal{D}^\Sigma$,
for each $\delta_1 \in \mathcal{D}^\Sigma$, for each $\delta_2 \in \mathcal{D}^\Sigma$, $[\delta_1 \wedge \delta_2] \in \mathcal{D}^\Sigma$,
for each $\delta_1 \in \mathcal{D}^\Sigma$, for each $\delta_2 \in \mathcal{D}^\Sigma$, $[\delta_1 \vee \delta_2] \in \mathcal{D}^\Sigma$.

$\mathcal{T}^\Sigma$ is a set of terms, consisting of either a variable or the reserved symbol ': ', which refers to the object being described, followed by a (possibly empty) string of attributes. The set of formulae, $\mathcal{D}^\Sigma$, provides sort assignments, path equations, and relations, closed under negation, conjunction, disjunction and a restricted form of existential and universal quantification (to which we return shortly). Implication and bi-implication can be obtained by combinations of these. Relations are expressed as tuples over variables. By using the aforementioned restricted quantification, and by requiring theories to consist only of descriptions with no free variables, *relations can only hold among components of a single object*. This allows us to interpret relations under the scope of negation, by restricting the set of objects in the denotation of a negated relation to exclude those over whose designated components the relation holds. The interpretation of the negation of relations is thus achieved, as elsewhere, by set complement.[4]

In the HPSG literature, some relations over lists have been used that, at first blush, seem to violate the componenthood restriction. Consider the description of a German verb phrase in Figure 1, adapted from (Kathol and Pollard, 1995, p. 176): compaction compacts the com-

$$
\begin{bmatrix}
phrase \\
\text{DOM} \quad \boxed{4} \; \Big\langle\, [\text{PHON}\ \langle las\rangle\,] \mid \boxed{0}\,\big\langle\boxed{2}[\text{PHON}\ \langle das,\ Buch\rangle\,]\big\rangle\,\Big\rangle \\
\text{H-DTR} \begin{bmatrix} word \\ \text{DOM}\ \boxed{3}\ \langle\, [\text{PHON}\ \langle las\rangle\,]\,\rangle \end{bmatrix} \\
\text{C-DTR}\ \boxed{1} \begin{bmatrix} phrase \\ \text{DOM}\ \langle\, [\text{PHON}\ \langle das\rangle\,],\, [\text{PHON}\ \langle Buch\rangle\,]\,\rangle \end{bmatrix}
\end{bmatrix}
$$

$\wedge\ \texttt{compaction}(\boxed{1},\boxed{2})\ \wedge\ \texttt{shuffle}(\langle\boxed{2}\rangle,\boxed{3},\boxed{4})$

FIGURE 1 Description of a German verb phrase.

plement daughter, $\boxed{1}$, into a single domain object, $\boxed{2}$, at the mother. shuffle, a relation between three lists, shuffles the lists in its first two arguments into the list in its third argument, preserving the relative order of their members. Under the componenthood perspective presented so far, all the list arguments of shuffle must be present in the described object for the relation to hold. With the given order of the elements on $\boxed{4}$, this is unproblematic: shuffle's first argument can (and must) be the list $\boxed{0}$. If $\boxed{4}$ is reversed, however, the described object no longer contains a list such as the one designated by $\boxed{0}$, a list whose single element is a domain object with the phonology *das Buch* (see Figure 2). Thus, of the conceivable phrase with the list $\boxed{4}$ reversed, shuffle would not hold. Note that the problem persists if we redefine compaction with the list in question built into its second argument and then use that second argument as the first argument of shuffle, i.e., shuffle($\boxed{0}$,$\boxed{3}$,$\boxed{4}$), as

---

[4]The fact that the syntax of RSRL in Definition 3 bears no apparent resemblance to the commonly used AVM diagrams as exemplified in figures 1 and 2 below, does not affect the suitability of our language for specifying HPSG grammars. For practical applications, Richter 1999 defines an AVM syntax for RSRL. The syntax in Definition 3 is more compact and, thus, more convenient for mathematical purposes.

$$\left[\begin{array}{l} \textit{phrase} \\ \text{DOM} \left\langle \boxed{2}[\text{PHON} \langle \textit{das, Buch} \rangle] \;\middle|\; \boxed{3}\langle[\text{PHON} \langle \textit{las} \rangle]\rangle \right\rangle \end{array} \right]$$

FIGURE 2 Description of a *phrase* with the DOM list $\boxed{4}$ reversed

is done by (Kathol, 1995, pp. 145ff). Although the list designated by $\boxed{0}$ in Figure 1 is then an argument of both relations, it might still not be a component of all phrases we wish to describe. In fact, in that case, Figure 2 has the same problem with not only `shuffle` but `compaction` also.

It is now crucial to realize that, for the use of the `shuffle` relation in our example and for similar cases in the literature, the problematic lists in question only contain objects that are themselves components of the described objects, and they never contain objects that are not components. In this sense, the componenthood restriction also applies to these constructions. This suggests that the notion of componenthood is on the right track even for these apparent counterexamples. The solution to the described problem consists in a natural generalization of the concept of components and quantification over components, and in replacing the problematic lists with *chains*, a kind of "virtual list", which can be constructed from a finite number of components, over which relations can then be defined and across which we can navigate using two logical symbols, the quasi-attributes † and ▷. The symbols *chain, echain* and *nechain* are the corresponding quasi-sorts, which are ordered in a hierarchy. We thus extend the set of species, $\mathcal{S}$, the set of attributes, $\mathcal{A}$, and the sort hierarchy, $\langle \mathcal{G}, \sqsubseteq \rangle$, as well as signature interpretations and the constraint language, to handle chains, as shown in Appendix 2. When we refer to these extensions, we write them as $\widehat{\mathcal{S}}, \widehat{\mathcal{A}}, \left\langle \widehat{\mathcal{G}}, \widehat{\sqsubseteq} \right\rangle$, and so forth. The crucial idea behind chains is that they provide a very simple recursive structure, namely (effectively) lists of objects, that enables us to quantify over not only single components of an object but also an arbitrary structured collection of components of an object, without granting the same status to these lists as to objects of genuine sorts.

The problem with `shuffle` pointed out above and all similar relations in the HPSG literature can now be solved very generally by simply defining the relations in question for chains in a parallel manner as they were defined for lists. In cases in which linguists find it more natural to talk about relations between recursively ordered components than about relations between single components of an object, they can do so without having to simulate their specification with new junk relations or junk objects.

In fact, we conjecture that corresponding, if in some cases quite complicated, reformulations without chains can be found for all uses in the linguistic literature of relations that violate the naive componenthood restriction. But even if that were proven correct, this approach would miss the point: The purpose of our formalism is not to codify the minimal necessary apparatus for linguistic analyses, but to give a mathematical interpretation to existing grammars that explains the meaning of and the intuitions behind these grammars as they stand. We are interested in how the actual language that people are implicitly using could be formalized.

15.3   Quantification

As mentioned above, we only use a restricted form of quantification in RSRL, by restricting it to components of the described object, which are those objects that are accessible by paths. The vast majority of linguistic principles are not concerned with whether some particular kind of object exists somewhere in the universe, but with whether a particular object within the same unembedded sign exists in order to license that sign. The Trace Principle (Pollard and Sag, 1994, p. 400) is an excellent example:

"The SYNSEM *value of any trace must be a (non-initial) member of the* SUBCAT *list of a substantive word."*

Which substantive word could that be? This principle, in fact, is not meant to be a constraint on traces, but rather a constraint on signs that contain traces. What Pollard and Sag (1994) meant to say is that for every sign, if there is a path from its root node to a trace, then there must also be a path from the root node to some substantive word on whose SUBCAT list the SYNSEM value of the trace appears as a non-initial member. It is irrelevant whether the trace's SYNSEM value appears on some other unrelated word's SUBCAT list. This principle is working, so to speak, inside an unembedded sign. Within that scope, of course, it is easy to formalize this principle. This perspective can be most saliently observed in Pollard and Sag (1994) in the Trace Principle, the Control Theory (which looks for potential controlled *local* objects), the Quantifier Binding Condition (which excludes occurrences of a quantifier's index not captured by the quantifier) and the Binding Theory (which looks for potential o-commanders). We may also notice that the quantification in the *être* example from Abeillé and Godard (1996) above is an instance of quantification over components as well.

There are a few proposed linguistic principles that have appealed to quantification over the world of objects, rather than over some particular sign, or more generally, over the components of a particular object. A crucial example is that of polarity items. At least in the tradition of Baker (1970) and Linebarger (1987), the grammaticality of a sentence that contains a Negative Polarity Item (NPI) may depend on the well-formedness of another sentence. The NPI *give a damn* in (1a) is licensed because it stands in the scope of a negation in the same sentence. In (1b), on the other hand, no such negation is present. In a Baker/Linebarger approach, the grammaticality of the sentence is accounted for indirectly by pragmatic licensing. (1b) has (1a) as one of its conventional implicatures. In this implicated sentence, the NPI is directly licensed, which also renders (1b) grammatical.

(1) a. John doesn't give a damn.

b. John is too tired to give a damn.

From this brief characterization of the theory of NPI-licensing, it can be seen that the grammaticality of one sentence can possibly depend on the grammaticality of a second sentence.

The relation between these two sentences, however, is not arbitrary, but one of what Linebarger (1987) calls conventional implicature.[5] It has been argued by (Pollard and Sag, 1994, p. 27) that implicatures of exactly this kind should be part of at least some linguistic signs. Conventional implicatures, in that approach, are explicitly mentioned as candidates for appearing as members of the BACKGROUND value. The existence of that value is motivated on independent grounds to account for the use of proper names and honorific forms. In our view, what few cases there are that would necessitate the more standard quantification can, and according to the philosophy of signs presented in Pollard and Sag (1994), should be reduced to instances of component quantification using this explicit BACKGROUND approach.

An alternative to explicit quantification in the description language could be the use of junk slots. On the one hand, this technique shares the assumption that linguistic theories need only to be able to talk about components of a given object. In the context of junk slots, however, this assumption includes the encoding of relations themselves, which also become components of the described objects. Even simpler formal systems such as SRL (King, 1989, 1999) can provide a means for a junk slot encoding of relations, including a junk slot encoding of "quantification,"

---

[5]The precise connection between the two sentences is, however, hard to state. See the differences among Baker 1970 and Linebarger 1987 as well as the criticism and alternative explanation put forward by Ladusaw 1979 and Giannakidou 1997 among others.

but only if the objects in question have only finitely many components. A straightforward junk slot encoding of member, for example, looks as follows:

:∼ *finished-member* → :ELT ≈ :LIST FIRST

:∼ *unfinished-member* → :ELT ≈ :REC ELT ∧ :LIST REST ≈ :REC LIST

Here, the sort *member* has two subsorts, *finished-member* (*f-mem*) and *unfinished-member* (*u-mem*). The attributes ELT and LIST are appropriate to *member*, with the values *top*, the most general sort, and *nelist*, respectively. *f-mem* and *u-mem* inherit these specifications from *member*; and *u-mem* has an additional attribute, REC, with value *member*. Notice that any element can be a member of any infinite list, as witnessed by an object with an infinite embedding of *u-mem* objects.

One of the problems of the junk slot method is that it cannot differentiate between the linguistically interesting components of an object and its junk components. A more serious shortcoming is their semantics. Junk slots cannot be negated with the negation of the description language; but their negation must be constructed with a negative junk slot, in our example, *non-member*. If the LIST value of the *member* junk slot is infinite, any value can occur in the ELT slot; and the same observation holds for *non-member*. The positive and negative junk slot encodings of a relation might, thus, have overlapping denotations. *Non-member* has the same problems with quantification as non-member discussed on page 283.

Objects with infinitely many components are not just an artefact of junk slots. In principle, linguistic objects can have an infinite number of components. In a linguistic object in a Hinrichs-Nakazawa-style analysis (Hinrichs and Nakazawa, 1994), nothing prevents the SUBCAT list of an argument raising verb, for example, from being infinite, if the argument from which it inherits SUBCAT elements is itself another argument raising verb; and argument inheritance can be formalized with an *append* junk slot. In RSRL, unlike junk slots, relations and their negations do not have overlapping denotations, because negation is classical. We can even impose a constraint that all linguistic objects contain only a finite number of components, thus eliminating the potential case of arbitrary membership of any element on an infinite list, or infinite argument raising in a Hinrichs-Nakazawa-style analysis. The legitimate question of whether linguists need to be concerned with the predictions of their theories in relation to objects with infinitely many components, particularly infinite phonology lists, will not be considered here.

We conjecture that most if not all of the linguistic principles of Pollard and Sag (1994) can be converted to junk slots, modulo problems with infinity, which cannot be excluded. While that might be the price to pay for computing with these principles, we have to be aware of how large that cost actually is. A junk slot encoding of principle B of the binding theory, for example, must look at the linguistic phenomenon from a completely different angle than the original formulation in Pollard and Sag 1994. For the purposes of explicating the language that linguists are using in their declarative theories, this cost is too much. RSRL eliminates that conversion step, and provides a direct formalization of the intended principle (see Appendix 1).

We are now ready to interpret our formulae:

Definition 4 For each signature Σ, for each Σ interpretation $I = \langle U, S, A, R \rangle$, $\mathsf{Ass}_I = \overline{U}^{\mathcal{VAR}}$ is the set of variable assignments in I.

Note that variable assignments in I assign objects or chains of objects of the universe to variables. This is why we can refer to chains of objects in the arguments of relations. To be able to fix the meaning of quantifiers, we need the usual notational convention for variable assignment functions:

Definition 5 For each signature Σ, for each Σ interpretation $I = \langle U, S, A, R \rangle$, for each $ass \in \mathsf{Ass}_I$, for each $v \in \mathcal{VAR}$, for each $w \in \mathcal{VAR}$, for each $u \in \overline{U}$,

$$ass\tfrac{u}{v}(w) = \begin{cases} u & \text{if } v = w \\ ass(w) & \text{otherwise.} \end{cases}$$

Definition 6 For each signature $\Sigma = \langle \mathcal{G}, \sqsubseteq, \mathcal{S}, \mathcal{A}, \mathcal{F}, \mathcal{R}, \mathcal{AR} \rangle$, for each Σ interpretation $I = \langle U, S, A, R \rangle$, for each $ass \in \mathsf{Ass}_I$, T_I^{ass} is the total function from $\mathcal{T}^\Sigma$ to the set of partial functions from U to $\overline{U}$, and D_I^{ass} is the total function from $\mathcal{D}^\Sigma$ to the power set of U such that, for each $u \in U$,

$T_I^{ass}(:)(u)$ is defined and $T_I^{ass}(:)(u) = u$,

for each $v \in \mathcal{VAR}$, $T_I^{ass}(v)(u)$ is defined and $T_I^{ass}(v)(u) = ass(v)$,

for each $\tau \in \mathcal{T}^\Sigma$, for each $\alpha \in \widehat{\mathcal{A}}$,

$T_I^{ass}(\tau\alpha)(u)$ is defined iff $T_I^{ass}(\tau)(u)$ is defined and $\widehat{\mathsf{A}}(\alpha)(T_I^{ass}(\tau)(u))$ is defined, and

if $T_I^{ass}(\tau\alpha)(u)$ is defined then $T_I^{ass}(\tau\alpha)(u) = \widehat{\mathsf{A}}(\alpha)(T_I^{ass}(\tau)(u))$,

$$\mathsf{Co}_I^u = \left\{ u' \in U \ \middle| \ \begin{array}{l} \text{for some } ass \in \mathsf{Ass}_I, \\ \text{for some } \pi \in \mathcal{A}^*, \\ T_I^{ass}(:\pi)(u) \text{ is defined, and} \\ u' = T_I^{ass}(:\pi)(u) \end{array} \right\},$$

for each $\tau \in \mathcal{T}^\Sigma$, for each $\sigma \in \widehat{\mathcal{G}}$,

$$D_I^{ass}(\tau \sim \sigma) = \left\{ u \in U \ \middle| \ \begin{array}{l} T_I^{ass}(\tau)(u) \text{ is defined, and} \\ \widehat{\mathsf{S}}(T_I^{ass}(\tau)(u)) \sqsubseteq \sigma \end{array} \right\},$$

for each $\tau_1 \in \mathcal{T}^\Sigma$, for each $\tau_2 \in \mathcal{T}^\Sigma$,

$$D_{\mathsf{I}}^{ass}(\tau_1 \approx \tau_2) = \left\{ u \in \mathsf{U} \left| \begin{array}{l} T_{\mathsf{I}}^{ass}(\tau_1)(u) \text{ is defined,} \\ T_{\mathsf{I}}^{ass}(\tau_2)(u) \text{ is defined, and} \\ T_{\mathsf{I}}^{ass}(\tau_1)(u) = T_{\mathsf{I}}^{ass}(\tau_2)(u) \end{array} \right. \right\},$$

for each $\rho \in \mathcal{R}$, for each $x_1 \in \mathcal{VAR}$, ..., for each $x_{\mathcal{AR}(\rho)} \in \mathcal{VAR}$,

$$D_{\mathsf{I}}^{ass}(\rho(x_1, \ldots, x_{\mathcal{AR}(\rho)})) = \{ u \in \mathsf{U} \mid \langle ass(x_1), \ldots, ass(x_{\mathcal{AR}(\rho)}) \rangle \in \mathsf{R}(\rho) \},$$

for each $v \in \mathcal{VAR}$, for each $\delta \in \mathcal{D}^\Sigma$,

$$D_{\mathsf{I}}^{ass}(\exists v\, \delta) = \left\{ u \in \mathsf{U} \left| \begin{array}{l} \text{for some } u' \in \overline{\mathsf{Co}}_{\mathsf{I}}^{u}, \\ u \in D_{\mathsf{I}}^{ass\frac{u'}{v}}(\delta) \end{array} \right. \right\},$$

for each $v \in \mathcal{VAR}$, for each $\delta \in \mathcal{D}^\Sigma$,

$$D_{\mathsf{I}}^{ass}(\forall v\, \delta) = \left\{ u \in \mathsf{U} \left| \begin{array}{l} \text{for each } u' \in \overline{\mathsf{Co}}_{\mathsf{I}}^{u}, \\ u \in D_{\mathsf{I}}^{ass\frac{u'}{v}}(\delta) \end{array} \right. \right\},$$

for each $\delta \in \mathcal{D}^\Sigma$, $D_{\mathsf{I}}^{ass}(\neg\delta) = \mathsf{U} \backslash D_{\mathsf{I}}^{ass}(\delta)$,

for each $\delta_1 \in \mathcal{D}^\Sigma$, for each $\delta_2 \in \mathcal{D}^\Sigma$, $D_{\mathsf{I}}^{ass}([\delta_1 \wedge \delta_2]) = D_{\mathsf{I}}^{ass}(\delta_1) \cap D_{\mathsf{I}}^{ass}(\delta_2)$,

for each $\delta_1 \in \mathcal{D}^\Sigma$, for each $\delta_2 \in \mathcal{D}^\Sigma$, $D_{\mathsf{I}}^{ass}([\delta_1 \vee \delta_2]) = D_{\mathsf{I}}^{ass}(\delta_1) \cup D_{\mathsf{I}}^{ass}(\delta_2)$.

T_{I}^{ass} interprets terms as partial functions from objects to objects or chains of objects in the interpretation. D_{I}^{ass} interprets formulae as sets of objects in the interpretation. $\overline{\mathsf{Co}}_{\mathsf{I}}^{u}$ is the set of components of an object, u, in an interpretation, I, closed under finite sequences. Notice the appeal to $\overline{\mathsf{Co}}_{\mathsf{I}}^{u}$ in the interpretation of quantification. This is where the restriction to quantification over components and chains of components is made. Notice also that an n-ary relational formula can simply be interpreted as the set of objects whose n-tuples of components or chains of components, as determined by a variable assignment under quantification, are in the denotation of that relation. Negation, of course, corresponds to set complement.

We restrict relations and variables to components and chains of components by requiring that, in grammatical principles, no free variables occur in formulae. Let $\mathcal{D}_0^\Sigma$ be the set of Σ formulae without free variables. We can easily prove that the denotation of each member of $\mathcal{D}_0^\Sigma$ is independent of variable assignments in I.

Definition 7 For each signature Σ, for each Σ interpretation $\mathsf{I} = \langle \mathsf{U}, \mathsf{S}, \mathsf{A}, \mathsf{R} \rangle$, D_{I} is the total function from $\mathcal{D}_0^\Sigma$ to the power set of U, and Θ_{I} is the total function from the power set of $\mathcal{D}_0^\Sigma$ to the power set of U such that

for each $\delta \in \mathcal{D}_0^\Sigma$, $D_{\mathsf{I}}(\delta) = \left\{ u \in \mathsf{U} \left| \begin{array}{l} \text{for each } ass \in \mathsf{Ass}_{\mathsf{I}}, \\ u \in D_{\mathsf{I}}^{ass}(\delta) \end{array} \right. \right\},$

for each $\theta \subseteq \mathcal{D}_0^\Sigma$, $\Theta_{\mathsf{I}}(\theta) = \left\{ u \in \mathsf{U} \left| \begin{array}{l} \text{for each } \delta \in \theta, \\ u \in D_{\mathsf{I}}(\delta) \end{array} \right. \right\}.$

Every object in our models of a grammar, $\langle \Sigma, \theta \rangle$, must satisfy every description in the theory, θ:

Definition 8 For each signature Σ, for each $\theta \subseteq \mathcal{D}_0^\Sigma$, for each Σ interpretation $\mathsf{I} = \langle \mathsf{U}, \mathsf{S}, \mathsf{A}, \mathsf{R} \rangle$,
I is a $\langle \Sigma, \theta \rangle$ model iff $\Theta_{\mathsf{I}}(\theta) = \mathsf{U}$.

The notion of a model formalizes the idea that, with a grammar, linguists want to characterize natural language by objects which, in all their components, obey every principle of the grammar. However, as King (1999) observes, arbitrary models are not adequate to characterize a natural language. The linguistically intended model is one that contains instances of all configurations of objects that are permitted by the theory. A trivial example of an uninteresting model is the model where U is the empty set. A less trivial example of a model that is too small is a model of Pollard and Sag's (1994) grammar which contains exactly the sentence *Kim likes bagels* and nothing else. We could say that the intended model is, in a linguistically significant sense, the largest possible model of the grammar. This is called an *exhaustive model*:

Definition 9 For each signature Σ, for each $\theta \subseteq \mathcal{D}_0^\Sigma$, for each Σ interpretation I,
I is an exhaustive $\langle \Sigma, \theta \rangle$ model iff
I is a $\langle \Sigma, \theta \rangle$ model, and for each $\theta' \subseteq \mathcal{D}_0^\Sigma$, for each Σ interpretation I',

  if I' is a $\langle \Sigma, \theta \rangle$ model and $\Theta_{\mathsf{I}'}(\theta') \neq \emptyset$ then $\Theta_{\mathsf{I}}(\theta') \neq \emptyset$.

Among the objects in an exhaustive model of a grammar are, of course, all sentences that are licensed by that grammar. In linguistic terms this means that a grammar is true of a natural language if the natural language is one of the exhaustive models of the grammar. For a more thorough discussion of exhaustive models and alternative mathematical characterizations in SRL — which, *mutatis mutandis*, carry over to RSRL —, see King (1999) and Pollard (1999). The following important result has been proven by Richter and King (1997) for RSRL:

Theorem 1 *For each signature Σ, for each Σ theory θ, there exists a Σ interpretation I such that I is an exhaustive $\langle \Sigma, \theta \rangle$ model.*

As a corollary of THEOREM 1, if a grammar has a nonempty model, it also has a nonempty exhaustive model. In other words, a non-vacuous grammar has a linguistically sensible meaning in the class of its exhaustive models.

15.4 Computation

RSRL was designed as a formal language for the precise specification of HPSG grammars, not for computations such as parsing per se. It is, natural, however, to ask whether it might be possible to use RSRL for computational purposes as well. Pollard and Sag (1994) certainly had this in mind when they wrote (p. 10) of the necessity for decidability in their view of linguistic theory.

The most basic question one can hope to answer in an implementation is whether there could possibly exist a non-trivial, i.e. non-empty, collection of objects that behaves in the way that the theory predicts. This question is formalized as the *satisfaction* problem:

Definition 10 An RSRL theory, θ, over a signature, Σ, is *satisfiable* iff there exists a Σ interpretation, I, such that $\Theta_I(\theta) \neq \emptyset$.

Theorem 2 *RSRL-satisfiability is not compact, i.e., there exists a signature, Σ, and theory, θ, for which every finite $\theta' \subset \theta$ is satisfiable, but for which θ itself is not satisfiable* (proven by Paul King).

This non-compactness result has the practical consequence that no finite sound and complete calculus can exist for RSRL-satisfiability, nor, therefore, for many of the other problems we would like an implementation to be able to solve for us.

Looking at the situation from a broader perspective, what this really shows is that the formalization of the requirements put forth by Pollard and Sag (1994) and other HPSG literature, simply taken at face value, cannot serve as the basis of a computational system. HPSG, ever since Pollard and Sag (1987), has led a dual existence, being not only a scientifically stated theory of language, but also a fairly precise specification of how to compute with a language, in particular, of how to parse the sentences of a language. The non-compactness of RSRL-satisfiability, in our view, is a mathematical proof that these two views of HPSG are fundamentally incompatible. There are, of course, feature logics over which one can design parsers. Contrary to the objectives of systems that aspire to "directly" implement HPSG grammars, however, e.g., Götz and Meurers (1995), Götz and Meurers (1997), some rephrasal or transformation of linguistic principles will inevitably be necessary. This rephrasal effort can be felt most acutely in the case of principles such as the Binding Theory, Control Theory, etc., mentioned earlier, that make significant use of the different interpretation that HPSG requires of quantification and relations, and in our own experience, is far from easy.

15.5 Conclusion

The task of this paper was threefold: First, by quoting examples from Pollard and Sag (1994) and others, we intended to bring to the reader's attention that an adequate formal language for HPSG grammars not only needs a means to express true relations and true negation, but also explicit quantification over components. Second, we defined a formal language, RSRL, that provides these means and has the linguistically desired kinds of models, namely exhaustive models. Third, we proved that a discrepancy exists between the apparent intended use of feature-based languages in HPSG linguistics and computational considerations for languages underlying practical systems. For HPSG, conceived of as a theory of language rather than as a theory of parsing, RSRL is the formal language which is by far the closest to the language implicitly used by HPSG linguists.

15.6 Appendix 1

We illustrate the suitability of RSRL to HPSG by a straightforward formalization of principle B of the binding theory as given in the appendix of Pollard and Sag (1994). We proceed by quoting the verbal descriptions of the components of principle B from Pollard and Sag (1994), followed by their formalization in RSRL.

Principle B relies on the auxiliary notions *member*, *more oblique than*, *locally o-command* and *locally o-bind*, which are defined in turn.[6]

The relation member is defined as usual:

$$\forall x \forall y [\texttt{member}(x,y) \leftrightarrow [x \approx y\text{FIRST} \vee \texttt{member}(x,y\text{REST})]]$$

"One *synsem* object is *more oblique* than another provided it appears to the right of the other on the SUBCAT list of some word." (Pollard and Sag, 1994, p. 401) In the formalization, x is more oblique than y on the SUBCAT list of w.

$$\forall x \forall y \ [\texttt{more-oblique}(x,y) \leftrightarrow$$
$$\exists w \ [w \sim word \wedge \texttt{2-the-right}(x,y,w\text{SS LOC CAT SUBCAT})]]$$

$$\forall x \forall y \forall z \ [\texttt{2-the-right}(x,y,z) \leftrightarrow$$
$$[[z\text{FIRST} \approx y \wedge \texttt{member}(x,z\text{REST})] \vee \texttt{2-the-right}(x,y,z\text{REST})]]$$

"One referential *synsem* object *locally o-commands* another provided they have distinct LOCAL values and either (1) the second is more oblique than the first, or (2) the second is a member of the SUBCAT list of a *synsem* object that is more oblique than the first." (Pollard and Sag, 1994, p. 401). In the formalization, x locally o-commands y.

$$\forall x \forall y \ [\texttt{loc-o-command}(x,y) \leftrightarrow$$
$$x\text{LOC CONT INDEX} \sim ref \wedge y\text{LOC CONT INDEX} \sim ref$$

---

[6]According to the definitions above, only variables are allowed as arguments in relational formulae. In this section, we use the following abbreviatory notation, where ρ is an n-ary relation symbol, $\tau_1, \ldots, \tau_n$ are terms, at least one τ_i is not a variable, and $v_1, \ldots, v_n$ are distinct variables that are not free in $\tau_1, \ldots, \tau_n$: $\rho(\tau_1, \ldots, \tau_n) \equiv \exists v_1 \ldots \exists v_n [\tau_1 \approx v_1 \wedge \ldots \wedge \tau_n \approx v_n \wedge \rho(v_1, \ldots, v_n)]$

$\wedge\neg\ x\text{LOC} \approx y\text{LOC}$
$\wedge\ [\texttt{more-oblique}(y, x)$
$\qquad \vee\ \exists v[\texttt{member}(y, v\text{LOC CAT SUBCAT}) \wedge \texttt{more-oblique}(v, x)\ ]]]$

"A referential *synsem* object *locally o-binds* another provided it locally o-commands and is co-indexed with the other." (Pollard and Sag, 1994, p. 401) The use of the relation `loc-o-command` in the definition of `loc-o-binds` makes sure that x and y are referential *synsem* objects.

$\forall x \forall y\ [\texttt{loc-o-binds}(x, y) \leftrightarrow$
$\quad \texttt{loc-o-command}(x, y) \wedge x\text{LOC CONT INDEX} \approx y\text{LOC CONT INDEX}]$

With these definitions to hand, we can formalize principle B of the binding theory directly: "Principle B: A personal pronoun must be locally o-free." (Pollard and Sag, 1994, p. 401)

$\forall x\ [x\text{LOC CONT} \sim ppro \rightarrow \neg\ \exists y\ \texttt{loc-o-binds}(y, x)]$

For every object o, for each *synsem* component, x, of o that is a personal pronoun, there is no component y of o such that y locally o-binds x.

15.7 Appendix 2

This section presents the necessary extensions of RSRL to chains, as discussed in Section 15.2. We extend the sort hierarchy by a chain hierarchy, and the set of attributes by the quasi-attributes in the obvious way:

Definition 11 For each signature $\Sigma = \langle \mathcal{G}, \sqsubseteq, \mathcal{S}, \mathcal{A}, \mathcal{F}, \mathcal{R}, \mathcal{AR} \rangle$,
$\widehat{\mathcal{G}} = \mathcal{G} \cup \{chain, echain, nechain, metatop\}$,
$\widehat{\sqsubseteq} = \sqsubseteq \cup \{\langle echain, chain \rangle, \langle nechain, chain \rangle\} \cup \left\{ \langle \sigma, metatop \rangle \;\middle|\; \sigma \in \widehat{\mathcal{G}} \right\}$,
$\widehat{\mathcal{S}} = \mathcal{S} \cup \{echain, nechain\}$, and
$\widehat{\mathcal{A}} = \mathcal{A} \cup \{\dagger, \triangleright\}$.

Note that $\left\langle \widehat{\mathcal{G}}, \widehat{\sqsubseteq} \right\rangle$ is a finite partial order. As with the sort hierarchy and attribute set, we extend the species assignment function, S, and the attribute interpretation function, A, to chains.

Definition 12 For each signature $\Sigma = \langle \mathcal{G}, \sqsubseteq, \mathcal{S}, \mathcal{A}, \mathcal{F}, \mathcal{R}, \mathcal{AR} \rangle$, for each Σ interpretation $\mathsf{I} = \langle \mathsf{U}, \mathsf{S}, \mathsf{A}, \mathsf{R} \rangle$,
$\widehat{\mathsf{S}}$ is the total function from $\overline{\mathsf{U}}$ to $\widehat{\mathcal{S}}$ such that for each $u \in \mathsf{U}$, $\widehat{\mathsf{S}}(u) = \mathsf{S}(u)$, for each $u_1 \in \mathsf{U}, \ldots$, for each $u_n \in \mathsf{U}$,
$$\widehat{\mathsf{S}}(\langle u_1, \ldots, u_n \rangle) = \begin{cases} echain & \text{if } n = 0, \\ nechain & \text{if } n > 0 \end{cases}, \text{ and}$$

$\widehat{A}$ is the partial function from $\widehat{\mathcal{A}}$ to the set of partial functions from $\overline{U}$ to $\overline{U}$ such that for each $\alpha \in \mathcal{A}$, $\widehat{A}(\alpha) = A(\alpha)$, and $\widehat{A}(\dagger)$ is the total function from U^+ to U such that for each $\langle u_0, \dots, u_n \rangle \in U^+$, $\widehat{A}(\dagger)(\langle u_0, \dots, u_n \rangle) = u_0$, and $\widehat{A}(\triangleright)$ is the total function from U^+ to U^* such that for each $\langle u_0, \dots, u_n \rangle \in U^+$, $\widehat{A}(\triangleright)(\langle u_0, \dots, u_n \rangle) = \langle u_1, \dots, u_n \rangle$.

$\widehat{S}$ is just like S, except that it assigns the quasi-sort *echain* to the empty chain, and *nechain* to each nonempty chain of objects. $\widehat{A}$ is just like A, except that it interprets the quasi-attribute $\dagger$ as mapping each nonempty chain to its first element, and the quasi-attribute $\triangleright$ as mapping each nonempty chain, c, to the chain that is just like c but with the first element missing.

Finally, the definitions of an interpretation and of the constraint language must be slightly modified to accommodate chains. To allow chains as arguments of relations, we redefine the denotation of relations, R, as a total function from $\mathcal{R}$ to the power set of $(\overline{U})^*$, and require for each $\rho \in \mathcal{R}$ that $R(\rho)$ be a subset of $\overline{U}^{AR(\rho)}$. For the description of chains, the quasi-sorts and quasi-attributes must be available in the formulae of our language. Therefore, we replace the lines 5 and 6 of definition 3 and say now that for each $\alpha \in \widehat{\mathcal{A}}$ and for each $\tau \in \mathcal{T}^\Sigma$, $\tau\alpha \in \mathcal{T}^\Sigma$, and for each $\sigma \in \widehat{\mathcal{G}}$ and for each $\tau \in \mathcal{T}^\Sigma$, $\tau{\sim}\sigma \in \mathcal{D}^\Sigma$.

References

Abeillé, A. and D. Godard. 1996. La complémentation des auxiliaires français. *Langages* 122:32–61.

Ait-Kaci, H. 1984. *A Lattice Theoretic Approach to Computation Based on a Calculus of Partially Ordered Type Structures*. Ph.D. thesis, University of Pennsylvania.

Baker, C. L. 1970. Double negatives. *Linguistic Inquiry* 1:69–96.

Carpenter, B. 1992. *The Logic of Typed Feature Structures*. Cambridge University Press. Cambridge, Massachusetts, USA.

Carpenter, B. and G. Penn. 1996. Efficient parsing of compiled typed attribute value grammars. In H. Bunt and M. Tomita, eds., *Recent Advances in Parsing Technology*. Kluwer.

Giannakidou, A. 1997. *The Landscape of Polarity Items*. Ph.D. thesis, University of Groningen.

Götz, T. and D. Meurers. 1995. Compiling HPSG type constraints into definite clause programs. In *Proceedings of the 33rd ACL*.

298 / Frank Richter, Manfred Sailer and Gerald Penn

Götz, T. and D. Meurers. 1997. Interleaving universal principles and relational constraints over typed feature logic. In *Proceedings of the 35th ACL / 8th EACL*, pages 1–8.

Hinrichs, E. and T. Nakazawa. 1994. Linearizing AUXs in German verbal complexes. In J. Nerbonne, K. Netter, and C. J. Pollard, eds., *German in Head-Driven Phrase Structure Grammar*, no. 46 in CSLI Lecture Notes, pages 11–37. Stanford University: CSLI Publications.

Höhfeld, M. and G. Smolka. 1988. Definite relations over constraint languages. LILOG Report 53, IBM Deutschland.

Kasper, R., A. Kathol, and C. Pollard. 1995. A relational interpretation of linear precedence constraints. *Paper presented at the Fourth Meeting on Mathematics of Language (MOL4)*.

Kathol, A. 1995. *Linearization-Based German Syntax*. Ph.D. thesis, Ohio State University.

Kathol, A. and C. Pollard. 1995. Extraposition via complex domain formation. *Proceedings of the 1995 Annual Meeting of the Association for Computational Linguistics* pages 174–180.

King, P. J. 1989. *A logical Formalism for Head-Driven Phrase Structure Grammar*. Ph.D. thesis, University of Manchester.

King, P. J. 1999. Towards Truth in Head-driven Phrase Structure Grammar. In V. Kordoni, ed., *Tübingen Studies in Head-Driven Phrase Structure Grammar*, Arbeitspapiere des SFB 340, Nr. 132. Universität Tübingen.

Ladusaw, W. 1979. *Polarity Sensitivity as Inherent Scope Relations*. Ph.D. thesis, University of Texas at Austin.

Linebarger, M. C. 1987. Negative polarity and grammatical representation. *Linguistics and Philosophy* 10:325–387.

Pollard, C. and I. A. Sag. 1987. *Information-Based Syntax and Semantics. Vol.1: Fundamentals*. CSLI Lecture Notes 13.

Pollard, C. and I. A. Sag. 1994. *Head-Driven Phrase Structure Grammar*. University of Chicago Press.

Pollard, C. J. 1999. Strong generative capacity in HPSG. In G. Webelhuth, J.-P. Koenig, and A. Kathol, eds., *Lexical and Constructional Aspects of Linguistic Explanation*, pages 281–297. CSLI Publications.

Richter, F. 1999. RSRL for HPSG. In V. Kordoni, ed., *Tübingen Studies in Head-Driven Phrase Structure Grammar*, Arbeitspapiere des SFB 340, Nr. 132. Universität Tübingen.

Richter, F. and P. J. King. 1997. On the Existence of Exhaustive Models in a Relational Feature Logic for Head-driven Phrase Structure Grammar. Manuscript.

16

Remnant Movement and Complexity

EDWARD STABLER

16.1 Remnant movement

Linguists in the transformational tradition have recently been exploring the extent to which previous empirical coverage can be maintained with fewer grammatical devices. For example, Kayne (1994) develops some analyses in a framework that requires constituents to begin in specifier-head-complement order, with only leftward movement, and Chomsky (1995) explores how the structure building operations in such a system can be bottom-up and driven by lexical features. In more recent work, Kayne (1998) begins the exploration of the possibility that there is no covert movement, and Koopman and Szabolcsi (1998) show how head movement is not needed in the analysis of verbal complexes.

With the restricted grammatical options these theories make available, "remnant movement" has come to have increasing prominence, where a "remnant" is a constituent from which material has been extracted. Moving a constituent from which material has already been extracted means that traces of earlier movements may be carried to positions where they are no longer c-commanded by their antecedents, something which was banned in earlier theories. Interest in remnant movement has a longer history. For example, den Besten and Webelhuth (1990) proposed analyses like the following:

(1) [t_i gelesen]$_j$ hat Hans [das Buch]$_i$ nicht t_j
     read   has Hans the book   not

Similar analyses are considered in Webelhuth (1992) and Müller (1996).[1]

---

[1] An alternative analysis is provided in Fanselow (1987), and a brief critical survey

Constraints and Resources in Natural Language Syntax and Semantics.
Gosse Bouma, Erhard W. Hinrichs, Geert-Jan M. Kruijff, and Richard T. Oehrle.
Copyright © 1999, Stanford University.

Nkemnji (1995) uses remnant movement in his analysis of the Bantu language Nweh,

(2) njikem a   ke? [te t_i akendɔŋ]$_j$ pfɛt$_i$ t_j
     he   Agr P1 neg   plaintains eat

And Koopman (1996) sketches a range of related analyses:

(3) 1. who$_i$ do you think [t_i came]$_j$ t_i t_j?

     2. who$_i$ [t_i came]$_j$ do you think t_i t_j?

With the renewed interest in remnant movement coming from theoretical shifts, a wide range of constructions involving negation and related things is considered in Kayne (1998), where it is proposed that alternative analyses like the following yield scope ambiguities:

(4) 1. I will force you to [marry t_i]$_j$ [no one]$_i$ t_j

     2. I will [force you to marry t_i]$_j$ [no one]$_i$ t_j

The first analysis of this example yields a narrow object scope reading, with the negative DP raising to the specifier of NegP, followed by a predicate raising step (cf. Koster 1994, Zwart 1994, 1997). The second, wide object scope analysis has longer movements.

The best-worked out remnant movement analysis is the account of verbal complex formation in Koopman and Szabolcsi (1998). Developing an observation of Kenesei, Koopman and Szabolcsi observe the following pattern in negated or focused sentences of Hungarian, schematized on the right where "M" is used to represent the special category of "verbal modifiers" like *haza-*:

(5) Nem fogok akarni   kezdeni haza-menni   V1 V2 V3 M
     not will-1s want-INF begin-INF home-go-INF
     V4

(6) Nem fogok akarni   haza-menni kezdenni   V1 V2 M V4
     not will-1s want-INF home-go-INF begin-INF
     V3

(7) Nem fogok haza-menni kezdenni akarni   V1 M V4 V3
     not will-1s begin-INF   want-INF home-go-INF
     V2

---

of remnant movement analyses is provided in De Kuthy and Meurers (1998).

All of these sentences mean roughly the same thing: "I won't want to begin to go home." Notice that the verbs following the modifier appear in inverted order. Other orders are not possible (on the readings indicated by the numbering of the verbs). In particular, it is interesting that while the pattern above suggests that a constituent [M V4 V3] can invert with V2 to yield [M V4 V3 V2], the uninverted form [V3 M V4] which we see in (5) cannot invert with V2 to yield V1 <u>V3 M V4</u> V2.

Koopman and Szabolcsi (1998) propose a very natural and uniform analysis of this paradigm which can be schematically represented as follows:

(8)   V1 V2 V3 [V4 M] $\Rightarrow$ (not a surface form)
      V1 V2 [V3 [M$_1$ [V4 t_1]]] $\Rightarrow$ =(5)
      V1 [V2 [M$_1$ [V4 t_1]]$_2$ [V3 t_2]] $\Rightarrow$ =(6)
      V1 [M$_1$ [V4 t_1]]$_2$ [V3 t_2]]$_3$ [V2 t_3]   =(7)

Notice that the various inverted orders are obtained by "rolling up" the predicates into increasingly complex constituents. Let's say that a grammar *rolls up* some category XP iff one XP$_1$ can move to a higher XP$_2$, with XP$_2$ in turn moving to a higher XP$_3$, and so on without bound. In the analysis (8), we see VP rolling up.

The verbal modifier M can be phrasal (e.g. *a szoba-ba* 'the room-into'), and so it is natural to assume that all the movements indicated here are phrasal. In fact, Koopman and Szabolcsi (1998) show that the idea that there are two different kinds of movement, head movement and phrasal movement, faces serious problems in the account of verbal complexes in Hungarian and Germanic: our best accounts do not work, and often we seem to need parallel accounts for very similar constructions that contain more than just heads.

These analyses have interesting formal properties, which can be revealed when they are cast into a natural generative framework.

16.2   Languages as closures

As in Keenan and Stabler (1996), we define a grammar as a pair $G = \langle Lex, \mathcal{F} \rangle$, where the lexicon *Lex* is a set of expressions and $\mathcal{F}$ is a set of structure building functions (functions from tuples of expressions to expressions). Then let the language defined by the grammar be the set of all expressions that can be built up from the lexicon by the structure building rules, $L(G) = closure(Lex, \mathcal{F})$.[2] In typical linguistic applications, as in this paper, both *Lex* and $\mathcal{F}$ are finite.

---

[2]Keenan and Stabler (1996) define languages this way in order to consider, for example, what relations are preserved by automorphisms of L that fix $\mathcal{F}$, just as as in semantics we can consider the similar question: what is preserved by automorphisms

Given a grammar that is formalized in this way, we will consider:

• What is the expressive power of grammars that derive the verbal complexes? (what sets are definable)

• What is the structural complexity of the verbal complexes in these grammars?

• Since structure building is driven by lexical features, is there a useful representation of derivations as graphs of feature checking relations?

Expressive power is familiar, but expression complexity is perhaps not so familiar, so we quickly review the ideas we will use. What is the size of a sentence like the following?

every student criticized some teacher

When comparing sentences, one possible measure is simply the count of the characters, the length of the sequence. In this case, we have 37 characters (counting the spaces between words). To get a slightly more universal measure, it is common to consider how many binary choices are required to specify each element of the sequence. In the ASCII coding scheme, each character is specified by 7 binary choices, 7 bits. So in the ASCII coding scheme, the sequence is represented with 359 bits.[3]

When we have a grammar that includes the sentence, we make available another way of specifying the sentence. The sentence can be specified by specifying its shortest derivation. Let's see how this works. Suppose we have the following grammar $G = \langle Lex, \mathcal{F} \rangle$, with 8 lexical items consisting of string-category pairs, and 4 structure building rules which operate as indicated here:

Lex:

every D	teacher N	praised V	and CONJ
some D	student N	criticized V	or CONJ

$\mathcal{F}$:

f: s D, t N $\longmapsto$ st DP h: s DP, t VP $\longmapsto$ st S

g: s V, t DP $\longmapsto$ st VP i: s S, t CONJ, u S $\longmapsto$ stu S

For example the function f takes a pair of expressions where the first is the string s of category D and the second is a string t of category N to yield the expression which is the concatenation st of category NP. The language $L(G)$ is clearly infinite, because we can form arbitrarily

---

of E that fix $E, (2, \leq)$. But in this paper, languages are defined as closures just for simplicity.

[3]The ASCII coding scheme is of course not an "optimal code" for a source of English text. We just use it as an example here because it is a well-known, standard code.

large sentential conjunctions, and it includes a derivation that can be depicted with a tree like the following:

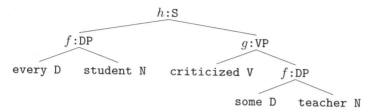

The written form of this sentence is specified by 359 bits, and the derivation tree looks larger, since when it is depicted this way it includes every character of the sentence, in addition to the indicated functions and constituent structure. But in fact there is a very natural grammatical coding scheme in which this derivation is specified by just 5 bits.

We can read off the elements of this tree by "traversing" the tree in a standard order. A standard "LR traversal" yields the derivation in a kind of reverse Polish notation:

every D, student N, f, criticized V, some D, teacher N, f, g, h

Now, we can calculate the size of this derivation by considering how many choices there are in this 9 element LR traversal. Since every sentence in the language begins with some determiner, and there are exactly 2 determiners, the first element represents one binary choice, one bit. After a determiner, we always have a noun, so that is a second binary choice. After a determiner and noun, the 2-place function f invariably applies. There is no choice here, so this is 0 bits. Considering our choices in this way, given each prefix p of the LR sequence, we easily calculate:[4]

$$size = \sum_{LR\ prefixes\ p} log_2|choices(p)| = 5 \text{ bits}$$

Notice that, whenever Lex and $\mathcal{F}$ are finite, the number of choices at each point in the LR enumeration of derivations will be finite. So in general, a grammatical code of this kind can be provided, and it will

---

[4]As in the input sequence, we are not counting the last choice of whether to continue to build a more complex form or not. Adding that choice into our size measure would not affect the points being made here.

The choice function will not be defined here, but this kind of function is familiar from parsing applications, where an "LR oracle" specifies the choices compatible with prefixes of the input (often focusing on the ideal deterministic case where there is exactly one choice at each point).

tend to be smaller than an input code (assuming that not all strings are grammatical). With any natural language grammar worth having, specifying an expression by its shortest derivation requires, on average, many fewer decisions than specifying it as an arbitrary sequence of sounds or typed characters. We will use this notion of size below.

Grammars like the one given above cannot specify "rolling-up" derivations of the sort mentioned earlier. The structure building rules here are essentially like context free rules, and we will see that these cannot possibly suffice. We now define transformational structure building rules that will do the trick.

16.3   A minimalist grammar formalism

The $\mathcal{MG}$ framework is defined by the restrictions it places on lexicons and generating functions.

16.3.1   Lexicon

An $\mathcal{MG}$ lexicon is a finite set of lexical items, where each lexical item is a finite sequence of features. There are four kinds of syntactic features, and there may also be non-syntactic (e.g. phonetic) features:

`c, t, d, n, v, p,...`	(selected categories)
`=c, =t, =d, =n, =v, =p,...`	(selector features)
`+wh, +case, +focus,...`	(licensors)
`-wh, -case, -focus,...`	(licensees)
`every,some,student,...`	(non-syntactic: phonetic,semantic)

Given the structure building rules of the next section, it will be easy to show that a lexical item that has a non-syntactic feature preceding any syntactic feature will be unable to play a role in any non-trivial derivation, because the structure building rules "check" syntactic features from left-to-right.[5]

16.3.2   Structure building rules

Our complex expressions will be trees, so it is convenient to regard lexical items as trees too. Lexical items are just 1-node trees, labeled with finite

---

[5]Allowing for the possibility of "useless" lexical items in order to obtain a maximally simple account is analogous to allowing "useless" categories to obtain a simple definition of context free grammars, where a category is "useless" if it has no yield in Σ^* or cannot be reached from the start category "S". It is of course possible to rule out such "useless" categories, just as we could rule out "useless" lexical items, but this complicates the definition of the grammar.

sequences of features.[6] A one node tree is both a root and a leaf.

We will also use a special tree notation which will make it easy to see how the structure building rules are feature-driven. We will not use traditional X-bar structures like

```
            DP
            |
            D'
           ╱╲
         D    NP
         |    |
        the   N'
              |
              N
              |
            idea
```

Rather, we will have trees like the following:

The internal nodes of these trees are labeled by the "projection order" of the daughters. In effect, the symbols <, > "point" towards the *head* of the phrase. So we can see that the tree just displayed is a determiner phrase by the fact that the order "points" to the left daughter which has the categorial feature d. Every leaf is a *head*, as usual. A *maximal projection* is a maximal subtree with a given head. So, for example, the right daughter of the tree just displayed is a head but also a maximal projection, since no larger subtree has that node as its head. Any right sister of a head will be called a *complement*. Any phrase attached to the left of a head in its maximal projection will be called a *specifier*.[7]

Let *exp* be the set of expressions, that is, the set of trees of this kind, in which internal nodes are labeled with < or > and leaves are labeled with (possibly empty) sequences of features.

Let's write $t_1\text{COMP}t_2$ to mean that the head of t_1 has t_2 as its complement (i.e. its right sister). That is, COMP signifies the "is a complement of" relation. We let COMP^+ be the transitive closure of COMP,

---

[6]Allowing complex trees as lexical items, as many linguists have proposed, does not change things substantially with respect to any of the issues considered in this paper.

[7]As will become clear below, a constituent can have at most one complement, but for the moment, no restriction is placed on the number of specifiers that a constituent can have.

and COMP* be the reflexive, transitive closure of COMP. We will say that t_2 is a comp$^+$ of t_1 if t_2 is a complement of, or a complement of a complement of, or ... of t_1.

Similarly, let's write t_1SPECt_2 to mean that the head of t_1 has t_2 as its specifier. That is, SPEC signifies the "is a specifier of" relation. We let SPEC$^+$ be the transitive closure of SPEC, and SPEC* be the reflexive, transitive closure of SPEC. We will say that t_2 is a spec* of t_1 if t_2 is t_1, or else it is a specifier of, or a specifier of a specifier of, or ... of t_1.

These relations do not depend on the node labels, but only on the structure of the tree and the < or > ordering. For example, consider the following tree:

The head of this tree is labeled 5. The constituent $[_<1[_>2,3]]$ is a specifier and hence also a spec$^+$ of 5. The constituent 1 is a specifier of 2, and so is also a spec$^+$ of 5. The constituent $[_<6[_<7,8]]$ is a complement of 5. The constituents $[_<6[_<7,8]]$, $[_<7,8]$ and 8 are comp$^+$'s of 5.

Now we define the two structure building rules: *merge* and *move*.

The partial function *merge* $:$ $(exp \times exp) \rightarrow exp$

The *merge* function applies to a pair of expressions when the head of the first begins with a selection feature =x for some x, and the head of the second begins with that category x. A 1-node head attaches the first constituent it selects on the right, in complement position. If it selects any other constituents, these are attached to the left in specifier positions, as we see in the following examples:

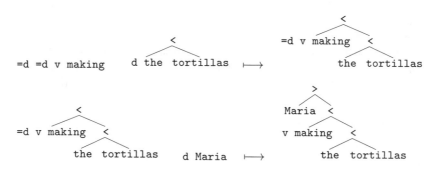

We also see in these examples that this structure building operation "cancels" a pair of features: the selection feature =x and the selected feature x are deleted, and do not appear in the result. In the first example, we see that the input trees have 4 syntactic features altogether, while the result has 2. In the second example, the inputs have 3 syntactic features, and the result has only 1.

We can define this structure building function in the following way, adapted from Cornell (1997a). Let $t[f]$ be the result of prefixing feature f to the sequence of features at the head of t. Then, for all trees t_1, t_2 and all $c \in Cat$,

$$merge(t_1[\text{=c}], t_2[\text{c}]) = \begin{cases} \overset{<}{\underset{t_1 \quad t_2}{\triangle}} & \text{if } t_1 \in Lex \\ \overset{>}{\underset{t_2 \quad t_1}{\triangle}} & \text{otherwise} \end{cases}$$

The partial function: $move : exp \to exp$

The function *move* applies to a single tree, when the head of that tree has a feature +f as its first element and when there is exactly one -f feature in the tree, where that feature is initial in some comp$^+$ of the tree or some specifier of a comp$^+$ of the tree. In this case, move applies by moving the maximal projection of the -f subtree to specifier position, and replacing the original occurrence of that tree by the empty tree λ (i.e. a single leaf node with no features). We see this operation applying in the following example:

Again, it is important to notice that each application of this function cancels exactly two features: the +f and -f are deleted and do not appear in the result. In this example, the input has 3 syntactic features, and the result has only 1.

We can define this structure building function in the following way. Let $t^>$ be the maximal projection of t. And for any trees t, t_1, t_2 where t properly contains t_1 but does not contain t_2, let $t\{t_1/t_2\}$ represent the result of replacing t_1 by t_2 in t. Then for any tree $t_1[\texttt{+f}]$ which contains exactly one exposed occurrence of $\texttt{-f}$, where $t_2[\texttt{-f}]^>$ is a comp$^+$ or a specifier of a comp$^+$ of $t_1[\texttt{+f}]$:

$$move(t_1[\texttt{+f}]) = t_2^{\overset{>}{\frown}} t_1\{t_2[\texttt{-f}]^>/\lambda\}$$

With this definition, all movement is overt, phrasal, and leftward.

The requirement that movement cannot apply when two outstanding $\texttt{-f}$ requirements would compete for the same position is a strong version of the "shortest move" condition Chomsky (1995). The other restriction on movement proposed here is from Koopman and Szabolcsi (1998): the moved tree must be a comp$^+$ or the specifier of a comp$^+$. Koopman and Szabolcsi (1998) say that the extracted constituent must be "on the main projection line," relating this idea to the treatment of the ECP in Kayne (1984).

$\mathcal{MG}$ grammars and languages

To summarize, in $\mathcal{MG}$, each grammar $G = \langle Lex, \mathcal{F} \rangle$ where the lexicon is a finite set $Lex \subseteq$ features*, and where $\mathcal{F} = \{merge, move\}$. As usual, a grammar of this kind defines a set $L(G) = closure(Lex, \mathcal{F})$. Let's say that the *sentences* in such a set are those $s \in L(G)$ with just one occurrence of one syntactic feature left, namely, the "start" category c.

We will use $\mathcal{MG}$ for the set of all minimalist grammars, and $\mathcal{ML}$ for the set of languages definable by these grammars, i.e. the string sets of the sentences of these languages.[8]

16.4   Formal grammars for Hungarian verbal complexes

The $\mathcal{MG}$ grammar formalism easily defines remnant movement. This paper will take three first steps towards the Koopman and Szabolcsi analysis of Hungarian verbal complexes. All three steps share the formal

---

[8]These grammars are weaker than the grammars studied by in previous work by Stabler, Cornell, and others. Cornell (1997a) shows how a derivational presentation of the sort given here, one in which traces and chains play no role, can equivalently be presented representationally, defining the language of expressions with traces, chains and constraints, more along the lines explored by Brody (1995). In other work Cornell (1997b, 1998a, 1998b) shows how grammars of this sort can be implemented in the type logical framework presented in Moortgat (1996) and Moortgat and Oehrle (1996). These demonstrations go through, even more easily, in the simpler framework described here. See also the related work of Lecomte (1998), Retoré and Lecomte (1997), Becker (1998), Michaelis (1998), Michaelis and Wartena (1998), Szalai and Stabler (1998), Vermaat (1998).

properties which will be explored later, but it is interesting to see how the beginnings of the more sophisticated analysis can be introduced.[9]

16.4.1 $G1$: rolling up VPs

The "rolling-up" of verb phrases schematically indicated in (8) can be defined with a trivial grammar. Let $G1 = \langle Lex, \mathcal{F} \rangle$ where Lex has the 9 lexical items listed here:

Lex:

```
=v  v  V1
=v  v  V2
=v  v  V3          =v +v  v  V2
=v  v  V3      =v +v  v  V3    =v +v  v -v  V3
=m +m  v  V4   =m +m  v -v  V4
m -m  M
```

$\mathcal{F} = \{merge, move\}$

In this lexicon, I use lower case for syntactic features, and upper case for the non-syntactic features. The first column of entries is used to derive (5), with obligatory inversion of the modifier M triggered by a movement requirement -m. The second column adds entries for (6), so that after M inverts with V4, the result still has a -v feature which forces M V4 to invert with V3. The third column adds entries for (7), so that after M V4 inverts with V3, it still must invert with V2.

Notice that V3 has three forms: the first just selects v; the second adds the +v feature so that it will invert the VP it selects, and the third adds -v so that its maximal projection must also invert. It is this third form that yields the distinctive, unbounded "rolling up" of structure. Notice that this form introduces two features =v,+m that it also consumes. – It is a common idea from categorial grammar that a category (e.g. a modifier) could yield the same resource that it consumes; what is novel here is that one of the resources with this status is one that triggers movement.

Here are the first steps of a derivation of a VP:

1. lexical: m -m M
2. lexical: =m +m v -v V4
3. merge(2,1):

```
        <
      +m v -v V4 -m M
```

4. move(3):

```
        >
      M   <
        v -v V4
```

[9]See Szalai (forthcoming) for more sophisticated formal models of these structures.

5. lexical: =v +v v -v V3 ⇐ this is the recursively moving category!
6. merge(5,4):

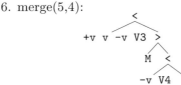

7. move(6):

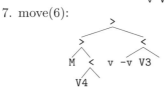

8. lexical: =v +v v V2
9. merge(8,7):   ⇐ next step, VP3 rolls up

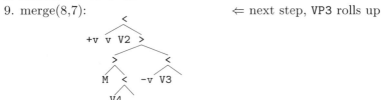

In step 5, the recursive category is introduced This first grammar allows derivations that we wanted to exclude, though, like: * V1 <u>V3 M V4</u> V2. So let's go to a slightly more interesting grammar.

16.4.2   G2: introducing PredP

To account for a wider range of facts, we need something a little more sophisticated. Following Koopman and Szabolcsi, we take another step. First, the contents of the position we are calling M are not all alike: they are classified into "bigger" and "smaller" types. A WP with a bigger M in its spec must be selected by PredP; with smaller M, PredP is optional. The modifier *haza* in our Hungarian examples (5)-(7) is "smaller," in this sense. The presence of PredP then determines a later step. When WP is selected by PredP, it cannot extract; the CP above it must extract. That is, PredP (our category **pr**) blocks inversion, and is always present when the modifiers are "bigger."

So in the following schematic representation, we see the derivation of the English form deviate from that of the inverted form after the first two steps. Two steps build a WP, but at that point the WP is optionally selected by PredP. If it is not selected by PredP, we get WP-to-WP movement for the inverted order. And if it is selected by PredP, we get CP-to-WP movement for the English order. The differences between the two derivations occur at the underlined steps.

(9)   1. V2 M $\Rightarrow$ invert M

2. $[_w$ M V2$] \Rightarrow$ For inverted order: build CP, VP1

3. V1 $[_c$ $[_w$ M V2$]] \Rightarrow$ WP to spec,WP

4. $[_w$ $[_w$ M V2$]$ V1 $[_c$ $]] \Rightarrow$ CP to licensor

5. $[_c$ $]$ $[_w$ $[_w$ M V2$]$ V1 $] \Rightarrow$ WP to higher WP or CP

6. $[_w$ $[_w$ M V2$]$ V1 $]$ $[_c$ $]$

(10) 1. V2 M $\Rightarrow$ invert M

2. $[_w$ M V2$] \Rightarrow$ for English order: WP selected by PredP

3. $[_{pr}[_w$ M V2$]] \Rightarrow$ build CP, VP1

4. V1 $[_c$ $[_{pr}[_w$ M V2$]]] \Rightarrow$ CP to spec,WP

5. $[_w$ $[_c$ $[_{pr}[_w$ M V2$]]]$ V1 $] \Rightarrow$ CP to licensor

6. $[_c$ $[_{pr}[_w$ M V2$]]]$ $[_w$ V1 $] \Rightarrow$ WP to higher WP or CP

7. $[_w$ V1 $]$ $[_c$ $[_{pr}[_w$ M V2$]]]$

To get just the aspects of the analysis indicated above, and continuing to ignore the arguments of the verbs, we use the following grammar with 12 lexical items. Th grammar introduces the categories **w, pr,** and the CP licensing category **lc.** Let $G2 = \langle Lex, \mathcal{F} \rangle$ where,

Lex: =lc +m c   =lc +m c -c
          =w +c lc
          =c v V1   =pr c -m
          =w c -c   =bw pr
          =v +m w -m   =v +bm bw
          =m v V2
          m -m M   m -bm M
   $\mathcal{F} = \{merge, move\}$

To derive the inverted order M V1 V2, lexical items in the first column suffice. To derive the English order V2 M V1, we add the second column, in which we see the feature -bm – the special requirement of "big modifiers", and the category **pr** (the category that heads PredP).

The following is a complete derivation of the inverted order M V2 V1 from this simple grammar:

1. lexical: m -m M
2. lexical: =m v V2
3. merge(2,1):

   v V2 -m M

4. lexical: =v +m w −m

5. merge(4,3):

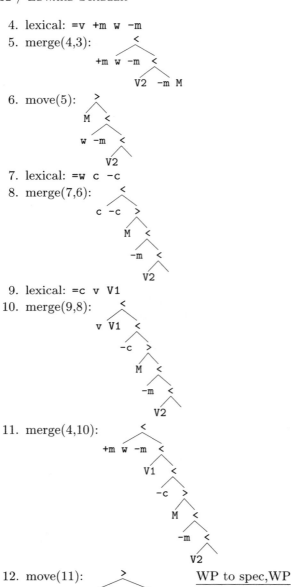

6. move(5):

7. lexical: =w c −c

8. merge(7,6):

9. lexical: =c v V1

10. merge(9,8):

11. merge(4,10):

12. move(11):   WP to spec,WP

13. lexical: =w +c lc

14. merge(13,12):

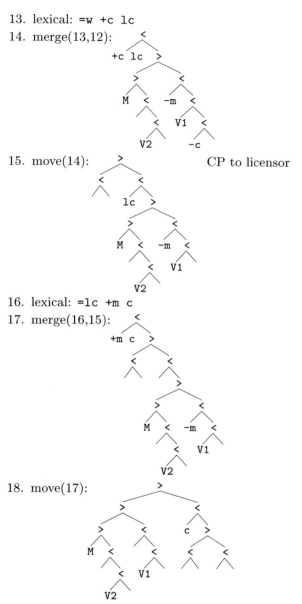

15. move(14):   CP to licensor

16. lexical: =lc +m c

17. merge(16,15):

18. move(17):

This derivation of the "inverted order" has 18 steps: 7 lexical items and 11 function applications. Notice that the derived structure 18 has only 1 syntactic feature left, namely the start category c. All the empty nodes are of little help in remembering how the derivation went, and so it is no surprise that linguists prefer richer labels! The traditional linguistic depiction (11) shows how the derivation went but obscures whether all features were checked:

(11)

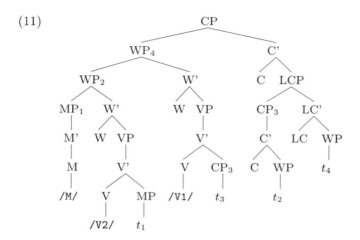

Looking at this tree, it is easy to see the course of the derivation, but it is very hard to see whether the derivation was successful – i.e. whether all features were checked! Having done the derivation we know: they were. (We will consider another, rather different representation of this derived structure below in section 16.7.)

The derivation of the English order V1 M V2 differs from the previous derivation at the first step and then, as a consequence of that first choice, later in the derivation:

1. lexical: m -bm M   ⇐ different from prev derivation here!

2. lexical: =m v V2

3. merge(2,1):
     <
   v V2 -bm M

4. lexical: =v +bm bw

5. merge(4,3):
       <
   +bm bw <
        V2 -bm M

...

21. move(20): This is the English order

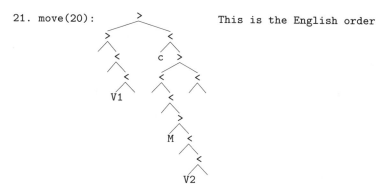

This derivation uses 9 lexical items, 12 function applications. It has 2 more lexical items than the derivation of inverted order, because (i) the inverted order uses `=v +m w -m` twice, while this one uses `=v +bm bw` in one of those positions, and (ii) this derivation has `=bw pr`. No surprise: this derivation has one more function application step than the inverted order, namely: the merging of PredP `=bw pr` with the "big" WP.

The traditional depiction of the derived structure is the following:

(12)

Koopman and Szabolcsi have a more elegant way to force CP movement when there is a PredP, and to allow the checked requirement to be the

-m feature of WP rather than a -m that is arbitrarily assigned to CPs with PredPs in them. One further step towards their analysis will be taken in the next section, where the extraction of spec,WP_3 gets some attention.

16.4.3 $G3$ and a conservative extension for pied piping

One of the interesting proposals in the Koopman and Szabolcsi proposal is the idea that we have been overly liberal in our assumptions about what can move and overly conservative in our assumptions about pied piping. They propose that pied piping and the movement of large structures is the normal occurrence. Let's see how we can adopt the following assumptions:

(13)   No projection has more than one specifier.

(14)   Only complements (that is, comp$^+$s) move.

(15)   A +f head triggers the movement of a comp$^+$ to check a -f feature in the spec* of that constituent.

To enforce the first restriction, we require lexical items to have the form:
$$(=f(\{+g,=g\}))\ c\ -r^*\ (phon)\ sem$$
where parentheses indicate optional choices (i.e. 0 or 1 occurrences), braces indicate the selection of exactly 1 element, and the star indicates 0 or more occurrences. (We neglect semantic features sem in the present study.)

To enforce the second two restrictions, we simply modify the definition of *move* so that a +f head triggers the movement of a comp$^+$ to check a -f feature in the spec* of that constituent.

Let $\mathcal{SMG}$ be the set of these "strict minimalist grammars," and let $\mathcal{SML}$ be the set of languages definable by these grammars, i.e. the string sets of the sentences of these languages.

The grammar G2 on page 311 already respects the lexical restriction: at most 1 specifier per head. However, with that grammar some sentences are derived by moving specifiers. For example, the "English order" structure with the derivation ending on page 315 involves specifier movement. The specifier movement is clearly visible when the derived structure is depicted as in the tree 12. To avoid this, the strategy is to redesign the grammar so that the VP in comp,WP_3 moves to some spec,ZP, so that then WP_3 can move to spec,LCP to check -c in its spec*, leaving us with the same English order of pronounced heads. That is, we will modify the grammar to yield the structure:

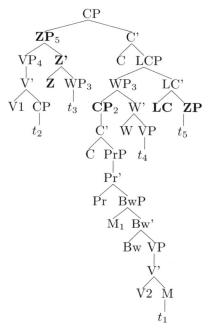

In this structure, all traces are in complement position. To empirically support any analysis of this sort, it of course remains to identify and independently motivate ZP, but the focus here is just on the formal options, so we provide a grammar which just uses the new projection ZP in the way indicated:

```
=lc +m c            =lc +m c -c
=z +c lc
=wz +v z -m         =v +m wz
=c v -v V1           =pr c -m
=w c -c             =bw pr
=v +m w -m          =v +bm bw
=m v V2
m -m M              m -bm M
```

Notice that category **wz** is introduced which is not −m, since **z** is −m instead.

With this grammar, the derivation of English order begins as usual, but gets to step 20, where a specifier triggers the movement of a complement:

1. lexical: m −bm M
2. lexical: =m v V2

3. merge(2,1):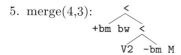

4. lexical: =v +bm bw

5. merge(4,3):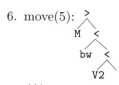

6. move(5):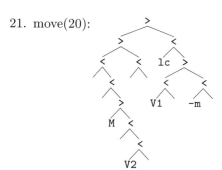

   . . .

20. merge(19,18):   ⇐ the −c phrase cannot move

21. move(20):

22. lexical: =lc +m c

23. merge(22,21):

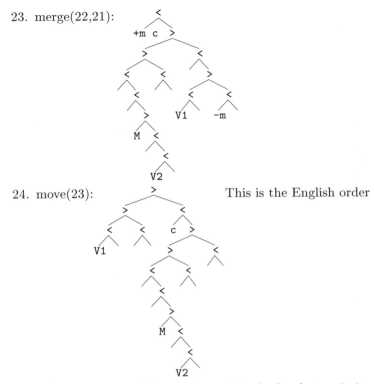

24. move(23):   This is the English order

Notice the movement of the complement to check a feature in its specifier in step 21.

16.5   Remnant movement and expressive power

First, it is easy to see that all context free languages can be defined in the $\mathcal{MG}$ formalism, and that the class of minimalist grammar languages is closed under unions:

(16) $\mathcal{CFL} \subseteq \mathcal{ML}$

(17)   If $L1, L2 \in \mathcal{ML}$, $L1 \cup L2 \in \mathcal{ML}$

Stabler (1997) showed that languages with 5 "counting dependencies" could be defined in a transformational grammar formalism with head movement and covert movement. It turns out that even without those mechanisms, we can still define these complex languages, very easily, as we see in the following grammar.

Theorem: $\{1^n 2^n 3^n 4^n 5^n \mid n \in \mathbb{N}\} \in \mathcal{ML}$

```
=1 +5 +4 +3 +2 +1 c            c
=2 1 -1 /1/                     =2 +1 1 -1 /1/
=3 2 -2 /2/                     =3 +2 2 -2 /2/
=4 3 -3 /3/                     =4 +3 3 -3 /3/
=5 4 -4 /4/                     =5 +4 4 -4 /4/
    5 -5 /5/                    =1 +5 5 -5 /5/
```

It is easy to check that all movements in derivations of clauses from this grammar are movements of complements, but the first lexical item allows a c to have 5 specifiers. The grammar is easily changed to a the "strict" $\mathcal{SMG}$ format, just by trading in the one offending lexical item for 5:

```
=1 +5 +4 +3 +2 +1 c   ⇒   =1 +5 c5
                          =c5 +4 c4
                          =c4 +3 c3
                          =c3 +2 c2
                          =c2 +1 c
```

Consequently, we have $\{1^n 2^n 3^n 4^n 5^n | n \in \mathbb{N}\} \in \mathcal{SML}$. In fact, it is plausible that the restrictions on the "strict" grammars are "conservative" in the sense that they do not change the class of definable languages:

Conjecture: $\mathcal{SML} = \mathcal{ML}$.

Vijay-Shanker and Weir (1994) show that languages with 5 counting dependencies cannot be defined by tree adjoining grammars (TAGs), nor by linear indexed grammars (LIGs), nor by head grammars (HGs), nor by categorial grammars (CGs) of a certain kind. Rambow (1994) points out that these languages can be defined by "multiset-valued linear indexed grammars" ($\{\} - \text{LIGs}$).

The following conjecture also seems plausible, though it has not yet been proven:

Conjecture: Grammars in $\mathcal{MG}$ can define languages with more than 2 counting dependencies only when some sentences in those languages are derived with remnant movements.

That is, it appears that the possibility of remnant movement is responsible for the great expressiveness of the framework. Prohibiting remnant movement, while leaving the framework unchanged in other respects, would yield a considerably less expressive system.

Many other basic questions remain open:[10]

(18) Open: Is $\mathcal{ML}$ closed under intersection with regular languages?

(19) Open: Is $\mathcal{ML}$ closed under intersection with ϵ-free concatenation?

(20) Open: Is $\mathcal{ML}$ closed under intersection with ϵ-free homomorphism?

16.6 The size of verbal complexes

The derived structures of the previous examples may appear to be rather complex, especially when depicted in the form that is familiar from mainstream theoretical linguistics, as for example in the tree (11). But in terms of grammar $G2$ and the size measure defined above, it has size: 2 bits. With grammar $G2$ one choice in the derivation of this tree comes in the selection of the verbal modifier. If m -m M is selected, then we cannot have a PredP, and we can only get the inverted order. If m -bm M is selected, then we must have a PredP, and we can only get English order. The other choice is whether to use the first (recursive) or second (non-recursive) c.[11]

16.7 Derivations as proof nets

Recent work on proof net representations of grammatical constructions suggests this much better representation of derivations.[12] The reason that the conventional depiction (11) looks complex is that it is showing too many things at once. All that is required for a successful derivation is that all features are checked in appropriate order, and this is something that can be depicted quite easily. For example, the successful derivation of the inverted form has the structure shown in Figure 1: It is a rooted, directed acyclic graph showing all the lexical items (from top to bottom in argument order, i.e. the order they have not in the derived structure

---

[10]Michaelis (1998) shows that minimalist languages are a subset of the multi-component TAG languages, $\mathcal{ML} \subseteq \mathcal{MC\text{-}TAL}$. If it could also be shown that $\mathcal{MC\text{-}TAL} \subseteq \mathcal{ML}$, then we would have positive answers to the questions (18-20).

[11]Without the first lexical item of our grammar $G2$, the grammar gets no other sentences than the two I have derived here because recursion through CP is then bounded. This can be seen by noticing that =lc +m c cannot appear in an embedded position, because c is only selected by a v which will always be dominated by a -c category: either w or pr. So then, notice that the recursive complementizers are both -c. But then recursion must be bounded because the only element that can cancel -c is lc, and lc is only selected by the non-recursive complementizer. If we had another complementizer in the lexicon to allow recursion here, the size of the trees would be 1 bit larger, given the choice of whether to use the recursive category.

[12]Retoré (1996); Lecomte and Retoré (1998); Lecomte (1998); Morrill (1997); Moortgat and Oehrle (1998).

(21)

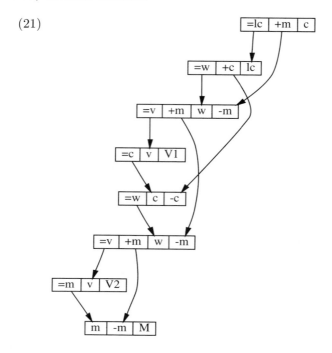

FIGURE 1 Matching graph for the derivation of inverted form

but in the derivation tree), and all the matchings. When "movement links" are ignored, i.e. the arcs connecting features +f to -f, the result is a tree, a tree of "merge links."

A detailed study of these matching graphs goes beyond the scope of this paper, but clearly, it will not be difficult to check such a graph to make sure that (i) features have been discharged in the required order, (ii) all movements are upward, (iii) all movements have applied to constituents that are either comp+ or spec,comp+, and (iv) no movement has applied to a constituent with two outstanding, matching requirements. Notice that there is no need to check for cycles as is required in the proofnets of the type logical tradition. In effect, we have only "tensor links" since all of our grammatical types are first order and there is no hypothetical reasoning.

16.8   Conclusions

The generative mechanisms of the "minimalist grammars" formalized here are assumed to be universal, so all language-specific constraints are given in the lexicon. These grammars can define interesting languages very easily, and at least some of the more interesting languages are defined using remnant movement, that is, movements of constituents from which material has already been extracted. Despite the appearance of conventional representations, the real size of the expressions derived by remnant movement can be perfectly reasonable, and the derivations in this framework are naturally represented by (rooted, acyclic) networks of matchings, for which we can provide direct admissibility criteria, phonetic and semantic denotations. Though a fully detailed, formal reconstruction of recent analyses of verbal complexes goes beyond the scope of this paper, the network representation of the basic outlines of the Koopman and Szabolcsi account reveals an extraordinary simplicity that is concealed in conventional representations of the derivational structures.

References

Becker, M. 1998. Acquiring grammars with complex heads. In *Proceedings, Twentieth Annual Meeting of the Cognitive Science Society*.

Brody, M. 1995. *Lexico-Logical Form: A Radically Minimalist Theory*. Cambridge, Massachusetts: MIT Press.

Chomsky, N. 1995. *The Minimalist Program*. Cambridge, Massachusetts: MIT Press.

Cornell, T. L. 1997a. Representational minimalism. SFB 340 Technical Report #83, University of Tübingen. Revised version forthcoming in U. Mönnich and H.-P. Kolb, eds.

Cornell, T. L. 1997b. A type logical perspective on minimalist derivations. In *Proceedings, Formal Grammar'97*. Aix-en-Provence.

Cornell, T. L. 1998a. A deductive calculus of categories and transformations. Forthcoming.

Cornell, T. L. 1998b. Island effects in type logical approaches to the minimalist program. In *Proceedings of the Joint Conference on Formal Grammar, Head-Driven Phrase Structure Grammar, and Categorial Grammar, FHCG-98*, pages 279–288. Saarbrücken.

De Kuthy, C. and W. D. Meurers. 1998. Incomplete category fronting in German without remnant movement. In *Konferenz zur Verarbeitung natürlicher Sprache, KONVENS'98*.

den Besten, H. and G. Webelhuth. 1990. Stranding. In G. Grewendorf and W. Sternefeld, eds., *Scrambling and Barriers*. NY: Academic Press.

Fanselow, G. 1987. *Konfigurationalität. Untersuchungen zur Universalgrammatik am Beispiel des Deutschen*. Tübingen: Gunther Narr Verlag.

Kayne, R. 1984. *Connectedness and Binary Branching*. Dordrecht: Foris.

Kayne, R. 1994. *The Antisymmetry of Syntax*. Cambridge, Massachusetts: MIT Press.

Kayne, R. 1998. Overt vs. covert movment. *Syntax* 1(2):128–191.

Keenan, E. L. and E. P. Stabler. 1996. Abstract syntax. In A.-M. DiSciullo, ed., *Configurations: Essays on Structure and Interpretation*, pages 329–344. Somerville, Massachusetts: Cascadilla Press. Conference version available at http://phonetics.ling.ucla.edu/.

Keenan, E. L. and E. P. Stabler. 1997. Syntactic invariants. In *6th Annual Conference on Language, Logic and Computation*. Stanford. forthcoming.

Kenesei, I. 1989. Logikus – e a magyar szórend? *Általános Nyelvézeti Tanulmányok* 17:105–152.

Koopman, H. 1996. The spec-head configuration. Syntax at Sunset: UCLA Working Papers in Syntax and Semantics, edited by Edward Garrett and Felicia Lee.

Koopman, H. and A. Szabolcsi. 1998. *Verbal Complexes*. UCLA. Forthcoming.

Koster, J. 1994. Predicate incorporation and the word order of Dutch. In G. Cinque, J. Koster, J.-Y. Pollock, L. Rizzi, and R. Zanuttini, eds., *Paths Towards Universal Grammar: Studies in Honor of Richard S. Kayne*, pages 255–276. Washington, D.C: Georgetown University Press.

Lecomte, A. 1998. Pom-nets and minimalism. In *Proceedings of the Roma Workshop*. INRIA, Nancy.

Lecomte, A. and C. Retoré. 1998. Words as modules. In C. Martin-Vide, ed., *Proceedings, International Conference on Mathematical Linguistics, Tarragonna, 1996*. Amsterdam: John Benjamins.

Michaelis, J. 1998. Derivational minimalism is mildly context-sensitive. In *Proceedings of Logical Aspects of Computational Linguistics, LACL'98*. Grenoble.

Michaelis, J. and C. Wartena. 1998. Unidirectional inheritance of indices: A weakly context free facet of LIGs. In *Proceedings of the Joint Conference on Formal Grammar, Head-Driven Phrase Structure Grammar, and Categorial Grammar, FHCG-98*, pages 258–267. Saarbrücken.

Moortgat, M. 1996. Categorial type logics. In J. van Benthem and A. ter Meulen, eds., *Handbook of Logic and Language*. Amsterdam: Elsevier.

Moortgat, M. and R. T. Oehrle. 1996. Structural abstractions. In *Proofs and Linguistic Categories: Applications of Logic to the Analysis and Implementation of Natural Language Theory: Proceedings 1996 Roma Workshop.*

Moortgat, M. and R. T. Oehrle. 1998. Proof nets for structured resources. Utrecht Institute of Linguistics. Forthcoming.

Morrill, G. V. 1997. Geometry of language. Universitat Politècnica de Catalunya.

Müller, G. 1996. Incomplete category fronting. SfS report 01-96, Seminar für Sprachwissenschaft, Universität Tübingen.

Nkemnji, M. A. 1995. *Heavy Pied-Piping in Nweh.* Ph.D. thesis, University of California, Los Angeles.

Rambow, O. 1994. *Formal and computational aspects of natural language syntax.* Ph.D. thesis, University of Pennsylvania. Computer and Information Science Technical report MS-CIS-94-52 (LINC LAB 278).

Retoré, C. 1996. Pomset-logic: a non-commutative extension of classical linear logic. In J. Hindley and P. de Groote, eds., *Typed Lambda-Calculus and Applications, TLCA '97*, pages 300–318. NY: Springer-Verlag (Lecture Notes in Computer Science 1210).

Retoré, C. and A. Lecomte. 1997. Logique des ressources et reseaux syntaxiques. In D. Genthial, ed., *Proceedings, Traitement Automatique du Langage Naturel, TALN'97*, pages 70–83. Grenoble.

Stabler, E. P. 1997. Derivational minimalism. In C. Retoré, ed., *Logical Aspects of Computational Linguistics*, pages 68–95. NY: Springer-Verlag (Lecture Notes in Computer Science 1328).

Szalai, T. A. 1998. Approaching a formal model of Hungarian. UCLA M.A. thesis.

Szalai, T. A. and E. Stabler. 1998. Formal analyses of the Hungarian verbal complex. In *TAG+ Workshop, Institute for Research in Cognitive Science, University of Pennsylvania.*

Vermaat, W. 1998. Derivational minimalism and MMCG. Universiteit Utrecht.

Vijay-Shanker, K. and D. Weir. 1994. The equivalence of four extensions of context free grammar formalisms. *Mathematical Systems Theory* 27:511–545.

Webelhuth, G., ed. 1992. *Principles and Parameters of Syntactic Saturation.* Oxford: Oxford University Press.

Zwart, J.-W. 1994. Dutch is head-initial. *The Linguistic Review* 11:377–406.

Zwart, J.-W. 1997. *Morphosyntax of verb movement: A minimalist approach to the syntax of Dutch*. Dordrecht: Kluwer.

Subject Index

Name Index